PEOPLES AND CULTURES
OF THE MIDDLE EAST

The Natural History Press, publisher for The American Museum of Natural History, is a division of Doubleday & Company, Inc. Directed by a joint editorial board made up of members of the staff of both the Museum and Doubleday, the Natural History Press publishes books and periodicals in all branches of the life and earth sciences, including anthropology and astronomy. The Natural History Press has its editorial offices at The American Museum of Natural History, Central Park West at 79th Street, New York, New York 10024, and its business offices at 501 Franklin Avenue, Garden City, New York 11530.

LOUISE E. SWEET received her training in anthropology and Near East studies at the University of Michigan and was awarded the doctoral degree in 1957. She has pursued ethnographic field research in Syria (1953–54), the Arab states of the Persian Gulf (1958–59), and Lebanon (1964–65), and has taught at a number of universities in the United States, Canada, and Lebanon. From 1966 to 1968 she served as the chairman of the Department of Anthropology at the State University of New York at Binghamton. She expects in 1969 to join the Department of Sociology and Anthropology at the American University of Beirut as Visiting Professor.

Dr. Sweet has written a monograph, *Tell Toqaan: A Syrian Village*, and a number of papers in professional journals. She is currently engaged in research focused on developing an ecological interpretation of the ethnohistory of the Druze people of the Levant.

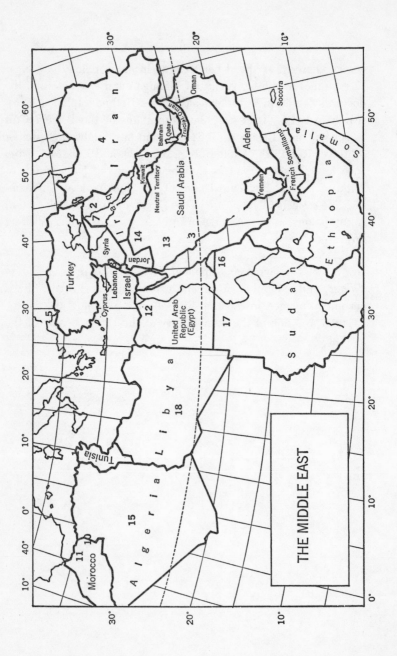

THE MIDDLE EAST

PEOPLES AND CULTURES
OF THE MIDDLE EAST

AN ANTHROPOLOGICAL READER

EDITED AND WITH AN INTRODUCTION BY
LOUISE E. SWEET

VOLUME I
Cultural Depth and Diversity

PUBLISHED FOR
THE AMERICAN MUSEUM OF NATURAL HISTORY
THE NATURAL HISTORY PRESS
GARDEN CITY, NEW YORK

The illustrations for this book
were prepared by the Graphic Arts Division of
The American Museum of Natural History

Preface

The new nations and new and old kingdoms of the Middle East, from Morocco to Afghanistan, descendants of old kingdoms and empires and of the earliest civilizations, today face multiple threats in their struggles for survival and integration. These are of two major kinds. There are, first, those threats to continuity that are of internal origin, inherent in the resources of their lands, peoples, and cultural heritages. There are, second, those threats that advance openly against them from the outside, or that infiltrate slowly and establish footholds for pressure and dominance.

The list of internal threats is long and I suggest only a few: exploding populations; harsh environments with often meager and unevenly distributed resources in water supply, soil fertility, or minerals; the legacies of colonial occupations in the present irrational political boundaries, entrenched ruling elites, façade parliamentary political bureaucracies; well-developed armies and poorly developed economies; and ethnic, linguistic, and religious diversities exacerbated by contacts of dependency to external political powers of the modern world.

But in the face of these there are also inherent traits of resiliency and strength, of adaptability to diversity and adversity, of ancient stores of wit and wisdom, of values of honor and responsibility, and of modes of strategic compromise that will stand Middle Eastern societies in good stead. And in the discoveries of new resources of vast oil reserves and in the steady acquisition of industrial technology lie many hopes for survival and independence in cooperation with the world of nations.

To understand and appreciate more fully the Middle Eastern

polities of today, close and detailed study of these and other aspects of the conditions for life and customs for meeting them of this vast area is an obvious requirement. In the main, anthropological perspectives on the cultural nature of the Middle East are presented in the selections in this *Reader*.

But the context of external threats to the integrity of these nations and peoples must not be forgotten. The Middle Eastern states face, as much of the world faces or has capitulated to, domination by the powerful, most fully industrialized nations or components of their systems, from the Americas, through those of Europe, to those of the Far East. The consequences of accepting dependency, or of resisting it even with force, or of attempting to industrialize their own economies, universalize their educational systems, and so on—and succeeding or failing—make the world's news headlines every day in one way or another, usually with very little perceptive comment.

Survival of these Middle Eastern polities will identify for the cultural anthropologist that process of adaptation to a world through which industrialized culture is spreading inexorably—as ten thousand years ago the domestication technology of the Neolithic Revolution began to proliferate inexorably from its earliest center of origin somewhere in the Middle East itself. The selections compiled here will indicate, I hope, the extent to which the research of modern anthropology into the inherent attributes of Middle Eastern sociocultural systems in all their variety can contribute to a more accurate understanding of this part of the world of man.

Together, the two volumes of this *Reader* assemble studies that sample the full range in time and space of cultural adjustments to the conditions for human life in the Middle East, from archaeological and historical depth to the niceties of intercommunal and interpersonal relations in different situations from traditional systems of relative stability to scenes of disorienting current change.

Volume I comprises selections that present the depth of Middle Eastern cultural heritages from the Neolithic to the current scene, samples of major social institutions or customs characteristic of the whole area, and studies of communities of the most well known type of society if not the most prevalent in the Middle East, the nomadic pastoralists.

Volume II focuses upon two community types of the Middle East, rural agricultural societies and urban societies, and their interrelations. It is especially useful for students of "urbanization."

Two major criteria guided my selections from the enormous literature that is available on the Middle East: the scholarly presentation of empirical data and the sophistication of analysis. It is my first concern that old, stereotyped ideas of the Middle East and North African peoples and their cultures should be challenged by these studies drawn from some of the best literature of anthropology, geography, and history that I have been able to assemble.

Most of the selections have been previously and recently published as independent papers in professional journals, or as parts of books or symposia, and in the cases of Ibn Khaldun and Charles M. Doughty, from classics. A few are published here for the first time, and I am most grateful to those who responded to my request for a revised publication or a new article that would fit the plan of the whole. They are in the order of their appearance: Volume I: Barbara C. Aswad, T. M. Johnstone, Safia K. Mohsen; Volume II: David M. Hart, Alex Weingrod, and Samih K. Farsoun.

I am also grateful to a number of colleagues in teaching the anthropology of the Middle East who responded to my queries as to which of a very long list of selections would be most useful for their own instructional needs, and who, in some cases, offered ideas for better examples or organization than I had listed initially: Harold Barclay, Harvey Goldberg, John Gulick, Fuad Khuri, Robert Murphy, Dorothy Wilner, and Alex Weingrod.

—Louise E. Sweet
January 1969

Contents

Introduction

The selections in the first volume of this *Reader* in Middle Eastern ethnology touch upon major aspects of the sociocultural systems of the area in such time depth and extent that it serves well to introduce the student to the area, and may well be used to represent the Middle East in broad surveys of "Asian" cultures in general. Time depth, diversity, and a sampling of institutions particularly characteristic of the Middle East are its themes, with attention given in particular to nomadic pastoralism, a major adaptation to the harsh and contrasting environments which prevail throughout the area.

Part One, a general section, opens with selections from Ibn Khaldun, the fourteenth-century Tunisian, whose insights into basic features of medieval Western Oriental society and man in general are as modern as today's anthropology.

The wealth of archaeological studies of crucial periods of culture change and adaptation in the Middle East is represented by Flannery's fine paper, "The Ecology of Early Food Production in Mesopotamia." Those distinctive patterns of transhumant economies and interaction between different ecological zones which he delineates for some ten thousand years ago are still to be observed today. And the staple crops and the food product animals of today are those with which he deals in their early stages of domestication.

Since writing was invented, there is abundant documentation of that recurrent phenomenon of "new" religion after "new" religion, each accompanied by its political expansion. The emergence of Islam has been specifically examined by anthropologists, as well as by many more traditionally oriented scholars. In this

volume Aswad's paper offers a cultural ecological interpretation
that should be read in conjunction with Eric Wolf's interpretation, cited in her notes and easily available in commercial reprint.

Professor Lambton's scholarly historical discussion of the features of Islamic society in Persia at once crosses time from the
Islamization of Iran to the present, and sets forth the traditional
Islamic structure of Iran upon which the forces of present in-
dustrialization are working. Apart from a few studies of the
great pastoral peoples of Iran, modern anthropological studies
of villages, cities, regions, and enclaves still wait to be done or
to be published, with one outstanding exception, a selection from
which is included in the second volume of this *Reader:* two chap-
ters from Paul W. English's *City and Village in Iran: Settlement
and Economy in the Kirman Basin* (Madison: University of Wisconsin Press, 1966). Here, together with the once autonomous
and now semi-autonomous hinterland Berber enclave in Morocco,
The Aith Waryaghar (see Hart in Volume II), two very distinct
sedentary cultural ecological types are presented, both of which
are recurrent sociocultural adaptations characteristic of the Middle East.

From Professor Bernard Lewis' *Istanbul and the Civilization
of the Ottoman Empire* a brief selection is included which
sets forth the ecclesiastical structure of Islam in the florescence of
the Ottoman Empire and which, in its setting in sixteenth-century
Istanbul, provides a framework of orthodox urban Sunni Islam
for comparison with developments in other parts of the Islamic
world described in other selections (cf. Gellner, in this volume).

Part Two of this volume offers samples of institutional features of the Middle East that have been of particular interest
for anthropological field observation and analysis. Still others are,
of course, represented in selections in both volumes (cf. the
résumé of the role of the *za'im*, "political leader," in Farsoun,
Volume II). Fredrik Barth's paper presents at once one of the
many recent analyses of a marriage form almost unique to the
area, parallel patrilineal cousin marriage, and, in Barth's attention to this feature in Kurdish society, a brief notice at least of
the great enclave of the Kurdish peoples. This type of marriage
is still vigorously discussed by anthropologists. Victor F. Ayoub's

"Conflict Resolution and Social Reorganization" calls attention to a most interesting role, the *waasta* or "intermediary," in a community which again signals in its microsetting the pressures of change engaging the Middle East.

In Alan Villiers' "Some Aspects of the Arab Dhow Trade" the reader will discover a sphere of activity which has scarcely been recognized in the anthropological literature, but which has for many centuries been a major feature of Arab culture—maritime commerce ranging out of the ports of the Persian Gulf to India, Southeast Asia, and East Africa—and it is still surviving today. Francisco Benet's "Explosive Markets: The Berber Highlands" presents another aspect of the rich commercial complex characteristic of this part of the world, a "rural" market exchange system to be distinguished from the urban bazaar system dominating a region exemplified in English's study of the Kirman basin in Iran (Volume II).

Gellner's "Saints of the Atlas" returns us to the chameleon forms of organization found in the Islamic world, to the role of the "saint" and the response of "tribal" Berber highlanders of Morocco to encroaching political power of a more complex and potent order.

And last, Mohsen's paper on aspects of the status of women among the Awlad 'Ali semi-nomads of Egypt serves to suggest that stereotypic ideas of the place of women in Middle Eastern society need re-examination.

Part Three of this volume focuses upon one of the major ecological adaptations of human societies to vast expanses of arid steppe and desert, nomadic pastoralism. Among the selections here I call attention particularly to the selection from the classic, *Arabia Deserta*, by Charles Doughty, to the ecological import of lineage structure and proliferation among Cyrenaican Bedouin of Libya by Peters, and to Asad's thesis of the rational and adaptive use of arid lands as pasturages by nomadic pastoral economies. This caveat is now well known if little attended to by the new states and old kingdoms with their policies of sedentarization of nomads.

PART I

Cultural Depth and Diversity

1. Selections from THE MUQADDIMAH: AN INTRODUCTION TO HISTORY, Vol. I (Translated by Franz Rosenthal)

FIRST PREFATORY DISCUSSION

Human social organization is something necessary. The philosophers expressed this fact by saying: "Man is 'political' by nature." That is, he cannot do without the social organization for which the philosophers use the technical term "town" (*polis*).

This is what civilization means. (The necessary character of human social organization or civilization) is explained by the fact that God created and fashioned man in a form that can live and subsist only with the help of food. He guided man to a natural desire for food and instilled in him the power that enables him to obtain it.

However, the power of the individual human being is not sufficient for him to obtain (the food) he needs, and does not provide him with as much food as he requires to live. Even if we assume an absolute minimum of food—that is, food enough for one day, (a little) wheat, for instance—that amount of food could be obtained only after much preparation such as grinding, kneading, and baking. Each of these three operations requires utensils and

These selections are reprinted here with the permission of the Bollingen Foundation of New York and Routledge and Kegan Paul Ltd. of London from Ibn Khaldun, THE MUQADDIMAH: AN INTRODUCTION TO HISTORY, Vol. 1 (Translated from the Arabic by Franz Rosenthal). New York: The Bollingen Foundation, 1958.

Footnotes of the translator and editor, Professor Franz Rosenthal, have been retained here from the published work when they serve as clarification of the passage selected. The reader is referred to the original translation and edition for the complete scholarly annotation that Professor Rosenthal provides therein.

Parentheses in text are also the translator's.

tools that can be provided only with the help of several crafts,
such as the crafts of the blacksmith, the carpenter, and the potter.
Assuming that a man could eat unprepared grain, an even greater
number of operations would be necessary in order to obtain the
grain: sowing and reaping, and threshing to separate it from
the husks of the ear. Each of these operations requires a number
of tools and many more crafts than those just mentioned. It is
beyond the power of one man alone to do all that, or (even)
part of it, by himself. Thus, he cannot do without a combination
of many powers from among his fellow beings, if he is to obtain
food for himself and for them. Through co-operation, the needs
of a number of persons, many times greater than their own
(number), can be satisfied.

Likewise, each individual needs the help of his fellow beings
for his defense, as well. When God fashioned the natures of all
living beings and divided the various powers among them, many
dumb animals were given more perfect powers than God gave
to man. The power of a horse, for instance, is much greater than
the power of man, and so is the power of a donkey or an ox. The
power of a lion or an elephant is many times greater than the
power of (man).

Aggressiveness is natural in living beings. Therefore, God gave
each of them a special limb for defense against aggression. To
man, instead, He gave the ability to think, and the hand. With
the help of the ability to think, the hand is able to prepare the
ground for the crafts. The crafts, in turn, procure for man the instruments that serve him instead of limbs, which other animals
possess for their defense. Lances, for instance, take the place of
horns for goring, swords the place of claws to inflict wounds,
shields the place of thick skins, and so on. There are other such
things. They were all mentioned by Galen in *De usu partium*.[1]

The power of one individual human being cannot withstand
the power of any one dumb animal, especially not the power of
the predatory animals. Man is generally unable to defend himself against them by himself. Nor is his (unaided) power sufficient to make use of the existing instruments of defense, because

[1] At the beginning of the work, ed. C. G. Kühn (Leipzig, 1821–33), III, 2.

there are so many of them and they require so many crafts and (additional) things. It is absolutely necessary for man to have the co-operation of his fellow men. As long as there is no such co-operation, he cannot obtain any food or nourishment, and life cannot materialize for him, because God fashioned him so that he must have food if he is to live. Nor, lacking weapons, can he defend himself. Thus, he falls prey to animals and dies much before his time. Under such circumstances, the human species would vanish. When, however, mutual co-operation exists, man obtains food for his nourishment and weapons for his defense. God's wise plan that man(kind) should subsist and the human species be preserved will be fulfilled.

Consequently, social organization is necessary to the human species. Without it, the existence of human beings would be incomplete. God's desire to settle the world with human beings and to leave them as His representatives on earth[2] would not materialize. This is the meaning of civilization, the object of the science under discussion.

The afore-mentioned remarks have been in the nature of establishing the existence of the object in (this) particular field. A scholar in a particular discipline is not obliged to do this, since it is accepted in logic that a scholar in a particular science does not have to establish the existence of the object in that science.[3] On the other hand, logicians do not consider it forbidden to do so. Thus, it is a voluntary contribution.

God, in His grace, gives success.

When mankind has achieved social organization, as we have

---

[2] Cf. Qur'ân 2.30 (28).

[3] The "object" (*mawḍû'*) of a science is the fundamental elements at its basis, such as quantities (measurements) in geometry, numbers in arithmetic, substances in physics, and so on. The object of Ibn Khaldûn's new science is human social organization, or civilization. . . . For the Avicennian basis of this theory, see, for instance, A.-M. Goichon, *Lexique de la philosophie d' Ibn Sînâ* (Paris, 1938), p. 439, and Abû l-Barakât Hibatallâh al-Baghdâdî, *Mu'tabar* (Hyderabad, 1357–58/1938–39), I, 221 ff. These fundamental elements of the individual sciences do not require proof of their existence. The pertinent Aristotelian passage in this connection (*Analytica posteriora* 76b 5 ff.), was quoted by de Slane. However, the Arabic translation, as published by 'Abd-ar-Raḥmân Badawî, *Manṭiq Arisṭû* (Cairo, 1948–49), II, 339, does not use the term *mawḍû'* in this context.

stated, and when civilization in the world has thus become a fact, people need someone to exercise a restraining influence and keep them apart, for aggressiveness and injustice are in the animal nature of man. The weapons made for the defense of human beings against the aggressiveness of dumb animals do not suffice against the aggressiveness of man to man, because all of them possess those weapons. Thus, something else is needed for defense against the aggressiveness of human beings toward each other. It could not come from outside, because all the other animals fall short of human perceptions and inspiration. The person who exercises a restraining influence, therefore, must be one of themselves. He must dominate them and have power and authority over them, so that no one of them will be able to attack another. This is the meaning of royal authority.

It has thus become clear that royal authority is a natural quality of man which is absolutely necessary to mankind. The philosophers mention that it also exists among certain dumb animals, such as the bees and the locusts. One discerns among them the existence of authority and obedience to a leader. They follow the one of them who is distinguished as their leader by his natural characteristics and body. However, outside of human beings, these things exist as the result of natural disposition and divine guidance, and not as the result of an ability to think or to administrate. "He gave everything its natural characteristics, and then guided it."[4]

The philosophers go further. They attempt to give logical proof of the existence of prophecy and to show that prophecy is a natural quality of man. In this connection, they carry the argument to its ultimate consequences and say that human beings absolutely require some authority to exercise a restraining influence. They go on to say that such restraining influence exists through the religious law (that has been) ordained by God and revealed to mankind by a human being. (This human being) is distinguished from the rest of mankind by special qualities of divine guidance that God gave him, in order that he might find the others submissive to him and ready to accept what he says.

[4] Qur'ân 20.50 (52).

Eventually, the existence of a (restraining) authority among them and over them becomes a fact that is accepted without the slightest disapproval or dissent.

This proposition of the philosophers is not logical, as one can see. Existence and human life can materialize without (the existence of prophecy) through injunctions a person in authority may devise on his own or with the help of a group feeling that enables him to force the others to follow him wherever he wants to go. People who have a (divinely revealed) book and who follow the prophets are few in number in comparison with (all) the Magians[5] who have no (divinely revealed) book. The latter constitute the majority of the world's inhabitants. Still, they (too) have possessed dynasties and monuments, not to mention life itself. They still possess these things at this time in the intemperate zones to the north and the south. This is in contrast with human life in the state of anarchy, with no one to exercise a restraining influence. That would be impossible.

This shows that (the philosophers) are wrong when they assume that prophecy exists by necessity. The existence of prophecy is not required by logic. Its (necessary character) is indicated by the religious law, as was the belief of the early Muslims.

God gives success and guidance.

1   Both Bedouins and sedentary people are natural groups.*

It should be known that differences of condition among people are the result of the different ways in which they make their living. Social organization enables them to co-operate toward that end and to start with the simple necessities of life, before they get to conveniences and luxuries.

---

[5] "Magians" originally meant the Zoroastrians. In later Islam they were considered as people who followed a kind of prophet but did not have Scriptures like the Christians and the Jews. Thus, they occupied a position somewhere between the latter and polytheists. The term was eventually used to denote the general idea of pagans. Cf. V. F. Büchner in *EI*, *s.v.* "Madjûs."

* From Chapter II: "Bedouin Civilization, Savage Nations and Tribes and their Conditions (of Life), Including Several Basic and Explanatory Statements." [Editor]

Some people adopt agriculture, the cultivation of vegetables and grains, (as their way of making a living). Others adopt animal husbandry, the use of sheep, cattle, goats, bees, and silkworms, for breeding and for their products. Those who live by agriculture or animal husbandry cannot avoid the call of the desert, because it alone offers the wide fields, acres, pastures for animals, and other things that the settled areas do not offer. It is therefore necessary for them to restrict themselves to the desert. Their social organization and co-operation for the needs of life and civilization, such as food, shelter, and warmth, do not take them beyond the bare subsistence level, because of their inability (to provide) for anything beyond those (things). Subsequent improvement of their conditions and acquisition of more wealth and comfort than they need, cause them to rest and take it easy. Then, they co-operate for things beyond the (bare) necessities. They use more food and clothes, and take pride in them. They build large houses, and lay out towns and cities for protection. This is followed by an increase in comfort and ease, which leads to formation of the most developed luxury customs. They take the greatest pride in the preparation of food and a fine cuisine, in the use of varied splendid clothes of silk and brocade and other (fine materials), in the construction of ever higher buildings and towers, in elaborate furnishings for the buildings, and the most intensive cultivation of crafts in actuality. They build castles and mansions, provide them with running water, build their towers higher and higher, and compete in furnishing them (most elaborately). They differ in the quality of the clothes, the beds, the vessels, and the utensils they employ for their purposes. Here, now, (we have) sedentary people. "Sedentary people" means the inhabitants of cities and countries, some of whom adopt the crafts as their way of making a living, while others adopt commerce. They earn more and live more comfortably than Bedouins, because they live on a level beyond the level of (bare) necessity, and their way of making a living corresponds to their wealth.

It has thus become clear that Bedouins and sedentary people are natural groups which exist by necessity, as we have stated.

2   The Arabs[6] are a natural group in the world.

We have mentioned in the previous section that the inhabitants of the desert adopt the natural manner of making a living, namely, agriculture and animal husbandry. They restrict themselves to the necessary in food, clothing, and mode of dwelling, and to the other necessary conditions and customs. They do not possess conveniences and luxuries beyond (these bare necessities). They use tents of hair and wool, or houses of wood, or of clay and stone, which are not furnished (elaborately). The purpose is to have shade and shelter, and nothing beyond that. They also take shelter in caverns and caves. The food they take is either little prepared or not prepared at all, save that it may have been touched by fire.[7]

For those who make their living through the cultivation of grain and through agriculture, it is better to be stationary than to travel around. Such, therefore, are the inhabitants of small communities, villages, and mountain regions. These people make up the large mass of the Berbers and non-Arabs.

Those who make their living from animals requiring pasturage, such as sheep and cattle, usually travel around in order to find pasture and water for their animals, since it is better for them to move around in the land. They are called "sheepmen" (*shâwiyah*), that is, men who live on sheep and cattle. They do not go deep into the desert, because they would not find good pastures there. Such people include the Berbers, the Turks and their relatives, the Turkomans and the Slavs,[8] for instance.

[6] As a sociological term, "Arab" is always synonymous with "Bedouin, nomad" to Ibn Khaldûn, regardless of racial, national, or linguistic distinctions.

[7] Ibn Khaldûn was familiar with this phrase for "preparing food in the open fire" through the *ḥadîth* literature. Cf. F. Rosenthal, *A History of Muslim Historiography*, p. 206.

[8] Though the Arabic text need not be understood as saying that there exists a relationship between the Slavs and the Turks, it is the most natural construction to understand it that way. It has been shown that Muslim geographers did not always mean precisely Slavs when they spoke about the Ṣaqâlibah. (Cf. A. Zeki Validi Togan, *Ibn Faḍlân's Reisebericht*, pp. 295 ff.) However, the above statement should not be taken too literally, and the term used for "relatives" (*ikhwân* "brethren") may perhaps be translated as "companions" or the like, implying no real relationship.

Those who make their living by raising camels move around more. They wander deeper into the desert, because the hilly[9] pastures with their plants and shrubs do not furnish enough subsistence for camels. They must feed on the desert shrubs and drink the salty desert water. They must move around the desert regions during the winter, in flight from the harmful cold to the warm desert air. In the desert sands, camels can find places to give birth to their young ones. Of all animals, camels have the hardest delivery and the greatest need for warmth in connection with it. (Camel nomads) are therefore forced to make excursions deep (into the desert). Frequently, too, they are driven from the hills by the militia, and they penetrate farther into the desert, because they do not want the militia[10] to mete out justice to them or to punish them for their hostile acts. As a result, they are the most savage human beings that exist. Compared with sedentary people, they are on a level with wild, untamable (animals) and dumb beasts of prey. Such people are the Arabs. In the West, the nomadic Berbers and the Zanâtah are their counterparts, and in the East, the Kurds, the Turkomans, and the Turks. The Arabs, however, make deeper excursions into the desert and are more rooted in desert life (than the other groups), because they live exclusively on camels, while the other groups live on sheep and cattle, as well as camels.

It has thus become clear that the Arabs are a natural group which by necessity exists in civilization.

God is "the Creator, the Knowing One."[11]

3 *Bedouins are prior to sedentary people. The desert is the basis and reservoir of civilization and cities.*

We have mentioned that the Bedouins restrict themselves to the (bare) necessities in their conditions (of life) and are unable to go beyond them, while sedentary people concern them-

---

[9] *Tall*, pl. *tulûl* "hills." The expression reflects the situation in northwestern Africa rather than in Arabia.

[10] Bulaq, apparently by mistake, has "to humiliate them" for the rest of the sentence.

[11] Qur'ân 15.86 (86); 36.81 (81).

selves with conveniences and luxuries in their conditions and customs. The (bare) necessities are no doubt prior to the conveniences and luxuries. (Bare) necessities, in a way, are basic, and luxuries secondary and an outgrowth (of the necessities). Bedouins, thus, are the basis of, and prior to, cities and sedentary people. Man seeks first the (bare) necessities. Only after he has obtained the (bare) necessities, does he get to comforts and luxuries. The toughness of desert life precedes the softness of sedentary life. Therefore, urbanization is found to be the goal of the Bedouin. He aspires to (that goal). Through his own efforts, he achieves what he proposes to achieve in this respect. When he has obtained enough to be ready for the conditions and customs of luxury, he enters upon a life of ease and submits himself to the yoke of the city. This is the case with all Bedouin tribes. Sedentary people, on the other hand, have no desire for desert conditions, unless they are motivated by some urgent necessity[12] or they cannot keep up with their fellow city dwellers.

Evidence for the fact that Bedouins are the basis of, and prior to, sedentary people is furnished by investigating the inhabitants of any given city. We shall find that most of its inhabitants originated among Bedouins dwelling in the country and villages of the vicinity. Such Bedouins became wealthy, settled in the city, and adopted a life of ease and luxury, such as exists in the sedentary environment. This proves that sedentary conditions are secondary to desert conditions and that they are the basis of them.[13] This should be understood.

All Bedouins and sedentary people differ also among themselves in their conditions (of life). Many a clan is greater than another, many a tribe greater than another, many a city larger than another, and many a town more populous (*'umrân*) than another.

It has thus become clear that the existence of Bedouins is prior to, and the basis of, the existence of towns and cities. Likewise, the existence of towns and cities results from luxury cus-

[12] Ibn Khaldûn is probably thinking of political exile and retirement in the country such as he experienced himself when writing the *Muqaddimah*.

[13] The pronouns are as ambiguous in Arabic as they are in English, and, were it not for the context, would be understood to mean the opposite of what they are intended to mean.

toms pertaining to luxury and ease, which are posterior to the
customs that go with the bare necessities of life.

4 *Bedouins are closer to being good than sedentary people.*

The reason for it is that the soul in its first natural state of creation is ready to accept whatever good or evil may arrive and
leave an imprint upon it. Muḥammad said: "Every infant is born
in the natural state. It is his parents who make him a Jew or a
Christian or a Magian." To the degree the soul is first affected
by one of the two qualities, it moves away from the other and
finds it difficult to acquire it. When customs proper to goodness
have been first to enter the soul of a good person and his (soul)
has thus acquired the habit of (goodness, that person) moves
away from evil and finds it difficult to do anything evil. The same
applies to the evil person when customs (proper to evil) have
been first to affect him.

Sedentary people are much concerned with all kinds of pleasures. They are accustomed to luxury and success in worldly occupations and to indulgence in worldly desires. Therefore, their
souls are colored with all kinds of blameworthy and evil qualities.
The more of them they possess, the more remote do the ways
and means of goodness become to them. Eventually they lose all
sense of restraint. Many of them are found to use improper language in their gatherings as well as in the presence of their su-
periors and womenfolk. They are not deterred by any sense of
restraint, because the bad custom of behaving openly in an improper manner in both words and deeds has taken hold of them.
Bedouins may be as concerned with worldly affairs as (sedentary
people are). However, such concern would touch only the necessities of life and not luxuries or anything causing, or calling
for, desires and pleasures. The customs they follow in their
mutual dealings are, therefore, appropriate. As compared with
those of sedentary people, their evil ways and blameworthy qualities are much less numerous. They are closer to the first natural
state and more remote from the evil habits that have been impressed upon the souls (of sedentary people) through numerous
and ugly, blameworthy customs. Thus, they can more easily be

cured than sedentary people. This is obvious. It will later on become clear that sedentary life constitutes the last stage of civilization and the point where it begins to decay. It also constitutes the last stage of evil and of remoteness from goodness. It has thus become clear that Bedouins are closer to being good than sedentary people. "God loves those who fear God." . . .

1 *Royal authority and large*[14] *dynastic (power) are attained only through a group and group feeling.**

This is because, as we established in the first chapter, aggressive and defensive strength is obtained only through group feeling which means (mutual) affection and willingness to fight and die for each other.

Now, royal authority is a noble and enjoyable position. It comprises all the good things of the world, the pleasures of the body, and the joys of the soul. Therefore, there is, as a rule, great competition for it. It rarely is handed over (voluntarily), but it may be taken away. Thus, discord ensues. It leads to war and fighting, and to attempts to gain superiority. Nothing of all this comes about except through group feeling, as we have also mentioned.

This situation is not at all understood by the great mass. They forget it, because they have forgotten the time when the dynasty first became established. They have grown up in settled areas for a long time. They have lived there for successive generations. Thus, they know nothing about what took place with God's help at the beginning of the dynasty. They merely notice that the coloring of the men of the dynasty is determined, that people have submitted to them, and that group feeling is no longer needed to establish their power. They do not know how it was at the beginning and what difficulties had to be overcome by the founder of (the dynasty). The inhabitants of Spain especially have forgotten group feeling and its influence, because so long a time has passed, and because as a rule they have no need of

---

[14] *'âmmah* "general," here and elsewhere refers to governmental power that is not restricted to a small unit, such as a tribe.

* Selections from Chapter III: "On Dynasties, Royal Authority, the caliphate, Government Ranks. . . ." [Editor]

the power of group feeling, since their country has been anni-
hilated and is depleted of tribal groups.

God has power to do what He wishes.

2 *When a dynasty is firmly established, it can dispense with group feeling.*

The reason for this is that people find it difficult to submit to
large dynastic (power) at the beginning, unless they are forced
into submission by strong superiority. (The new government) is
something strange. People are not familiar with, or used to, its
rule. But once leadership is firmly vested in the members of the
family qualified to exercise royal authority in the dynasty, and
once (royal authority) has been passed on by inheritance over
many generations and through successive dynasties, the beginnings are forgotten, and the members of that family are clearly
marked as leaders. It has become a firmly established article of
faith that one must be subservient and submissive to them. People will fight with them in their behalf, as they would fight for
the articles of faith. By this time, (the rulers) will not need much
group (feeling to maintain) their power. It is as if obedience to
the government were a divinely revealed book that cannot be
changed or opposed. It is for some (good reason) that the discussion of the imamate is placed at the end of works dealing
with the articles of faith, as if it were one of them.[15]

(The rulers) maintain their hold over the government and
their own dynasty with the help, then, either of clients and followers who grew up in the shadow and power of group feeling,
or (with that) of tribal groups of a different descent who have
become their clients.

Something of the sort happened to the 'Abbâsids. The group
feeling of the Arabs had been destroyed by the time of the reign
of al-Mu'taṣim and his son, al-Wâthiq. They tried to maintain
their hold over the government thereafter with the help of
Persian, Turkish, Daylam, Saljûq, and other clients. Then, the

[15] Ibn Khaldûn refers to the numerous catechisms and creeds where the
caliphate is discussed, usually near the end. Cf., for instance, al-Ash'arî's
Kitâb al-Luma', ed. and tr. R. J. McCarthy, *The Theology of al-Ash'arî*
(Beirut, 1953).

Persians (non-Arabs) and clients gained power over the provinces (of the realm). The influence of the dynasty grew smaller,
and no longer extended beyond the environs of Baghdad.
Eventually, the Daylam closed in upon (that area) and took
possession of it. The caliphs were ruled by them. Then (the
Daylam), in turn, lost control. The Saljûqs seized power after
the Daylam, and the (caliphs) were ruled by them. Then (the
Saljûqs), in turn, lost control. Finally, the Tatars closed in. They
killed the caliph and wiped out every vestige of the dynasty.

The same happened to the Ṣinhâjah in the Maghrib. Their
group feeling was destroyed in the fifth [eleventh] century, or
before that. Dynastic (power), but of decreasing importance,
was maintained by them in al-Mahdîyah, in Bougie, in
al-Qal'ah,[16] and in the other frontier cities of Ifrîqiyah. Frequently, some rival aspirant to royal authority would attack these
frontier cities and entrench himself in them. Yet, they retained
government and royal authority until God permitted their dynasty to be wiped out. Then the Almohads came, fortified by
the strong group feeling among the Maṣmûdah, and obliterated
all traces of the (Ṣinhâjah dynasty).

3 *Members of a royal family may be able to found a dynasty
that can dispense with group feeling.*

This is because the group feeling in which (a member of a
royal family) shares may have much power over nations and
races, and the inhabitants of remote regions who support his
power may be obedient (to that family) and submissive. So,
when such a person secedes, leaving the seat of his rule and
the home of his might, and joins those inhabitants of remote
regions, they adopt him. They support his rule and help him.
They take care of establishing his dynasty on a firm basis. They
hope that he will be confirmed in his family (rights) and take
the power away from his kinsmen.[17] They do not desire to share
in any way in his rule, as they subject themselves to his group

[16] The ancient capital of the Banû Ḥammâd, northeast of Msila.
[17] Bulaq adds: "and reward them for helping him by choosing them for
royal ranks and positions, such as the wazirate, the army command, or the
governorship of a frontier district."

feeling and submit to the coloring of material superiority firmly
belonging to him and his people. They believe, as in an article
of faith, in being obedient to (him and his people). Were they
to desire to share his rule with him or to rule without him, "the
earth would be shaken."[18]

That is what happened to the Idrîsids in Morocco and the
'Ubaydid(-Fâtimids) in Ifrîqiyah and Egypt. Abû Tâlib's descendants had left the East and removed themselves from the
seat of the caliphate, to go to remote regions of the Muslim
realm. They aspired to deprive the 'Abbâsids of the caliphate
whose coloring had (throughout the years) firmly established itself in the descendants of 'Abd-Manâf, first among the Umayyads
and then among the Hâshimites ('Abbâsids). They seceded (from
the ruling 'Abbâsid dynasty) in the western part of Islam and
made propaganda for themselves. The Berbers supported their
rule time after time. The Awrabah and Maghîlah (supported)
the Idrîsids, and the Kutâmah, the Sinhâjah, and the Hawwârah
(supported) the 'Ubaydid(-Fâtimids). These (Berber tribes)
cemented the dynasties of (the Idrîsids and 'Ubaydids) and
firmly established their rule through the group support they gave
them. They detached the whole Maghrib and then Ifrîqiyah from
the realm of the 'Abbâsids. The influence of the 'Abbâsid dynasty
grew steadily smaller and that of the 'Ubaydid(-Fâtimids) larger.
Eventually, the latter took possession of Egypt, Syria, and the
Hijâz, and shared the Muslim empire half and half with the
'Abbâsids. Nonetheless, the Berbers who supported the dynasty
submitted their own affairs to the 'Ubaydid(-Fâtimids) and
obeyed their rule. They merely vied for positions under them.
They subjected themselves to the royal authority that had become the established coloring of the Hâshimites (the family of
Muhammad, the 'Alid-Fâtimids as well as the 'Abbâsids), and to
the superiority over all nations of the Quraysh and the Mudar.
Royal authority, therefore, remained with their descendants
down to (the time of) the complete destruction of Arab rule.

"God decides, and no one can change His decision."[19]

[18] Qur'ân 99.1 (1).
[19] *Ibid.* 13.41 (41).

5 *Religious propaganda gives a dynasty at its beginning another power in addition to that of the group feeling it possessed
as the result of the number of its (supporters).*

As we have mentioned before, the reason for this is that religious coloring does away with mutual jealousy and envy among
people who share in a group feeling, and causes concentration
upon the truth. When people (who have a religious coloring)
come to have the (right) insight into their affairs, nothing can
withstand them, because their outlook is one and their object
one of common accord. They are willing to die for (their objectives). (On the other hand,) the members of the dynasty they
attack may be many times as numerous as they. But their purposes differ, in as much as they are false[20] purposes, and (the
people of the worldly dynasty) come to abandon each other,
since they are afraid of death. Therefore, they do not offer resistance to (the people with a religious coloring), even if they
themselves are more numerous. They are overpowered by
them and quickly wiped out, as a result of the luxury and hum-
bleness existing among them, as we have mentioned before.

This happened to the Arabs at the beginning of Islam during
the Muslim conquests. The armies of the Muslims at al-Qâdisîyah
and at the Yarmûk numbered some 30,000 in each case, while
the Persian troops at al-Qâdisîyah numbered 120,000, and the
troops of Heraclius, according to al-Wâqidî, 400,000.[21] Neither

[20] Whereas the truth is only one, and means unity of purpose. Cf., for
instance, the saying attributed to Plato in al-Mubashshir b. Fâtik, *Mukhtâr
al-ḥikam*, No. 227 in the edition prepared by me; cf. H. Knust, *Mittheilungen
aus dem Eskurial*, p. 229: "Justice in something is one form, whereas injustice is many forms. Therefore it is easy to commit an injustice, and difficult
to pursue justice. Justice and injustice are like hitting and missing (the tar-
get) in shooting. Hitting (it) requires practice and experience, while it does
not require anything of the sort to miss."

[21] The very high figures given here and in some of the historical examples
mentioned on the following pages, are not usually found in the old sources,
such as aṭ-Ṭabarî, al-Mas'ûdî, etc. This might have warned Ibn Khaldûn
against using them—had it been as easy for him to check the sources as it is
for us.

The *Futûḥ ash-Sha'm*, a novelistic elaboration of the conquest of Syria
ascribed to al-Wâqidî, speaks of four armies, the first three of which consisted of 100,000 knights each. This may have given rise to the figure of

of the two parties was able to withstand the Arabs. (The Arabs) routed them and seized what they possessed.

Another illustration is the Lamtûnah (Almoravid) and Almohad dynasties. In the Maghrib, there existed many tribes equaling or surpassing them in numbers and group feeling. However, their religious organization doubled the strength of their group feeling through (their) feeling of having (the right religious) insight[22] and (their) willingness to die, as we have stated, and nothing could withstand them.

This can also be illustrated (by the situation existing at the time) when the religious coloring changes and is destroyed. The power (of the ruling dynasty) is then wiped out. Superiority exists then merely in proportion to (the existing) group feeling, without the additional (power of) religion. As a result, the dynasty is overpowered by those groups (up to this time) under its control, that are equal or superior to it in strength. It had formerly overpowered the groups that had a stronger group feeling and were more deeply rooted in desert life, with the help of the additional power that religion had given it.

An illustration of this is the relationship of the Almohads with the Zanâtah. The Zanâtah were deeply rooted in the desert and more savage than the Maṣmûdah, but the Maṣmûdah had the religious call to follow the Mahdî. They took on (his religious) coloring. As a result, the strength of their group feeling increased many times over. Therefore, they were at first able to overpower the Zanâtah and to make them their followers, even though (the Zanâtah) were more strongly rooted in the desert and had a stronger group feeling than they. But (later on) when the Maṣmûdah lost their religious coloring, the Zanâtah rose up against them from every side and took their power away from them. "God has the power to execute His commands."[23] . . .

400,000 mentioned by Ibn Khaldûn. However, Pseudo-Wâqidî also mentions 600,000 and 700,000 as the number of Heraclius' troops. Cf. *Futûḥ ash-Sha'm* (Cairo, 1354/1935), I, 102 f.

[22] *Istibṣâr,* . . . The term, based on Qur'ân 29.38 (37), is quite frequently used in religious literature. In this passage one might be tempted to read *bi-l-intiṣâr* "through their willingness to win and die."

[23] Qur'ân 12.21 (21).

7 Each dynasty has a certain amount of provinces and lands, and no more.

The reason for this is that the group to which a given dynasty belongs and the people who support and establish it, must of necessity be distributed over the provinces and border regions which they reach and take into possession. Only thus is it possible to protect them against enemies and to enforce the laws of the dynasty relative to the collection of taxes, restrictions,[24] and other things.

When the (various) groups have spread over the border regions and provinces, their numbers are necessarily exhausted. This, then, is the time when the territory (of the dynasty) has reached its farthest extension, where the border regions form a belt around the center of the realm. If the dynasty then undertakes to expand beyond its holdings, it(s widening territory) remains without military protection and is laid open to any chance attack by enemy or neighbor. This has the detrimental result for the dynasty of the creation of boldness toward it and of diminished respect for it. (On the other hand,) if the group is a very large one and its numbers are not exhausted when distributed over border regions and territories, the dynasty retains the strength to go beyond the limit (so far reached), until its expansion has gone as far as possible.

The natural reason for this (situation) lies in the fact that the power of group feeling is one of the natural powers. Any power resulting in any kind of action must proceed in its action in such manner.[25]

A dynasty is stronger at its center than it is at its border re-

24 The translators disagree as to who is to be restricted. De Slane: "to contain those who are defeated." Issawi: "to awe the population." Schimmel (p. 78): "to drive back enemies." The term used here is not common with Ibn Khaldûn, but it appears to refer to the restraining influence which is to be exercised upon the native population. The word *rad'* used here occurs also elsewhere in the same sense in which Ibn Khaldûn preferably uses *wz'*. Cf., for instance, Ibn al-Ukhuwwa, *Ma'âlim al-qurbah*, p. 195, l. 19, or al-Mubashshir, *Mukhtâr al-ḥikam*, sayings of Socrates, Nos. 7 & 277 (in the edition prepared by me).

25 That is, it must follow its natural course. Each power can have only the effects depending on its inherent character.

gions. When it has reached its farthest expansion, it becomes too weak and incapable to go any farther. This may be compared to light rays that spread from their centers, or to circles that widen over the surface of the water when something strikes it.

When the dynasty becomes senile and weak, it begins to crumble at its extremities. The center remains intact until God permits the destruction of the whole (dynasty). Then, the center is destroyed. But when a dynasty is overrun from the center, it is of no avail to it that the outlying areas remain intact. It dissolves all at once. The center is like the heart from which the (vital) spirit spreads. Were the heart to be overrun and captured, all the extremities would be routed.

This may be observed in the Persian dynasty. Its center was al-Madâ'in (Ctesiphon). When the Muslims took over al-Madâ'in, the whole Persian empire dissolved. Possession of the outlying provinces of the realm was of no avail to Yazdjard.

Conversely, the center of the Byzantine dynasty in Syria was in Constantinople. When the Muslims took Syria away from the Byzantines, the latter repaired to their center in Constantinople. The loss of Syria did not harm them. Their rule continued there without interruption until God permitted it to be ended.[26]

Another example is the situation of the Arabs at the beginning of Islam. Since they were a very large group, they very quickly overran neighboring Syria, 'Irâq, and Egypt. Then, they kept on going, into Western India (as-Sind), Abyssinia, Ifrîqiyah, and the Maghrib, and later into Spain. They spread over many provinces and border regions, and settled in them as militiamen. Their numbers were exhausted by that expansion. No further conquests could be made by them, and the Muslim empire reached its farthest extension. Those borders were not passed, but the dynasty receded from them, until God permitted it to be destroyed.

The situation of later dynasties was the same. Each dynasty depended on the numerical strength of its supporters. When its numbers were exhausted through expansion, no further conquest

[26] The past tense is used here! The word "there" certainly does not refer to Syria, but to the Byzantine center in Constantinople. This anticipation of the fall of Constantinople may have something to do with traditions and predictions to that effect. . . .

or extension of power was possible. This is how God proceeds with His creatures.

8 *The greatness of a dynasty, the extent of its territory, and the length of its duration depend upon the numerical strength of its supporters.*

The reason for this is that royal authority exists only through group feeling. Representatives of group feeling are the militia-men who settle in the provinces and territories of the dynasty and are spread over them. The more numerous the tribes and groups of a large dynasty are, the stronger and larger are its provinces and lands. Their royal authority, therefore, is wider.

An example of this was the Muslim dynasty when God united the power of the Arabs in Islam. The number of Muslims who participated in the raid against Tabûk, the Prophet's last raid, was 110,000,[27] (consisting of) Muḍar and Qaḥṭân horsemen and foot soldiers. That number was augmented by those who became Muslims after the (raid) and down to the time of the Prophet's death. When (all these people) then set out to seek for them-selves the royal authority held by (other) nations, there was no protection against them or refuge. They were allowed (to take possession of) the realms of the Persians and the Byzantines who were the greatest dynasties in the world at that time, (as well as the realms) of the Turks in the East, of the European Christians and Berbers in the West (Maghrib), and of the Goths in Spain. They went from the Ḥijâz to as-Sûs in the far west, and from the Yemen to the Turks in the farthest north. They gained possession of all seven zones. . . .

The real reason why (large dynasties last longer) is that when collapse comes it begins in the outlying regions, and the large dynasty has many such provinces far from its center. Each de-fection that occurs necessarily requires a certain time. The time required (for collapse of the dynasty) will be long in such cases, because there are many provinces, each of which collapses in its own good time. The duration of a large dynasty, therefore, is long.

[27] . . . Lower figures are given, for example, by Ibn Sayyid-an-nâs, *'Uyûn al-athar*, II, 216, who has 30,000 men and 10,000 horses.

This (fact) may be observed in the Arab Muslim dynasty. It lasted the longest of (all Muslim) dynasties, counting both the 'Abbâsids in the center and the Umayyads far away in Spain. Their rule collapsed only after the fourth [tenth] century.[28] The 'Ubaydid(-Fâṭimids) lasted about 280 years. The Ṣinhâjah dynasty did not last as long as that of the 'Ubaydid(-Fâṭimids), namely, from the time when Ma'add al-Mu'izz entrusted Ifrîqiyah to Buluggîn b. Zîrî in the year 358 [969], up to the time when the Almohads took possession of al-Qal'ah and Bougie in the year 557 [1162]. The contemporary Almohad (Ḥafṣid) dynasty has lasted nearly 270 years.

Thus, the life of a dynasty depends upon (the number of) its supporters. "This is how God formerly proceeded with His servants."[29]

9 *A dynasty rarely establishes itself firmly in lands with many different tribes and groups.*

The reason for this is the differences in opinions and desires. Behind each opinion and desire, there is a group feeling defending it. At any time, therefore, there is much opposition to a dynasty and rebellion against it, even if the dynasty possesses group feeling, because each group feeling under the control of the ruling dynasty thinks that it has in itself (enough) strength and power.

One may compare what has happened in this connection in Ifrîqiyah and the Maghrib from the beginning of Islam to the present time. The inhabitants of those lands are Berber tribes and groups. The first victory of Ibn Abî Sarḥ[30] over them and the European Christians (in the Maghrib) was of no avail. They continued to rebel and apostatized time after time. The Muslims massacred many of them. After the Muslim religion had been

[28] The "Arab Muslim dynasty" comprises the 'Abbâsids and the Umayyads. Since, for Ibn Khaldûn, the 'Abbâsid dynasty as an independent power ended in the ninth/tenth century . . . , he had to include the Spanish Umayyads, in order to give the "Arab Muslim dynasty" the longest duration of all Muslim dynasties.

[29] Qur'ân 40.85 (85).

[30] 'Uthmân's governor of Egypt, who tried to conquer Tripolitania shortly after 647.

established among them, they went on revolting and seceding, and they adopted dissident (Khârijite) religious opinions many times. Ibn Abî Zayd said that the Berbers in the Maghrib revolted twelve times and that Islam became firmly established among them only during the governorship of Mûsâ b. Nuṣayr and thereafter. This is what is meant by the statement reported on the authority of 'Umar, that "Ifrîqiyah 'divides'[31] the hearts of its inhabitants." The statement refers to the great number of tribes and groups there, which causes them to be disobedient and unmanageable. The 'Irâq at the time was different, and so was Syria. The militia of the ('Irâq and Syria) consisted of Persians and Byzantines (respectively). All (the inhabitants) were a mixed lot of town and city dwellers. When the Muslims deprived them of their power, there remained no one capable of making a defense or of offering opposition.

The Berber tribes in the West are innumerable. All of them are Bedouins and members of groups and families. Whenever one tribe is destroyed, another takes its place and is as refractory and rebellious as the former one had been. Therefore, it has taken the Arabs a long time to establish their dynasty in the land of Ifrîqiyah and the Maghrib.

The same was the case in Syria in the age of the Israelites. At that time, there existed (there) a very large number of tribes with a great variety of group feelings, such as the tribes of Palestine and Canaan, the children of Esau, the Midyanites, the children of Lot, the Edomites, the Armenians[!], the Amalekites, Girgashites, and the Nabataeans from the Jazîrah and Mosul. Therefore, it was difficult for the Israelites to establish their dynasty firmly. Time after time, their royal authority was endangered. The (spirit of) opposition (alive in the country) communicated itself to (the Israelites). They opposed their own government and revolted against it. They thus never had a continuous and firmly established royal authority. Eventually they were overpowered, first by the Persians, then by the Greeks, and finally by the Romans, when their power came to an end in the Diaspora. "God has the power to execute His commands."[32]

---

[31] This is a play on words, connecting Ifrîqiyah with the Arabic root *f–r–q* "to divide." . . .

[32] Qur'ân 12.21 (21).

On the other hand, it is easy to establish a dynasty in lands that are free from group feelings. Government there will be a tranquil affair, because seditions and rebellions are few, and the dynasty there does not need much group feeling. This is the case in contemporary Egypt and Syria. They are (now) free from tribes and group feelings; indeed, one would never suspect that Syria had once been a mine of them, as we have (just) stated. Royal authority in Egypt is most peaceful and firmly rooted, because Egypt has few dissidents or people who represent tribal groups. Egypt has a sultan and subjects. (Egypt's) ruling dynasty consists of the Turkish rulers and their groups. They succeed each other in power, and the rule circulates among them, passing from one branch to another. The caliphate belongs in name to an 'Abbâsid, a descendant of the 'Abbâsid caliphs of Baghdad. . . .

10   *By its very nature, the royal authority claims all glory for itself and goes in for luxury and prefers tranquillity and quiet.*[33]

As to claiming all glory for itself, this is because, as we have mentioned before, royal authority exists through group feeling. Group feeling (such as leads to royal authority) is something composite that results from (the amalgamation of) many groups, one of which is stronger than all the others. Thus, (a group feeling) is able to overcome and gain power over (all the others), and, eventually, brings them all under its sway. Thus, social organization and superiority over men and dynasties come about. The secret here is that a group feeling extending over the entire tribe corresponds to the temper in the things that come into being. Temper is the product (of the mixture) of the elements. It has been explained in the proper place[34] that, when the ele-

[33] This section is the consolidation of three sections, as the earlier texts presented the material. The second, entitled "Luxury belongs to royal authority by nature," begins on p. 338, l. 1 and the third, entitled "Tranquillity and quiet belong to royal authority by nature," begins on p. 328, l. 21. C still has the old division in the text but also contains corrections and slight changes made at the beginning of the original sections and these are incorporated in the text of D. [Page and line references to original text. Editor]

[34] This seems to be meant as a general reference to works on physics where the subject is treated. However, Ibn Khaldûn had made the same statement . . . in an early stage of the text later deleted.

ments are combined in equal proportions, no mixture can take place. One (element) must be superior to the others, and when (it exercises) its superiority over them, mixture occurs. In the same way, one of the various tribal group feelings must be superior to all (others), in order to be able to bring them together, to unite them, and to weld them into one group feeling comprising all the various groups. All the various groups are then under the influence of the superior group feeling.

This highest group feeling can go only to people who have a "house" and leadership among (the tribe). One of those people must be the leader who has superiority over them. He is singled out as leader of all the various group feelings, because he is superior to all the others by birth. When he is singled out for (the position of leadership), he is too proud to let others share in his leadership and control over (the people) or to let them participate in it, because the qualities of haughtiness and pride are innate in animal nature. Thus, he develops the quality of egotism (*Ta'alluh*), which is innate in human beings.

Moreover, politics requires that only one person exercise control. Were various persons, liable to differ among each other, to exercise it, destruction of the whole could result. "If there were other gods except God in the two (heaven and earth), they (heaven and earth) would have been destroyed."[35]

Thus, the aspirations of the various group feelings are blunted. People become tame and do not aspire to share with the leader in the exercise of control. Their group feeling is forced to refrain (from such aspirations). The leader takes charge all by himself, as far as possible. Eventually, he leaves no part in the power to anyone else. He thus claims all the glory for himself and does not permit the people to share in it. This may come to pass already with the first ruler of a dynasty, or it may come to pass only with the second or the third, depending on the resistance and strength of the various group feelings, but it is something unavoidable in a dynasty. This is how God proceeds with His servants. . . .

[35] Qur'ân 21.22 (22).

15 *The stages of dynasties. How the desert attitude differs among the people in the different stages.*[36]

It should be known that a dynasty goes through different stages and encounters new conditions. Through the conditions that are peculiar to a particular stage, the supporters of the dynasty acquire in that stage traits of character such as do not exist in any other stage. Traits of character are the natural result of the peculiar situations in which they are found.

The conditions and stages of a dynasty are as a rule no more than five (in number).

The first stage is that of success, the overthrow of all opposition, and the appropriation of royal authority from the preceding dynasty. In this stage, the ruler serves as model to his people by the manner in which he acquires glory, collects taxes, defends property, and provides military protection. He does not claim anything exclusively for himself to the exclusion of (his people), because (such an attitude) is what is required by group feeling, (and it was group feeling) that gave superiority (to the dynasty), and (group feeling) still continues to exist as before.

The second stage is the one in which the ruler gains complete control over his people, claims royal authority all for himself, excluding them, and prevents them from trying to have a share in it. In this stage, the ruler of the dynasty is concerned with gaining adherents and acquiring clients and followers in great numbers, so as to be able to blunt the aspirations of the people who share in his group feeling and belong to his group, who are of the same descent as he himself and have the same claim to royal authority as he has. He keeps them from power and bars them from the sources of (power). He stops them from getting to it, and, eventually, all the power is in the hands of his family. He reserves all the glory that he is building up to the members of his own house. He spends as much, or more, care to keep (his people) at a distance and to subdue them, as the first members

---

[36] The earlier texts had a different title, namely, "The stages of a dynasty and its varying conditions. The desert attitude of the people in the different stages." The old title is replaced in C by the new one, which then occurs in D.

of the dynasty expended in the search for power. The first (members of the dynasty) kept strangers away, and all the people who shared in their group feeling supported them in this. He, on the other hand, keeps (his) relatives away, and he is supported in this effort only by a very small number of people, who are not related to him. Thus, he undertakes a very difficult task.

The third stage is one of leisure and tranquillity in which the fruits of royal authority are enjoyed. (These fruits are) the things that human nature desires, such as acquisition of property, creation of lasting monuments, and fame. All the ability (of the ruler) is expended on collecting taxes; regulating income and expenses, bookkeeping and planning expenditures; erecting large buildings, big constructions, spacious cities, and lofty monuments; presenting gifts to embassies of nobles from (foreign) nations and tribal dignitaries; and dispensing bounty to his own people. In addition, he supports the demands of his followers and retinue with money and positions. He inspects his soldiers, pays them well, and distributes fairly their allowances every month. Eventually, the result of this (liberality) shows itself in their dress, their fine equipment, and their armor on parade days. The ruler thus can impress friendly dynasties and frighten hostile ones with (his soldiers). This stage is the last during which the ruler is in complete authority. Throughout this and the previous stages, the rulers are independent in their opinions. They build up their strength and show the way for those after them.

The fourth stage is one of contentment and peacefulness. The ruler is content with what his predecessors have built. He lives in peace with all his royal peers. He adopts the tradition of his predecessors and follows closely in their footsteps. He imitates their ways most carefully. He thinks that to depart from tradition would mean the destruction of his power and that they knew better (what is good for the preservation of) the glory they themselves had built.

The fifth stage is one of waste and squandering. In this stage, the ruler wastes on pleasures and amusements (the treasures) accumulated by his ancestors, through (excessive) generosity to his inner circle and at their parties. Also, he acquires bad, low-class followers to whom he entrusts the most important matters (of state), which they are not qualified to handle by themselves, not knowing which of them they should tackle and which they should leave alone. (In addition,) the ruler seeks to destroy the great clients of his people and followers of his predecessors. Thus, they come to hate him and conspire to refuse support to him. (Furthermore) he loses a number of soldiers by spending their allowances on his pleasures (instead of paying them) and by refusing them access to his person and not supervising them (properly). Thus, he ruins the foundations his ancestors had laid and tears down what they had built up. In this stage, the dynasty is seized by senility and the chronic disease from which it can hardly ever rid itself, for which it can find no cure, and, eventually, it is destroyed. We shall explain that in connection with conditions to be discussed later on.

God is the best heir.[37]

[37] Cf. Qur'ân 21.89 (89).

KENT V. FLANNERY

2. *The Ecology of Early Food Production in Mesopotamia*[1]

Greater Mesopotamia—broadly defined here as the whole area drained by the tributaries of the Shatt al-Arab—has long been the scene of popular interest and scholarly research. In recent years attention has been drawn to the fact that this was one of the few areas in the world where agriculture and animal husbandry seem to have arisen autonomously. A number of excellent cultural-historical reconstructions of the way food production began in the Near East are already available,[2, 3] but most of these reconstructions do not deal directly with some of the ecological questions most commonly asked by the interested nonspecialist. This article examines some of those questions.

THE ENVIRONMENT

From the standpoint of agriculture and grazing potential, the area under consideration includes four main environmental zones: the alluvial plain of Mesopotamia proper, the steppeland of Assyria, the woodland belt of the Zagros Mountains, and the

Permission to reprint this selection is granted by the author and by the American Association for the Advancement of Science, © 1965 by the American Association for the Advancement of Science in *Science,* March 12, 1965, Vol. 147, pp. 1247–56.

[1] Much of the research leading to discoveries mentioned in this article was made possible by National Science Foundation grants to R. J. Braidwood of the University of Chicago (1959–60) and Frank Hole of Rice University (1963). Hans Helbaek, Frank Hole, and James Neely made suggestions which led to the formulation of many of the ideas presented.

[2] R. J. Braidwood and B. Howe, in *Courses Toward Urban Life,* R. J. Braidwood and G. R. Willey, eds. (Aldine, Chicago, 1962), pp. 132–46.

[3] J. Perrot, *ibid.,* pp. 147–64.

edge of the high central plateau of Iran (see Figs. 2-1 and 2-2).
The first three of these zones have already been described by
Hatt;[4] I have added the high plateau, although it is not actually
drained by the Shatt al-Arab system, because its mineral resources figured prominently in the early village period.

1) *The central plateau of Iran.* Central Iran is an interior drainage basin at altitudes of 900 to 1500 meters, with annual rainfall
as low as 100 to 230 millimeters. The basin is filled with sierozem
and desert soils, overlain in places by shallow brackish lakes surrounded by salt-crusted flatland. Rugged mountains jut unexpectedly from the plain, some of them ore-bearing; there are
veins of copper just east of the prehistoric site of Tepe Sialk, and
one of the world's major turquoise sources lies in the northeast
corner of the plateau near Meshed. Both turquoise and copper
were traded as far away as the Assyrian steppe zone by 6500
B.C.[5]

Herds of gazelle (*Gazella subgutturosa*) and wild ass (*Equus
hemionus*) would have been available to hunters in the area, but
without irrigation the high plateau is very marginal agricultural
land; the only source of hope for the early farmer would have
been the alluvial aprons of mountain soil produced where
streams break through the Zagros to enter the salt lake basins.
Despite the uncertain rainfall, some of these "oasis" locations appear to have been permanently settled by 5500 B.C., especially
those near copper sources.

2) *The oak-pistachio woodland belt.* The Zagros Mountains
break away from the eastern edge of the high plateau and descend in tiers toward the Tigris-Euphrates basin. In places the
mountains form parallel ridges which are separated by long,
narrow, synclinal or anticlinal valleys, frequently poor in surface
water; in other areas there are irregular mountain masses bordering wide flat valleys. Acting as aquifers, these porous mountain
masses may trap tremendous quantities of winter snow or rain
and release it through springs, which in turn feed permanent
poplar-bordered streams. At elevations of 600 to 1350 meters
there are alluvial valleys of chernozem, chestnut, brown, or

---

[4] F. Hole, K. V. Flannery, J. A. Neely, "Early Agriculture and Animal
Domestication at Deh Luran, Iran," *Current Anthropology* [in press].
[5] *Ibid.*

reddish-brown soils, with alpine meadows scattered through the surrounding peaks. Summers are warm and dry, winters cool and wet; depending on altitude and topography, the annual rainfall varies from 250 to 1000 millimeters, and hillsides have varying densities of oak, maple, juniper, hawthorn, pistachio, and wild pear. On well-watered slopes grow hard-grained annual grasses like wild emmer wheat (*Triticum dicocoides*), barley (*Hordeum spontaneum*), and oats (*Avena fatua*).

FIG. 2-1 Map of Greater Mesopotamia and adjacent areas today.

Much of the area is too rugged for large-scale agriculture, but even the narrower and drier valleys have been used for sheep or goat grazing since at least 8500 B.C.; broad valleys with annual rainfall in excess of 300 millimeters have been farmed for at least the same length of time.

3) *The Assyrian steppe.* The Zagros Mountains fall away
through a series of foothills and eventually level off onto a steppe
region of great natural winter grassland at elevations of 150 to
300 meters; these plains have reddish-brown or brown prairie
soils of high fertility. Here the mountain streams have collected
into larger rivers like the Tigris, Karkheh, Diz, and Karun, which
flow into the area through erosional valleys and have wide, farm-
able floodplains. Hot and dry in the summer, the Assyrian
steppe is transformed by 250 to 380 millimeters of winter rain
into meadows of Bermuda grass, canary grass, and wild narcissus.
Herds of gazelle, wild ass, and wild cattle once roamed the
plain, and the rivers had carp and catfish. The Assyrian steppe is
oil country, and one of its most widely traded commodities in
prehistoric time was bitumen or natural asphalt, used for cement-
ing flint tools into their handles.

Some parts of the steppe, too salty for effective agriculture, are
used for winter grazing. Other areas are real breadbaskets for
winter wheat (like the upper Khabur plain; the area near Mosul,
Iraq; or the Khuzistan plain of southwest Iran), and the density of prehistoric villages in these regions is staggering. Adams'
comments on northern Khuzistan[6]—that the adequate rainfall,
underlying gravels, and consequent good drainage in this zone
facilitated the crucial transition from dry farming to irrigation—
may apply to other favored parts of the steppes.

4) *Southern Mesopotamia.* Below 150 meters the Assyrian
steppe gives way to the lower drainage of the Tigris, Euphrates,
and Karun, as they flow together and empty into the Persian
Gulf. Here the annual rainfall is under 250 millimeters (an
amount usually inadequate for dry farming) and the grassland is
replaced by two kinds of biotopes: alluvial desert and blowing
sand dunes on higher ground, and reed-bordered swamps in the
low-lying areas. The delta area is a subsiding geosyncline, slowly
settling and filling with river alluvium, across which the big
rivers run between their own natural levees, flooding and changing courses periodically.[7] Contrary to what was once believed,
the area has never been under the waters of the Persian Gulf
(at least not since the Pliocene), and in prehistoric times it must

[6] R. M. Adams, *Science 136*, 109 (1962).
[7] G. M. Lees and N. L. Falcon, *Geograph. J. 118*, 24 (1952).

have looked much as it does today. It was in this environmental
zone that urban life, civilization, and writing began, about 3000
B.C. When permanent settlement began here is undetermined,
but villages dating back to 5500 B.C. are known even in the bleak
area west of the Euphrates. Surely these villages must have followed the old swamps and watercourses, beyond which agriculture would have been impossible and grazing difficult.

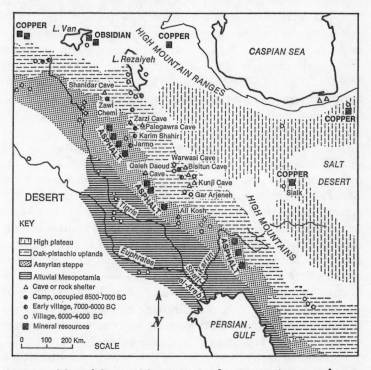

FIG. 2-2   Map of Greater Mesopotamia, showing environmental zones,
mineral resources, and archeological sites. Only sites mentioned in
the text are labelled.

THE LOCAL CLIMATIC SEQUENCE

The possibility that the environment in the Near East might have been different during the beginnings of agriculture has intrigued archeologists for generations. The few prehistoric pollen sequences we have suggest that, although some climatic fluctuations did occur, they were not on a scale capable of creating or destroying the complex of plants and animals that were eventually domesticated. The facts we have are too few to permit us to say dogmatically that climatic change played *no* role, but it appears that the problem is cultural rather than climatic; the inescapable conclusion is that agriculture began in an area where, then as now, only about 10 percent of the land surface is suitable for dry farming.[8]

One pollen sequence comes from Lake Zeribar in the wooded mountains of western Iran, at an altitude of about 1200 meters. Studies by van Zeist and Wright[9] show that during the late Pleistocene the area was steppe, characterized by the sagebrush-like *Artemisia*, which implies a cool dry climate. About 11,000 B.C., at the end of the Pleistocene, the area became warmer and the vegetation made the transition to savanna, with scattered oaks and pistachios. The savanna thickened to oak forest about 3500 B.C., either through increased precipitation or through lowered temperature. Cereal-type pollen (possibly wild wheat and barley?) is present throughout the entire sequence, so climatic fluctuation would seem not to have been a determining factor in the beginning of agriculture there.

Six hundred meters lower, in the Zagros Mountains of Iraq, a slightly conflicting pollen story is available from human occupational debris in Shanidar Cave. More striking climatic fluctuations are implied, one of which Solecki interprets as the "shock stimulus" which triggered the beginnings of food production.[10] Actu-

[8] G. B. Cressey, *Crossroads: Land and Life in Southwest Asia* (Lippincott, New York, 1960), pp. 158–60.
[9] W. van Zeist and H. E. Wright, Jr., *Science 140*, 65 (1963).
[10] R. S. Solecki, *ibid.*, 139, 179 (1963).

ally, however, the late-Pleistocene to early-Recent pollen sequence from Shanidar is not in much conflict with that from Lake Zeribar: at about 10,000 B.C. a "relatively cool climate" changed to "a warmer one similar to the present climate." Cereal pollen is known at least as early as 14,000 B.C., and potential animal domesticates (sheep and goat) are present in the cave debris even at 40,000 B.C.

Neither of these pollen sequences supports the age-old myth that the Near East was once lush and well watered, then suffered from desiccation. Nor do any of the inferred climatic fluctuations imply the sudden, overnight appearance of wheat, barley, sheep, or goats. I do not feel qualified to evaluate the "shock stimulus" theory, but I suspect that, although drastic climatic change explains why certain plants and animals become extinct, it does not explain how or why cultures change.

PRE-AGRICULTURAL SUBSISTENCE PATTERN

Scattered caves, rock shelters, and open-air sites have given us only hints of how man lived in this part of the world before domestication of plants and animals. All appearances are that his way of life conformed to a flexible, "broad-spectrum" collecting pattern, keyed to the seasonal aspects of the wild resources of each environmental zone, with perhaps a certain amount of seasonal migration from zone to zone. The less mobile members of society appear to have collected such resources as snails, turtles, fresh-water clams and crabs, and the seeds of wild annuals and perennials, while more mobile members pursued wild ungulates by special techniques, according to the species involved. Although cave remains include fish, birds, and small mammals, the bulk of the meat diet—often more than 90 percent[11]—came from ungulates, like the wild sheep, goat, ox, pig, wild ass, gazelle, and deer. Note that the first four were early domesticates.

Hunting patterns were influenced by the topography of the region. In the steep, rugged rockslide area around Shanidar Cave,

[11] See, for example, D. Perkins, Jr., *ibid.*, 144, 1565 (1964).

wild goat (*Capra hircus*) was the animal most frequently taken. The goat, a resident of the limestone crags, is difficult to hunt by means of drives; it is best pursued by small groups of agile men who know their country well and are equipped with light projectiles. Rock-shelters or caves overlooking broad, flat valleys are usually rich in the bones of the wild ass, a plains-dwelling animal which could best have been hunted by drives or surrounds, then dispatched with a larger weapon, like a thrusting spear. Gazelles and hares are also creatures of the flat valley, while the wild sheep of the Near East (*Ovis orientalis*) frequent rolling, round-top hills and are hunted today by ambush in the brushy stream-canyons where they hide during the noon hours. Some of the smaller rock-shelters excavated in the Zagros Mountains seem to have been stations or overlooks used mainly for hunting or butchering a single species of ungulate, or two species at most.[12]

In recent years the oak-pistachio uplands, in the 400- to 1000-millimeter rainfall belt at altitudes of 450 to 900 meters, have been singled out as an "optimum" zone which includes all the potential domesticates.[13] Actually, topography is a much more important ecological factor for wild sheep and goats than either altitude or rainfall; sheep range down to sea level along the Caspian Sea, and up to 2700 meters in the Zagros Mountains, if rolling mountain meadows are available. Goats reach sea level on the foothills flanking the Persian Gulf, and are as much at home on the last rugged sandstone hills separating southwest Iran from

[12] The foregoing discussion is based in part on published studies of faunas from the sites of Shanidar Cave and Zawi Chemi (footnote 11), Zarzi Cave, and Palegawra Cave, all in Iraq [for a summary see R. J. Braidwood and B. Howe, "Prehistoric Investigations in Iraqi Kurdistan," *Studies in Ancient Oriental Civilization No. 31* (Univ. of Chicago Press, Chicago, 1960), pp. 169–70], and Bisitun Cave in Iran [see C. S. Coon, *Cave Explorations in Iran in 1949* (Univ. of Pennsylvania Museum, Philadelphia, 1951)]. It is based, also, on personal examination of unpublished faunal collections from Karim Shahir in Iraq (footnote 13) and from the following Iranian sites: Qaleh Daoud Cave [see F. Hole, *Science 137*, 524 (1962)]. Warwasi Rock Shelter [see R. J. Braidwood and B. Howe, *Courses Toward Urban Life* (footnote 2), p. 135], and Kunji Cave and Gar Arjeneh Rock Shelter (F. Hole and K. Flannery, unpublished data).

[13] R. J. Braidwood and B. Howe (*et al.*), "Prehistoric Investigations in Iraqi Kurdistan," *Studies in Ancient Oriental Civilization No. 31* (Univ. of Chicago Press, Chicago, 1960).

southern Mesopotamia (180 meters above sea level) as they are on the 3000-meter crags of the northern Zagros. Pigs range over a wide area, from sea level to timberline, and if we knew more about the ecologcial requirements of wild cattle we might find their range equally broad.[14] The crucial factor for hunters of wild ungulates, or early herders of semiwild ungulates, would have been the ability to move from upland to lowland as seasonal pasture was available, a pattern known as "transhumance."

Let me give one example. Khuzistan, the Iranian arm of the Assyrian steppe, is lush winter grassland from December to April while many of the mountains to the east are covered with snow. Through late spring and summer the steppe becomes blisteringly hot and dry, while the melting snow on the mountains gives rise to good spring and summer grassland. The Persian herder classifies the steppe as *quishlaq* (winter pasture) and the mountains as *yehlaq* (summer pasture), and he moves his herd from one to the other as the season demands. Prehistoric hunters may have followed game over the same route; and as for prehistoric herders, Adams reminds us:[15] "It is, in fact, erroneous to consider the upper plains as a zone of occupance distinct from the surrounding uplands. Both together constitute a single natural ecosystem, whose seasonal alternation of resources provides as strong an inducement to migratory stockbreeding as to intensive, settled agriculture."

The wild plants of southwestern Asia have much the same seasonal aspect. MacNeish's work in the New World[16] has shown that a long period of intensive plant collecting preceded agriculture there; archeologists have long assumed that this was the case in the Near East, but preserved plant remains were not available to tell us which specific plants were used in the pre-agricultural era. New light was thrown on the problem in 1963 by a collection of some 10,000 carbonized seeds from basal levels at the site of

[14] For a good summary of the differences in ecology between sheep and goat, see D. Perkins, Jr., "The Post-Cranial Skeleton of the Caprinae: Comparative Anatomy and Changes under Domestication," thesis, Harvard University, 1959. Perkins explains the skeletal differences, especially differences in metapodial length, which reflect the somewhat different habitats occupied by *Ovis* and *Capra*.

[15] R. M. Adams, *Science 136*, 109 (1962).

[16] R. S. MacNeish, *Science 143*, 531 (1964).

Ali Kosh in lowland southwestern Iran.[17] The area, a part of the Assyrian steppe, lies outside the range of wild wheat and barley, but locally available plants were intensively collected; the most common were wild alfalfa (*Medicago*) and the tiny-seeded wild legumes *Astragalus* and *Trigonella,* as well as fruits like the wild caper (*Capparis*), used today mainly as a condiment. These data indicate that intensive plant collecting may have been the pattern everywhere in southwest Asia, not merely at the altitude where wild wheat grows best. Moreover, the fact that *Astragalus* and *Trigonella* occur in the mountains as well as the lowlands suggests that prehistoric collectors could have harvested one crop on the Assyrian steppe in March, moved up to 600 meters for a harvest in April or May, and arrived at 1500 meters for another harvest in June or July. Somewhere between 600 and 1200 meters these migrant collectors could have harvested the seeds of the annual grasses ancestral to domestic wheat, barley, and oats. These cereals, which are dependent on annual rainfall of 400 to 750 millimeters, do not range down to the Assyrian steppe today, although they are available over a surprisingly wide area; according to Helbaek,[18] wild barley "grows in the mountain forest, on the coastal plain, in the shade of rock outcrops in semidesert areas, and as a weed in the fields of every conceivable cultivated crop" from Morocco to Turkestan.

Other plants useful to the collector—and eventually, in some cases, to the primitive cultivator—were ryegrass (*Lolium*), *Aegilops* grass, wild flax (*Linum bienne*), and large-seeded wild legumes like lentil, vetch, vetchling, chick pea, and *Prosopis* (a relative of mesquite). The lowlands had dates; the foothills had acorns, almonds, and pistachios; and the northern mountains had grapes, apples, and pears.

Most of the important species occurred in more than one zone, and their months of availability were slightly different at different altitudes—key factors from the standpoint of human ecology. An

[17] The plants were identified by Dr. Hans Helbaek of the Danish National Museum (see footnote 4).

[18] H. Helbaek, in "Prehistoric Investigations in Iraqi Kurdistan," *Studies in Ancient Oriental Civilization No. 31* (Univ. of Chicago Press, Chicago, 1960).

incredibly varied fare was available to the hunter-collector who knew which plants and animals were available in each season in each environmental zone; which niche or "microenvironment" the species was concentrated in, such as hillside, cliff, or stream plain; which species could be stored best, and which it was most practical to hunt or collect. From 40,000 to 10,000 B.C., man worked out a pattern for exploiting the natural resources of this part of the world, and I suspect that this pre-agricultural pattern had more to do with the beginnings of food production than any climatic "shock stimulus."

BEGINNINGS OF FOOD PRODUCTION

Leslie White reminds us[19] that "we are not to think of the origin of agriculture as due to the chance discovery that seeds thrown away from a meal subsequently sprouted. Mankind knew all this and more for tens of thousands of years before cultivation of plants began." The cultivation of plants required no new facts or knowledge, but was simply a new kind of relationship between man and the plants with which he was most familiar.

One striking aspect of the late pre-agricultural pattern in the Greater Mesopotamian area was the trading of obsidian from its source in central and eastern Turkey to cave sites in the central Zagros, such as Zarzi and Shanidar.[20] Natural asphalt was traded in the opposite direction, up from the tar pits of the Assyrian steppe to campsites in the mountains, wherever flints had to be hafted. By 7000 B.C., handfuls of emmer wheat from the oak-pistachio belt had reached the lowland steppe of Khuzistan.[21] Typical of the prehistoric Near Easterner was this penchant for moving commodities from niche to niche within environmental zones, and even from zone to zone.

It has been argued that the last millennia of the pre-agricultural era were a time of "settling in" to one's area, of increasing inten-

[19] L. A. White, *The Evolution of Culture* (McGraw-Hill, New York, 1959), pp. 283–84.
[20] Solecki, 1963. See also footnote 13.
[21] See footnote 4.

sification and regionalization of the exploitation of natural resources.[22] This is indeed reflected in the flint tools, but such "regional specialization" may not be the essential trend which led to food production. From the standpoint of human ecology, the single most important factor may have been the establishment of the above-mentioned pattern of interchange of resources between groups exploiting contrasting environmental situations—a kind of primitive redistribution system. It was this pattern that set the stage for the removal of certain key species of edible grasses from the niches in which they were indigenous, and their transferral to niches to which they were foreign.

With the wisdom of hindsight we can see that, when the first seeds had been planted, the trend from "food collecting" to "food producing" was under way. But from an ecological standpoint the important point is not that man *planted* wheat but that he (i) moved it to niches to which it was not adapted, (ii) removed certain pressures of natural selection, which allowed more deviants from the normal phenotype to survive, and (iii) eventually selected for characters not beneficial under conditions of natural selection.

All that the "settling in" process did for the prehistoric collector was to teach him that wild wheat grew from seeds that fell to the ground in July, sprouted on the mountain talus in February, and would be available to him in usable form if he arrived for a harvest in May. His access to those mature seeds put him in a good position to bargain with the goat-hunters in the mountain meadow above him. He may have viewed the first planting of seeds merely as the transfer of a useful wild grass from a niche that was hard to reach—like the talus below a limestone cliff—to an accessible niche, like the disturbed soil around his camp on a nearby stream terrace. Happily for man, wild wheat and barley both grow well on disturbed soils; they will sprout on the back-dirt pile of an archeological excavation, and they probably did equally well on the midden outside a prehistoric camp.[23] It is obvious from the rapid spread of agriculture in the Mesopotamian area that they grew as readily on the midden outside the forager's

[22] R. J. Braidwood and B. Howe, *et al.*, p. 180.
[23] H. Helbaek in "Prehistoric Investigations in Iraqi Kurdistan."

winter camp at 180 meters as they did in his summer camp at 900 meters, in the "optimum" zone.

Viewed in these terms the advent of cultivation may have been a rather undramatic event, and the concept of "incipient cultivation"[24] becomes rather hard to define. Was it a fumbling attempt at cultivation, or only the intensification of an already existent system of interregional exchange?

BIOLOGICAL OBSTACLES TO EARLY FOOD PRODUCTION

The transfer of species from habitat to habitat made the products of all zones available to all people; but it was a process not without difficulty, since some of the plant and animal species involved had not yet developed the most tractable or productive phenotypes, from man's point of view.

Some of the biological obstacles faced by early agriculturalists were as follows.

1) The difficulty of harvesting wild, brittle-rachis grains. One adaptive mechanism for seed dispersal in wild wheat and barley is a brittle rachis or axis which holds the seeds together in the mature head of grain. When a dry, ripe head of wild barley is struck by a twig or a gust of wind, the rachis disintegrates and the seeds are spread far and wide.[25] The disadvantages of this mechanism for the prehistoric collector are obvious: the slightest tug on the stem of the plant or the slightest blow with a flint sickle might send the seeds scattering in every direction.

2) The difficulty of removing the grain from its husk. Even after a successful harvest, the prehistoric collector's troubles were not over. Primitive grains like emmer or einkorn wheat have a tough husk, or glume, which holds each kernel in a stubborn grip long after the brittle rachis has disintegrated. Even vigorous

[24] R. J. Braidwood and B. Howe (*et al.*).

[25] This, and all subsequent discussion of the ecology of the early cereals, is based on personal communications from Hans Helbaek or on one of the following articles by Dr. Helbaek: "Paleo-Ethnobotany," in *Science in Archaeology*, D. Brothwell and E. Higgs, Eds. (Thames and Hudson, London, 1963); *Iraq* 22, 186 (1960); "The Paleoethnobotany of the Near East and Europe," in "Prehistoric Investigations in Iraqi Kurdistan" (see footnote 13).

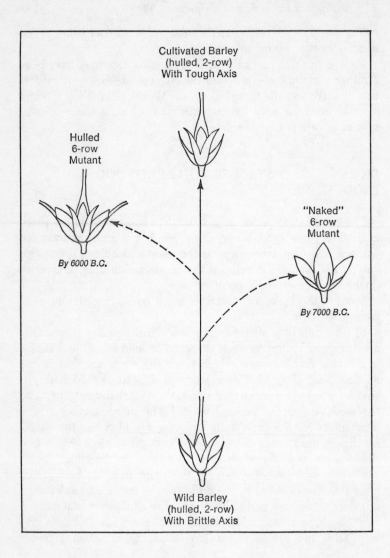

FIG. 2-3 Simplified diagrams of barley spikelets, showing some of the changes which took place after domestication. Data courtesy of Helbaek (see text).

threshing will usually not release these primitive grains from the glume so that they can be eaten.

3) The difficulty of farming in the niche to which the grain was adapted. Both wild wheat and barley are grasses of hillsides and slopes, and they usually do not occur on the flat stream flood-plains, where it would have been most convenient for prehistoric man to farm. The deep alluvial soils in the valley centers, prime areas from an agricultural standpoint, were already occupied by competing grasses and wild legumes.

Research on archeological grain remains by Danish botanist Hans Helbaek has shown us some of the ways in which early farmers either consciously or unconsciously overcame these three obstacles.

1) Selection for tough-rachis grains. Within the gene pool of wild wheat and barley were variants whose rachis was tough enough so that it did not shatter on contact. Normally these variants would have left few descendents, because of the inadequacy of their seed-dispersal mechanism. When man harvested with sickles or flails, however, he automatically selected *for* the tough-rachis grains because their heads stayed intact despite the rough treatment of the harvest. When seeds from the harvest were planted, the next generation of plants contained an abnormally high proportion of tough-rachis individuals, and each successive generation reinforced the trend.

2) The development of techniques for removing the seeds from their glumes. Sometime before 7000 B.C. man discovered that by roasting the grain he had collected he could render the glumes so dry and brittle that they could be crushed by abrasion; roasting, moreover, killed the wheat or barley germ so that it would not sprout, and the grain could be stored even through the winter rainy season. Many of the preceramic villages excavated throughout the Near East contain clay ovens appropriate for roasting grain in this manner, and nearly all seem to have stone grinding slabs of one kind or another on which the dry grain could be abraded out of its glume. Further grinding resulted in "groats," or coarse grits of grain which could be cooked up into a mush or gruel. (By and large, the tough-glumed primitive grains were unsuitable for bread-making.)

3) Actual genetic change in the grain species themselves, re-

sulting in new strains. Because early cultivated grain was somewhat shielded by man from the natural selection pressures to
which uncultivated grain was subjected, the chance that random
mutants would survive was much greater. One of the first mutations that occurred, apparently, was a change from the standard
adhering-glume kernel to a "naked" kernel which could be easily
freed by threshing. According to Stubbe,[26] a single gene controls
the difference between "hulled" and "naked" barley, and when a
mutation took place at that locus, sometime before 7000 B.C.,
free-threshing barley was born. A second genetic change was that
which transformed standard wild barley (*Hordeum spontan-
em*), which has only two fertile kernel rows, into mutant barley
with six fertile rows (*Hordeum hexastichum*). Helbaek, who has
actually produced the six-row mutant in his laboratory by sub-
jecting wild two-row barley to x-rays,[27] feels that ecological factors probably determined the early distribution of these two
strains: two-row barley is adapted to the fairly late (April and
May) rainfall of the cool Zagros Mountain uplands, while mutant
six-row barley may be more successfully adapted to much drier
spring weather and the irrigation farming of the Mesopotamian
plain.[28] Archeological remains tend to support this. The two-row
form seems to be the only one known so far from the highlands
before 5000 B.C., while six-row barley is known from lowland
Khuzistan by 6000 B.C.; the two-row strain does not seem to have
caught on in the lowlands, possibly because it was poorly adapted
to the climate there. Present data, in fact, suggest that although
the cool uplands probably contributed the original ancestor (two-
row hulled barley) it may have been the lowland ecology which
stabilized the important "naked" and "six-row" strains (see
Fig. 2-3).

Another important early genetic change was polyploidy, an
actual increase in the chromosome number, which produced new
strains of wheat. Wild emmer wheat (*Triticum dicoccoides*) is
tetraploid—that is, it contains 4×7 chromosomes and has tough
glumes enclosing the kernels. A native annual grass of well-
watered mountains, it prefers the 400- to 750-millimeter rainfall

[26] H. Stubbe, *Cold Spring Harbor Symp. Quant. Biol. 24*, 31 (1959).
[27] H. Helbaek, *Iraq 22*, 186 (1960).
[28] *Ibid.*, in "Prehistoric Investigations in Iraqi Kurdistan."

zone, from Palestine and Syria to the Zagros Mountains of Iran and Iraq. By 6000 B.C., however, on the Anatolian plateau of central Turkey, a mutant had been produced which was free-threshing: this was hexaploid wheat (*Triticum aestivum*), with 6×7 chromosomes.[29] Such polyploid strains, together with irrigation, were instrumental in the spread of free-threshing wheat throughout southwest Asia.

Mutations and changes in gene frequency also played a role in the establishment of races of domestic animals, and once again there were biological obstacles to be overcome by early herders. Some of the adaptive and nonadaptive changes which took place were as follows.

1) A change in the sex and age ratios within the captive population. If early herds of domesticated sheep or goats were small,

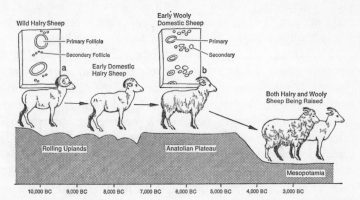

FIG. 2-4 Simplified diagram showing some of the steps in the evolution of domestic sheep. (a) Section, as seen through a microscope, of skin of wild sheep, showing the arrangement of primary (hair) and secondary (wool) follicles; (b) section, similarly enlarged, of skin of domestic sheep, showing the changed relationship and the change in the size of follicles that accompanied the development of wool. [After Ryder; see text]

as we assume they were, how did the animals avoid being eaten during the winter and survive until the spring lambing season?

[29] See footnote 25.

Work by Charles A. Reed[30] and Dexter Perkins[31] on archeological bones from early villages in Kurdistan suggests that some kind of conservation may have been practiced. Perkins notes that the proportion of immature sheep relative to adult sheep at Zawi Chemi, Iraq, was far higher than that in any normal wild herd, an observation from which he infers domestication.[32] Evidently the young animals were eaten, while the older breeding stock was saved. The practice was much the same at the village of Jarmo, where Reed noted a high proportion of butchered young males, as if the females were being held back for breeding. Such practices would have resulted in an abnormally high proportion of adult females in the herd, and consequently in milk surpluses in late winter and early spring. Although wild sheep and goats produce very little milk in comparison to today's domestic breeds, such seasonal surpluses may eventually have been exploited by early herders. Today, milk, yogurt, and cheese are part of the whole trading complex of southwest Asian pastoralists.

2) Changes leading to wool production. Wild sheep (*Ovis orientalis*) have a coat like a deer or gazelle, and are no woolier than the latter. Microscopic examination of their skin reveals two kinds of follicles: "primaries," or hair follicles which produce the visible coat, and "secondaries," which produce the hidden, wooly underfur. In the skin of wild *Ovis* the secondary follicles lie intermingled with the primaries in groups of three to five. After domestication, genetic changes moved the secondaries out to the side, away from the primaries, and greatly increased their numbers; while wild strains of sheep or goat may have a ratio of only two to four secondaries for each primary, the ratio may be as high as seven to one in fine Merino sheep. The wool of the domestic sheep grows from these dense clusters of secondary follicles.[33] Wool may already have been spun as early as 6000 B.C. at Catal Hüyük in Anatolia.[34] Both "hairy" and "wooly" sheep

[30] C. A. Reed in "Prehistoric Investigations in Iraqi Kurdistan," see footnote 13.
[31] See footnote 11.
[32] See also R. H. Dyson, Jr., *Am. Anthropologist 55*, 661 (1953).
[33] M. L. Ryder, *Nature 182*, 781 (1958).
[34] J. Mellaart, *Sci. Am. 210*, 99 (1964).

were known by 3000 B.C. in Mesopotamia,[35] and the now-famous Dead Sea Scrolls, dating to the time of Christ, have been shown by Ryder[36] to have been written on parchment made both from hairy and from wooly sheep (see Fig. 2-4).

3) Nonadaptive genetic changes, such as the twisted horns of domestic goats. One of the most interesting (if poorly understood) changes which followed domestication was one affecting the horns of the goat (*Capra hircus*). The wild goat of the Near East has scimitar-shaped horns whose bony cores are quadrangular or diamond-shaped in cross section near the skull. Sites dating from 8500 to 7000 B.C. are known where goat domestication is inferred from the ratio of immature animals to adult animals, but no changes in the cross section of the horn during this period are noted. By 6500 B.C., from the Jordan Valley to the Zagros Mountains, there are scattered occurrences of goats whose horn cores show a flattening of the medial surface, and thus a triangular or almond-shaped cross section. By 6000 B.C. in the Mesopotamian area, from the Assyrian steppe to the oak-pistachio woodlands, a new type of horn core makes its appearance: the core is medially flattened in section, and it also shows signs of a corkscrew twist like that of the modern domestic goat in southwest Asia. The irregular geographic distribution of the trait suggests that it was strongest in the Iran-Iraq area, occurring only sporadically elsewhere before 4500 B.C.; even at 3500 B.C. not all sites in the Palestinian area show goats of a uniformly "twisted horn" type.[37] Possibly its rapid spread in the Zagros was due to transhumant herding (see Fig. 2-5).

4) The problem of pig domestication. One of the questions most frequently asked is why the pig was domesticated at 6000 B.C. in some parts of the Near East, like the Zagros Mountain valleys,[38] but was apparently never domesticated in prehistoric time in other areas, such as the Khuzistan steppe.[39] The most common answer is that this was the result of religious or dietary

[35] M. Hilzheimer, *Studies in Ancient Oriental Civilization No. 20* (Univ. of Chicago Press, Chicago, 1941).

[36] M. L. Ryder, *op. cit.*

[37] C. A. Reed, in "Prehistoric Investigations in Iraqi Kurdistan" (see footnote 13).

[38] *Ibid.*, Z. *Tierzüchtung Züchtungsbiol.* 76, 32 (1961).

[39] F. Hole, K. V. Flannery, J. A. Neely (see footnote 4).

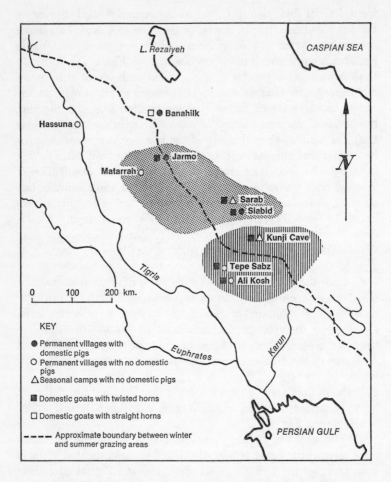

FIG. 2-5 Map of Greater Mesopotamia, showing areas where transhumance is believed to have been of importance in prehistoric times. Ceramic objects from sites in the stippled area (Jarmo, Sarab, Matarrah) all have one set of traits; those from sites in the hachured area (Kunji, Ali Kosh, Tepe Sabz) all have another set. The rapid spread of the twisted-horn goat in both areas suggests that flocks may have been moved from one elevation to another seasonally; so does the almost complete absence of the domestic pig, an animal unsuitable for transhumant herding. In the summer grazing area (northeast of the dashed line), many sites appear to be seasonal shepherds' camps

laws; but in fact, the reasons may be ecological. According to Krader,[40] "the disappearance of the pig from Central Asia is not the clear-cut case of religious determination that might be supposed. The pig is not a species suitable to pastoral nomadism . . . it is nomadism with its mastery of the steppe ecology and movements of herds and herdsmen which is the decisive factor in the disappearance of pigs from this part of the world." Figure 2-5 shows the sites where domestic pigs are known either to have been, or not to have been, present in the Mesopotamian area between 6000 and 5000 B.C. Since pigs seem to be incompatible with transhumant herding, the areas where they do *not* occur may be those where there was greatest reliance on seasonal movement of flocks.

EFFECTS ON HUMAN LIFE AND CULTURAL ECOLOGY

In the past it has been customary to treat each of the Mesopotamian environmental zones as if it were a "cultural and natural area"—a region characterized by a certain flora and fauna and exploited by a certain group of inhabitants who knew it particularly well.[41] There are hints that such a situation obtained in Palestine, for there Perrot[42] has distinguished two archeological traditions, one adapted to the moist Mediterranean side of the mountains, the other adapted to the arid eastern foothills.

In 1956 Fredrik Barth pointed out that the "cultural and natural area" concept did not fit northern Pakistan, and there are a considerable number of data to suggest that it does not fit the Mesopotamian area at 6000 B.C. either. Barth showed that a single valley system might be occupied by three distinct ethnic

[40] L. Krader, *Southwest J. Anthropol. 11*, 315 (1955).
[41] For the origins of the "cultural and natural area" hypothesis see A. L. Kroeber, *Cultural and Natural Areas of Native North America* (Univ. of California Press, Berkeley, 1947).
[42] *Courses Toward Urban Life,* R. J. Braidwood and G. R. Willey, Eds., p. 162.

---

in caves or on valley floors. These camps seem to have stronger ties, from the standpoint of traits of ceramic objects, with sites in the adjacent winter grazing area (southwest of the dashed line) than with other sites in their own environmental zone (see text).

groups, each of which occupied only a portion of the total resources, leaving the rest open for other groups to exploit. The
first group consists of sedentary agriculturalists who practice intensive irrigation agriculture on the river floodplain, growing two
crops a year and never moving to a higher elevation. A second
group raises one crop a year in this same floodplain area, but its
members also migrate annually with their flocks up through five
seasonal campsites to high mountain meadows. Still a third group
is made up of pastoral nomads who are assimilated into the society of the intensive agriculturalists as a special "herder caste,"
contributing milk and meat in exchange for grain; they are permitted to use prime grazing land not needed by the sedentary
farmers.[43]

At 6000 B.C. there are striking contrasts between archeological
sites in the oak-pistachio belt and the Assyrian steppe of the
Greater Mesopotamian area which suggest Barth's model. Jarmo,
at an elevation of 750 meters in the oak woodlands, was a village
of permanent, mud-walled houses with courtyards and ovens;
Tepe Sarab, at an elevation of 1260 meters, has no obvious houses,
and only the kind of ashy refuse beds that might occur around a
tent camp. The pottery objects at the two sites are nearly identical, but Jarmo has goats, sheep, and even domestic pigs, along
with two strains of wheat and one of barley, whereas Tepe Sarab
has only goats and sheep, and no grinding stones suggestive of
local agriculture. The ages of the domestic goats show that Tepe
Sarab was occupied in late winter or early spring. In this case
we suspect that the camp at 1260 meters may have been occupied
by seasonal herders who obtained their grain from more permanent farming villages at 750 meters.[44]

From the Assyrian steppe of Khuzistan, southwestern Iran,
come further data of the same type. From 7000 to 6500 B.C. at
the site of Ali Kosh, goat grazing and tiny amounts of agriculture
supplemented the collection of wild legumes; from 6500 to 6000
B.C. the growing of wheat and barley greatly increased at the

[43] F. Barth, *Am. Anthropologist* 58, 1079 (1956).
[44] R. J. Braidwood and B. Howe in *Courses Toward Urban Life;* and K. V.
Flannery, in *Proc. Spring Meeting Am. Ethnol. Soc. 1961, Columbus,* V. E.
Garfield, Ed. (Univ. of Washington Press, Seattle, 1962), pp. 7–17; C. A.
Reed, in *Science in Archaeology,* D. Brothwell and E. Higgs, Eds. (Thames
and Hudson, London, 1963), p. 214.

expense of wild plants. At 6000 B.C. a striking expansion of sheep and goat grazing occurred, and amounts of wild wheat and wild barley lessened, while the pod-bearing perennial *Prosopis* came to the fore.[45] We doubt that this was a simple case of abandonment of agriculture; *Prosopis,* Helbaek reminds us, is intimately associated with herding peoples in southwest Asia, and the increase in domestic sheep and goats suggests that this was a time when, in conformity with Barth's ecological model, Ali Kosh became primarily a "herding village" coexisting in a symbiotic framework with "farming villages" in adjacent areas.

Finally, we have the occurrences of typical Khuzistan pottery at a shepherds' camp in Kunji Cave, 1200 meters up, in the mountains of western Iran.[46] This part of Luristan seems to have stronger cultural ties with lowland Khuzistan than with other mountain areas in the same environmental zone, suggesting that at 6000 B.C. some valleys in Luristan were summer grazing land for herds that wintered in Khuzistan.

SUMMARY AND SPECULATION

The food-producing revolution in southwestern Asia is here viewed not as the brilliant invention of one group or the product of a single environmental zone, but as the result of a long process of changing ecological relationships between groups of men (living at varying altitudes and in different environmental settings) and the locally available plants and animals which they had been exploiting on a shifting, seasonal basis. In the course of making available to all groups the natural resources of every environmental zone, man had to remove from their natural contexts a number of hard-grained grasses and several species of ungulates. These species, as well as obsidian and native copper, were transported far from the biotopes or "niches" in which they had been at home. Shielded from natural selection by man, these small breeding populations underwent genetic change in the environment to which they had been transplanted, and favorable changes

[45] F. Hole, K. V. Flannery, J. A. Neely (see footnote 4).

[46] F. Hole (of Rice University) and I made a test excavation of Kunji Cave in 1963; the data have not been published.

were emphasized by the practices of the early planter or herder.

Successful cultivation seems to have intensified exchanges of natural resources and cultivars between groups, and there are hints that the diversity of environments made village specialization in certain commodities the best means of adapting to the area. We have suggestive evidence that by 4000 B.C. the redistributive economy had produced regional temple-and-market towns which regulated the produce of a symbiotic network of agriculturists engaged in intensive irrigation, transhumant herders, and perhaps even traders who dealt in obsidian, copper, salt, asphalt, fish, and regional fruits.[47]

[47] F. Hole, K. V. Flannery, J. A. Neely (see footnote 4).

BARBARA C. ASWAD

3. Social and Ecological Aspects in the Formation of Islam[1]

The nature of the development of Islam has been a subject of much interest and discussion among Orientalists. Of equal interest to anthropologists are the conditions under which state organizations are formed. This paper attempts to analyze the development of the rudimentary Islamic state apparatus as a secondary state formation; that is, one which arose as a consequence of economic and political conditions in other state centers.[2] This particular case involved the integration of pastoral society and oasis society as a result of external forces. The paper also attempts to show that the ecological position and the conditions of disequilibrium present at the oasis of Medina favored the development of a higher form of integration than did those of the more highly integrated, but more ecologically specialized oasis city of Mecca, whose social organization reflected stability and resisted change. As will be discussed later, the ecological and historical conditions which governed the integrative process in the Medina oasis characterize an empire-oasis-nomadic complex which greatly resembles the forces described by Owen Lattimore in Central Asia. He associates the power struggle accompanying the symbi-

This paper is a revision of "Social and Ecological Aspects in the Origin of the Islamic State," *Papers of the Michigan Academy of Science, Arts, and Letters*, 48:419–42, 1963 (1962 Meeting). It is included here with the permission of the author and the Michigan Academy of Science, Arts, and Letters.

[1] The ideas for this paper were initially presented in a seminar conducted by Dr. Eric Wolf at the University of Michigan in 1961. The paper was then delivered in its first version before the Michigan Academy of Sciences, Arts, and Letters, Spring, 1962.

[2] For a discussion and definition of pristine and secondary states, see Fried, 1960, 1961.

otic relationship of oasis and nomadic life in Central Asia with
the rise and fall of the central Chinese empires.

Among the writers who neglect important indigenous social
elements in their analyses, are those who attribute primary importance to the diffusion of foreign ideologies. Richard Bell ana-
lyzes the Christian influences, C. C. Torrey the Jewish, and others
emphasize South Arabian elements.[3] These writers appear to
treat Islam mainly as an ideology rather than a process of socio-
cultural integration. Indeed, ideological aspects do spread and
influence the content of ideologies on other social systems, as
Christianity and Judaism were doing in Arabia. A functional
analysis of the indigenous ideological process, however, will be
found to reflect the local milieu, especially where foreign influences are not accompanied by political control, but rather are
brought in through trade and minorities, as in this instance. One
is, moreover, tempted to ask the diffusionists why in fact the
Mecca and Medina Arabs did not convert to Christianity or
Judaism. Opposing the above interpretations, Wolf has isolated
the internal evolution of Meccan urban society as the impetus
for the formation of the state,[4] thereby minimizing external
forces, even to the extent of excluding the importance of the
Medina situation. In this he has overlooked important points of
history, notably the weakening of the Byzantine and Sassanid
Empires to the north and the fact that the development of the
initial Muslim state occurred at Medina and maintained its capital there rather than at Mecca. Although several important members of the newly emerging Medina community were in fact
Meccans who had accompanied Muhammad to Medina, the city
organization of Mecca itself in effect strongly resisted change.

Montgomery Watt has characterized the state of society immediately prior to Muhammad as one of discord between the set
of social relations changed by the economic evolution of Mecca
and Medina, and the ideologies which reflected an earlier nomadic state.[5] George Bousquet's criticism[6] of Watt's writings as
Marxist lacks foundation and could be more productively leveled

[3] Bell, 1926; Torrey, 1933.
[4] Wolf, 1951.
[5] Watt, 1960, 1961a, 1961b.
[6] Bousquet, 1954.

at E. Belaiev, who has created an exaggerated class struggle in Mecca.[7] Bousquet's own tendency toward the great man theory neglects the importance of social and economic factors.

The approach of this paper most closely follows that of Watt (1956, 1960, 1961a, 1961b) and draws on his excellent discussions while also taking into account ecological and evolutionary aspects which seem causal to the changes which occurred. The historical position of Arabia at the time of Muhammad will be considered first. This is followed by an analysis of the ecological and socio-economic aspects of both Mecca and Medina in their bearing on the role of Muhammad and the development of Islam. The evidence suggests to the writer that the state might not have been formed at Mecca, an environmentally specialized trade center lacking indigenous agricultural support, unless directly backed by a stronger political power. In addition, the less highly specialized and integrated Medina society, occupying a rich agricultural oasis will be shown as possessing more organizational and ecological potential than Mecca, which resulted in its eventual conquest of Mecca.[8]

HISTORY OF ARABIA

All trade between eastern countries such as India and China to Africa, Egypt, Syria, Greece, and Rome had passed through Arabian hands on the three main trade routes in the period before Islam. As a result of its position on one of these routes and its agricultural potential, the Southern Arabian coast was the location of monarchies based on irrigation agriculture. By the time of Muhammad, the last of these states had fallen into ruin with the general decline in the entire Mediterranean economy in the 3rd Century A.D., which led to the decrease in the demand for

[7] Beliaev, 1954.
[8] This instance of social change might be exemplary of "The Law of Evolutionary Potential" as stated by Service (1960) as "The more specialized and adapted a form in a given evolutionary stage, the smaller is its potential for passing to the next stage" (p. 97) and ". . . a sudden leap forward is apt to be accomplished by a different relatively unspecialized culture . . ." (p. 106).

Oriental products.[9] The following invasion by the Abyssinians and later by the Persians brought the final collapse of South Arabia. Traditionally, the breaking of the Ma'rib Dam is used as a symbol of the collapse, as well as for the consequent migration of South Arabian tribes to the north. Although the date of the migrations is uncertain, 300 A.D. is used by some writers.

On the eve of the development of Islam, and accompanying the migrations of the tribes toward the north, there was an increase in trade along the inland routes passing through the oases of Mecca and Medina. The cause is not easily documented. Watt attributed it to ". . . wars between the Byzantine and Persian empires which interfered with the route through Iraq."[10] . . . We do see that as the struggles between the empires made both the Red Sea and Persian Gulf unsafe for trade, the inland trade route cities were strengthened and possibly became competitive centers of distribution.

In the north, the two great empires had become weak through the increasing warfare between them. Persia, which had previously tried to control the local and trading population of Medina, was threatened by Byzantium and by internal revolts, and it seems probable that support for Medina was weak at this time. Associated with this is the increased pressure of the desert society onto that of the oasis, a situation analogous to an ecologically similar situation in Central Asia described by Owen Lattimore. His main theme shows that when China was strong as an empire, it could dominate the oasis regions, but could never fully integrate them because of their "cellular" structure, the distance of communication, and "above all (because of) the intervals of arid 'un-Chinese terrain.'"[11] During periods of empire strength the oasis would encroach upon the steppe, but when the empire weakened, the steppe would encroach upon the oases and empire borders. Similarly in Arabia, perhaps, Medina, located closer to the empires, was more integrated into this empire-oasis-steppe complex than was Mecca.

Another important relationship in the complex that involved Medina is that between the empires and their Arab buffer states,

9 Hourani, 1952: p. 294.
10 Watt, 1961a: p. 6.
11 Lattimore, 1951: pp. 169–70, 205.

the Ghassanids and Lakhmids, whose populations consisted of migrants from Southern Arabia. The strength of the empires determined their relations with the buffer states and thereby the relation of the buffer states with the oases and nomads of Arabia. The weakness of the empires at this time resulted in the dysfunction and dislocation of these buffer states. Bernard Lewis states that in the period just before the rise of Islam, ". . . the subsidies hitherto paid by Byzantium to the Ghassanids were stopped by Heraclius as a measure of economy after the exhausting Persian war, and the Muslim invaders consequently found Ghassanid in a state of resentment and disloyalty to Byzantium."[12] Regarding the Lakhmid dynasty, Delacy O'Leary writes: "In 605 A.D., the Lakhmid dynasty came to an end. Hira was reduced to the status of an ordinary province. This was sorely resented by the Arabs of Hira and rendered them disposed to join the confederation of tribes which the Prophet formed in the course of his ministry at Medina. . . ."[13]

In sum, we find the collapse of the Southern Arabian complex sending tribes toward the borders of the northern empires in the 4th century A.D. followed by the weakening of the northern empires in the next centuries and their consequent loss of control over their buffer states and oasis trading communities. This occurred during a time when the trade was shifting to the internal trade route passing through Mecca and its northern neighboring oasis, Medina. Because Medina was closer to the buffer states and empires, it felt the impact of both the loosening of empire control and the building up of trade, and it seems to be this combination which was responsible for the great social upheaval in that oasis at the time of Muhammad. Mecca, on the other hand, was primarily influenced by the increasing trade, and due to its distance from the empires as well as its lack of an agricultural base, became more specialized and stabilized in its adaptation as a trade city.

[12] Lewis, 1950: p. 32.
[13] O'Leary, 1927: p. 161.

NOMADIC SOCIAL ORGANIZATION

The changes in the two oases, resulting from the conditions described above, brought about a modification of the social organization in each area, but in different ways. The occupation of Mecca by desert groups resulted in the beginnings of stratification around the control of trade. In Medina, it caused a transfer of power from the cultivators to the encroaching semi-herders who, with Muhammad and his exiled friends, occupied the oasis of Medina and later conquered Mecca. Since the reorganization at Medina constituted the initial stage in the beginnings of Islam and the Islamic state, more importance should be attributed to elements of nomadic social structure in its effect on Islam than is allowed by such writers as Wolf and those who minimize the influence of the desert on Islam.

Ecology acts as a maximizing factor on Bedouin herding patterns and social organization. Due to the sparse and sporadic rainfall patterns of their desert environment, to the instability of herd sizes, and to their migratory subsistence patterns, large groupings are not the constant form of organization. Yet grazing lands cannot be held by small groups and there is a need for cooperation of larger groups, for higher levels of organization to coordinate migration and the sharing of water supplies during dry seasons, for defense and for dealing with settled society. The nature of their relations with settled society fluctuates as the urban centers expand and contract their borders of control. To meet these diverse and unstable requirements, desert society appears at various levels of organization, and has organizational principles which allow this necessary flexibility. Accordingly, in areas of sparse resources there exist smaller groupings with lower level organization. As the resources and proximity to higher level societies increase, such as in oases, along trade routes and regions bordering empires, the density and complexity of Bedouin organization increases. Ranked societies arise that associate with settled groups through caste and semi-caste relations. In their symbiotic relationship with settled society, tribute and taxes are collected by the stronger member of the relationship.

In the desert, raiding and redistribution of booty by the chief help to offset the unreliability of camel herding.[14] Land is not exclusively owned and camels are never bought and sold among Bedouin.[15] Tribute is offered from the weaker sections to stronger sections and the chief keeps a store of one-fifth of all booty for purposes of redistribution. Therefore, although certain elements of temporary economic imbalance are represented in the form of tribute payment, and although there are differential amounts of wealth in different hands, the circulation of wealth through raiding, hospitality, and kinship channels does not permit significantly restricted and impaired access by all to strategic resources, a measure used by Morton Fried for identifying the presence of social stratification.[16]

The ranked hierarchy of Bedouin society is under continual modification, as strong lineages split and weaker groups are absorbed into alliances which center around a strong lineage section and chief. The process of segmentation in lineages is between powerful, close agnates, and partially resembles Fredrik Barth's analysis of the Swat Pathans. These competing agnates form alliances with distant agnates and divisions of other lineages as in the case of the Pathans; however, in addition, Bedouin also rely on forming alliances with other close agnates.[17] The processes of fusion and fission in combination with the mechanisms of economic distribution, allow therefore for the adjustment of population size to the uneven resource base.

The qualities of a Bedouin chief include success as a leader in raids and alliance making, good judgment concerning movement and settlement of groups, generosity and qualities of arbitration. The position normally remains in one line and is contested by the sons of the previous chief. Hence we find that lineages are

[14] Sweet, 1965. For a discussion of raiding and warfare, and the ecology of camel herding see the following articles: Sweet, 1965; Irons, 1965.

[15] *Ibid.,* 1965a: p. 1137.

[16] Fried, 1960: p. 722.

[17] Evans-Pritchard's interpretation was accepted by the author in the original version of this paper. Recent fieldwork has provided further insights into the dynamics of Near Eastern ranked societies. See Evans-Pritchard (1949), Aswad (1967), Barth (1959), Peters (1959), Sahlins (1961), Cunnison (1966).

not politically corporate and the followings of the lineage rivals
are heterogeneous.

In the oasis areas, however, with which we are especially concerned in this paper, social organization adapts to a change in
subsistence, and a new interaction with other forms of society.
The oases are centers of redistribution of a more stable nature
than is possible in nomadic Bedouin society, and consequently
they can support higher levels of organization. In Mecca, the
trade alliances were organized by criteria other than ranking
through prestige. Wealth differentiation between and within lineages emerged as a competing organizational principle. A tendency toward primogeniture in the tribal chiefdoms of the desert
became more pronounced in the oases as the desire to concentrate wealth continued. The emphasis upon actual patrilineal
descent likewise increased, thus causing unrest among weaker
clans, clients, and other individuals affected by the beginnings
of unequal distribution and access to resources. It is important
to note in this respect that the early followers of Muhammad in
Mecca, according to Watt's analysis, did not primarily consist of
the lowest segments of society, but of younger members of the
leading families and clients.[18] For more evidence, let us now examine the historical discussion of these two oases.

MECCA

Mecca was organized around a religious shrine in an area
which the Qur'an describes as an uncultivable valley.[19] Rain falls
only twice a year and is tropical in violence; there is only one
well, and water is still brought from outside springs at Jebal
Arafat.[20] The city's specialization and dependence upon trade
can be seen in many statements, such as, "The absolute sterility
of the soil brought another scourge, that of famine. The slightest
irregularity of the convoy of grain from Syria or Sarat was enough
to cause it. A drought would last up to four years."[21]

[18] Watt, 1961a, p. 36.
[19] Qur'an, 14, 40. (Richard Bell, the Qur'an Translated . . . 1937–39).
[20] *Handbook of Arabia,* 1923: p. 124.
[21] Lammens and Winsinck, 1953: p. 369.

Caravans traded skins and leather, frankincense, silks, and aromatic goods to the north, bringing back cotton, arms, cereals, and oils.[22] It was a center of redistribution as well as of worship; however, as long as the Meccans were obliged to import all their own subsistence items, their power to monopolize the redistribution of subsistence goods around Mecca was highly vulnerable to outside forces. This fact would seem to constitute a definite limitation in the city's potential for statehood without the backing of a stronger organization.

It is difficult to estimate the degree of economic stratification or the importance of money in the Meccan economic structure, since money was essentially a foreign element. Reports of selling are numerous. The Persian and Byzantine coins in use, however, had no universal value; they were weighed for use. It is probable that bartering remained the predominant form of exchange. That there were indications of wealth differentiation cannot be denied. Al-Wakidi, the eighth-century biographer of the Prophet and chronicler of early Islam, speaks of villas in neighboring Ta'if for the wealthy,[23] mention is made of a voluntary fund for the poorer members of the Quraysh, and "slaves" existed. Henri Lammens mentions the *nádí*, or ward councils, where foreigners were affiliated with a family, and commercial caravan activities were generated.[24]

In matters of jurisdiction and political control, the feud, defined through the bonds of agnatic and client affiliation backed by trade alliances, was the effective rule. There was no control institution with power operating above agnatic and client institutions, and opposing groups attempted to control each other through the use of boycott. When the Quraysh group first took over Mecca, Qusayy became the chief, and his word was followed.[25] Due to increasing trade and stratification, an institution was formed of the heads of several strong subgroups or clans, but this institution, called the *mala'*, lacked coercive authority. The trading clans were competitive and alliances were formed, despite the strong competition between groups within the city. The elaborate de-

[22] Lammens, 1928: p. 223.
[23] Wakidi, 1882: p. 303.
[24] Lammens, 1928: pp. 224–83.
[25] Ibn Ishaq, 1955: p. 25.

velopment of ritual in Mecca helped maintain the peace necessary for trading purposes.

Another form of control which has been reported is the
"army," which Lammens characterized as consisting of Abyssinian
slaves.[26] Watt theorizes however that they were a "weak quasi-
tribal group from the neighborhood of Mecca."[27] Abd Rabbini
said that ". . . when there was a war, they took ballots among
the chieftains and elected one as a king, be he a minor or a grown
man."[28] From these statements, it might be concluded that there
existed the beginnings of a group designated for fighting, but obviously it cannot be said to be a permanent institution in its own
right.

In the development of social systems, the situation at Mecca
presents a departure from kinship organization in a religious and
trade center, and also an apparent attempt to maintain stability,
but at a level below that of a state organization. It had no centralized authority or administrative staff; there was no monopoly
of force; and the basic control system was based on blood revenge
modified by trade alliances and stratification, although not
enough to effectively displace kinship mechanisms.

The position of Muhammad and Islam in Mecca reflected these
conditions of stabilization and the increased reduction in kinship
mechanisms. As a prophet and warner, Muhammad himself criti-
cized the importance the Meccans were giving to individual
power, and urged people to give to the poor.[29] Muhammad, who
grew up as an orphan, undoubtedly felt the effect of a decrease
in kinship ties.

Initially, Muhammad's concept of God was an admission of the
idea of God as known in other religions, an awareness created
by the increased number of foreigners in Mecca and his own
experience on trading expeditions. He did not insist on the oneness of God, and conceded at one point, the existence of the
three goddesses of the Meccans,[30] but later he retracted this

26 Lammens, 1928.
27 Watt, 1956: pp. 154–57.
28 Abd Rabbini (al-Iqd al Farid, p. 226) quoted by Hamiddullah, 1938:
p. 273.
29 Qur'an, 74, 96, 92, 5–11.
30 *Ibid.*, 53, 19–23. Watt, 1960, pp. 101–9.

statement. With trading alliances as its primary control and serving as a center for polytheistic tribes upon whose existence it depended, Mecca in fact resisted the innovation of monotheism and the disruption Muhammad was causing. Finally he and his group of followers were forced from its limits. It also seems that the acceptance of another religion such as Christianity would cause a loss of neutrality in Mecca's position as a trade center between the Byzantine and Sassanian Empires.[31]

From the historical references and discussions, it can be deduced that the Meccan society was not the exclusive or even principal environment for the initial development and organization of Islam. Had it not been for the Medinan situation, Muhammad and his group of followers might never have been heard of again, after their departure from Mecca.

MEDINA

What conditions in Medina, then, were causal in the establishment of Islam? An examination of the available literature reveals some illuminating ecological factors, but also a lack of data on pre-Islamic social conditions there. Hartwig Hirschfeld states, regarding the Jewish cultivators: "At just this moment, the century before the Hegira, the historical sources relative to the Jews of Medina are totally lacking. . . ."[32] Consequently there are references to an earlier period when the Jewish agriculturalists were dominant, with small local Arab groups serving them in a client relationship; and mention is made of the newly arrived Southern Arabian tribes who occupied the outlying waste areas on the border of the oasis. One hundred years later, members of the outlying tribes, the Aus and Khazraj, are described as successfully wresting the cultivable land from the Jews, and in some cases the Jewish tribes are mentioned as being in alliances with the Aus and Khazraj.[33] The situation was one of constant feuding, first between the cultivators and the encroaching herders, then, as

[31] Watt, 1960: p. 15.
[32] Hirschfeld, 1883: p. 175.
[33] Ibn Ishaq, 1955: p. 462.

the Arab tribes gained strength, among themselves. Before discussing the process which led to the expulsion of the agriculturalists and traders, and the unification of the herders with the
emigrants from Mecca under Muhammad, the background of
these two ecologically diverse and competing groups at Medina
should be briefly mentioned, for there is a feature of the South
Arabian tribes which, although not often mentioned by histo-
rians, possibly furnishes an important link in the creation of the
state.

The date of the first Jewish settlement in Medina and their
origin is uncertain. Sources disagree as to whether they came
from Palestine at the time of the conquest of Nebuchadnezzar,
or that of the Greek or Romans. J. Horowitz concludes from the
Kitab al-Aghani that it might be the 1st or the 2nd century A.D.
and again later in the 5th century.[34] They brought new methods
of cultivation and new plants, iron goods and weapons with them,
and by the 3rd century had absorbed the local Arab inhabitants,
and had built large forts in different regions of the oasis.

From the reports of Al-Baladhuri, the ninth-century chronicler
of the rise of Islam, it appears that the Aus and Khazraj tribal
units were related to the Ghassanids of the Byzantine buffer
state, who had migrated from South Arabia at approximately the
same time.[35] There are reports that the Ghassanids gave these
Arab tribes occasional support in Medina. For example the important Jewish leaders were killed by the Ghassanid Emir, Abu
Dhobayla, when the latter came to Medina upon request.[36] In
the alternating power struggle involved in an empire-oasis-
nomadic complex, this connection would seem to be of importance when the power relationship shifts, as it was doing at the
time of Muhammad.

Ecologically, Medina held a crucial position in Northern Arabia. As one of the largest oases in the Hejaz, it was well known
for its great water resources which resulted from the convergence
of numerous wadis. Wheat was the predominant crop grown; also
there were vines, barley, and clover. In respect to the abundance
of water, it is interesting that many of the quarrels brought to

[34] Horowitz, 1939: p. 178, and quoting Diwan of Quis Ibn al-Khatan.
[35] Baladhuri (tran. by Hitti and Murgotten) 1916–24: pp. 32–33.
[36] Caussin de Perceval, 1948: p. 660.

Muhammad for arbitration by the new cultivators concerned the distribution of water currents.[37]

The Medinan Jews also monopolized the trade in the northern Hejaz.[38] This trade was predominantly in subsistence goods, in contrast with numerous luxury items that formed the base of Meccan trade. The fact that the inhabitants could provide for their own subsistence needs from indigenous sources would indicate they could operate as an independent and enduring center for the redistribution of subsistence goods to the surrounding tribes, which Mecca could not, due to its own dependency upon imported cereals. The controlling position of Medina on the Meccan trade route therefore obviously provided this oasis with an element of crucial importance in the ensuing power struggle between the early Islamic community in Medina and the Meccans.

Part of the organization of the oasis may be deduced from its settlement patterns. It was not centralized; rather, numerous lineage groups with their clients were scattered among the heavy palm groves, and forts were reported to have been situated in each settlement. Fighting ceased once those attacked got inside their forts. Presumably the forts were used as protection against Bedouin raids and as a means of internal control as well. The oasis was isolated enough to be free from the direct control of the empires, yet in previous periods there had been evidence of indirect support from the Persians. In 583 A.D., 50 years before Muhammad came to Medina, a Prince Amar was authorized by the king of the Lakhmid buffer state to rule Medina, but this attempt by the Persian Empire to control the oasis also failed.[39] Even at the time of Muhammad's arrival, a strong man was unsuccessfully negotiating with Persia to have himself crowned "king."

With the orientation of the agriculturalists toward the Persian buffer state, the relationship of the herding Aus and Khazraj with the Ghassanids of the opposing Byzantine buffer state seems to provide further evidence of the influence of the empires on the events in the Medina region.

At the time of the Hejira, the Ansar or "helpers" as the Aus and

[37] Baladhuri, pp. 24–25, 27.
[38] Lammens, 1914: p. 82.
[39] Caussin de Perceval, 1948: p. 650.

Khazraj were later called, had taken control of much of the land. The Jewish tribes had been able to maintain some of their independence because of the feuding between the Arab tribes; however, they finally were reduced to joining the Aus against the stronger Khazraj. This resulted in a large scale battle won by the Aus and the Jews just five years before Muhammad was invited to Medina.[40]

The events of the Medinan period and the organizational transition are particularly discussed in three sources. The first is the Qur'an. The second is "The Constitution of Medina"[41] which is a contract drawn between the Emigrants from Mecca and the Arab tribes, the Aus and Khazraj, shortly after Muhammad's arrival there. It was also a convenant with the Jews, whereby their possessions and religion were confirmed for them, although this part of the agreement soon became obsolete. The third reference is the biography of Ibn Ishaq (1955) which gives a detailed description of the events of the period.

From these sources, the early *umma* or community of believers may be described as a function of the patterns established among the Arab tribes in Medina, with the exception that Muhammad was to be the arbiter of the community. Initially the Emigrants were paired with members of the Khazraj tribe as brothers who were to support each other morally, economically, in war and in inheritance.[42] This is the same method by which clients were adopted in Bedouin society. By the time of the writing of the "Constitution," the Meccan Emigrants were fashioned into a "tribe" with Muhammad in the role of its chief as well as arbiter for the community. The "Constitution" lists nine clans, of which the Emigrants form the first named. These nine groups were responsible for providing their own blood money in feuds and for the ransoming of prisoners. However, it provided for the protec-

[40] An interesting comment on the historical implication of this victory is that the Jews had often mentioned that their God, Allah (as Arabian Jews and Christians also called their God before Islam) was going to send them a prophet to help them against the newcomers. Subsequent to the battle which the Jews helped win, we find the defeated Khazraj going to Mecca, asking Muhammad if he were this prophet, and inviting him to arbitrate their dispute. It may also be of interest that Muhammad's grandmother was a Khazrajite.

[41] Ibn Hisham, 1375 A. H.: pp. 501–4.

[42] Lichtenstaedter, 1942: pp. 47–48.

tion of each member against those outside the *umma*, and it stated that peace was not to be concluded separately by any member with the enemies of the *umma*. All important matters were to be brought to Allah and Muhammad. Of the remaining eight groups, five were Khazraj clans and three were Aus; the Jewish groups were mentioned as attached to one or another Arab clan, except for the three main Jewish clans, which were omitted completely. Gertrude Stern reports that the Ansar were not anxious to intermarry with the Emigrants and very few marriages between the two resulted.[43] It is possible that with Muhammad's ruling which provided women with inheritance, marriage of Ansar women with Emigrant men could mean the loss of part of the Ansar's newly occupied agricultural lands.

The organization was dependent upon voluntary contributions during the early period and in the Qur'an there is a stress on contributions with the threat of divine punishment.[44] The term *zakāt* (alms) was used for these contributions, which were mainly given to the poor, who happened to be the Emigrants at the beginning. Blood revenge was maintained, although rules in the Qur'an attempted to prevent cumulation of feuding.[45] Muhammad tried to encourage the payment of blood money in all cases of killing.

As we noted, Muhammad came to Medina as an arbiter; his powers were not great and although the "Constitution" indicated that all disputes should be taken to him, there were other strong leaders. He had no military power. "He waged wars at the head of groups of men who followed their own will."[46] Muhammad's message in the Qur'an reflects his change from the position of a prophet to that of an arbiter. "His emphasis is less on the conversions to the religion of Allah than upon submission to prophecy; conversions were of a political nature."[47]

After the Emigrants from Mecca lived off their "brothers," the Aus and Khazraj for a short period at the beginning, Muhammad attacked the Meccan caravans, partially to obtain support for his

[43] Stern, 1939: pp. 77–82.
[44] Watt, 1956: p. 252. Qur'an, 3. 175; 4. 41–44.
[45] Qur'an, 5. 49; 2. 173–74.
[46] Schacht, 1955: p. 30.
[47] *Ibid.*, 1932: p. 338.

group. But he had also traveled the trade route himself, and was undoubtedly aware of the potential ruin which the presence of an enemy in Medina could bring to Mecca. The looting was successful and encouraged the participation of the Khazraj and Aus, thereby uniting the *umma* temporarily and for the first time; eventually, as the fighting increased, the union became stronger. After the first few raids, the Muslims expelled the Jewish tribe which controlled the trade and blacksmithing, thereby putting themselves into one of the strongest positions in the oasis. Watt's analysis of the struggle between the sections of the Aus and Khazraj before the arrival of Muhammad at Medina, as well as during the unification period, shows the splitting of lineage and clan segments which join rival alliances, the process we mentioned in describing nomadic social organization.[48]

The most important events which created a response of alignment were the successful raids on Meccan caravans, the expulsion of the agricultural populations, and the defense against the enraged Meccans. In this power struggle, it is important to note the comparative lack of flexible alignments which both the Jews and Meccans displayed in organizing themselves against this growing new threat. In their battle with the Meccans, the Muslims were strongly outnumbered, but had the advantage of better organization. Watt mentions two items concerning the Meccan performance in these wars. First, after they had begun a siege of Medina, they suffered from a lack of sufficient food needed for themselves and their horses. Secondly some clans withdrew from the battle for what Watt considers reasons of rival economic interests.[49] The Ansar had also had the advantage of recent involvement in warfare, with the total group participating in the fighting force. The Meccans, on the other hand, had only an incipient form of specialized fighting force, and therefore when the entire Meccan community was involved in warfare, it lacked efficiency as a total military unit. It is also probable, in view of the assistance which we mentioned that the buffer states gave to the Ansar of Medina, that this outside aid helped to increase the strength of the new Muslim community at this time. This relationship could assist in the displacing of the cultivators not only through military meas-

[48] Watt, 1956: pp. 153, 156, 161, 164.
[49] *Ibid.*, p. 11.

ures, but in addition, the buffer states could also influence trading operations since the Meccan and Jewish trade routes passed through their territories.

Muhammad's achievements as a raid leader and redistributor of surplus wealth in the form of booty established his leadership. Initially, the booty had gone to the Emigrants who had no means of support, and who were clients of the Ansar. Later it went to all of the men who fought and to a public fund.

The rapid growth of the Muslim community is suggested from the figures of participants in the following battles fought under Muhammad's leadership: at Badr in 624 A.D., there were over 300 men and two horses; at Hunayn in 628 A.D. there were 4,700 men and 800 horses; on an expedition at Tabuk in Jordan in 630 A.D. there were 30,000 men with 10,000 horses.[50] The last figure greatly surpasses the largest number of men which the Meccans were ever said to have brought together.[51]

The influence of the Meccan followers became evident just before the conquest of Mecca when several leaders of Mecca joined Muhammad and hence made the conquest relatively peaceful. With this conquest and the final expulsion of the Jews from Medina, the *umma* began to acquire the form of an embryonic state with Muhammad at its head. In the Qur'an the word *umma* is replaced by *hisb Allah* (party of God).[52] Joseph Schacht mentions in regard to Muhammad's position that when Muhammad was head of the *umma,* he was called *hakam* (judge): however, when the verb from this noun and the word *qada',* which referred to a sovereign ordinance either of Allah or the Prophet, are found together, there appears the first indication of the emergence of the new Islamic idea of the administration of justice.[53]

By 631 A.D. a new political order was formed, Muhammad's name appeared, coupled with God's, and he had representatives of the Ansar, the Emigrants and local chiefs acting as governors and tax collectors in most of Arabia.[54] Such specialists were needed to arrange the increasing number of alliances.

[50] Watt, 1961a: p. 215.
[51] *Ibid.*
[52] Qur'an, 5.61; 58.22.
[53] Schacht, 1955: p. 30.
[54] Ibn Ishaq, 1955: p. 652. Watt, 1956: pp. 235, 239.

The term *zakāt* actually did not mean legal alms until after Muhammad's death, but there was a change during his rule from voluntary to fixed alms.[55] Booty still provided an important source for the new organization's expenses. Minorities payed a fixed amount of alms; Muhammad still received a fifth portion of the booty; and there are reports of his increased need to pay for the representatives and agents of redistribution, for the expeditions, and for subsidies to certain tribes to gain their assistance. Watt's mention of the numerous men needed merely to collect and to redistribute goods, points to an important factor in transcending the chiefdom level of organization.[56] The people of the Peninsula were well aware of the growing weakness of the northern Empires, for already a plundering Arab group had unexpectedly defeated a Persian army division in 610 A.D.

Therefore, we see the formation *at Medina* of an embryonic primitive state, with tax collection, administrative agents, representatives, and a concentration of force. Taxes went directly to the center, and although this was a centralized organization, the use of alliances was evident on the peripheries of power where tribal leaders were agents. Muhammad's power had become considerable and his agents consisted of the Emigrants, Ansar and local leaders. Their previous organization was similar to that of a chieftainship, the important difference being that the Emigrants were not a kin-based unit, and they were forced to combine with the Ansar initially as clients, not conquerors. We may assume that the fact the Emigrants came from a stratified community might have affected the rate of state formation, and Eric Wolf's emphasis upon the urbanization processes of Mecca becomes important at this point. However, it seems evident from the discussion above that the Islamic state formation did not emerge directly from Meccan society and it is doubtful whether the Meccans alone could have formed a state organization without direct backing from an empire.

The frailty of the new polity under Muhammad was demonstrated at his death: the wars of the Riddah caused the state to collapse temporarily as factions led by tribal leaders and former

[55] Watt, 1956: p. 253.

[56] Qur'an, pp. 255–56, for a discussion of early taxes, see Yahya (tran.) 1958.

agents fought each other for succession. Muhammad had no direct heir and in the question of heredity versus ability and seniority, the latter characteristics were used by a board of electors for selecting the subsequent caliphs, all of whom were of Meccan origin.

The Meccans who came to the capital of Medina after the formation of the incipient state came into conflict with the Ansar, but the threats from outside brought these two groups together and once again unified the organization so that in a short time its energies were transferred to the conquests which ultimately spread from Libya to Iran.

SUMMARY

The creation of a secondary primitive state under Muhammad at Medina through the influence of external political factors and ecological elements, reveals certain interesting aspects in this particular case. First the origins of this state are seen to derive from a struggle between nomadic and oasis societies under the pressure of the externally induced factors of increased trade and the deterioration of the northern empires. Therefore it has been necessary to look outside of the local area for some of the causes and influences which directed the change. These external factors were found to create a different cultural response in Mecca than they did in Medina due to the differing environments of these two cases. Mecca, distant from the influence of the empires, lacked agriculture and had become a highly specialized trading and religious center. Resulting from this adaptive specialization and the presence of new wealth resources, low level stratification and stabilization characterized the organization of the city at the time of Muhammad. These factors which had made the oasis less vulnerable to nomadic or other pressures, caused it to lose an element of flexibility and potential for advancement. The city resisted ideological and social innovation and expelled the reformer and prophet Muhammad from its midst. Medina, on the other hand, was characterized by a change in the balance of power in the symbiotic relation between the cultivators and traders of the oasis, and the encroaching nomads of the desert. The strategic location of this oasis on the trade routes that provided Mecca with its subsistence and commercial base, as well as Medina's own fertility, provided the context for a new level of integration to emerge when the northern empires weakened. The dissipation of these empires had lessened their support for the original Medina oasis dwellers, thereby allowing a steppe encroachment onto the oasis; and, simultaneously, the empires alienated their own buffer states which provided sporadic assistance for the new conquerors and organizers of this rich center of redistribution at Medina.

The brief examination of Bedouin social organization and the review of the conditions in the two oases, suggest that elements from these three social levels combined into the unit that eventually emerged as the incipient Islamic state power with its members serving as the political and military rulers that gained control over most of Arabia. The features of nomadic society which permit flexibility by continual modification through permutation, shifting alliances, and allowances for individual achievement, both weakened and strengthened the community under Muhammad. This flexibility provided the sedentarizing pastoralists at Medina (the Ansar) with an advantage in expelling the indigenous oasis cultivators at Medina, and in combining with the Emigants of Mecca and accepting Muhammad as their leader. It also aided them in their warfare and conquest of Mecca. Mecca did not show the same flexibility. The organization in which the Emigrants and Ansar merged to lay the basis of the new Islamic polity at first operated at a quasi-chiefdom level of organization, with the Emigrants forming a dominant if fictive kin group among the clans. Muhammad's role was that of a judge and chief. He initially achieved the loyalty of his followers as a raid leader and redistributor of surplus wealth in the form of booty. Later, his name was coupled with God's, and he ruled over the majority of Arabia through agents from the Ansar, the Emigrants, and local tribes who acted as governors and tax collectors. Before his death, the organization under Muhammad had captured the city of Mecca and had organized an expedition of 30,-000 men into Jordan.

The influence of the Meccan Emigrants grew particularly after the death of Muhammad. It seems probable that neither the

Ansar of Medina nor the Meccans alone, would have provided the basis for the later Islamic Empire. It is not the purpose of this paper to argue whether the conditions of Mecca or Medina were the most influential. I have sought, rather, to illuminate the integrative factors, to show that the process did not come directly out of Meccan stratification and urbanization, nor primarily from the high quality of Muhammad's statesmanship, but rather that the incipient stages of the state organization of Islam took place at Medina and resulted from the interaction of ecological and external forces with indigenous socio-cultural factors.

ANN K. S. LAMBTON

4. Islamic Society in Persia

[Inaugural Lecture delivered March 9, 1954]
The ideal society, as described in the expositions of the philosophers in medieval Islamic times, was a hierarchic society, with mankind graded into various classes. The function of government was to maintain a just balance between the various classes. The philosophers in their expositions are influenced both by Greek thought and by Persian. The Persian influence is naturally strongest in the Eastern part of the Islamic world. In Sasanian Persia society was divided into four estates, namely, (i) the religious classes; (ii) the warriors; (iii) the bureaucracy, among whom were included also biographers, doctors, poets, and astronomers; and (iv) peasants, shepherds, merchants, and artisans.[1] Naṣīr ud-Dīn Ṭūsī, who wrote his famous work, the *Akhlāqi Nāṣirī*, shortly before the fall of the caliphate, similarly resolves society into four estates, each of which was to be kept in its appropriate place and within which each person was to be employed in that occupation to which he was best fitted, so that he would, so far as the possibility lay within him, attain to perfection. These orders were (i) men of the pen, among whom were included scholars, *fuqahā*, *qāẓīs*, scribes, mathematicians, geometricians, astronomers, doctors, and poets; (ii) men of the sword; (iii) men of affairs, such as merchants, craftsmen, artisans, and

[1] See A. Christensen, *L'Iran sous les Sassanides* (Copenhagen, 1936), pp. 93 ff., and *Tansar Nāma* (ed. M. Minovi, Tehrān, 1932–33), p. 12.

tax-collectors; and (iv) husbandmen.² Jalāl ud-Dīn Davvānī, who closely follows the work of Naṣīr ud-Dīn, maintains that temporal sovereignty consists in the maintenance of the classes in their proper places.³ A later work, the *Jāmi'i Mufīdī*, belonging to the seventeenth century A.D., makes a slightly different classification, while retaining the fourfold division. The first class consists of the chief military and civil officials and the court; the second comprises the religious classes; the third class is composed of landowners, merchants, craftsmen, such as architects and goldsmiths; and the fourth class of artisans, other craftsmen, the people of the bazaar, and workmen.⁴ It is noteworthy that the exposition of Naṣīr ud-Dīn Ṭūsī, in spite of the militarization of the state which had taken place, puts men of the pen apart from and in front of men of the sword, whereas in the exposition of Muḥammad Mufīd the leading military and civil officials are placed together in the first class.

This tendency towards classification is not peculiar to the philosophers. It is also found in the manuals of statecraft such as the *Siyāsāt Nāma* of Niẓām ul-Mulk; diplomas issued to governors and others moreover contain frequent injunctions to 'maintain the people in their proper ranks'. That the philosophers should construct a neat theory of society is natural, but I would suggest

² Lith., Lahore, 1865, pp. 180–81; see also Maḥmūd Āmulī, *Nafā'is ul-Funūn* (lith., Tehrān, 1891–92), ii. 24. Naṣīr ud-Dīn Ṭūsī, having established that men are naturally impelled to congregate with their fellows, states such congregation demands a proper regulation of affairs. Left to themselves men would not achieve mutual co-operation. Provision, therefore, had clearly to be made so that each would be content with his rightful position, fulfil that function to which he was suited, and so that no one should transgress the rights of another (p. 144). This proper regulation of affairs was secured by the establishment of a law-giver, divinely inspired, who was called by the 'moderns' the *imām*, and his work the 'imamate', whereas Plato according to Naṣīr ud-Dīn, called him the controller of the world, and Aristotle the 'man of society' (pp. 145–46). Elsewhere Naṣīr ud-Dīn divides the population of the 'good city' into five (and not four) classes: (i) philosophers; (ii) men of eloquence; (iii) those who preserved equity among the people, the sciences in which they were skilled being computation, accountancy, geometry, medicine, and astronomy; (iv) warriors; and (v) those who provided the food of the other classes, whether this was derived from trade, crafts, or the collection of taxes (p. 168).

³ *Practical Philosophy of the Muhammadan People* (translated by W. F. Thompson, London, 1839), pp. 377 ff.

⁴ B.M. Or. 210, f. 332 b.

that their classification is more than a theoretical abstraction and that it reflects in some measure the underlying structure of Islamic society in general and Islamic society in Persia in particular. In Persian society there was a tendency towards group organization at many levels. Some of these groups persist from earliest times down to modern times; some are found throughout the country; others have a more limited existence in time or place or both. Only by belonging to a group did the individual acquire security and status. Further, this corporate structure of society gave to medieval Persia stability and an astonishing recuperative power. On the other hand, the attempt to maintain the balance of society by group organization carried with it certain penalties. The groups at times degenerated into mobs. There was also a tendency towards a hardening into separate communities. So far as this tendency became strong it caused the once potent force to become a stumbling block to the advancing civilization. Within the various groups of society, especially within the craft gilds and religious orders, there was a spirit of fellowship, but there is little evidence of any wider spirit of fellowship transcending these groups. In this respect there is a striking difference between the medieval Persian city and the medieval European city.

One of the effects of the Islamic conquest of Persia was to bring about, to some extent, a fusion of races. The theoretical basis of the new political structure was the *'umma*, 'the community', which was a group of individuals owing allegiance to one another by ties of religion. Within the *'umma* all were equal. There were no distinctions of rank, but there were distinctions of function. Externally the *'umma* was sharply divided from all other communities. The Muslim and the non-Muslim remained permanently separated. Non-Muslim communities, although geographically within the *dār ul-islām*, were never assimilated.[5] In

[5] The principles governing the relations of Muslims and non-Muslims were laid down in the first centuries of the Hijra. The juristic basis of these relations was (i) the treaties between Muḥammad and non-Muslim communities, and (ii) the capitulations of non-Muslim communities made during the conquests, especially that of Egypt. By these contracts the non-Muslim communities enjoyed certain privileges. In internal affairs they remained autonomous in civil and judicial matters. Their contractual rights included security of life and property, security of defence and freedom of religious cult in return for loyalty to the Muslim state and payment of taxes. These rights were acquired

practice, even within the community of true believers itself, there were cleavages. There were various reasons for this. One was the fact that the Arabs brought with them into the conquered territories their tribal loyalties and also their feuds. Moreover, in Persia there very soon arose a dichotomy between Arab and 'Ajam, or non-Arab, which cut across the division between Muslim and non-Muslim. Later under the Seljūqs there was a dichotomy between Turk and Tājīk, or non-Turk, while under the Mongol Īlkhāns there was a marked segregation between the conquerors and the conquered. Even today fusion between the various racial and religious groups is limited. The Armenian communities remain unassimilated, as also do the Assyrians. The Kurds, Balūch, and Turkomāns remain distinct communities, separated from their neighbours. Further, in the centre of Persia, in Fārs, there are a number of Turkish tribes in a province of which the settled population are predominantly Persian, and the old dichotomy between Turk and Tājīk is still clearly apparent. Similarly in Khūzistān the cleavage between Arab and non-Arab persists.

The most widespread group organizations in time and place are the tribal group and the village group, both of which have played an immensely important role in Persian history. The tribal groups have, during Islamic times, for the most part, formed self-governing communities under their own leaders and elders. Control of the tribal element has been and is one of the perennial problems of government in Persia. All except the strongest governments have delegated responsibility in the tribal areas to the tribal chiefs. One aspect of Persian history is that of a struggle between the tribal element and the non-tribal element, a struggle which has continued in a modified form down to the present day. Various Persian dynasties have come to power on tribal support. In almost all cases the tribes have proved an unstable basis on which to build the future of the country. The Seljūqs, who came to power as the leaders of a tribal migration, were quickly faced with the problem of incorporating the tribal element into the structure of the state, and their failure to solve this problem satisfactorily was one of the causes of their fall. The

by an individual only by virtue of membership of a protected community and not as an individual, and they could only be enjoyed as long as that individual was under the jurisdiction of that community.

Ṣafavids, like the Seljūqs, came to power on tribal support. Before long, however, tribal ambitions and jealousies threatened the existence of the state. Shāh Tahmāsp accordingly began to disband the tribal forces which had until then formed the backbone of the Ṣafavid army.[6]

Under the Qājārs, who were also, by origin, tribal leaders, attempts were made by the government of the day to control the tribes by nominating the tribal leaders. The Īlkhānī and the Īlbegī were appointed over the larger tribes. They collected government taxes, provided military contingents, and were generally responsible for tribal affairs. These officers were usually, but not always, tribal chiefs; and there was a tendency for the office to become hereditary. When the government was strong it was able to reduce the power of the tribal leaders, sometimes leaving them only the titular rank of Īlkhānī.[7] More often, however, the government was forced to bow to the wishes of the tribe in its selection of the Īlkhānī and Īlbegī. In so far as the tribal leaders were able thereby to reinforce the power they derived from their position as tribal chiefs their power *vis-à-vis* their followers was increased, the condition of the ordinary member of the tribe depressed, and the element of consultation reduced.[8]

The village group like the tribal group has also played an important role in Persian society.[9] The Arab conquest destroyed

[6] See *Tadhkirat al-Mulūk*, translated and explained by V. Minorsky (E. J. W. Gibb Memorial, New Series, 1943), p. 30.

[7] Curzon, travelling in Persia in 1889–90, mentions that Sulṭān Muḥammad Khān Īlkhānī of the Qashqā'ī had been deprived of his power and only held the titular rank of Īlkhānī (*Persia and the Persian Question*, London, 1892, ii. 112–13).

[8] This appears to have happened among the Qashqā'ī, the Khamseh, and the Bakhtīārī, and in modern times among the Balūch. The element of consultation probably remained stronger among the Turkomāns. Sayf ud-Dawla, when governor of Astarābād in 1320–1/1902–4, wrote an account of the Guklān and Yamūt, in which he states that each tribe was composed of several *auba*, each of which had its leader. There was no leader over the whole tribe and when necessary the shaykhs and elders of the *aubas* assembled for consultation (unnumbered manuscript in the library of the National Consultative Assembly, Tehrān).

[9] Al-Fārābī in his classification of societies counts as imperfect societies those formed by the quarters of a city and villages. The latter he regards as merely there to serve the state (F. Dieteriei, *Die Staatsleitung von Alfarabi*, Leiden, 1904, pp. 50–51).

the political structure of the former Sasanian empire and by removing the pressure of the former imperial bureaucracy and the feudal aristocracy which had impeded the free growth of village communities, stimulated the growth of local associations. Not only, however, was the association of local groups fostered in this way by the conquest: administrative convenience also caused the Arabs to leave local administration to the leaders of local groups.

From early Islamic times the villages in general appear to have enjoyed a considerable degree of autonomy and to have been organized as self-contained and virtually self-governing communities. This was especially the case where the inhabitants retained their former religion; in such cases they remained autonomous in civil and judicial affairs. The Muslim village communities also throughout the pre-Mongol period enjoyed autonomy to a considerable degree. The tendency to treat the village as a corporate unit for tax purposes continued down to the twentieth century A.D. The village headman, or *kadkhudā*, acted as the representative of the village in its relations with government officials, or, in areas which the government had alienated from direct control, with the *muqṭaʿ*, or assignee. There was little movement from one village to another, though large-scale resettlement sometimes took place. Neighbouring villages often spoke, as they still do today, different dialects.

With the rise of military government in the ninth century A.D. the position of the village communities was depressed. When the central power was no longer able to discharge its public duties it surrendered public rights to powerful individuals. The village communities were accordingly in large measure forced to seek the patronage of these persons. Gradually they became burdened with services and found themselves in political and economic bondage to the military classes who had become by the ninth century the main landholders. As long as a certain balance was maintained between the various classes of society the position of the village communities was not, however, intolerable, and they still retained a certain measure of self-government. With the rise of the Mongol Īlkhāns in the thirteenth century the village communities became subject to a greater degree of interference by the civil and military authorities. This in turn involved a weakening in local self-government. Under the Ṣafavids and Qājārs the autonomy of the village communities was further reduced by the pressure exerted on them by the *tuyūldārs*. The increased tendency towards absolutism which ran through society and the changed position of the religious class also exerted an adverse affect on the position of the village communities. Finally, with the spread of administrative centralization in the twentieth century the earlier village organization was largely destroyed. Traces of it still persist, notably the custom in certain areas of making deductions from the harvest for the village craftsmen and others, the arrangements for distribution of water (though in many areas this has now been taken over by the government), the appointment of certain local officials, and in the arrangements made in some areas for communal shepherds.[10]

The towns, also, enjoyed a considerable measure of self-government. In the larger cities the quarters were largely self-contained, having their own mosque, bazaar, and public bath. Each quarter was often enclosed within its own walls. For example, Nāṣiri Khusraw mentions that all the bazaars, streets, and quarters of Iṣfahān had strong bars and gates in A.D. 1052.[11]

The role of the merchant communities was important. They were in many cases wealthy bodies, and the government was often forced to have recourse to them for loans. Hence, although they were taxed at times heavily, the government was usually careful not to tax them so heavily as to interfere with their trade or to drive them to migration. Merchant gilds as distinct from craft gilds were, however, a late growth in Persia and not widely found until the late nineteenth century.

From early times the administration of cities appears to have been largely in the hands of local officials chosen by the local population. In the eleventh and twelfth centuries under the Seljūqs the most important local official was known as the *ra'īs*. He was, in effect, the link between the government and the people. He received his appointment from the government but was

---

[10] For a more detailed discussion see my *Landlord and Peasant in Persia* (O.U.P., 1953).

[11] *Sefer Nameh, Relation du Voyage de Nassiri Khosrau* (ed. C. Schefer, Paris, 1881), Persian text, p. 92.

in many cases a local man.[12] In spite of the militarization of the state which had by that time taken place, he was nevertheless a man of considerable local importance.

The larger cities were divided into wards, which had their own heads, known as *kadkhudās*. Under the Ṣafavids in the sixteenth and seventeenth centuries the *kadkhudās* received their appointment from an official known as the *kalāntar*. The inhabitants of each ward appointed among themselves the person whom they considered most trustworthy, drew up a testimonial for him, and fixed his salary. The document was then legalized by the *naqīb's* seal, and brought to the *kalāntar*, who would issue a certificate and robe of honour for their nominee.[13] Waring, writing in 1802, states that in Shīrāz the most respectable man of the ward was usually given the office of *kadkhudā*, which was an unpaid one. His duties were to acquaint himself with the trade and occupation of the different persons who resided in the ward and of their means of subsistence. It was his duty to arrange for the billeting of troops and the allocation among the inhabitants of any contribution laid upon the ward by the governor.[14] It was also the *kadkhudā's* duty to bring minor disputes in the ward to an amicable termination. His business was to be a peacemaker and to exert himself for the good of the community over which he presided. The *kadkhudās* were, moreover, the mediators between the government and the people. Often a degree of weight attached to their representations which served as a strong restraint on the oppression of the governor.[15] Malcolm, writing somewhat later, states that although the *kadkhudās* were not formally elected the voice of the people always pointed them out: 'if the king should appoint a magistrate disagreeable to the citizens, he could not perform his duties, which require all the weight he derives from personal consideration to aid the authority of office. In small towns or villages the voice of the inhabitants in nominating their *kutkhodah*, or head, is still decided: if one

[12] Cf. *'Atabat al-Kutabat* (ed. 'Abbās Iqbāl, Tehrān, 1950–51), pp. 21 ff. There are numerous references in the documents in the *'Atabat al-Katabat* to the *ra'īs*.

[13] *Taḏhkirat al-Mulūk*, p. 81.

[14] *A Tour to Sheeraz by the Route of Kazroon and Feerozabad* (London, 1807), p. 64.

[15] Ibid., p. 65.

is named of whom they do not approve, their clamour produces either his resignation or removal.[16] It sometimes happened that a *kadkhudā* became an instrument of tyranny but on the whole his power tended to be used for the protection of his fellow citizens.[17] There was a tendency for the office of the *kadkhudā* to become hereditary in certain families.

The *kalāntar*,[18] who is first commonly found in the large towns in Ṣafavid times, was in charge of the *kadkhudās* of the wards and the affairs of the craft gilds.[19] John Fryer, writing about 1677, calls him the Clerk of the Market and states that 'he fixes the Price of Corn, has the Oversight of all Bakers, Cooks, etc., and by his own Authority can not only confiscate their Goods to the Poor, but mulct with loss of Life such Offenders as are notoriously irreclaimable otherwise; many times throwing a Baker into his own Red-hot Furnace, that vends poysonous Corn, or cheats in the Weight; and the Cook into his own Boiling Caldron, for imposing on the People Carrion, or ill-nourished Flesh, found in Highways or Ditches.[20] Tavernier compares the *kalāntar* to the Prévôt des Marchands in France. He states that the *kalāntar* was answerable only to the king, and that he was responsible for the defence of the people against the injustices and vexatious measures of the governor.[21] Corneille le Brun states that the authority of the *kalāntars* 'only extends over the lower classes in the large towns, especially Isfahan. They are the protectors of the people and defend their cases in the tribunals of justice. They are in charge of ordinary and extraordinary taxes which they adjust according to the means and capacity of the inhabitants.'[22]

Two diplomas for the *kalāntar* of Tabrīz issued by Karīm Khān Zand, dated 1764 and 1773 respectively, show clearly that the wishes of the inhabitants were at least in theory considered in

[16] *History of Persia* (John Murray, 1892), ii. 324–25.

[17] Ibid., ii. 350.

[18] The term *kalāntar* is used at the present day to denote the head of a tribal group.

[19] *Tadhkirat al-Mulūk*, pp. 81–82.

[20] Hakluyt, Series II, vol. xxxix; *John Fryer's East Indies and Persia*, iii. 24.

[21] *Voyages en Perse* (Pascal Pia, Paris), p. 250.

[22] *Voyages de Corneille le Brun par la Moscovie, en Perse, et aux Indes Orientales* . . . (Amsterdam, 1718), i. 209.

the appointment of the *kalāntar*. His duties included the over-
seeing of the affairs of the craft gilds in Tabrīz and the appointment of the *kadkhudās* of the wards.[23] There was a tendency
for the office of *kalāntar*, like that of the *kadkhudā* to become
hereditary.[24] Morier, in 1809, wrote that the *kalāntar* was a man
of consequence and an officer of the crown, from whom he received wages. He was 'the medium through which the wishes and
wants of the people are made known to the King; he is their
chief and representative on all occasions, and brings forward the
complaints of the *Rayats*, whenever they feel oppressed. He also
knows the riches of every *Rayat*, and his means of rendering the
annual tribute; he therefore regulates the quota that every man
must pay; and if his seal be not affixed to the documents which
the *Rayat* brings forward in the time of the levy the assessment
is not valid, and the sum cannot be received.'[25] Towards the
end of the nineteenth century the office of *kalāntar* declined in
importance and eventually died out. His duties were in part
transferred to the *dārūgha*.[26]

The affairs of the citizens were also closely affected by the
muhtasib, who since early times had been in charge, among other
things, of weights and measures, the fixing of prices and the affairs of the bazaar in general.[27] His functions were largely concerned with the enforcement of the provisions of the *sharī'a*.
There was, however, some clash of jurisdiction between the

[23] Lisān ul-Mulk Sipihr, *Tārīkh Dār as-Saltana-yi Tabrīz* (lith., Tehrān,
1808–09), pp. 291–93.

[24] Cf. two diplomas for the *kalāntar* of Tabrīz, dated 1835 and 1876 (ibid.,
pp. 294, 296).

[25] *A Journey through Persia* (London, 1812), pp. 235–36.

[26] In 1877 there was still a *kalāntar* in Isfahān. He resided in the Yazdā-
bād quarter, which accordingly had no *kadkhudā*. The other quarters, numbering thirty-one in all, each had a *kadkhudā*, who was under the authority
of the *dārūgha* (Husayn b. Ibrāhīm Khān Isfahānī, *Tārīkh-i Isfahān* (Archives of the Ministry of Finance Secondary School, No. 726), f. 526).

[27] Cf. Nizām ul-Mulk, *Siyāsāt Nāma* (Persian text, ed., Schefer, Paris,
1891), p. 41; *'Atabat al-Katabat*, pp. 72–73. See also Ibn al-Ukhuwwa,
Ma'ālim al-Qurba (ed. R. Levy, G.M.S. 1938); *Staatsschreiben der Timuri-
denzeit* (ed. H. R. Roemer, Wiesbaden, 1952), pp. 150 ff.; *Tadhkirat al-
Mulūk*, p. 83; Tavernier, *Voyages en Perse*, 1632–37 (ed. Pascal Pia, Paris,
1930), p. 257; Du Mans, *Estat de la Perse en 1660* (Paris, 1890), pp. 36–
37; Corneille le Brun, i. 210; and K. 'Awād for a bibliography of the *hisba* in
Revue de l'Académie Arabe, Sept.–Nov. 1943, pp. 417 ff.

muḥtasib and the 'civil' officials. In Seljūq times this clash was mainly with the *ṣāḥib ush-shurṭa,* and in the later period with the *kalāntar* and the *dārūgha.* From early Islamic times down to the seventeenth century the *muḥtasib's* powers were broadly speaking unchanged. According to a diploma for the office of *muḥtasib* of Tabrīz dated 1662 the *muḥtasib* was charged with the preservation of public morality, including the prevention of drinking, gambling, and other offences against the *sharīʿa,* the collection of *khums* and *zakāt* and the distribution of the proceeds of these taxes among those who had a right to them, and the upkeep of mosques, schools (*madāris*), and charitable endowments; he was also to control weights and measures and public highways, and to supervise certain groups and gilds, such as the *mullās, muʿizzins,* and washers of the dead. The civil officials such as the *kalāntars, kadkhudās, dārūghas,* and officials administering customary law (? *ʿummāl-i ʿurf*) were ordered to refrain from interfering in the fixing of prices.[28] Towards the end of the Ṣafavid period, however, it seems that those functions of the *muḥtasib* which had concerned the prevention of offences against the *sharīʿa* were taken over by the *dārūgha.*

During the nineteenth century the office of *muḥtasib* disappeared in some cities. Thus, Binning, writing about 1857, states that the office of *muḥtasib* had recently been abolished in Shīrāz.[29] On the other hand, the office appears to have continued to exist in some other areas for some years. Among the taxes abolished in 1926 by the law of 20 Āzar 1305 was an item of 150 kr. levied on the gild of the butchers of Tehrān for the *muḥtasib.*[30]

The *dārūgha* was a kind of police officer.[31] In the nineteenth century he was especially concerned with the settlement of disputes in the bazaar.[32] According to the History of Iṣfahān, writ-

[28] Diploma in the possession of Ḥājjī Muḥammad Āqā Nakhjavān of Tabrīz.

[29] *A Journal of Two Years' Travel in Persia, Ceylon, etc.* (London, 1857), i. 337–38.

[30] The Second Yearbook of the Municipality of Tehrān: Statistics of the city of Tehrān for the years 1925 to 1929.

[31] Tavernier, pp. 221, 237. Don Juan, however, likens him to the mayor of a town (*Don Juan of Persia,* ed. Le Strange, London, 1926, p. 46). See also Chardin, *Voyages* (ed. Langlès, Paris, 1811), v. 259 ff.

[32] Cf. Waring, p. 67; Binning, i. 337–38.

ten by Ḥusayn b. Ibrāhīm Khān Iṣfahānī in 1877, the *dārūgha*
of Iṣfahān was in charge of the *kadkhudās* of the wards. He
had forty to fifty *farrāshes* and subordinates. In the daytime he
sat with his stocks at the Sekūya Sang in the Qaysariyya, where
he inflicted summary punishment. Subordinate officials known as
pākārs and *sar-gazmas* paraded the bazaars and streets in the
daytime and at night respectively. Any untoward occurrences
were reported to the *kadkhudās*, who reported them to the
dārūgha, who, in turn, referred them to the governor.[33] In
Tabrīz, at the end of the nineteenth century, the *dārūgha* was in
charge of the bazaar only; he was appointed by the *beglarbegī*.[34]

The head of the night-watchmen was known in Shīrāz as the
mīr 'asas in the nineteenth century. His duty was to preserve the
peace of the city, to take up people who were out of their houses
at improper hours, and to prevent robberies. He had a number
of persons under him who patrolled the streets. Each shop-
keeper in the bazaar contributed to the upkeep of these officials.
The *mīr 'asas* was accountable for any robbery and had to recover the property or refund the amount.[35] In Ṣafavid times it
appears that the night-watchman paid for anything stolen and
not recovered, and received one-third of anything recovered.[36]

Local patriotism was a marked feature of medieval Persia.
This would manifest itself in times of disorder, when it frequently
happened that the citizens would band themselves together for
defence. For example, when disorders broke out in the neighbourhood of Bayhaq after the death of Malikshāh in 1092 a local
sayyid arranged for nightly armed patrols round the city, paying
those who took part from his own property.[37] The leaders of
such movements for self-help were frequently members of the

[33] f. 613.

[34] Terminology varied from place to place. In Qazvīn about the same period, the *dārūgha* was an official under the *kadkhudā* of the district. Under
the *dārūgha* were a number of watchmen, known as *bābās* or *chirāghchīs*,
who patrolled the streets and bazaars at night.

[35] Waring, p. 68. A similar system still prevailed in many other cities at the
end of the century; in Qazvīn, for example, the *kadkhudā* of a district was
responsible to the governor for any stolen property.

[36] Du Mans, p. 41.

[37] Ibn Funduq, *Tārīkh-i Bayhaq* (ed. Aḥmad Bahmanyār, Tehrān, 1929–
30), pp. 274–75.

religious class. The existence of a spirit of corporate feeling among the inhabitants of a city is also shown in the ability of a town to make a settlement with individual leaders without reference to the central government or its officials.

There was also a tendency for local patriotism to manifest itself in factional strife. This frequently took the form of rioting between the different religious rites; or between different wards or groups in the city, or between neighbouring towns or villages.[38]

Under the Ṣafavids the factional strife between the Sunnī rites was replaced by rivalry between the Ḥaydarī and Ni'matī factions. The former take their name from Sulṭān Ḥaydar of the Ṣafavid order and the latter from Shāh Ni'matullāh of Māhān. Alessandri, who travelled in Persia in the sixteenth century, states that Qazvīn was divided into two factions (which were presumably the Ḥaydarī and the Ni'matī), all the nine wards and all the citizens belonging to one or other of the factions. These factions, he writes, had always been at enmity and slaughtered each other every day, nor could the king or any other put a stop to it, as the hatred between them had lasted more than thirty years.[39] Malcolm notes that the strife between the Ḥaydarīs and Ni'matīs still existed and continued to excite as much animosity as formerly, and that no effort was made to abolish the usage. He states that during the last three days of Muḥarram in particular the factions would attack each other with violence. If a mosque was decorated by one party, the other, if they could, would drive them from it and destroy their flags or ornaments. If they forced their opponents from their houses, they did not enter them or plunder them, but made a mark on each door with a hatchet, as

[38] Factional strife in Sīstān in the tenth and eleventh centuries appears to have been between tribal groups rather than between cities or wards of cities. The two main factions were known as Ṣadaqī and Samakī respectively. They had a religious colouring in that the former were supported by the *aṣḥāb ar-ra'ī* and the latter by the *aṣḥāb al-ḥadīth,* but appear to have derived their origin from the Tamīmī and Bakrī factions into which the Arab conquerors of Sīstān were divided (*Tārīkh-i Sīstān,* ed. Malik ush-Shu'arā Bahār, Tehrān, 1935–36, pp. 275–76).

[39] Hakluyt, Ser. I, vol. 49, p. 224; according to the version in *Chronicle of the Carmelites* (Eyre and Spottiswoode, 1939), the two factions, between whom was a 300-year-old rivalry, were at peace when Alessandri visited the city (i. 51).

a token of victory. These affrays were often very serious and many lives were lost.[40] Factional strife between the Ḥaydarīs and the Niʿmatīs continued in Shīrāz until the middle of the nineteenth century.[41] The Ḥaydarī and Niʿmatī factions took part in the celebration of the ʿid-i qurbān, and, with the people of certain quarters and certain craft gilds, had a traditional right to different parts of the camel. The custom of slaughtering a camel on the occasion of this festival in the large cities was instituted by Shāh ʿAbbās[42] and continued in force until the twentieth century.[43]

Factional strife, in one form or another, has remained a feature of Persian life down to modern times. Usually, but not always, the factions in modern times have been local rather than religious factions; in Bushire, however, until relatively recent times, there were two rival factions, the *akhbārī* and *uṣūlī*, who were divided by minor differences of dogma.

Among the corporate organizations in the cities may be counted the ʿ*ayyār* movements, which were linked up on the one hand with the craft gilds, and on the other with the *futuwwa* orders, and through both with the *darvīsh* orders. The basis of the *futuwwa* orders was a moral one, in which survived perhaps something of the old Arabian spirit of chivalry and its social ideal. Al-Bīrūnī defines a man possessing *futuwwa* as one who takes upon himself the causes of others and bears their difficulties in order to ease their way, does not hold greedily to that which God has placed at his disposal, and is known for forgiveness, patience, gravity, forbearance, and his aspiration to become great through humility. He goes on to state that the *fatā* will sacrifice his own life rather than bear a disgrace or in order to avert an injustice. He compares a *fatā* in his magnanimity and generosity to Ḥātim aṭ-Ṭāʾī and Kaʿb b. Māma al-Iyādī.[44] The eleventh-century conception of a *fatā*, or *javānmard* (the Persian equiva-

[40] Malcolm, op. cit. ii. 429.

[41] Fasāʾī, *Fārs Nāma-yi Nāṣirī* (lith., Tehrān, 1894–96), ii. 22.

[42] Chardin, ix. 6 ff.; Ḥusayn b. Ibrāhīm Khān Iṣfahānī, *Tārīkh-i Iṣfahān*, ff. 582–84.

[43] Cf. E. Aubin, *La Perse d'aujourdhui* (Paris, 1808), p. 147.

[44] F. Taeschner, Der Anteil des Sufismus an der Formung des Futuwwai-deals, in *Der Islam*, Bd., 24, Ht. i, pp. 69 ff.

lent of *fatā*), was that of a man who was brave, manly, and patient in everything, faithful to his promises, pure and single-minded; one who did not desire another man's loss for his bene-fit, but considered his own loss legitimate for the benefit of his friends, did not oppress the weak or commit extortion against prisoners, and repelled evil from the oppressed; one who as he spoke the truth, also listened to it, gave justice even to his own detriment and did not do wrong to him whose salt he had eaten, did not repay evil for good, considered hypocrisy shameful, and did not regard calamity as vexatious.[45] Among those who pos-sessed this quality, according to the author of the Qābūs Nāma, were the *sipāhiyān* (i.e. the gilds of 'regular' warriors for the faith, the *ghāzī* or the *murāviṭ*), the *'ayyārān* (i.e. 'auxiliaries' who took upon themselves various duties of a more local nature), and the people of the bazaar.[46] The object of these associations of *'ayyār* in so far as they were found in the cities was the preserva-tion of the good name of the inhabitants and the protection of the weak. They were found in many of the big cities from the ninth to the twelfth century. Abu'l Faraj b. Jawzī, writing at the end of the twelfth century, identifies the *'ayyār* with the *futuwwa* and makes it clear that they had a gild organization.[47] There was in practice, however, a tendency for the associations of *'ayyār* to degenerate into mobs of mere hooligans, and in some works the term *'ayyār* is used synonymously with robbers and seditious persons.[48]

In East Persia associations of *'ayyār* were widespread in the ninth, tenth, and eleventh centuries. They had to some extent the nature of popular movements, and their leaders acquired something of the quality of Robin Hood. Ya'qūb b. Layth, as the leader of one of these groups in Sīstān, made himself master of the province in the middle of the ninth century. In Seljūq times and at the time of the Mongol invasion in the thirteenth century

[45] Kay Kā'ūs b. Iskandar, *Qābūs Nāma* (ed. R. Levy, London, 1951), p. 142.

[46] p. 143.

[47] *Tablīs Iblīs* (ed. Cairo, 1928), p. 392. See also *I.A.* xi. 41–42.

[48] Cf. Gardīzī, *Zaynal-Akhbār* (ed. Muḥammad Naẓim, *Iranschähr*, Berlin, 1928), p. 105, and *'Atabat al-Katabat*, p. 61.

there was from time to time renewed activity by the *'ayyār* in East Persia.[49]

There is evidence of the existence in the nineteenth century of associations which are not dissimilar to the earlier associations of *'ayyār*, namely the associations of *lūṭīs* or *dāshhā*. These were local associations, whose objects were the preservation of public morality in the district to which they belonged, the protection of the district from robbers, to which end they would patrol the district at night, and the education of the orphans and the poor children of the district. They caused levies to be made on the rich people of the district and distributed the proceeds to the poor. They had a gild organization. Only persons of good character were admitted. Candidates for admission had to undergo a period of trial, after which, if they proved themselves worthy, they were admitted to membership of the association at a special banquet or *valīma* and girded with a belt.[50] On feast days the associations would take part in religious and other celebrations as corporate groups. The leaders of these associations, known variously as *sar-jumbān, pīsh-dāsh, lūṭī-bāshī,* or *pātūq-dār*, would frequently engage in single combat with each other.

The *zūrkhānas*, institutions where a certain type of wrestling and gymnastic exercise were practised, were in many cases run by these local associations.[51] The members of the *zūrkhānas* also had a gild organization and initiation rites. Purity of character was demanded of those who wished to be initiated. These associations, like the craft gilds and the *futuwwa* orders, had an 'Alid tinge.

As in the case of the gilds of *'ayyār* these associations of *lūṭīs* also frequently degenerated into bands of hooligans, and as such would levy toll upon the people of the quarter in which they were. Binning speaks unfavourably of associations of *lūṭīs* in Shīrāz and Iṣfahān in the middle of the nineteenth century.[52] In more modern times the term *lūṭī* and *dāsh* has become some-

---

[49] See Sayfī Haravī, *Tārīkh Nāma-yi Harāt* (ed. Muḥammad Zubayr aṣ-Ṣadīqī, Calcutta, 1943), pp. 81 ff.

[50] Cf. the initiation ceremonies of the *futuwwa* orders and the *'ayyār* associations.

[51] Cf. Mustawfī, *Sharḥ-i Zindagī-yi Man* (Tehrān, 1945–46), i. 408–9.

[52] Binning, i. 273 ff.; ii. 119–20.

thing of a term of abuse, but even among the *lūṭīhā* and *dāshhā* of the modern Persian city the old conception of chivalry is not wholly absent, and a certain *esprit de corps* prevails among them.

The most highly organized and clearly defined associations in the cities were the craft gilds. Their origin is obscure. There is no evidence of their evolution from gild merchants which preceded them in some cases in Europe.[53] Some writers believe that the origin of the Islamic craft gild is to be ascribed to the Carmathian movement.[54] While the organization of the craft gilds was in all probability affected by the Carmathian movement, it seems more doubtful whether the actual beginnings of the Islamic craft gild can be ascribed to it. It seems more probable that the craft gilds were a natural consequence of the constitution of Islamic society, and were a development of the *'āqila* system.[55] Fellow craftsmen thus formed a closed community, which both answered in a body for any one of its members involved in a punishable offence[56] and also offered its members protection in times of insecurity.

Most of the craft gilds had their own bazaars, which fact no doubt strengthened their sense of corporate life. Throughout the Middle Ages the craft gilds played an important part in the life of the cities.[57] Ibn Baṭṭūta, travelling through Persia in the four-

[53] See W. J. Ashley, *An Introduction to English Economic History and Theory* (London, 1909), i. 67 ff. Nor does the craft gild appear to be a legacy from Sasanian times. The merchants and craftsmen were included in the fourth estate but there is little evidence of gilds within this classification. Moreover, whereas trade was regarded in Islamic times as an honourable and respected occupation to which the efforts of the Muslim citizen could be worthily devoted, in Sasanian times trade held no such respected position and the attention of the citizens was concentrated primarily on agriculture. Sauvaget considers the recrudescence of corporate life in Syria in 'Abbasid times to have been a survival of Roman and Byzantine organization ('Esquisse d'une Histoire de la ville de Damas', in *Revue des Études Islamiques*, 1934, iv. 451–52).

[54] See 'Enquête sur les corporations musulmanes d'artisans et de commerçants au Maroc', in *Revue du Monde Musulman*, lviii. 2, p. 99, and Massignon in article 'Sinf' in the *Encyclopedia of Islam*.

[55] See article on ''Āḳila' in *E.I.*

[56] Von Kremer, *Culturgeschichte des Orients* (Vienna, 1877), ii. 186–87.

[57] One of the earliest literary references to the gilds is in the writings of the Ikhwān as-Ṣafā which belong to the tenth century. Here the gilds are classified according to place, time, membership, and the type of movement. F. Dieterici, *Die Logik und Psychologie der Araber im zehnten Jahrhundert n. Chr.*, Leipzig, 1868, pp. 85 ff.; see also 'Enquête sur les corporations musulmanes d'artisans et de commerçants au Maroc', in *Revue du Monde Musul-*

teenth century, mentions the rivalry between the various corporations of artisans in Shīrāz and Iṣfahān.

> The Sultan of Shīrāz at the time of my visit [he writes], was Abū Ishāq one of the best of sultans. . . . At one time Sultan Abū Ishāq desired to build a palace like the Aywān Kisrā and ordered the inhabitants of Shīrāz to undertake the digging of its foundations. They set to work on this, each corporation of artisans rivalling the other, and carried their rivalry to such lengths that they made baskets of leather to carry the earth and covered them with embroidered silk. They did the same with the donkey panniers. Some of them made tools of silver, and lit numerous candles. When they went to dig they put on their best garments, with girdles of silk, and the Sultan watched them work from a balcony. When the foundations were dug the inhabitants were freed from service, and paid artisans took their place.[58]

Of Iṣfahān he writes,

> the members of each trade form corporations, as also do the leading men who are engaged in trade, and the young unmarried men; these corporations then engage in mutual rivalry, inviting one another to banquets, in the preparations for which they display all their resources. I was told that one corporation invited another and cooked its viands with lighted candles, then the guests returned the invitation and cooked their viands with silk.[59]

It was no doubt partly the shortcomings of Islamic law which encouraged the gilds to carry out certain judicial functions. The limitations of the *sharī'a* made it difficult to take cognizance of many trading disputes. These were, thus, in the first instance referred to the gilds. The city authorities moreover looked to the heads of the gilds to keep the men under their charge in order

---

man, lviii. 41. In the law books in the section on equality in marriage certain crafts are mentioned as having a lower status than others.

[58] Ibn Battūta, *Travels in Asia and Africa 1325–1354* (ed. H. A. R. Gibb, London, 1929), p. 94.

[59] Ibid., p. 91.

and through them to bring home responsibility for misdemeanours and fraudulent actions. Each gild had a kind of gild court, formed by the elders, or *rīsh safīd,* and presided over by the head of the gild, or *kadkhudā.* This court tried members who had committed petty offences or broken the laws of the gild.[60] Any disputes between the members were also settled by this court. Chardin records that in the sixteenth century the chiefs of the trades were the police judges of their trades in small affairs.[61] In the nineteenth century disputes which the elders of a gild were not able to resolve were referred to the *kalāntar* of the town and by him, if necessary, to the governor. Disputes between gilds were settled by a joint court. In Shīrāz in the early twentieth century four persons of either gild would assemble in an appointed place and try the case. In the period immediately following the establishment of a modern police administration in Shīrāz the findings of the gild court were referred to the police (*nazmiyya*) or the municipality (*baladiyya*) for execution.

The internal organization of the craft gilds was in the hands of the elders, or *rīsh safīd,* and the head of the gild, known variously as the *kadkhudā, ra'īs* or *bāshī.* The head of the gild was normally chosen by the members. In many gilds the office tended, however, to be hereditary.[62] In some cases the government of the day endeavoured to exert a closer control over the gilds by the appointment of the head of the gild. Ghāzān Khān, the Īlkhān ruler (1295–1304), attempted to bring those crafts engaged in the manufacture of weapons, and which were under obligation to provide the court with a certain number of weapons annually, under closer control by the appointment of an *amīn* over each craft.[63] In Ṣafavid times the heads of those gilds which were subject to corvées for the king were paid by the king. Chardin maintains that they had greater power than the heads of other crafts because of the power they had to oblige those under them to

---

[60] The regulations of the Persian gilds appear to have been handed down orally for the most part.

[61] Chardin, op. cit. vi. 119; cf. also iv. 93.

[62] Cf. Chardin, vi. 119.

[63] Rashīd ud-Dīn, *Tārīkh-i Mubārak-i Ghāzānī* (ed. K. Jahn, Gibb Memorial Series, 1940), pp. 336–39.

work.[64] In the late nineteenth century the *kadkhudās* of the gilds in Iṣfahān were elected at an annual assembly of all members, but their appointment was subject to the approval of the governor.[65]

The functions of the *kadkhudā* were to preside at the meetings of the gild, which were held to discuss matters affecting the craft, to settle disputes among the members, to punish those who had infringed the rules of the gild, to apportion the tax quota among the members, or for some other purpose. He also acted as the intermediary between the government and the gild.

Entrance to the gilds, in cases where the gilds were not hereditary, depended in modern times upon the acquisition of the goodwill of the other members of the gild. No trace remains, except possibly among the *shāṭirān-i nānvā* (a section of the bakers' gild) in Tehrān, of the elaborate initiation ceremonies which, according to Massignon, prevailed among the Islamic gilds of artisans in the Middle Ages.[66] In some cases on the admission of a new-comer to the gild the elders, or alternatively the new-comer, gave a reception or *valīma*.

The majority of the gilds in Persia were not apparently interconfessional. Conditions varied, however, from place to place and from gild to gild. The head of the carpenters, the *najjārbāshī*, in Iṣfahān in the seventeenth century was, according to Tavernier, an Armenian. He states that 'since the post of chief of the carpenters can only be filled by a Muhammadan the king has often urged this Armenian to renounce Christianity, which he has always steadfastly refused to do, and he is only suffered in this office by the excellency of his genius and the protection of the king'.[67] In modern times in Kirmānshāh the gilds accepted both Sunnīs and Shī'īs. In Qazvīn the cloth merchants, or *bazzāz*, had among their members Muslims, Jews, and Zoroastrians. In Tabrīz Armenians and Muslims belonged to the gild of the goldsmiths (*zargar*) and in 1936 an Armenian was the head of the gild. In

[64] Chardin, op. cit. vi. 119–20.

[65] At the present day the election of the head of a craft gild is subject to confirmation by the municipality.

[66] See article on 'Shadd' in *Encyclopedia of Islam* (1st edition).

[67] *Voyages en Perse*, pp. 224–25.

Kāshān so far as Jews belonged to the gilds they were under the Muslim *ra'īs* but had their quarters in separate bazaars.

One of the functions of the medieval European craft gild was to see that each member had a fair share of the available employment. Regulations forbidding the wealthier craftsmen from acquiring large stocks of material or compelling them to share their bargains at cost price, or even making it incumbent upon the members to obtain their materials through the officers of the gild so that the rich and poor might be served alike were not uncommonly made by the French and German crafts in the fourteenth and fifteenth centuries.[68] There is little trace of such regulations among the Persian gilds in recent times, with the exception of certain gilds in Iṣfahān, including the *urusīdūz* (a gild of shoemakers), the *qannād* (the makers of cone-sugar), and the butchers. In these gilds the right of each member to trade was known as *ḥaqq-i bunīcha*. An outsider could only obtain entrance to the gild by buying this right from a member, who thereby lost his right to carry on the craft. Moreover this right could only be sold with the consent of the other members of the gild. These restrictions remained in force until some forty-five years ago.

The practice of treating the gilds as corporate bodies for purposes of taxation continued until 1926, when by the law of 20 Āzar 1305, taxes levied on the gilds were abolished. In 1948 this tax was reimposed. It is uncertain when this custom of taxing the gilds as a body began. Under the Ṣafavids it was the duty of the *naqīb* to fix the assessment of the gilds in the first quarter of each year.[69] Under the Qājārs there was a great variety of practice both as to the number of instalments in which the government was paid and the way in which the quota was fixed. In Iṣfahān the *kalāntar* was responsible for the collection and payment of the tax. In the case of those gilds, the members of which did not have a *ḥaqq-i bunīcha*, the members were at liberty to pay their share individually to the *mustawfī*. On 1 Farvardīn the *kalāntar* informed each gild which was under his jurisdiction what was its assessment for the coming year, and obtained the signature of one or two of the leading men of the gild in confirmation of this.

[68] See Unwin, *Industrial Organization in the Sixteenth and Seventeenth Centuries* (Oxford, 1904), p. 149.
[69] *Tadhkirat al-Mulūk*, p. 83.

The amount due was paid in twelve monthly instalments. In the case of those gilds, the members of which had a *ḥaqq-i bunīcha*, the share of the tax quota to be paid by each member was allotted under the supervision of the *kalāntar* and the amount of business each member should be allowed to do during the coming year was at the same time decided. The division of the tax quota among the members of other gilds, known as *bunīcha-bandī*, was usually made by the *kadkhudā* and *rīsh safīd*. In Kirmān the members of the gilds paid their share of the tax quota in seven instalments to their respective heads.

Various gilds were from time to time granted exemption from taxation.[70] In Ṣafavid times exemption was granted to the carpenters and masons but in return they performed services for the king, which in Tavernier's view were fully equal to the due paid by others.[71] There were seventeen other gilds which were exempt from taxation in Ṣafavid times. These included doctors, washers of the dead, grave-diggers, singers, midwives, *rawżakh-wāns*, bath-keepers, barbers, blood-letters, story-tellers (*ma'-rikagīrān*), wrestlers (*varzishgarān*), and darvishes. They were under the *naqīb*.[72] The government used them as spies and propaganda agents. In Qājār times also, certain gilds, including the carpenters (*najjār*), stone-cutters (*sangtarrāsh*), and sword-makers (*shamshīrsāz*), were also exempt from taxation. Tradition alleges that this exemption goes back to the reign of Shāh 'Abbās. In the case of the sword-makers the story runs as follows. Shāh 'Abbās is said to have received a helmet from the Ottoman sultan, who offered a sum of money to whoever could break the helmet with a sword. No one was able to do this until a certain 'Asad, a sword-maker, made a sword with which he cut through the helmet. Shāh 'Abbās was delighted and remitted the tax of the sword-makers. In memory of this event the sword-makers assembled once a year at the grave of 'Asad, the *shamshīrsāz*, at

---

[70] Numerous inscriptions are to be found in mosques recording the grant of tax exemptions to different craft gilds, e.g. in the Gawharshād mosque in Mashhad, the Friday mosques in Iṣfahān and Yazd respectively, and the *masjid-i shāh* in Iṣfahān.

[71] p. 239.

[72] The *naqīb ul-ashrāf* was the head of the corporation of *sayyids* and Hāshimites in 'Abbāsid times. Under the Seljūqs the head of the corporation of *sayyids* was appointed by the *sulṭān* (cf. *'Atabat al-Katabat,* pp. 63–64).

Sīchān near Iṣfahān. This practice was still current in 1937. Taxation was reimposed on the sword-makers some thirty-three years ago, although the craft was then virtually dying out.

The craft gilds were concerned not only with questions of security and matters related purely to the craft. Like the English gilds they also provided for mutual assistance in difficulties and for common worship.[73] In some cases the gilds also took part as corporate groups in religious ceremonies, notably the Muḥarram processions and the celebrations of the *'īd-i qurbān*. In Tehrān, for example, certain craft gilds had their own places according to tradition in the procession which took place on the occasion of the *'īd-i qurbān,* and the right to represent the gild in the procession was hereditary in certain families.[74]

On the death of a member mourning ceremonies were attended by the gild as a body and the dead man's heir escorted from the house of the deceased and installed in his premises in the bazaar. Among the butchers of Tehrān a special ceremony was held until recent times on the death of a member, at which a *kashmīrī* shawl, bought out of gild funds, was placed by one of the members on the shoulder of the nearest male relative of the deceased man.[75]

The relations between the religious class and the craft gilds have always been close. In modern times in so far as the gilds have played a part in political affairs they have frequently acted together with the religious class. Further, the craft gilds have

[73] Cf. Köprülü, who shows that the professional morale of the craft gilds of Anatolia in late Seljūq times was inspired by traditions in part mystical and religious and in part chivalrous, and that the relations between the employer and the worker were comparable with those of the shaykh and his disciple (*L'Origines de L'Empire Ottoman,* Paris, 1935, p. 77).

[74] Four days before the *'īd* the representatives of the gilds would tour the town on specially caparisoned horses. A shawl would be given by the gild to its representative and on the day of the *'īd* the representatives of the gilds who took part in the procession would receive a shawl from the *shāh.* Each craft, moreover, had a traditional right to a different part of the camel's body when it was slaughtered. After the camel had been distributed, the gilds would hold a feast in the house of the individual who had represented them in the procession.

[75] In Yazd a similar custom prevailed but was not confined to the gilds. The most important man present at a funeral ceremony would place a hat and special clothes on the nearest male relative of the deceased.

since early times had a connexion with the Ṣūfī orders.[76] The *futuwwa* orders were also in all probability connected with certain gilds. Unfortunately it is impossible to discuss here all the many forms of association which played an important part in Islamic society.

Through the various groups which existed, the citizen in Persia exercised to some extent civic virtues and this enabled him to express, to a limited degree, his sense of social purpose. Moreover, jealous preservation of hereditary rites became the frame of great traditions. During the nineteenth century, however, the traditional bulwarks of society began to crumble. The main factor in bringing about this disintegration was increased contact between Persia and the West. Trade relations with Europe became important in the Ṣafavid period. Envoys from Queen Elizabeth had attempted to foster amicable trade relations with Persia. The resultant relationship fluctuated in warmth and depth in the succeeding centuries. By the nineteenth century a fundamental change had taken place in Persia's relationship with the major Powers. At this juncture Persia began to seek from European Powers knowledge, as traders, three centuries earlier, had sought Persian goods and raw materials, whilst the major Powers were now seeking strategic advantages. Persia in order to maintain her position in this new situation became aware that she would have to undertake certain reforms. First and foremost was the need for improved military technique to enable Persia to withstand the encroachments of her neighbours and the attempts of the major Powers to increase their influence in the country. New military technique meant reorganization of recruitment, pay and equipment, and also greater centralization. This resulted in a weakening of the position of the local leaders and inaugurated a complete decline in the autonomy of the tribal and village communities. Secondly, there was about the middle of the century a considerable movement in the intellectual sphere: westernization and modernization were being sought not only for military reasons but also for the material and intellectual benefits which were assumed to be inherent in western systems of government.

Meanwhile, with increased centralization the influence of the

[76] See W. Ivanow, Introduction to the *Dīwān of Khākī Khurāsānī* (Bombay, 1933), p. 12.

government came to be felt on a far more widespread scale than
had previously been the case. The immediate result was to emphasize the autocratic nature of the government, because the new
technique was not accompanied by the checks and counter-
checks which had developed with it in the West. The government, moreover, to provide money for its new undertakings and
to replenish its treasury, now depleted by extravagance and in-
efficiency, began to give concessions and monopolies to foreign
governments and companies. This, coupled with the fact that an
increasing number of people were affected by the activities of the
government, and believed these activities to be oppressive,
caused opposition to the government to become vocal. So effective, however, had the intellectual movement for modernization
been that the form this opposition took was, broadly speaking,
not a demand for a return to the old system and for less westernization, but a demand for more westernization. The full implica-
cations of this demand were, however, neither realized nor
followed up. The leaders of the movement of revolt were, in the
beginning, the intellectuals. Alone they would have been impo-
tent to achieve success, but they succeeded in rallying to their
support both the religious class, the smaller merchants, and the
craft gilds. Thus they forced the government to become cognizant
of the movement. As the basis from which the movement drew its
support widened, however, so the nature of the movement itself
changed. Popular support could only be won if the aims of the
movement were expressed in terms of Islam. Accordingly nationalism, to which the West had given a stimulus both by its
examples and by its intrusion, was expressed by the leaders of
the movement in terms of Islam and made the main weapon
against the oppression of the government. The movement, therefore, had two main aspects; it was a movement for modernization
and it was also a vigorous protest against oppression by the ruling
classes. These expressions came through the medium of the traditional groupings of society. During the period immediately
preceding the grant of the Constitution the gilds constituted
themselves into associations known as *anjuman-i aṣnāf*, and for a
brief period they exerted considerable political influence. The
Tehrān *anjuman* was formed after the constitutionalists had taken
asylum in the British legation in July 1906. It was constituted by

seventy gilds, each electing one member. From these, twelve representatives were elected to serve as an executive committee. They did not confine their activities to political affairs only, but did much of the work now carried out by the municipality. In Yazd there was a similar body known as the *hay'at-i aṣnāf*, formed by representatives of all the gilds. In Kirmān there was a general assembly known as the *majma'-i ittifāq-i 'umūmī*, formed by various craft gilds and corporations, each of which elected two members. The head of the assembly was chosen from their ranks, and generally was a member of the religious class. The life of the Tehrān *anjuman* coincided with the period of political emergency, and it disappeared shortly after the grant of the constitution. Noteworthy is the *Kirmānī* assembly, which continued to meet until 1930.

How far the new ideas could really have been put into effect by Persian society in its traditional form is highly doubtful. But that there was enthusiasm and some organization is quite clear. That there was an understanding of the problems involved is much less certain. The issue is obscured owing to the fact that the experiment in constitutional government was interrupted after only a brief period by factors beyond the control of the nation. These factors were, the rivalry of the Great Powers in Persia, and the active intervention of Russia.

Many years later a new phase of modernization began under Riẓā Shāh, and the corporate structure of society was still further weakened. Riẓā Shāh aimed at a rapid modernization of the country, to achieve which centralization was essential. Thus local autonomies, whether regional or tribal, were ruthlessly suppressed, because they were obstacles to centralization, and also because the local groups formed potential centres of resistance. The social and religious activities of the craft gilds were virtually nullified.[77] In the economic field the regulation of conditions of work and output was increasingly taken over by the government. Modern methods of industry also inevitably brought about a change.

---

[77] If they wished to hold meetings they had first to report this fact to the local police station and a policeman would be deputed to attend the meeting. The government used the gilds to some extent to implement their social policy, but this policy was dictated from higher authority and was bereft of consultation or discussion.

In the rural areas the autonomous village and tribal communities were broken up even more effectively owing to these modern governmental devices. Government officials from different offices now intervened in areas which formerly had contact with the government only by the offices of the tax collector. Greatly improved means of transportation and communication brought the outlying areas into contact with the capital and the provincial centres. These various developments created conditions which made it possible to foster a sense of national unity. But these were not natural developments: on the contrary they were imposed by force, and executed by a bureaucratic cadre newly trained to put the new methods into operation. The traditional abysmal chasm of doubt and mistrusting of governments by the people, always a marked feature of Persian society since early Islamic times, remained.

Since the abdication of Riẓā Shāh in 1941 the activity of both the gilds and religious orders has been renewed. Conditions of modern life, however, are such that a revival according to the tenets of tradition has become nigh impossible. Various politicians have endeavoured to enlist the support of the gilds, believing in their potency. The influence exerted by the gilds is now, however, a mere phantom of the influence which they wielded at the time of the Constitutional Revolution. It is interesting to note that the sequence of events in recent manifestations of nationalism in Persia in many respects was similar to the manifestations at the turn of the nineteenth and twentieth centuries. The original leaders of the movement were the intellectuals, but it was not until the movement appeared under the guise of Islamic nationalism that it attracted the unstinting support of the populace. Here again the appeal was weaker than at the turn of the century. I would suggest, moreover, that the loudness of the appeal of the more extreme elements of the movement was due in part to an attempt to compensate a loss of vitality by greater external organization, and by frantic calls for greater loyalty to a way of life which no longer has a nationwide appeal. It is meet to suggest also that the development of secret societies, the main political weapon of which is the threat of assassination, is a measure of the breakdown in society which has recently been made manifest. It seems not unreasonable to ascribe this breakdown in part to the dissolution of the corporate structure of society. Whereas formerly the people, even though they had little direct contact with the government, still had an opportunity for the exercise of civic virtues through the various corporations, this was no longer the case with the dissolution of the corporate structure of society. Formerly the citizen had a certain group responsibility. With the dissolution of the corporate structure of society this also ceased to be the case, and the citizen does not yet feel in place of the old group responsibility an individual responsibility. In medieval Persia governments were frequently oppressive and inefficient, but conditions nevertheless existed in which the traditions of civilization were handed down, and in which, at times, civilization flowered. This was possible only because the purpose of Persian society was expressed irrespective of the government. The new technique of government in destroying the traditional corporate structure of society has unfortunately deprived the citizen of the possibility of exercising his civic virtues effectively in a familiar context.

The primary and fundamental problem facing the Persians, both as a nation and individually, is this: how to express a sense of social purpose now that the modern governmental system has virtually caused traditional mediums to atrophy. Persia in the past has shown herself adept at adapting herself to new conditions. It is of interest to orientalists and others to watch the lines along which a solution to this problem will be sought. For myself, I can say that it is my earnest wish to see Persia, a land steeped in tradition and culture, rise like the fabulous Phoenix, and in so doing recovering the art of constructive individual expression through mediums compatible with the age and attaining to new heights of glory.

5. Faith and Learning (a selection from Chapter VI, IS-TANBUL AND THE CIVILIZATION OF THE OTTOMAN EMPIRE)

Among the Christian peoples of Europe it was the common practice, at one time, to use the word Turk as a synonym of Muslim, and to speak of a convert to Islam, of whatever nationality, as having "turned Turk." This usage was not without good reasons. The Ottoman Empire from its foundation to its end was an Islamic state, dedicated first to the advancement, then to the defense of Islam against the infidels. From the sixteenth century its territories included the old heartlands of Islam—the holy cities of Mecca and Medina, the capitals of the ancient caliphs in Damascus and Baghdad. This was the last, perhaps the greatest, certainly the most enduring of the great universal Islamic empires. In the parlance of its writers and officials, its sovereign was the sovereign of Islam, its armies were the armies of Islam, its laws were the laws of Islam, which it was the sultan's duty to uphold and administer. In this task, he was assisted by a great hierarchy of scholars and divines, the custodians of the Holy Law.

It has often been said that there is no priesthood in Islam—that is to say, there is no sacerdotal office, no priestly mediation between man and God. It might also be said that there are no lawyers in Islam, in the sense that Islam recognizes no human legislative function, and no valid system of law other than the law of God. In fact, however, there grew up from early times a class of professional men of religion who fulfilled the task of both lawyers and priests—the doctors of the Holy Law, the jurist-divines of Islam. In Islam there is no clear division between law and

Reprinted by permission of the author and publisher from *Istanbul and the Civilization of the Ottoman Empire*, by Bernard Lewis. Copyright 1963 by the University of Oklahoma Press.

religion, nor between crime and sin. The dogmas of the faith, the rules of ritual and worship, the civil and criminal law—all emanated from the same authority and were buttressed by the same ultimate sanctions. Those who were professionally expert in them followed different specializations in the same basic discipline of knowledge. That knowledge, in Arabic *Ilm*, was the preserve of the ulema—those who know. In Ottoman times their hierarchy was called *Ilmiye*.

The scholarship of the ulema was concerned with two main subjects, theology and law; their talents were exercised in two great professions, education and justice. The two were closely related, and indeed formed part of the same ladder of professional advancement. The holder of the highest offices were known as *Mollas*, an Arabic word meaning lord or master. It was applied to the chief religious dignitaries in the capital, and to the occupants of certain posts in other places, graded in rank and status.

In the strict theory of the Muslim jurists there is no legislative power in the state. God alone makes law, and promulgates it by revelation. The Holy Law of Islam, the *Shari'a*, thus rests on the Koran and on the traditions of the Prophet, as assembled and interpreted by the ancient doctors. The function of the sovereign is not to make or even to amend the law, which antedates and determines his own office, but to uphold and enforce it. The duty of the jurists similarly is not to revise or reform, still less to change the law, which is divine and eternal, but to expound and apply it.

The practical need to interpret and administer the law gave rather greater scope to the will of the sovereign and the skill of the lawyer than the strict letter of the law would suggest. The customary law of the peoples and provinces of the Empire often survived, to play no small part in the system of justice as actually administered; the will of the ruler, as expressed in decrees, dealt simply and efficiently with problems, notably financial and criminal matters, for which the treatises of the Holy Law provided no clear and immediate guidance. From time to time sets of rules were issued, known as *kanun*, and collected in *kanunnames*, some of them general, others dealing with particular areas or matters. These were not usually laws or enactments in the strict sense— rather tabulations, for administrative convenience, of existing law, and resting on *Shari'a*, custom, and decree. Many *kanuns* were promulgated during the reign of Süleyman the Magnificent, who is known in Ottoman annals as Süleyman Kanuni. The legal ulema were of two kinds—*kadis,* judges, and muftis, jurisconsults. The former, by far the more numerous in the Ottoman Empire, tried and adjudicated cases; the latter gave rulings, *fetva,* on points of law when consulted.

The first Ottoman ulema were scholars from the East, whom the sultans appointed as *kadis* in the various towns that they conquered. Murad I appointed a chief *kadi,* to whom he gave the title *kadi-asker—kadi* of the army. A second was appointed by Mehemmed II. From this beginning a great hierarchy of juridical-religious offices grew up, the like of which had never been known in Islamic history. At first it was headed by the two *kadi-askers;* then the chief mufti of Istanbul, who came to be known as the *Sheyh ül-Islam,* began to rise in power, and in the early sixteenth century came to be acknowledged as the senior religious dignitary. His power and influence are expressed in the rules of court ceremonial; according to these he ranked immediately after the grand vizier, to whom alone he was required to pay courtesy calls. Later he seems to have ranked as the equal of the grand vizier, and even the sultan was required on occasion to pay him visits. His chief political function was to issue rulings—*fetva*—in accordance with the Islamic law, on questions of public policy. Thus he might be called upon to authorize a declaration of war, the deposition of the sultan, or to approve the issue of new rules and regulations. In the sixteenth century, when the Islamic influence was growing very rapidly, the chief muftis and their staffs played an important role in harmonizing the rules of the *Shari'a* with the administrative practice of the Ottoman state.

He presided over a vast army of *kadis* and muftis with territorial jurisdictions like those of Christian justices and bishops. Also under his jurisdiction were the mosques, with their staffs of imams, muezzins, and preachers, and the schools, with their own hierarchy of schoolboys, students, tutors, teachers, professors, and principals. In these schools the bureaucratic as well as the religious classes received their education, and many of the high bureaucratic offices were normally held by members of the ulema class.

Many of the ulema were engaged in the teaching profession, at the summit of which were the senior professorships at the great medreses in Istanbul. Such were the great colleges founded by Mehemmed the Conqueror and Süleyman the Magnificent, as well as many lesser figures. Their syllabus consisted chiefly of religion and law, but also gave some—if dwindling—attention to the so-called rational sciences, such as natural history, astronomy, and mathematics. Medicine—of the medieval Islamic school—was also taught, and the profession of medicine was regarded as a branch of the *Ilmiye*. The professors of the medreses were graded in ranks, the highest of which were an acknowledged stage on the way to a judgeship or to one of the state offices, such as *nishanji* and defterdar, held by ulema. The *kadis*, though nominally judges, were also the keepers of many of the provincial records, and in the smaller provincial centers were in fact representatives of the executive power. The chief mufti had no temporal power; he could not initiate but only answer questions put to him. Nevertheless, as chief authorized exponent of the Holy Law, to which the sultan himself was subject, he enjoyed tremendous prestige; as head of an organized hierarchy he wielded great effective power.

This hierarchy enjoyed undisturbed control of law, justice, religion, and education. It also enjoyed financial independence. The ulema themselves were exempt from taxation, and, unlike their colleagues in the slave establishment, could transmit their possessions and even, in effect, their professional status from generation to generation, thus forming a real hereditary possessing class. Moreover, they were in effective control of the vast *wakf* revenues—lands or other revenue-producing properties consecrated as pious foundations for more or less religious purposes. These included of course many established for genuinely pious purposes; they also included a growing number of so-called civil or family *wakfs*, the enjoyment of which passed from father to son for generations with a degree of security unknown to any other form of tenure. In course of time vast properties became *wakf*, and their revenues were controlled by administrators appointed by and drawn from the ulema class. As Lady Wortley Montagu acutely remarked, in a letter of 1717:

This set of men are equally capable of preferments in the law or the church, those two sciences being cast into one, and a lawyer and a priest being the same word in the Turkish language. They are the only men really considerable in the Empire, all the profitable employments and church revenues are in their hands. The Grand Signior, tho' general heir to his people, never presumes to touch their lands or money, which go, in an uninterrupted succession, to their children. 'Tis true, they lose this privilege by accepting a place at court, or the title of Bassa; but there are few examples of such fools among them. You may easily judge of the power of these men, who have engrossed all the learning, and almost all the wealth of the Empire.

In the early period the heads of the Ottoman ulema were often immigrants from countries of older Islamic civilization—from Persia and the Arab lands—or else had gone there for their education. By the sixteenth century however they consisted largely of Ottoman Turks, and disposed of their own centers of higher learning in the capital and the provincial centers. Despite the tendency for religious offices to become hereditary, they never became a closed priestly caste. Men of the second generation in the slave establishment—the sons of military and palace officers —often found a career in religion; also freeborn Muslims of humble origin—clerks and artisans, sometimes even tribesmen—found their way through the schools into the ranks of the ulema. Education, though far from universal, was free and endowed, and the promising student without means could rise through the ladder of the ulema class to the highest office.

The ulema were jurists and theologians, and their religion was legal, dogmatic, and severe. To the people, they appeared as judges and masters, powerful and often rich. Behind them were the majesty of the law and the might of the state, and a God who, even more than His representative the sultan, was immeasurably remote.

The ritual of the mosque is simple and austere. Orthodox Islam, like Christianity and Judaism, has rejected dancing from its worship and ritual. Going even further than its sister faiths, it has also rejected music and poetry, and confined its liturgy to a few

simple, pious texts, taken chiefly from the Koran. The mosque
has no altar and no sanctuary, for Islam has no sacraments or
ordination. The Imam is neither priest nor pastor, but a leader
in prayer. He may guide the believer in matters of religious law
and ritual, but cannot interpose between him and God. Public
prayer is a disciplined, corporate act of submission to the One,
remote and transcendent God. It admits of no drama and no mystery, and has no place for liturgical music or poetry, still less for
representational painting or sculpture, which Muslim piety re-
jects as blasphemy verging on idolatry. In their place Muslim
artists used abstract designs, with elaborate decorative patterns
based on sacred inscriptions in Arabic writing, mostly quotations
from the Koran. In the hands of the great masters, calligraphy
reached a summit of artistic achievement not easy of access for
those brought up in another aesthetic and religious tradition.

The privileged aloofness of the orthodox ulema, the austerity
of their worship, the cold legalism of their doctrines, failed to
satisfy the spiritual and social needs of many Muslims, who
turned elsewhere for sustenance and guidance. In earlier days,
they had often followed the teachings of the Shi'a, regarded as
heretical by the Sunni ulema, and many traces of Shi'ite belief
still remained in popular religion. More important was the influence of the sufis, the mystics of Islam who since mediaeval
times were organized in dervish brotherhoods, each dedicated
to a different mystical way, called *tarikat*. These *tarikats* added
much that was lacking in orthodox Islam. Dervish saints bridged
the gap left by orthodoxy between man and God; dervish leaders
served as pastors and guides; dervish meetings offered brotherhood and communion in the search for God and, on occasion, in
the struggle for human needs. Their faith was warm, mystical,
and intuitive; their worship was passionate and ecstatic, using
music, song, and dance to bring the believer to mystical union
with God. Unlike the ulema, the dervishes remained part of the
people, wielding immense influence among them. In earlier days
they were often leaders of movements of religious and social
revolt—for charity and sanctity against legalism and learning, for
the people against the state and the hierarchy. At times they were
able to penetrate even the palace and the army themselves, and
to challenge the ulema in the very centers of power. They were

present at the birth of the Ottoman state, as religious mentors and preceptors of the frontier warriors. They spread with the Turkish armies to the newly conquered lands and cities, building up a far-flung system of lodges and branches that came to include a large part of the Turkish population. Their centers were the *tekke,* a kind of cloister or convent where the *sheyh* of the order resided, with a number of celibate followers. Married dervishes lived out and attended ceremonies at the *tekke,* as did also the lay-brothers, called *muhibb,* lover (of God). Each order had its own form of ecstatic worship, called *zikr,* and its own discipline and rule. Some of their practices may well retain traces of the dance cults of antiquity and the shamanistic rituals of the heathen Turks; some of their beliefs reflect the impact of the Islamic heresies which the Turks encountered on their way from Central Asia across Iran to Anatolia, and which flourished in the relative freedom of the Anatolian frontier. Yet another influence appears in the preservation, among converts to Islam, of some Christian beliefs, and in the honor accorded, sometimes under disguised names, to Christian saints, festivals, and holy places. The relative importance of Turkish, local shi'ite, and Christian elements in the faith and observances of the brotherhoods has been variously assessed.

It is not surprising that the orthodox ulema regarded the *tari-kats* with suspicion, and not infrequently denounced them. In particular they disliked their pantheistic doctrines, which seemed to impugn the transcendental unity of God; their idolatrous worship of saints and holy places; their thaumaturgic practices and suspect methods of inducing ecstasy; their laxness in observing the divine law. Another ground for suspicion was the strong element of Shi'ism in the beliefs of almost all the brotherhoods—not enough, perhaps, to label them as Shi'a, but enough to arouse the fear and anger of Sunni orthodoxy. There were other fears, too, of the dangerous, pent-up energies which the dervish leaders controlled, and could, if they desired, release. Under both Seljuk and Ottoman rule, the dervishes led numerous rebellions, in the name of religious ideals, and at times offered a deadly threat to the established order. The first great dervish rising was that of Baba Ishak, in the thirteenth century. Another, led by the famous Sheyh Bedr ed-Din, almost destroyed the Ottoman Empire before being crushed in 1416. In 1519, Selim I, following his victories against Persia and Egypt, had to suppress a rebel called Jelali, with messianic pretensions, in the neighborhood of Tokat; in 1527, Süleyman the Magnificent, soon after his triumph over the Hungarians at Mohács, had to send the grand vizier with an army to Anatolia, to crush a rebellion in Karaman led by a dervish known as Kalender oglu, and claiming descent from Hajji Bektash. Yet another series of risings followed in the late sixteenth and early seventeenth centuries, one of them, in 1608, led by another Kalender oglu, called Mehmed Aga.

Kalender oglu means son of a Kalender, a familiar figure in the writings of the early European travellers to the Ottoman Empire, as well as in the stories of the *Thousand and One Nights*. The Kalenders were wandering mendicant dervishes, who deliberately flouted Muslim opinion by shaving their beards, hair, and eyebrows and by throwing off the restraints of the Holy Law and most others. The term *Baba*—father—was applied to dervish leaders generally, and particularly to those who, from the eleventh century onwards, inspired the Turkish frontiersmen and tribesmen who conquered and colonized Anatolia.

It was from these circles that the first great Turkish brotherhood, that of the Bektashi dervishes, emerged. Their patron and eponymous founder was Hajji Bektash, an immigrant from Khurasan who was probably a disciple of Baba Ishak, leader of the Anatolian rebellion of 1240. The order drew its inspiration from various sources, Central Asian and local, and, after a long development in the course of which it absorbed considerable Christian elements, seems to have reached its classical form at the beginning of the sixteenth century. Their Grand Master, or *Chelebi,* resided at the mother convent by the tomb of Hajji Bektash, between Kayseri and Kirshehir; their branches spread over Anatolia and Rumelia. They soon established themselves in the capital where, at the time of their dissolution in 1826, they were reported as having fourteen convents. According to an old legend, Hajji Bektash was the founder of the corps of Janissaries, to whom he gave their name and distinctive headdress. Though certainly untrue in this form, the story probably reflects an early link between the corps and the Anatolian dervishes. In the fifteenth and sixteenth centuries the Bektashis acquired a dominant influence over the religious life of the Janissaries, serving as preceptors and chaplains to their cadets and soldiers and giving them the character of a religious-military fraternity.

In spite of their connection with the Janissaries, the Bektashis retained something of their popular and radical character, and frequently aroused the suspicion of the state and the ulema. A story told by the historian Esad Efendi at the time of their dissolution is very revealing, if not of the attitudes of the Bektashis themselves, then of the charges brought against them by their opponents. In 1690, he says, during the war with Austria,

> an accursed Bektashi went among the Muslim troops when they were encamped for the night and went from soldier to soldier saying: "Hey, you fools, why do you squander your lives for nothing? Fie on you! All the talk you hear about the virtues of holy war and martyrdom in battle is so much nonsense. While the Ottoman Emperor enjoys himself in his palace, and the Frankish king disports himself in his country, I can't think why you should give your lives fighting on these mountain-tops!"

In spite of such accusations, of frequent charges of heresy, impiety and, what was worse, of sedition, the Bektashis continued to flourish, their connection with the corps of Janissaries assuring them of a position of power and influence at the very center of the Ottoman state.

It was perhaps in order to counteract this influence that the Ottoman authorities gave some encouragement to another, rival *tarikat*, which also came to play a major role in the life of the Ottoman Empire. This was the great brotherhood of the Mevlevis, known to the West as the Dancing Dervishes. Their name comes from the famous mystic and poet Jelal ed-Din Rumi, known as *Mevlana*, "our lord," who lived in the Seljuk capital of Konya, in the thirteenth century. Their Western name derives from part of the discipline of the *zikr*, when they whirled round and round on the right foot, to the music of reed flutes and other instruments, until they achieved ecstasy. The Grand Master of the order, the *Chelebi*, resided at Konya, in the central convent by the tomb of their eponymous founder. The Mevlevis were the nearest to orthodoxy among the *tarikats*. Their following was urban and middle or upper class, and included many famous Turkish poets and musicians; their doctrines were sophisticated, and could be so presented as to minimize their divergence from orthodoxy. By the end of the sixteenth century they had won the favor of the sultans, and in 1648 their Grand Master officiated, for the first time, at the ceremony of the girding on of the sword of Osman, which marked the accession of a new sultan. This later became a recognized privilege of the order.

The Bektashis and Mevlevis were both of Anatolian Turkish origin, and in the main restricted to territories subject to Ottoman rule or influence. Other orders were introduced from elsewhere in the Islamic world. Such for example were the Kadiris, founded in Iraq in the twelfth century, and probably the oldest surviving dervish brotherhood. This comparatively orthodox order seems to have been introduced into Turkey at the time of the Ottoman conquest of Iraq in the sixteenth century, and was soon strongly established in Istanbul. Another and earlier importation from Iraq was the *tarikat* of the Rifais, known in the West as the Howling Dervishes. Their followers stabbed, gashed, and burned themselves without suffering injury, and practiced a *zikr* based on rhythmic shouts and cries.

The Nakshbendi order was of Central Asian origin; it is said to have been introduced in Turkey in the late fifteenth century by the poet Ilahi, who visited the tomb of the founder in Bukhara, was initiated into the order, and brought a Bukharan *sheyh* back with him to Istanbul, where he set up the first Nakshbendi lodge in Turkey. Several Turkish authors of the time were among the disciples of the Nakshbendi order, notably the poet and mystic Lamii of Bursa (d. 1531), author of innumerable works in verse and prose. At a later date the Nakshbendi order was reintroduced from India in a more militant form, and acquired a considerable lay following. Its beliefs were closer to Sunni orthodoxy than those of most of the other orders, and its followers were strict in their observance of the prayers, fasts, and other observances prescribed by the Holy Law. Evliya Chelebi, writing after the middle of the seventeenth century, recognizes the importance of the Nakshbendis, and remarks that "the great *Sheyhs* may be classed in two principal orders; that of the Halveti and that of the Nakshbendi."

The Halveti order, which Evliya Chelebi also mentions, was for a while of special importance. Its name comes from the Arabic word *Khalwa,* meaning solitude, and refers to the rule of the order which required members to go once a year into solitary retreat for up to forty days in a cell, fasting and praying from dawn to dusk. The order was founded in the first half of the fifteenth century by a mystical Sheyh of Shemakha, in the eastern Caucasus. It soon won a following among the Turcoman tribes of Azerbayjan and eastern Turkey, and was carried westward by a group of active and devoted missionaries. Very soon after the capture of Istanbul, the Halvetis were strongly established there, under a leader who enjoyed great influence and authority among the people. The militant attitude, extensive following, political ambitions and dubious orthodoxy of the Halvetis made them an object of recurring suspicion to both the Sultan and the ulema. Mehemmed the Conqueror soon "advised" the Halveti leader to leave the city, but the order was already well entrenched, and able to play a considerable if rather obscure political role under several of his successors.

During the early seventeenth century a series of significant clashes occurred between the Halvetis and their orthodox opponents. The two opposing leaders were the Halveti *Sheyh* Sivasi Efendi (d. 1639) and the orthodox preacher and teacher Mehmed Efendi, usually known as Kadizade, "the *Kadi's* son" (d. 1635–36). The rivalry between the two was well described by their contemporary, the famous Kâtib Chelebi:

> These two sheyhs were diametrically opposed to one another; because of their differing temperaments, warfare arose between them. In most . . . controversies . . . Kadizade took one side and Sivasi took the other, both going to extremes, and the followers of both used to quarrel and dispute, one against the other. For many years this situation continued, with disputation raging between the two parties, and out of the futile quarrelling a mighty hatred and hostility arose between them. The majority of sheyhs took one side or the other, though the intelligent ones kept out of it, saying, "This

is a profitless quarrel, born of fanaticism. We are all members
of the community of Muhammad, brothers in faith. We have
no warrant from Sivasi, no diploma from Kadizade. They
are simply a couple of reverend sheyhs who have won fame
by opposing one another; their fame has even reached the
ear of the Sultan. Thus have they secured their own advantage and basked in the sunshine of the world. Why should we
be so foolish as to fight their battles for them? We shall get
no joy of it."

But some foolish people persistently attached themselves
to one side or the other, hoping to become famous like
them. When the cut and thrust of verbal contention from
their several pulpits was near to bringing them into real warfare with sword and spear, it became necessary for the Sultan
to discipline some of them and administer a box on the ears
in the shape of banishment from the city. It is among the
duties of the Sultan of the Muslims to subdue and discipline
ranting fanatics of this sort, whoever they may be, for in the
past manifold corruption has come about from such militant
bigotry.

These conflicts were based on something more than personal
rivalries and jealousies, however, and continued long after the
deaths of both protagonists. A little later in the century a notable
battle was fought over coffee and tobacco, which the dervishes
defended and which the orthodox condemned, together with music and dancing, as impious and licentious. The struggle between
mystics and dogmatists was a principal theme in the religious
life of the Ottoman Empire, and has not entirely ceased even at
the present day. . . .

6. The Languages of the Middle East

In the huge area ordinarily described as the Near and Middle East many languages of different families are spoken. By far the most important of these languages however is Arabic, with its estimated fifty million speakers and its great and extensive literature.

Spread by the great outward surge of the Arab nation in the early days of Islam, Arabic replaced the native languages in Syria, Egypt, and much of North Africa. Although it did not replace Persian as the language of Iran and the lands beyond it, it was for centuries the main literary medium in Iranian lands and many of the great writers of the early Islamic period were Persians who spoke one language and wrote another.

Arabic is a Semitic language; indeed, literary Arabic is not radically different from proto-Semitic, though it is clear that Arabic has developed certain proto-Semitic tendencies analogically in nominal and, more especially, plural formations. The most important idiosyncrasy of the Semitic languages is the triliteral nature of the root. Thus root *KTB* gives the idea of writing, *KRB* the idea of being great or large, *ŠRB* the idea of drinking, *NZL* the idea of going down or descending, and so on. The precise aspect of the action is conveyed by prefixation, suf-

Dr. T. M. Johnstone, Reader in Arabic in the University of London, provided this sketch of Middle Eastern languages especially for this *Reader*. In his discussion of variations of the triliteral root structures of Semitic languages, the patterns are presented, for example, as CaCaCa: C stands for one of the roots or radical consonantal sounds, i.e. a "consonant." By this means the linguist can demonstrate the patterns of a language, as Dr. Johnstone does on the following pages. [Editor's note] fixation and by internal vowel pattern. The simple perfect verb has in the 3rd person masculine singular the pattern CaCaCa/CaCiCa/CaCuCa; thus *KaTaBa* means in English, 'he wrote, has written', *NaZaLa* 'he descended', *ŠaRiBa* 'he drank', *KaBuRa* 'he was great, became great'. Broadly speaking the pattern CaCuCa occurs in verbs of permanent state (as, for example, being great, noble, small) and CaCiCa in verbs of temporary state (as, for example, being sad, glad, satisfied).

The perfect tense of the verb denotes all complete actions, the imperfect all incomplete actions. The 3rd person masculine singular of the simple verb has the pattern yaCCiCu/yaCCaCu/yaCCuCu. In general the perfect pattern CaCiCa has the imperfect pattern (with prefix ya-) yaCCaCu, and CaCuCa the imperfect pattern yaCCuCu; thus *ŠaRiBa/yaŠRaBu* (He drank/he is, was drinking, will drink) and *KaBuRa/yaKBuRu* (He became big/is, was becoming great, will become great).

The perfect is inflected by suffixation, the imperfect mainly by affixation; thus:

KaTaBtu	'I wrote'	*aKTuBu*	'I write'
KaTaBTa	'you (s.) wrote'	*taKTuBu*	'you (s.) write'
KaTaBa	'he wrote'	*yaKTuBu*	'he writes'
KaTaBat	'she wrote'	*taKTuBu*	'she writes'
KaTaBnā	'we wrote' &c.	*naKTuBu*	'we write' &c.

The "triliteral" verb can be modified in meaning in many ways by various modifications of the basic pattern. By doubling the second radical an intensive pattern is formed, as *KaSaRa* 'he broke', *KaSSaRa* 'he smashed'; *QaTaLa* 'he killed', *QaTTaLa* 'he murdered'. By prefixing *'a* to the root, a causative pattern (aCCaCa) is formed, thus *SaQaṬa* 'he fell' and *'aSQaṬa* 'he felled'. Such derived verbs have the same system of personal prefixes and suffixes as simple verbs, thus *KaSSaRat* 'she smashed', *tuKaSSiRu* 'she smashes'.

In the noun also many patterns have specific meanings. Thus, for example, maCCa/iCun indicates the place in which the action of the verb is performed; as *maJLiSun* 'sitting place, council' (from *JLS* 'to sit'), *maXZaNun* 'store room' (from *XZN* 'to store'), *maRKaBun* 'ship' (from *RKB* 'to ride').

So also the pattern CaCCāCun denotes the trader, and CiCā-Catun the trade: thus *XaBBāZun* 'a baker', *XiBāZatun* 'baking' (from *XBZ* 'to bake'), and *ZaRRā'un* 'a farmer' *ZiRā'atun* 'agriculture' (from *ZR'* 'to sow (seeds), cultivate').

Arabic, as was mentioned above, gradually replaced the native languages of most of its new provinces. In Egypt Coptic finally died out as a community spoken language in the sixteenth century. In Syria and Iraq and in parts of Persia Syriac was gradually replaced till today New Syriac is spoken only by small communities, though the older language is still preserved as a liturgical language by Arabic-speaking Christians.

In the further provinces however the native languages survived. Thus in Morocco it is estimated that half the population is Berber-speaking; in Algeria Berber (Kabyle) is spoken by a substantial minority. As we move eastwards however the number of speakers declines till, on the borders of Egypt, the Siwa Oasis is the last little pocket of Berber speakers. Nowhere, however, is Berber a literary medium.

In the Sudan which was settled later by the Arabs, Arabic is the dominating language, but there are large communities still speaking Nubian (once a literary language), on the Nile between Aswan (in Egypt) and Meroe.

On the Red Sea coast there are many speakers of Beḍauye (Beja), a Cushitic language akin to Somali, Galla and 'Afar. In the South, where Arab penetration is comparatively recent, Arabic is little understood and the most important languages are of the Nilotic group (Dinka, Nuer, Shilluk). Dinka and Nuer are used in schools and administration and to this extent are literary languages. It seems unlikely that this trend will continue however, though recent events in the area have shown that attempts at Arabisation are not without opposition.

In Iran the Persian language re-asserted itself as a literary medium, and although even to-day there are still small pockets of Arabic speakers in the area of Bukhara and Qashqadarya in Central Asia, Arabic never replaced the native languages in the Islamic lands beyond Iran.

Even in Arabia itself Arabic has not completely replaced the other Semitic languages of ancient times. As we have seen, some New Syriac is still spoken in the North, and in the South, formerly dominated by languages like the Sabaean, Minaean and Qatabanian of the South Arabian inscriptions, we still have, driven back to the coast and offshore islands by the pressure of the Arabic, Semitic languages which are similar to those of Ancient South Arabia. The most important of these are the Mehri, Šxawri and Soqoṭri languages.

Re-introduced into the Arabian Peninsula about the turn of the last century is the Hebrew language which had to all intents disappeared from it, even before the rise of Islam, except as a liturgical language. Its success in re-establishing itself as a language undoubtedly rests upon the fact that the immigrant Jews were a multilingual community, whose choice of a state language was limited to Hebrew or Yiddish. Clearly, since Yiddish is essentially a German dialect, Hebrew was the preferable choice, but it is interesting that the ultra-conservative in Israel continue to speak Yiddish, believing that the Hebrew language should be preserved for religious purposes, and is too sacred to be used as a secular language.

It may be of some interest to compare with the verbal flexions given above for Arabic, corresponding forms from the other Semitic languages discussed.

Thus from Hebrew *šāMaR* 'he guarded'; Mehri *ĠaLōQ* 'he saw'; Šxari *KeTéB* 'he wrote' and Soqoṭri *QōFoD* 'he descended':

	Hebrew	*Mehri*	*Šxawri*	*Soqoṭri*
Perf. tense,				
sing.:				
1 c.	šāMaRti	ĠaLaQk	KeTóBk	QoFóDk
2 m.	šāMaRtā	ĠaLaQk	KeTóBk	QoFóDk
3 m.	šāMaR	ĠaLōQ	KeTóB	QoFoD
3 f.	šāMRāh	ĠaLQōt	KeTeBót	QeFēDoh
plural:				
1 c.	šāMaRnū	ĠaLōQen	KeTóBen	QoFōDen

Imperf. tense,

sing.:

1 c.	ešMōR	aĠūLaQ	eKóTeB	eQāFeD
2 m.	tišMōR	tiĠūLaQ	tiKóTeB	tQāFeD
3 m.	yišMōR	yiĠūLaQ	yiKóTeB	yQāFeD
3 f.	tišMōR	tiĠūLaQ	tiKóTeB	tQāFeD

plural:

| 1 c. | nišMōR | niĠūLaQ | tiKóTeB | tQāFeD |

In Modern Syriac the old Semitic verbal flexions have disappeared and their place is taken by participial constructions.

As we have seen before, Arabic is the most extensively spoken of the Semitic languages. It would be wrong, however, to think of all these speakers as speaking a language close in structure and vocabulary to literary Arabic. Within the Arab world there is great variation in the spoken word and the learning of literary Arabic imposes a very considerable strain on the speakers of colloquial Arabic. This is particularly true in the West where the difference between the spoken and written standard is at its greatest.

Indeed it is true to say that literary Arabic, which has been so tenaciously conserved because of its immense cultural significance as the language of the Quran and Islam, has always been in danger from the natural processes of linguistic change. We know that spoken varieties of Arabic different from the literary language had developed early in the history of the language, though this we know (almost exclusively) only from the writings of Christians and Jews who were not bound by the tabus of Islam or by those of nationality. It also seems probable that in the later period of the Ottoman Empire the literary language came near to complete extinction, and was being replaced by a number of languages based on the more important of the dialects.

That this should happen would seem natural to a Westerner, the expected product of many centuries of linguistic change. This danger, as it would certainly be conceived by educated Arabs, began to recede with the *nahḍa* (Renaissance) in the nineteenth century, a determined, and successful, attempt to turn the tide, and to make neo-Classical Arabic a flexible instrument

of literary expression. This movement began in Syria and Lebanon and in its early days those involved were mainly Christians.
It is only more recently however that a simple, expressive kind of
literary Arabic has been evolved, mainly in Egypt and Syria, and
largely through the medium of the press.

This has been, in a way, the greatest positive achievement of
Arab nationalism, which in its earlier days was not so closely to
be identified with Islam as it now is. And indeed it would be
difficult to put forward arguments for the unification of the Arab
world if the regional dialects had in fact developed into literary
media.

Despite this success, however, the situation is essentially unstable. The neo-Classical language has shown itself to be a simple
and effective medium of reaching the masses, but it is not widely
used as a spoken medium except by the intelligentsia. Even with
these, a heated argument usually brings a relapse into the spoken
idiom, and in Egypt where neo-Classical is at its simplest and
most refined, a great deal of spoken Egyptian Arabic is broadcast,
and most films are made in Egyptian. It is also noticeable that
political speakers, while they may begin a speech in Classical
Arabic, usually soon fall into Egyptian or into a highly Egyptian-
ised lingua franca. This trend has spread widely the understanding of Egyptian in the Eastern Arab world, and it may be that we
see here the first stage of the development of a new language out
of a dialect. It will however be a long time before educated Arabs
will encourage the development of such a new language, which
they feel would cut them off from their literary heritage, impair
their understanding of Islam, and which would certainly affect
their aspirations to Arab unity.

The most important of the Iranian languages spoken in the
Middle East are Persian and Tajik (which may be classed together), Kurdish, Balochi and Pashto. Less important are Ossetic
in the Caucasus, Tāti in the North and Tālishi in the South-east
of Soviet Azerbaijan, Gōrānī and Zāzā in the area of Kermanshāh,
the Pamir languages, Yaghnob (Neo-Soghdian) in Tajikistan,
and Parachi and Ormuri in Kabulistan.

In the first centuries after the defeat of Persia by the Arabs,
Arabic was almost the only literary language of the new province,
though the native language was still used to some extent in the

writing of poetry. The Sāmānids, however (874–999), and later
the Buwayhids (932–1055) strongly supported the emergent literature in the national language, doubtless from local patriotism
but also because the re-emergence of Persian as a literary medium
to some extent buttressed their separatism. However, it was not
until about 1000 A.D. that the Persian language became widely
used in literary composition, and indeed it was not till after the
Mongol invasion in the thirteenth century that Persian replaced
Arabic outside the field of belles-lettres.

Persian belongs to the Indo-European language family and its
general structure is therefore similar to that of the European languages. There are also similarities in some of the most basic vocabulary. Thus *pidar* 'father', *mādar* 'mother', *birādar* 'brother',
duxtar 'daughter', *tu* 'thou'. In the numerals compare *do* 'two',
šiš 'six', *nuh* 'nine'.

Persian is on the whole an analytical rather than a synthetic
language. The accusative of a definite noun is designated by the
element *rā*, as for example, *mard rā,* 'the man (*virum*)'. The
verbal system is not complex. Thus the simple present of the verb
pursīdan 'to ask' is inflected:

	Sing.	Plur.
1 pers.	pursam	pursīm
2 pers.	pursī	pursīd
3 pers.	pursad	pursand

The 1st person singular of the continuous present is *mī pursam,*
of the present subjunctive *bipursam,* of the simple past *pursīdam,*
continuous past *mī pursīdam,* of the perfect (with the verb *būdan*
'to be' as an auxiliary) *porsīde am,* etc.

The difficulties of Persian lie in its flexibility and its idiomatic
structure. In the Classical literature the multiplicity of Arabic
words adds much to the difficulty of texts.

Like almost all of the languages of Islamic peoples, Persian is
written in the Arabic script with the addition of symbols for *p,*
č, Ž and *g* which do not occur in Arabic. A number of symbols representing distinct sounds in Arabic have the same realisa-
tion in Persian. Thus Arabic *ḥ* and *h* are pronounced the same by
Persians, as are *t* (th), *ṣ* and *s.*

Persian does have a great advantage however in that the literary and spoken languages are not seriously divergent.

Tajik, the language of Soviet Tajikistan and of about 30 per cent of the population of Afghanistan (mainly in the area of Herat and Kabul), does not differ greatly from the Persian of Iran. It is in some ways more conservative, having preserved more of the vowels of early Classical Persian, as e.g. compare *sēr* (Pers. *šīr*) 'a lion' but *dīd* (Pers. *dīd*) 'he saw'. In the Soviet Union, Tajik is written in the Cyrillic alphabet, which has facilitated a great influx of Russian words, mainly of a technical nature.

Balochi is a non-literary language spoken in two main dialects, a Western dialect spoken mainly in Iran, and an Eastern in Pakistan. The Eastern dialect shows some phonological assimilation to the Indian languages, but on the whole Balochi is the most conservative of the Iranian languages with regard to phonetics. Its nominal and verbal system is more complex than that of Persian. There are large Balochi colonies in Oman where they play an important part in the economy of the country.

Pashto, which since 1936 has been an official language of Afghanistan, is spoken by about 60 per cent of its population, mainly in the East and South-East of the country from Jalalabad to Kandahar. It is also spoken in the neighbouring parts of Pakistan. Although Persian was for long the principal literary language of the country, Pashto has been a literary language for many centuries.

It is the least conservative of the Iranian languages in regard to phonetics. Its phonological system is complex and not well suited to the Arabic alphabet, to which substantial additions have had to be made.

The Kurdish language is spoken in Turkey, Iraq, Iran and the U.S.S.R. As might be expected, its development as a literary language has been severely restricted by the division of the Kurdish nation between various countries. Although Kurdish has been used for literary productions for two or more centuries, it has been difficult if not impossible to create a standard literary language. In Iraq there has been considerable effort to make the Sulaimani dialect a literary medium, and this has had considerable success in its home province and the neighbouring Arbil. It is also likely that the conflict with the Arabs in Iraq will further stimulate the development of a regional national language.

The Turkic languages are spoken in parts of Eastern Europe, in Asia Minor and in Asia proper. In spite of the vast area over which they are distributed, the Turkic languages, with some exceptions such as Chuvash, exhibit a remarkable degree of uniformity.

There is no general agreement among scholars on how the Turkic languages are to be classified, but the most important members of this language family are: Ottoman and Azeri (Azerbaijani) in the S.W. of the area, Uzbek and Turki in the S.E., Kazakh, Nogai and Volga Tartar in the N.W., and Uighur, Tuvin and Yakut in the N.E.

Turkish is earliest known from the Orkhon (eighth century) and Yenisei inscriptions, written in a script which, from a superficial resemblance to Scandinavian runes, is generally called 'runic'. An extensive Buddhist literature was written in the Uighur script. The earliest Islamic writings date from the eleventh century, notably a didactic poem called the *Kutadgu Bilig*, and a most important dictionary of Turkish (written in Arabic) by Mahmud Kashgari.

The Eastern literary tradition can be traced without interruption from this period through Khwarezmian and Chaghatai Turkish to present-day Uzbek and Turki, reaching its peak in the late fifteenth century. The earliest surviving works of the Western literary tradition—Anatolian and Azeri—belong to the late thirteenth century. Anatolian (Ottoman) literature reached its highest development in the sixteenth century, with the apogee of the Ottoman Empire.

The Turkic languages are agglutinative languages, one of whose main characteristics is vowel harmony. The system of affixation, though complex, is regular and the difficulties of a Turkic language for a Westerner lie more in its unfamiliar syntax, which makes extensive use of verbal nouns and of adverbial derivates from verbs, usually (and misleadingly) called 'gerunds'.

The Turkish of Turkey has been written in Latin characters since 1928. Though this often makes it difficult to recognise Arabic and, perhaps even more so, French words, there is no doubt that this has simplified the reading of Turkish. The Arabic alphabet, in which the short vowels are not normally written, was entirely unsuited to a language which had many more short vowels than the Arabic *a*, *i* and *u* and in which vowel harmony is an essential feature. The fact that the abandonment of the Arabic script to some extent cut off the people from their Islamic legacy and the literature of their past was in any case no drawback in the eyes of the secular, anti-irredentist regime of Kemal Atatürk.

PART II

Examples of Middle Eastern Institutions

7. Father's Brother's Daughter Marriage in Kurdistan

The prevalence of preferential father's brother's daughter marriage in the Middle East, and its association with Islam, has frequently received reference. Yet no clear picture of the possible
structural implications of this form of preferential marriage has
emerged, nor of the actual distribution and frequency of the
practice. The present paper attempts to analyze the relationship
between the Kurdish form of segmentary lineage organization
and this marriage pattern.

Any chart of unilineal descent in a stable or expanding population constitutes a ramifying system where succeeding generations in many lines tend to be larger and more inclusive than the
preceding. It is this chart, generally in compressed form, which is
utilized to organize a descent group in the form of a segmentary
lineage organization. This organizational form was named by
Gifford and later by Firth, who called it a "ramage," and first
analyzed fully by Evans-Pritchard.[1] Recent work on this type
of organization has been lucidly summarized by Fortes.[2]

In almost all the lineage systems described in the literature,
the lineage, or the clan of which it is a part, is an exogamous
group. This fact of exogamy has important implications, e.g. for

Reprinted with the permission of the editors of the Southwestern Journal
of Anthropology from Volume 10, pp. 164–71 (1954), and with the permission of the author.

[1] E. W. Gifford, Miwok Lineages and the Political Unit in Aboriginal California (American Anthropologist, vol. 28, pp. 389–401, 1926); Raymond
Firth, We, the Tikopia (London, 1936); E. E. Evans-Pritchard, The Nuer:
Tribe and Clan (Sudan Notes and Records, 1933–35), and The Nuer (London, 1940).

[2] Meyer Fortes, The Structure of Unilineal Descent Groups (American
Anthropologist, vol. 55, pp. 17–41, 1953).

the development of dispersed clans and normalizing of a "daughter's son" relationship as a mechanism for grafting foreign lineages to the dominant lineage of an area (as described for the Nuer), and it is further frequently reflected in the whole construction of kinship terminology.[3]

Lineage exogamy is, however, no essential feature of lineage systems. No matter what the marriage pattern in a population may be, a strict chart of *uni* lineal descent offers an equally clear framework on which a segmentary lineage organization may be based. In a patrilineal system, matrilineal ties may be regarded as totally irrelevant to the political relations of segments and whole lineages—marriage patterns may, so to speak, be "liberated" from their role in defining the relations between political groups. This lack of association of lineage organization and exogamy is common among Semitic and Iranian tribes of the Middle East, and in the same area possibly also among some Caucasian groups.[4] However, though marriage patterns do not function to define the relations between lineages, this does not assume that marriage relations and maternal ties have indeed no relevance of a structural or specifically political nature. The present paper presents an hypothesis regarding these implications in the Kurdish lineage organization, specifically the meaning of a pattern of father's brother's daughter marriage, for the consideration of students working with similar problems in the Middle East.

Features of Kurdish culture and society have been described elsewhere,[5] but might be summarized briefly. The Kurds are a linguistic and ethnic group, nearly exclusively Moslem by religion, totalling some three million people.[6] They occupy a semicontinuous territory along the hills and mountains east and north of the Fertile Crescent, divided between the modern states of Persia, Iraq, Turkey, the U.S.S.R., and Syria. Some few groups of Kurds have remained nomadic till the present day, following their

[3] F. Eggan, *Social Organization of the Western Pueblos* (Chicago, 1950).
[4] Louis J. Luzbetak, *Marriage and the Family in Caucasia* (Vienna, 1951).
[5] V. F. Minorsky, "Kurds and Kurdistan" (in *The Encyclopedia of Islam*, London, 1913); E. R. Leach, *Social and Economic Organization of the Rowanduz Kurds* (Monographs in Social Anthropology, no. 3, London, 1940); Fredrik Barth, *Principles of Social Organization in Southern Kurdistan* (Universitetets Etnografiske Museum, Bulletin no. 7, Oslo, 1953).
[6] *The Middle East* (Royal Institute of International Affairs, London, 1950).

herds of sheep, goats, and large cattle into the mountains in the summer and down on the plains in the winter. The great majority are today subsistence farmers, many of whom practice a pattern of localized transhumance. The present discussion relates to the southern districts of Iraq Kurdistan, where material was collected in the field from February to August, 1951.

Two basic types of organization were found: a tribal system, based on descent, and a feudal system, based on class and land ownership. The latter is progressively becoming assimilated into the modern structure of the state of Iraq; the former, a patrilineal lineage system, survives only among the nomads and a minority of the farmers in the more isolated territories.

Kurdish tribal organization is a segmentary lineage organization of very simple type. The largest kinship unit, the *tira*, is a maximal lineage, divisible into segments according to the charter of patrilineal descent. The genealogical depth of the tira varies. For the sedentary Hamawands (location: Kirkuk Liwa, Iraq), the apical ancestor is nine generations removed from the present adult generation; for the nomadic Wurda Shatri (location: centering in Suleimani Liwa, Iraq), twelve generations.

Several tiras may be united, though not necessarily, in a political confederacy of variable endurance, the most important in southern Kurdistan being at present the Jaf confederacy of nomadic as well as sedentary tiras. The following discussion will, for the sake of simplicity, relate only to the Hamawands, an independent tira of population ca. 1000–1500, which became sedentary some two or three generations ago.

The lineage organization has two main areas of relevance: land ownership, and defence and offence in war. Property rights to land and grazing area are held jointly by the tira as a whole; exclusive usufruct rights are vested in its localized segments, inhabiting compact villages with a population of 50 to 200 individuals. Within the village territory, men have traditional rights to certain fields. These rights are passed on from father to son, but are not inalienable, and land is freely redistributed by the village council when the need arises. If a segment becomes extinct, its territory passes as normal inheritance to the other segments of the lineage, according to the degrees of kinship (on any

one level of segmentation, "brothers" exclude "cousins" from
inheritance).

Further, until successful pacification in 1932, the lineage was,
and still is potentially, also a military unit, mobilized in toto if a
segment were attacked from without, and divided in opposition
according to the segmentary charter when conflicts arose within
the group. Conflicts relating to territorial rights were rife, both
within, where they led to fission, and without, where they led
to conquest or loss of territory.

There is a clear contrast between the Kurdish and most African
systems in the readiness with which the problems of fission and
fusion are solved. A man's rights to land are limited to the territory of the village segment of his lineage; a stranger or a person
from another lineage segment is accepted into a village only as
hired farm help ("sapani") of degraded status. The territorial
exclusiveness of lineage segments thus tends to be maintained to
high degree, and there are no kinship mechanisms for developing
"attached" lineages with local territorial and political rights.[7] The
segmentary nature of the maximal lineage expresses itself directly
in geographical distribution, and the respective territories of major and minor segments, inhabited nearly exclusively by them,
down to the village level, can be plotted on a map or clearly seen
where one has a view of the valley bottom. The main integrative
factors relevant to segments larger than the village seem to be
territorial contiguity, knowledge of common descent, and the
importance of the tira as a defensive unit—this last probably being of most weight. No religious or ritual mechanism exists for
bringing together any group larger than the village, and no symbiotic relations of a practical or ritual nature have been
developed.

This organizational form is associated with a strong emphasis
on the father's brother's daughter as preferred spouse, and
marked tendency to close family endogamy. The strength of em-

[7] A permanent relationship may occasionally be established between a con-
quering lineage group and a conquered, non-tribal peasant population, who
retain certain rights as serfs of the ruling lineage. In these cases, a caste
barrier is set up, preventing intermarriage between the two groups. This relationship, observed on the northern margins of Hamawand territory, does
not seem to be very stable.

phasis is indicated by (1) expressed norms, (2) relative bride-price, and (3) actual statistical occurrence.

(1) Informants agree that paternal cousins have first rights to a girl, and where the father of a girl contemplates giving her in marriage to anyone else, the paternal cousin must first release her by renouncing his claim. Cases of violence resulting from breach of this obligation on the part of the father were collected in the field and have been recorded by others in the literature.[8] Giving one's daughter to a brother's son is further considered thoughtful and proper: the father knows his daughter's spouse well, and will also be able to exert some control over his actions toward her after marriage; marriage should be between equals, and no one is closer in status and sentiments than a paternal cousin. Small children are pleasantly embarrassed when teased for being "in love" with their paternal cousin. The importance of endogamy in maintaining family property is also recognized, though the problem only arises with any degree of gravity where Koranic laws of inheritance, giving stipulated fractions of the estate to female descendants, are strictly followed, and this does not generally seem to be the case.

(2) It is an agreed privilege for paternal cousins, to less extent also other near kin, to receive the girl at a reduced brideprice. The normal brideprice for village girls ranges between £30–100. Paternal cousins generally pay only wedding expenses.

(3) The actual frequency of father's brother's daughter, and other cousin, marriage is high, apparently ranging around fifty percent. The degree of relationship between all living spouses in two normal sized Hamawand villages fall into the following categories:

Fa and Mo					Other village	Total
FaBrDa (amoaza)	MoBrDa (khaloaza)	SiDa (purza)	Other relative	Unrelated, in village		
9	1	2	3	2	4	21

TABLE 1.

Taking the normal fluctuations in size and sex distribution of sibling groups into account, this probably approximates the maximal

[8] E.g. W. R. Hay, *Two Years in Kurdistan* (London, 1921), p. 71.

frequency that marriage with actual, non-classificatory paternal cousin can reasonably attain.

Where the cost of marrying an unrelated, "stranger" girl is so high and the normative preference for near kin clear, the inducement for the young man to seek a bride among his cousins is evident. Consequently, the young men make the "right" choice though they appear subjectively to feel, and invariably express the opinion, that they are entirely free to seek any bride they might wish. The problem in this situation centers around what the motivation of the girl's father is, that he should forego his right to a brideprice which, to the Kurdish farmer, constitutes a minor fortune. Or put somewhat differently, the central problem is: what are the advantages gained in this system by giving one's daughter to a brother's son which compensate one for the loss of the brideprice.

The answer would seem to lie in the political structure. In the Kurdish lineage system, all groups are subject to a constant pressure towards segmentation and fission, unmodulated by the interlocking circles of identification normally associated with segmentary descent systems (among the Nuer, territorial vs. descent groups, cross-cutting age-grades; among Tallensi, further the ritual collaboration between lineages, etc.). This pressure is painfully evident in factional activity within the villages, and emerges in all first-hand descriptions of Kurdish life.[9] Kurdish villages are characterized by a constant struggle for political power on the part of a majority of the adult men, at times even women. Such political power is proportional to the number of riflemen one can mobilize to support one's claims. In a patrilineal lineage system, a man can expect political support only from his agnatic relatives, those who by descent belong to his political sub-section; and the factions in the village tend to be alignments of the younger men of a small lineage segment around an older leader. These segments consist primarily of brothers, sons, and brothers' sons. The relation to the latter is most critical: it crosses the first potential line of cleavage between collateral branches.

[9] E.g. C. J. Rich, *Narrative of a Residence in Koordistan* (London, 1836); E. B. Soane, *Through Mesopotamia and Kurdistan in Disguise* (London, 1926); Hay, *op. cit.*

If a man alienates his nephews by refusing them their traditional rights, he loses their political support. If he, on the other hand, gives them his daughters in marriage, the ties are reinforced and lineage solidarity maintained. The girl's father creates an obligation on the part of his brother's son to give him political support by exempting him from paying the brideprice. No other son-in-law can, in the lineage system, fill this role as political supporter; consequently they must invariably pay brideprice. The transaction may thus be regarded as constituting a type of delayed exchange: the father receives political allegiance in his lifetime from his brother's son in return for the daughter which he gives him. In this way, the pattern of preferential father's brother's daughter marriage serves to reinforce the political implications of the lineage system.

If this view is generally correct, one would expect to find a high frequency of father's brother's daughter marriage associated with a developed lineage organization in the Middle East, and the frequencies to be appreciably lower in villages with a different type of organization. In the southern Kurdish area, this is clearly so: for other areas, the literature gives no conclusive evidence.

In the southern Kurdish feudally organized territory, neighboring on the above discussed Hamawand territory, the comparative picture might be summarized as follows: (1) The expressed norms are modified, though not basically changed. First rights of paternal cousins are not as strongly emphasized, and the ideal of equality between spouses tends to be interpreted in terms of village endogamy rather than with reference to descent group. (2) Brideprices tend to be lower for all categories of husbands, especially those of the local community (this holds true for the villages, not for the larger towns, where great variations in class and wealth intervene); some villages have made formal agreements that no brideprice should be charged within the village unit. An alternative and moderately popular way of avoiding brideprice is the sister exchange between two indifferently related men. (3) The actual frequency of father's brother's daughter marriage clearly drops, while village endogamy (in villages generally larger than those with a lineage organization) remains high. A complete census of marriages in one such non-tribal village may serve as an example:

Fa and Mo						
FaBrDa (amoaza)	MoBrDa (khaloaza)	SiDa (purza)	Other relative	Unrelated, in village	Other village	Total
6	1	1	9	19	10·	46

TABLE 2.

This picture would seem to be consistent with the views expressed above.

Hilma Granqvist[10] gives some comparable material from an Arab village in Palestine, where the local community is divided into patrilineal descent groups, called clans, apparently of a segmentary type; but where several of these descent groups reside together in a large village, and have no wider political or territorial importance. She offers the following frequencies of degree of relationship between spouses in one village:[11]

FaBrDa	Total marriages within clans	Between unrelated co-villagers	With strangers	Total
35 13.3%	89 33.7%	62 23%	113 42.8%	264

TABLE 3.

There is some suggestion that clan endogamy has similar factional implications in this situation as lineage segment endogamy has in the Kurdish system, but that the emphasis centers on the opposition between co-resident clans—witness the discrepancy between 33 percent marriages within own clan vs. 23 percent with unrelated co-villager, in a village where four major and six smaller clans co-reside. Yet Granqvist prefers the standard explanation: ". . . marriage with the father's brother's son is preferred to any other marriage in order to prevent a stranger

[10] Hilma Granqvist, _Marriage Conditions in a Palestinian Village_ (Helsingfors, 1931).

[11] _Idem_, pp. 81, 92, 194–95.

taking possession of the property and inheritance of the family."[12]
This even though her argument is further weakened by the fact
that her villagers do not observe the proper Koranic rule[13] of
giving both male and female relatives of the same degree a share
of inheritance, in the proportion 2:1—". . . even if it be seldom
that a man die without leaving any sons, yet the possibility affects
it so far as to allow marriage between the children of brothers
to appear specially desirable."[14]

Chapple and Coon offer a theoretical analysis of parallel
cousin marriage, with special reference to the Bedouin[15] which,
if I have understood their argument correctly, emphasizes the
incompatibility of a subordinate son-in-law relation to a non-
relative with a system of strong political and economic identification with the lineage segment—in this case seen as composed as
father, son, and father's brother. This incompatibility is then
resolved by a pattern of establishing the son-in-law relationship
with the father's brother, though marriage with a father's
brother's daughter. This appears as a rather round-about way
of attacking the problem from the point of view developed here;
but their discussion indicates that the present viewpoints are not
inapplicable to this marriage pattern among the Bedouin.

The points of view expressed above might be summarized
briefly. As contrasted to most African systems, marriage patterns
among the Moslem peoples of the Middle East are liberated
from their role in expressing the relations between segments of
a larger lineage system. The potential relevance of these patterns
to social structure may then theoretically be utilized in various
ways.

In many areas of the Middle East, a pattern of close family
endogamy and preferential father's brother's daughter marriage
has been assumed to be associated with a desire to maintain family property in the face of Koranic rules of inheritance. The apparently exceptionally high frequency of father's brother's
daughter marriage among the Kurdish tribes with lineage organi-

[12] *Idem*, p. 78, where further references to this view are given.
[13] A. S. Tritton, *Islam, Belief and Practices* (London, 1951), p. 66.
[14] Granqvist, *op. cit.*, p. 78.
[15] E. D. Chapple and C. S. Coon, *Principles of Anthropology* (New York,
1942), pp. 305–6.

zation, and possibly among other groups with a similar organization, requires separate explanation. The thesis of this short discussion has been that such a pattern of father's brother's daughter marriage plays a prominent role in solidifying the minimal lineage as a corporate group in factional struggle. Marriages of this type thus serve to reinforce the political implications of the lineage system, *not,* as in most African systems, relative to the relations between whole lineages, but here, on the contrary, relative to the first potential lines of fission and segmentation within the minimal lineage itself.

VICTOR F. AYOUB

8. Conflict Resolution and Social Reorganization in a Lebanese Village

I

A change of considerable magnitude has occurred throughout
the world during the past two decades. Populations and the
territories they inhabit, previously under the hegemony of others,
have attained the status of sovereign states. The evidence has
become apparent, however, that to be a state does not necessarily mean to be a nation. Within their territories, many of these
states have not yet welded through law and sentiment an internal hegemony which is a mark of national identity.

The present discussion may be taken as a case study reflecting
something of this transformation in process. The subject is the
reorganization of social relationships and accompanying sentiments seen in the context of adjudication. The locale is a Lebanese village.

A general statement of the situation would run as follows: a
territory in recent times has fallen under the partially effective
authority of a sovereign state with a central administrative organization controlled ultimately by the indigenous population.
It is characterized by political institutions, including legal ones,
whose jurisdiction over people is legitimized on the basis of territory rather than kinship, religion or other possible principles
through which the organization and control of individuals can
be made effective. The smallest territorial units within the country, that is, the villages, are administratively linked to the central
organization through intermediary administrative bodies. How-

Reprinted by permission of the author and the editors of *Human Organization* from Vol. 24, pp. 11–17 (1965).

ever, they continue to reflect the dominance of a social structure based on other principles of organization in the social relationships of their inhabitants, such as kinship and religion. These modes of organization are, of course, less inclusive.

Legal action (that is, legislative, adjudicative and enforcement behavior) is associated with each type of organization. In operation, although not necessarily in purpose, such action may be markedly different within the less inclusive structures from what it is when linked with the more inclusive one embodied in the governing institutions of the state. A choice, at least in the area of adjudication, becomes possible. Specifically, a villager disputing with another may find himself in a position which permits him to choose between resorting to the courts associated with the central administration or accepting the adjudicating procedures consistent with the indigenous social structure.

I suspect that the postwar creation of independent states in Africa and Asia, usually resulting in new political institutions being superimposed upon, rather than thoroughly displacing, old ones, has made a choice of this kind common enough. However, I shall be concerned in documenting this situation in one country, Lebanon, and on the basis of studying one village in that country.

It may be argued that Lebanon hardly represents the situation I have generalized. A central authority and adjudicating procedures associated with it were part of its social structure long before independence. However, for the Lebanese villager an appeal to an agency of the state was not a viable alternative. The recognition that the authority of the state was alien and therefore to be feared was not likely to promote a genuine choice. This attitude toward the state persists among many villagers even now. However, the objective basis for it is no longer present. Therefore, other attitudes may more easily share currency with it. A genuine choice has become possible.

The empirical basis of this discussion will rest on the documentation of three disputes which occurred in the village and of which I was later informed.

II

Lebanon, a small country on the eastern coast of the Mediterranean and bounded elsewhere by Syria and Israel, became a fully independent state after World War II. However, the political institutions of a modern nation-state were established after World War I, while the territory was under a French mandate.

Lebanon is a nation of religious minorities, of which Sunni Moslems and Maronite Christians are the two largest. Each community of believers retains a significant degree of political autonomy, clearly affecting the institutions of the state as a governing body. For example, the law of personal status, covering such matters as marriage, divorce and inheritance, falls within the jurisdiction of the religious community as a political entity. More directly, recruitment to legislative, executive, and other offices of the central government, elected and appointed, is based on proportional representation according to religious affiliation. The policy does not rest upon a constitutional premise. It is a matter of agreement. Thus, the relatively new political institutions of the nation-state are articulated with, and partially assimilated to, an aspect of the indigenous social structure, that is, the presence of significantly autonomous religious communities. In like manner, but at the village level, the national political administration and the religious affiliation which extend the bonds among individuals beyond the local scene are often woven into the fabric of kinship organization which dominates the village social structure.

The majority of inhabitants in the village from which my material is drawn are adherents of the Druze religion, members of which can be found in three states of the Middle East, Lebanon, Syria, and Israel. The Druze faith stems from eleventh century Islam origins, but its most devout initiates today would disclaim the status of Moslem sectarians and most jealously guard their spiritual as well as their political autonomy. This attribute does not significantly set them apart from the other religious minorities. It is rather their comparatively greater success in maintaining social autonomy which most distinguishes them. Good reasons may be suggested for this success. Endogamy is virtually prescribed for the religious congregation and is preferred within the kin groups. This practice helps to perpetuate insularity. A closed-door policy, dating back to the eleventh century has made formal conversion to the Druze religion an impossibility. This policy complements the effects of endogamy. Thus, the Druze religious community has been virtually coterminous with a community of clans. A strong pride in being a Druze and a strong commitment to maintain the solidarity of the religious group derive from the social relationships which have emerged as these principles have been applied. Such sentiments have helped, in turn, to perpetuate the principles and consequent social relationships.

I can turn my attention now to the village itself. It is located on the western slopes of Mount Lebanon. The population is approximately 1200, of which some 1100 are Druze. The remaining inhabitants are of the Maronite Christian confession.

Within the confines of the village, the chief occupation has been freehold agriculture. Taken as a whole, the village is wealthy. However, agriculture cannot be accounted responsible. A considerable proportion of the wealth has been generated by the capital input of villagers who have emigrated to West Africa and South America, principally, while retaining close bonds with kinsmen within the village. Most of them have been temporary emigrés. They have accumulated capital to enhance their status in Lebanon, not elsewhere. The affluence of the community is due principally to the financial success of a few men during the decade of World War II and its aftermath.

Kinship affiliation, real and putative, determines the most significant relationships within the village. Kinship organization conforms broadly to a general Middle Eastern pattern including patrilineal descent, patrilocal residence, and preferred endogamy within the kin groups. The Druze population is divided into two clans, and each of these is subdivided into a series of graded lineages reflecting a segmentary organization of kin groups.

A brief description of the organization should suffice for the purpose of this paper. The inhabitants of the village who acknowledge themselves, and are acknowledged, as members of the same clan do so through the claim that all of them ultimately share the same ancestor in the male genealogy. The primary symbol of this claim is a common surname. "Al Ayli" identifies this most inclusive grouping although the name is usually extended in use as it is applied to the subdivisions as well.

The clan members are further differentiated into several sections known as *zhibs*. The same claim of agnatic relationship affiliates members of each *zhib* but at a lesser genealogical depth than that of clan association. The *zhibs* have equal organizational status, although they vary in size and the constellation of attributes which might be abstracted from the individual members of each. A common surname is also an important mark of identity at this level.

Again, the members of each *zhib* can be clustered into a set of less inclusive units called *ahl el lezim*. The same principles of descent and organizational equality apply to this level at which the clan is segmented. Here there is no question that an adult can state the precise genealogical links that bind members of his own *ahl el lezim*. There is a unit between *zhib* and *ahl* which was discriminated for me as *asaba*, but it appeared to have very little organizational currency. In any case, it reflects the same process of segmentation discussed here. This paper does not require raising subtler problems of organization.

Clearly, the image of a pyramid is projected by this description, each level of segmentation, as one moves from the clan downward, involving more units of its type but decreasing in inclusiveness. Individual households, the core of each of which may be an elementary family or extended family, form the base of the pyramid. It is the action of, and interaction between, siblings and children of siblings which give substance to this organizational shell.

It should be added that the presence of women who are members of the household by virtue of marriage does not contradict the application of the patrilineal descent principle for determining the composition of kin groups within this organizational framework. The principle of preferential endogamy applies throughout the organization of kin groups, not only to marriage within the clan but within the *ahl el lezim* as well, that is, specifically marriage between the children of brothers. Thus the composition of the household remains consistent with the principle of affiliating on the basis of patrilineal descent. Frequently enough, this is not in fact the case, since women are taken in marriage from outside the clan as well. However, ideologically the principle continues to be affirmed. The loyalty of a woman is expected to be unequivocally directed to her husband and his family. It is also a reasonable inference that something of this ideological affirmation is manifest in terminology. *Bint el 'amm* (daughter of father's brother) is the most acceptable term of reference for "wife" (Bint 'ammi:my wife). It is used whether the consanguineal relation it indicates is actual or not. Even when the situation is too remote to allow the comfortable use of this form (as when a reference was made to my wife or when the speaker became self-conscious of the provincialism of the accepted form), the substitute is not usually an Arabic equivalent. For example, *mara, woman* (marti:my wife) is considered coarse. The term most frequently adopted when *Bint el 'amm* is sensed as inappropriate comes from the French. It is "Madame" (madamti:my wife). Thus, either the ideological recognition embodied in the linguistic usage is consistent with the patrilineal and endogamous principles of organization, regardless of the actual relationship between spouses, or there is recourse outside the appropriate linguistic order entirely.

Although social intercourse between the two clans and between the two religious communities occurs, it has been minimal both in frequency and significance. The most important relationships are those within the kin groups localized in the village.

III

One more point must be covered before I present the disputes which represent the central core of the paper.

A procedure of adjudication based on mediation of differences is the favored means of reestablishing order within the clan when conflict between any of its members occurs. It is known as a *waasta*, a procedure of mediation consistent with the segmentary organization of kin groups within the clan. All forms of dispute (whether stimulated by differences over politics, women, land or resulting from theft, assault, homicide) have fallen under its jurisdiction.

The conditions which align the procedure with the clan organization can be outlined briefly. There is a strong commitment to support one's nearest kinsman in a controversy, brothers against cousins and nearer cousins against more distant ones. At the very least, one does not actively support the other party against a nearer kinsman. The question of the rightness of one claim over the other is not a paramount issue so far as one's obligation to support is concerned. Thus, if members of different *ahls* quarrel, each can expect support (or neutrality at the very least) from others in his own kin group at that level of organization. The same condition would hold if the quarrel were between individuals of different *zhibs*.

At the same time, whatever level of kin group organization the disputants represent, there are always others for whom the commitment to support is not binding. They can be disinterested in that one party is no closer to them than the other. On the other hand, they can be very interested in resolving the conflict in order to reconstitute the solidarity of the more inclusive association to which their own and the disputants' respective kin groups belong. Mediators are recruited predominantly from such a cluster of individuals. Anyone nearer to one disputant than the other is not likely to be acknowledged a disinterested party by both. Outsiders are likely to be uninterested.

The primary aim of the adjudication procedure which the mediators institute is reconciliation through compromise. They, too, are neither expressly interested in determining the guilt or innocence of any party in the dispute nor the rightness or wrongness of one claim over the other. They mediate. They do not arbitrate. They do not judge. The courts can make judgments and have them enforced regardless of any disputant's objections. However, the courts reflect a principle of organization coexisting with but, in important respects, incompatible with that of the clan, and an appeal to them has not been a popular alternative. In fact, an individual who resorts to the courts does not solve the problem of the group. Whatever the result of the court action, the need for mediation persists because reconciliation of the disputants continues to be considered important in maintaining the solidarity of the group. Adjudication must serve this purpose. Thus, the appeal to the courts not only does not eliminate or supersede the mediation procedure, but makes the success of the latter more difficult to achieve. It is not surprising, then, that there is considerable resistance to the use of courts. Nevertheless, the alternative is there, and some have chosen it. The choice reflects a process of transformation in important social relationships affecting village life.

IV

In this section I shall describe three disputes which prompted an appeal to the adjudication procedures of the state. In each case, the principals were kinsmen. Consequently they fell within the jurisdiction of the *waasta*.

The first case occurred a few years prior to my fieldwork in 1953. It concerned workman's compensation. With but two exceptions, some land was owned by each household in the village. Its distribution, however, has been far from equitable. It has been common practice for those whose own land resources did not provide subsistence, or did not take up all their time and energy, to work as agricultural laborers for landowners, primarily their own kinsmen, who needed hired help. Thus it happened that a man working for a relative was injured on the job. They belonged to the same clan but came from different *zhibs*. The worker was hurt while repairing terrace walls which often break down during the winter season when rain and snow soften their foundations. He was bent over when the terrace wall on the level above the one on which he was standing collapsed. Several rocks struck his back. The accident temporarily disabled him. The resulting medical costs he could not easily afford. He sued his employer in court. There were witnesses to the accident, fellow employees who were fellow kinsmen as well. When the case was brought before the magistrate, however, the witnesses denied that the accident had occurred under the conditions specified. The magistrate declared his helplessness under the circumstances. The case was dropped. He recommended that the disputants resort to the clan mode of adjudication, the *waasta*. The suggestion is not uncommon, I was told by a lawyer in Beirut. Litigation between villagers is often difficult to administer in the courts. Both judges and lawyers, in anticipation of an impasse when a case is brought to trial, urge resolution by means of the *waasta*. In this instance, once back in the village, the witnesses were prepared to cooperate with the injured party. Through the process of mediation, he received compensation from his kinsman-employer to cover his medical bill and some loss of time as a breadwinner, although the amount was less than he had hoped to get through the courts.

The second case concerned an "abduction." This time, the disputing parties were from the same *ahl el lezim*. A young man wished to marry his father's brother's daughter. As I remarked before, this type of union is included in the general pattern of preference for marriage within the clan. More than that, it is said, attested to in folklore and literature, that a young man has always been free to invoke strong claims upon his cousin.

The claim in this case was not acknowledged. Neither the girl nor her parents (the father, I was told, mainly in deference to her) favored the match. Although they were residents of the same village and close kin, there were social differences of some significance between the boy and the girl. She was comparatively well-educated. She had attended secondary school outside the village and was thinking of further study at the American University of Beirut. Her father, an emigré at the time, assured the family a comfortable style of life. In contrast, the boy's family was less prosperous. More important, he was barely literate. The girl and her mother, in particular, would have none of him. However, refusal did not discourage him. Hearing that his cousin was to be betrothed to a man from outside the village, he planned, with the help of friends, to kidnap her. The abduction was successfully managed, and the boy took his cousin to a village several miles away where he asked for protection. This is a request which cannot with honor be refused. The girl was kept there by the boy for two days without a word to their kinsmen. It was thought at the time that she must have been forced to submit to him. I was told that the boy either led others to believe she had submitted or did not disabuse anyone of the

thought. The manoeuvre is clear. Who would contest an accomplished fact?

After a lapse of two days, a delegation from among those who
were serving as protectors went to the young couple's village.
They sought out a close kinsman of the girl's father who was also
an influential leader within the clan and told him that they
would disclose the girl's whereabouts if they were promised that
the matter would not be taken to court nor the boy threatened
with jail. These assurances were given. At the same time, the girl
diplomatically assured the boy that she was reconciled to the
fact that she now belonged to him, but that she wanted to return home so that they could be married in the proper manner.
The boy took her back to the village. However, as soon as she
was home again, the girl refused to marry her cousin. With the
full support of her mother she wanted to take legal measures
against him. Through his consulate, the father sought the intervention of the state on kidnapping charges.

Mediators from other lineages within the clan interceded in an
effort to convince the girl's parents that her cousin should have
her so that a reconciliation might be effected. They invoked the
standard principle of the cousin's rights over his father's brother's
daughter. When this did not move the family, they pointed out
that, after all, the girl had been with the boy for two days. Consequently, it would be shameful to bring her back to her home
as a maiden. Nothing availed.

When the family acted to bring the matter to court, however,
no witnesses would come forward to affirm that the girl had
been taken by force. There was the suggestion that the girl had
been a party to the whole affair. It had been an elopement. Even
gendarmes stationed in the village, who had been called immediately after the abduction, and, among other things, had found the
door of the girl's home battered down, denied that their investi-
gation had revealed any evidence of the use of force. There the
matter rested. One mark of progress did help clarify an important issue. A medical examination, for those who would believe,
confirmed the young lady's maiden status. This incident occurred
in 1952. The girl was still unmarried in 1954, although there
were rumors of a suitor from outside the clan. In 1961, I learned
that she was married to a young man whose education far ex-

ceeded her own. They were social peers, too. Reconciliation of the contending parties had also been effected.

A land dispute is the subject of the third case. The disputants were from different *zhibs*. The climax of this dispute was reached while I was in the village (1953–54), although the situation provoking it had occurred before I became a resident.

A man who had sold a piece of land to a kinsman early in the 1930's laid claim to it again by attempting to plow it for himself. He may have reasoned that sufficient ambiguity existed in the original sale to make it worth a try. Mediation would get him something. However, the son of the original purchaser decided to take the issue to court rather than accept the inevitable compromise of mediation. He did so and won a judgment.

This case has two features of special interest that mark it off from the others. It is the only one of the three in which litigation was successfully administered through the courts. It is also a kind of dispute not likely to occur again, for a cadastral survey and clear registration of land holdings were well underway during my 1961 fieldwork. On a brief visit early in 1964, I learned that the survey and registration had been completed.

The details of the case are interesting. The land transaction occurred during the French mandate. A simple statement affirming the sale was the only contract. It had been confirmed by a village official, representing the state. At that time the legal status of an agreement provided that if after five years the parties involved made no effort to rescind, it could be registered as a legitimate contract. In this case, the man had allowed twenty years to elapse before challenging the sale. He began claiming that the land had not belonged to him alone, but to his brothers as well. Therefore, he had had no right to sell their share. They were emigrés.

The then current owner of the land, a man of more than eighty years, no longer concerned himself much with the mundane. He was a devout man. He had turned over responsibility for such matters to his son, a man of thirty who was a schoolteacher and so better educated than most in the village. More important, he had the intelligence of the wise. He was greatly respected in the community, although often politely scornful of the manners and mores associated with the dominance of clan sentiments.

When his father's rights to the land were first challenged, this young man went to an intermediary and suggested that the former owner write to his brothers in Brazil, so that if they confirmed that they wanted the land back by granting him the power to speak and act for them, some justification for his claim might be assumed. The intermediary, a close kinsman of the former owner, agreed that the proposal was fair and passed it on. The letter was never written. It was not held likely that the men in Brazil would have given their brother in Lebanon the power to act on their behalf. On other occasions he had been irresponsible in the disposal of land which they, in fact, did hold jointly.

Perhaps unhappy at the prospect of discord, the schoolteacher's father, without informing his son, showed the contract to three eminent members of the clan. One of them, a village official at the time, concluded that the former owner did have a claim because his brothers' agreement to sell had not been obtained. The father then thought that perhaps the claim ought to be given some consideration. He was prepared for mediation. So, apparently, he informed his son.

When the schoolteacher learned what his father had done and what the response had been, he took the contract to a lawyer in Beirut. He was advised to needle the former owner into an attempt at taking the land so that court action could be brought against him. The teacher let the word spread that he would welcome any attempt the former owner might make to work the land. This was in the spring of 1953. The challenge was not accepted then. The following spring the former owner again threatened that he would take his land back. The teacher let it be known that he would be pleased to have him try. This time the bait was taken. One day, the former owner began to plow the contested strip. The teacher immediately turned the matter over to the lawyer. He initiated court proceedings. After the first postponement of the case on the court docket, the former owner sought out an intermediary to induce the plaintiff to drop the action. No success. I asked the young man why he had not been willing to effect a resolution through the usual procedures of mediation. Why appeal to the courts? He answered in the following manner:

. . . most of the time people like to do things that way. . . .
Someone will come to the people who are in disagreement
with one another and try to bring them together and compromise . . . for example, they may come to us and talk
and say that we shouldn't have this kind of bad feelings between us and we should try to find some way to come to an
agreement . . . and then maybe they will suggest that I give
him a small piece of the land back to satisfy him and everything will be all right. . . . No one will say that I have right
all on my side or he has right all on his side or that he is
responsible for what he is doing. They will only try to find
someway to make everyone satisfied. But I would rather
take it to court like I am doing, and either lose the whole
land or keep it all, rather than give him one-tenth of it
[through mediation] . . .

As I remarked before, the former owner may have reasoned that
this mediation procedure would be operative and so he could
garner something for his efforts. If this was his expectation, he
was disappointed. The case was finally aired before a judge, who
declared against him. In 1964, I asked the teacher whether his
quarrel had been mediated after the court case in an effort to
patch up differences. He said that it had not been necessary.
Sometime after, he visited the man in his home, quite uncere-
moniously. Apparently there was nothing for the loser to do but
acknowledge the teacher's presence and talk to him. It was an
act of deference on the latter's part to be the first to make such a
visit, doubly significant in that it was not gained through a
formal effort at reconciliation. A most unusual act. A most unusual young man.

V

The incidents just described hint at a process of transformation
in village life. The act of choosing the court as the source of conflict resolution is an outward mark of that transformation. What
happened that made it happen? The reciprocal expectations that
define the substance and limits of particular social relationships,

between kinsmen in these instances, were in a measure unful-
filled. Therein lies the significance of the alternative taken. There
is a change going on in the definition of important social relationships. In this final section I want briefly to elaborate these remarks into a possible manner of interpreting this change.

It was assumed earlier that there was a fitness between a
given type of legal process and a given type of social structure.
In this village, mediation, an aspect of the legal process concerned with adjudication, is consistent with the indigenous social
structure of the village, of which the extension of kinship organization is a vital part. Use of the court as an adjudicating agent is
part of the territorially determined political structure which has
been superimposed on that of the older village organization. It
offers a recognized alternative to individuals for resolving disputes.

The social structure of the village is changing. This conclusion
is an obvious one to be drawn in explaining the fact that the
choice in favor of court proceedings had been made in these
cases and others as well. I can simply relate the fact of the choices
made to the assumption cited above and adduce the conclusion.
Not very satisfactory. What we have in mind when we say
"the social structure is changing" is more to the point.

Empirically, there can be little doubt that there are events al-
tering village life. The increase in capital available in the village
due to successful commercial ventures of inhabitants who have
temporarily emigrated helps promote such events. So, too, does
the increased availability of goods and services for those who can
afford them. And, not the least, the increased exposure of villagers to new ideas, a different style of life provided by Beirut, the
movies there, by radio and, more recently, television.

It might be said that the villagers are internalizing at different rates of assimilation new values and value-orientations, resulting in the transformation of social structure. However, when
concerned with change, the concept of values is an inadequate
source of understanding.

A consideration of values may assuredly reflect a process of
change in social structure. But it is not dealing directly with that
process. If a set of social relationships comprising some sector
of a society (or, were it possible, the total set of social relation-

ships making up the society) is abstracted to be analyzed as a system in a stationary state, then reference to values can prove a profitable basis of understanding. They serve as symbolic statements affirming such relationships and acting as motive power to perpetuate them. In this context, they are an ideological image of the relationships.

However, values as objectified statements of preference for specific objects and relations are derivative. I believe social scientists are committed to the position that they have a natural derivation, emerging out of man's social and cultural experience. To speak of a transformation in social structure is to speak virtually in the same breath of the transformation of values. The latter do not account for anything, in this context. They must be accounted for themselves.

I shall therefore turn to the concept of role as a sounder basis for developing an interpretation of a changing social structure. A set of fixed relationships between individuals constitutes an aspect of the social structure of a community at any moment in time. A role is the basic unit determining the content of any relationship. It provides the basis for defining the behavior expected by one individual of another.

He is a kinsman, therefore I expect him to accept mediation.

The mutual expectations derived from two or more related roles determine a social relationship.

The definition of any given role is derived from the cognition of a limited constellation of attributes drawn from an objectively wider collection by which any individual can be characterized by another. For example, any individual may be *perceived* as having the attributes of being kin, of being wealthy, of being educated, of having flat feet, dark skin or red hair, but only those which are cognized define a role. A role, then, is a set of distinctive features drawn from a collection of attributes which at any time include a large number of nondistinctive features. The linguistic analogy I have in mind is, I believe, clear. For example, the phoneme as a "sound that matters" represents the cognition of a limited set of sounds from a larger set of physiologically perceivable ones. Similarly, a role is defined by the attributes that matter, and not all the attributes which can be perceived matter.[1] The distinctive attributes provide the substance of the expectations which determine a social relationship. Again,

he is a kinsman, therefore I expect him to accept mediation.

If he is not a kinsman, the expectation is not present. I am pointing to a situation in which "kinsman" becomes a non-distinctive feature replaced by some other attribute that matters. The individual with all his characteristics remains, but the role is changed and so is the relationship.

When we speak of a changing social structure, then, we mean ultimately the selection of a new set of distinctive attributes drawn from a larger store of perceivable ones. A man may go on being a kinsman, but it is no longer a significant attribute. His wealth may become a distinctive feature. The new set of attributes determines new relationships, that is, a different content to the mutual expectations. Such a set of new relationships represents a modification in the social structure.

The cases presented suggest that the decision to use the courts reflected this process of transformation in the village. There is, however, the problem of a reasonable basis for inference in using the incidents I have described to illustrate the argument. I have certainly not presented the kind of material in the first case which would permit a direct inference. With the exception of a few young men, none of them agricultural laborers, there was no marked indication of class consciousness that would transform the kinship attribute that defined important relations between employer and employee from a distinctive to a non-distinctive feature. And I had no personal acquaintance with anyone in this case.

There is, however, some basis for an indirect inference. It rests in the laborer's failure to implement the choice he made. It seems obvious and certainly well within credibility that pressures were exerted to prevent a court trial and to invoke mediation proceed-

[1] The analogy may have more than metaphoric significance, considering the semantic function of language in the process of human behavior as it classifies relationship and indicates the content of action.

ings. The fact that witnesses did not stand behind the laborer in court indicates an assertion of power in controlling his actions. It was a coercive act. The legitimate basis of control, recognized as authority and the ability to influence, was obviously inoperative. Where the effort to control no longer has a legitimate basis, the disruption of a relationship may be reasonably posited. In effect, expectations were no longer being fulfilled, suggesting a change in the cognition of the relationship.

My evidence in the second case offers more leeway for reasonable inference. The marriage rights of a man over his father's brother's daughter is a classic feature of Middle Eastern social organization. The force of this right, it has been claimed, exhibits itself as virtually a duty imposed on the girl's family to give her to the patri-parallel cousin, if he chooses. This attitude is well-authenticated in the literature.[2]

A curious reversal has taken place in the village. Stories of "abductions" as love's only way out are not uncommon in the Middle East. However, in the past, it was a lover without jural rights to his beloved who did the abducting, with the cousin in hot pursuit. There has been a change in the village. As always, some families have sought suitors for their daughters elsewhere than within the *ahl* even when a father's brother's son was available. However, the number of abductions as a consequence of rights denied the cousin have increased. It was reported to me that between 1943 and 1953 there had been twenty such abductions by the father's brother's son, while for the preceding fifty years only one such case could be recalled. Most of these cases were successfully resolved through mediation, which meant, by and large, that the cousins married.

In the case presented, there is no doubt that the attribute of the man as cousin was evident, as were other qualities, predominantly intellectual ones. In the context of marriage, the binding force of the claim to his cousin's hand would suggest that kin was the distinctive feature determining the relationship. Obviously, expectations based upon it were not met. The attribute of kin ceased to be a significant determinant of the behavior of the girl and her parents toward him. It should be added

[2] Raphael Patai, "Cousin-Right In Middle Eastern Marriage," *Southwestern Journal of Anthropology*, XI (1955), 371–90.

that there have always been some wealthier than others, and some better educated than others, within the clan. It should not be assumed that these characteristics were not hitherto conceived as equally significant because they have only recently become perceivable.

The third case can be dealt with briefly. The teacher's behavior was consistent with his own frequent and explicit objections to what he called "the family system." He often expressed the view that obligations based merely upon the fact of kinship were insincere. He would stress the attribute of "friend" to distinguish some of his kinsmen. And he explained, not as a matter of genealogical information but as some justification for his opposition to the family system, that the members of the clan were not all related in any case. In short, he was more interested in stressing attributes other than kin in determining the relationships he had with his kinsmen.

CONCLUSION

At the beginning of this paper I referred to the problem of welding the internal elements of newly independent states into a national identity. The discussion of adjudication and the process of transformation in a village's social structure is not so remote from that point of departure as it may seem.

I began with the assumption that there was a consistency between types of legal action and types of social structure, noting in some detail the fitness between the mediation procedures in the village and the kinship organization, but simply accepting that a similar fitness could be described between court adjudication and the political structure of the state. The appeal to court proceedings, in effect, illustrated a movement toward bringing village organization into a consistent relationship with the territorially founded organization of the state. On the one hand, the choices which were made reflect the process of dissolving old roles and relationships as a basis of community organization. On the other hand, they indicate the process of reconstituting community organization in new roles and relationships consonant with the greater community, the nation.

9. *Some Aspects of the Arab Dhow Trade*

At the end of 1939, there were 106 large ocean-going dhows on the registry of the Persian Gulf port of Kuwait. They averaged about 100 tons, the largest being 300 and the smallest about 75 tons, by European standards. Their average value, at that time, was perhaps 10,000 rupees, the approximate equivalent of $3,000. They made trading voyages with Iraqi dates, loaded in the Basra river, to the coasts of India and East Africa, generally making either two Indian, or one East African, voyage annually. The majority were in the trade to India, with an occasional diversion to East Africa. From India they were accustomed to bring back shipbuilding materials, coir for cordage, and Malabar teak; from East Africa they brought mangrove poles from either the delta of the Rufiji River, in Tanganyika, or from the port of Lamu, in Kenya Colony. These poles were used for building, and the dimensions of the rooms in most of the Kuwait houses depended upon the length of the mangrove poles brought from East Africa.

In addition to these deep-sea dhows, there were also, at that time, between 100 and 150 pearlers, and some 50 or 60 smaller dhows in the local trade to the Basra river, many of them engaged in bringing fresh water (for Kuwait has no satisfactory supply of its own). New vessels were building at the rate of two

Alan Villiers, deep-sea sailor and author, spent over twelve months in 1938–39 studying firsthand the Arab dhow trade of the Persian Gulf and the coasts of southern Arabia and East Africa. His experiences are described in his *Sons of Sinbad* (Scribner's) published in 1940; Mr. Villiers here presents further information on the social and economic aspects of the trade. This material is reprinted by permission of the editor of *The Middle East Journal* from Vol. 2, pp. 399–416 (1948).

or three a month, for deep-sea, and a similar number for coast-wise trade.

The port of Kuwait was then, and is still, the principal dhow-building and trading port of the Persian Gulf, though offering little trade itself. Its only real rival in the deep-sea trade was the ancient port of Sur, near Ras al-Hadd, on the Gulf of Oman. Figures for the port of Sur were unobtainable, but there must have been at least 100 deep-sea dhows sailing from there, the majority to Mogadishu, Mombasa, and Zanzibar. Several ports on the Trucial Coast of Oman also sent their quota of deep-sea ships to Africa and India; and Muscat and Mutrah Bay, and the ports of Lingeh and Qishm, in Iran, contributed a few. But the flag of Iran was a rarity in both Indian and African ports, compared with the Arab.

In addition to the Persian Gulf and Omani ports, Mukalla in the Hadhramaut, Ma'alla by Aden, Hodeida, Mocha, and Luhaiya in the Yemen, and Qizan on the coast of Asir in the Red Sea, all build and maintain considerable fleets of dhows. These I have seen, personally; there are many ports I was unable to visit. It is probable that the dhow trade round the Arab coasts employs upwards of 2,000 vessels of one sort or another, in which at least thirty or forty thousand men gain some sort of livelihood.

For many years, steamers of the British India Company have been trading in the Persian Gulf. Kuwait is still well served by steamers from Karachi, and an occasional long-voyage vessel used to put in from New York and London, even before the oil resources began to be exploited in 1940. American, German, Italian, and British lines, none of them likely to overlook any cargoes, all traded to the Gulf. The African East Coast and the Indian coasts are even better served. How is it, then, that a dhow trade of such importance still survives? How is it organized, and how managed?

One reason—perhaps the chief—why the ancient trade with the monsoons down the Indian Ocean not only survives but flourishes is that the dhows warehouse the goods they carry as well as transport them, and it suits the merchants better to have 10,000 packages of new season's dates divided among a fleet of dhows, than in the hold of one steamer which will unload the lot in a day or two, and flood the market. Ten thousand packages provide cargoes for at least five large dhows; the dhow master does not care how long he takes to discharge his cargo, for his overheads are trifling, his crew works on shares and handles all cargo, and his vessel pays practically no port dues. His dates can therefore be warehoused in the dhow, until the market can easily absorb them.

The dhow trade is "native" trade, a stubborn plant which has been growing a long, long time. Nearly all the cargoes carried in dhows are for the native bazaars, and almost never for European account. Much of the cargoes consists of goods which the dhow captain himself, or some merchant or merchants travelling with him, sells for his own profit. The dhow is a peddler, as well as a carrier; a storehouse, as well as a ship; a means of livelihood to travelling merchants, as well as to her crew proper. Basra dates, though the most important outward cargo,[1] are only one source of revenue: there are a host of others, not necessarily always legitimate.

Kuwaiti owners of date plantations on the nearby Basra river play a considerable part in the financing of deep-sea dhows, though in most cases the captains, called *nakhodas*, are at least the nominal owners. It suits the merchants well that the *nakhodas* should regard themselves as the owners, for this provides them with a cheap form of insurance. If the dhow be lost it is the *nakhoda's* loss, and not the merchant's, for the poor captain must pay back not only the value of the dhow but the advance of freight given him to finance his voyage. Since Islam forbids all forms of ordinary insurance, this arrangement is to the merchant's liking. The *nakhodas* must accept it, for in most cases there is no other way by which they can acquire a big dhow.

In Kuwait, immediately prior to the outbreak of World War II, there was beginning to be some restiveness about this, and an association of the *nakhodas* had the temerity to issue its demands upon the merchants. These included payment of demur-

---

[1] Crew requirements and the very measurements of the dhows themselves are reckoned in terms of dates. A sailor to each 100 packages is the general rule, in Kuwait, and a dhow is spoken of there as having a capacity for 2,000 packages of dates, rather than as being of 100 tons burden.

rage when unduly delayed at the loading berths in Basra (a dhow might be kept for weeks waiting for her cargo), a sliding scale of freights for different ports instead of the customary flat rate of 1.5 or 2 rupees a package regardless of destination, liability for the return of advances to cease with the loss of the ship, two competent officers for every seagoing dhow, and so forth. The demands represented a bare minimum, surely, and

FIG. 9-1   Arab Boom.

no more than a *nakhoda's* right, but the merchants' answer was that if the *nakhodas* could make new rules, so also could they; and they had the real power. I do not think the attempt of the *nakhodas* got them very far.

While the dates are generally carried both to India and East Africa on a freight basis, nearly all other cargo is bought to the ship's own account and peddled to best advantage. The merchants have a substantial share in the dhow's earnings, apart from the sailors' own ventures, which are limited to what they can stow in a sea chest on the poop. As far as I was able to discover—and I was more than twelve months sailing in deep-sea dhows—the freight from the dates, on the typical African voyage, is used to finance a cargo of salt from Aden and to purchase odds and ends which might earn a profit in the bazaars of the Benadir coast and Kenya Colony. At the same time, the dhow carries all the passengers she can prevail upon to make a voyage, anywhere, for the Arab of Oman, and the Hadhramaut in particular, is an inveterate wanderer, and every dhow is a passenger vessel by the mere possession of deck enough to lie upon.

The salt is sold in the best market that offers between the Hadhramaut coast and Zanzibar. At the same time, the *nakhoda* does what trading he can in anything which he knows, from past experience, will command a market. The average dhow never leaves the Gulf without at least some carpets, allegedly Persian but generally of either Italian or English origin, which are used both as trade and as bribes. Cooking stones, ghee, live sheep, cows, sacks of rice and flour, dried fish, haberdashery of all sorts, brassware, cheap enamelware, Arab confectionery—all these may be aboard, either as ship's ventures or as the crew's, generally the latter.

Every man of the crew concentrates on goods which can be bought cheaply in the free port of Aden, adulterated if possible in transit, and sold to the Somali or Swahili shopkeepers whose little stores abound in every port along the coast of East Africa, from Haifun in the north (which the Italians called Dante) to Mikindani in the south, which is about as far south as the Arabs sail in these days. Only Indian dhows go further, to Madagascar and the Comorin Islands. Gaily coloured turbans of the correct style (for the manner of headdress worn in the different parts of Arabia and East Africa varies considerably; what will sell well at Mukalla, for instance, will find no buyers at Kuwait; and the Arab is a stickler for style), sarongs from Java and Japan, amber and artificial beads of the kind the true Moslem loves to fondle, cigarettes in gay packages but of no advertised brand, cheap perfumes (which I have several times seen the sailors laboriously adulterating with water from the ship's tanks), small crocheted caps to go under turbans, money belts, caps of artificial leather and pullovers of extremely artificial wool, veils for the harem, basketware from the Hadhramaut, sometimes a little hashish or qat[2]—these are the sailors' ventures, and the profits are their own.

[2] A bush common to southern Arabia, especially the Yemen. The leaves, when chewed, are somewhat intoxicating.

The sailors are inveterate smugglers; almost none of the goods they bring—apart from the main cargo—is declared. Since they leave from small ports along the coast of Arabia where official supervision, while thorough, is not organized to conform with the Europeans' idea of how trade should be conducted, and since so much of their more highly dutiable goods are private ventures, such manifests as they produce to the authorities are useless. The mariner buys his goods himself, and sells them himself (though he does not mind disposing of them to boats alongside). He sees no point in accepting any official interference, and to him the European on the East African coast is still an interloper, recently arrived and wholly unnecessary.

The passenger trade is an important one, particularly in the East African voyaging. Though the Italians in their colonies tried to regulate the movement of Arabs, and the growth of Indian influence in Mombasa and Zanzibar has much lessened Arab trade and opportunities, still thousands of Omani and Hadhramaut Arabs travel down the Benadir coast and to Zanzibar annually. Every dhow fit to go to sea—and quite a few which look as if they are not—carries her quota, and some of the overcrowding is incredible. Among 35 Arab dhows which were lying together at Mogadishu, in Italian Somaliland, in the season of 1939, the Italian immigration authorities checked 4,000 passengers. They missed at least another 600, for no list which the dhows supply is really reliable, and each ship carries many persons who are without European documents. As a new dhow arrives, sometimes dozens of her passengers will drop quietly over the side and disperse themselves among the dhows already in the harbour. As with the disposal of the seamen's ventures, all Arabs take a delight, regardless of their ports of origin, in the general defeat of European regulations.

II

At first glance, the whole deep-sea trade in dhows seems unorganized and almost unregulated. In point of fact, it is very well organized indeed, and has a tradition going back, probably, some thousands of years. There is no association of dhow owners in

Arabia as there is a Country Craft Organization on the west coast of India, for the Arab of today is too inherently disunited and fiercely individualist to make this type of co-operation possible. But he can organize his own trade very well, nevertheless. The typical wealthy business family of Kuwait maintains offices, almost always managed by sons of the house who frequently rotate on the circuit, in all the more important centers of Arab coastal trade. The head office is at Kuwait or perhaps Basra, with branches at Aden (in the Crater, not at Steamer Point), Bombay, possibly one other west coast of India port, and Mukalla. Where there is not an actual branch of the family conducting business on a permanent footing, there is either a trusted agent (probably a relative), or one of the younger sons sent in the trading season to watch the family interests. This, for instance, is done at Berbera, in British Somaliland, which, when times are good, can absorb a surprising quantity of Iraqi dates carried there in dhows. The agent or family member is primarily responsible for the collection of debts—always a problem in a trade which is carried on without banking. A family carrying on business on such a scale will have a finger in perhaps a score big dhows, all nominally "owned" by their own *nakhodas*. The cash resources of some of these families must be enormous, and behind them stands the Sheikh of Kuwait, who was a wealthy man even before oil was discovered in his territory.

When a deep-sea dhow is built, at least some of the money is put up by the *nakhoda* himself and his family. It is the first essential of the *nakhoda* that he should be from a family of standing in the community, which will pay its debts. Just why such families cannot finance a dhow by themselves I was unable to discover, but the Arab, apparently, has no objection to carrying on business under a cumbersome structure of debt. The merchant, backed by the Sheikh or the ruling family, backs the *nakhoda's* family, who support in turn a trusted and experienced member to take command of the dhow.

It is customary for the boys in such families to go to sea while very young, but they never work as sailors. They are always privileged: no sailor can become a deep-sea *nakhoda*, since obviously if his family is of standing, he would never serve before the mast. The children sail with him sometimes from the age of six or seven, though not regularly. They will make one or two long voyages, looking on and learning but not actually doing anything; then they will remain at home a year or two before going out again. They take command very young. Schooling, at least in 1939, was normally restricted to the local Koranic schools, and rarely occupied more than three months in the year. Only merchants' sons went to the colleges of Iraq, Egypt, and Syria.

Gradually the head of a *nakhoda's* family may attain the status of a lesser merchant himself, though his merchandise is generally limited to the wherewithal to build ships, which comes up in his own dhows from the Malabar coast. But a *nakhoda* himself almost never becomes a merchant, and a merchant's son never becomes a *nakhoda*. Nevertheless, the profession of conducting deep-sea dhows about the waters of the Indian Ocean is a highly respected one, and the shipmasters of Kuwait are, on the whole, a very competent and knowledgeable class, though few of them can practice much astronomical navigation. Even their long voyages down to Zanzibar or to Calicut are coasting, really down with one monsoon, and back with the other, almost always in sight of land. Their real ability consists in their local knowledge, both of ports and trade.

In Kuwait, in 1939—as now—there were upwards of 10,000 qualified deep-sea sailors. An astonishingly high proportion is of Negro origin, the descendants of slaves, though not now slaves themselves. Many others are of Iranian origin. Almost none are Bedouin, for the Arab Bedouin is not a seafaring man. In Kuwait, the callings open to the low-class Iranian are restricted to portering, pearling (either as diver or as tender), and sailing. Both Iranians and Negroes work splendidly, are loyal, competent, and well disciplined.

As the *nakhoda* class is tied to the merchant by a structure of debt, so also are the sailors tied to the *nakhoda* class in the same way. All deep-sea sailing is paid for on a shares system, and there are no wages. Often the *nakhoda* of the deep-sea dhow has an interest in a pearling vessel (though not now to anything like the same extent as in former years), and the sailor may be bound to him through pearling debts, either his own or inherited. The more iniquitous practices in the pearling business structure have long been on the way out, largely because of the excellent example set at Bahrein, but the debt tradition stands and is almost impossible to eradicate.

The sailors go to sea because they know no other life, and they make a wretched living by incredibly difficult methods. They have no possessions other than the clothes they stand in, and one or two spare gowns, a good headcloth, and a few sarongs. Their toothbrush is the twig of a tree; their ablutions are made five times daily at a mosque well, or in the sea; they know no shelter and rarely have a bed. The younger seamen, I have noticed, often have no home other than the *suq,* or native bazaar, where they coil down in their rough cloaks for a night's sleep on a bench in a cheap coffee shop, or in the sand. At sea, they stretch out on the deck, beneath the stars, for there is no such thing as accommodation for the seamen or anyone else in most dhows. The officers and the more important merchants live on a bench round the wheel, in the stern of the ship; the seamen lie down anywhere.

What keeps the seaman a disciplined and more or less contented worker is his hope of reward, principally from smuggling or his own ventures, and his ambition to get hold of a tiny shop in the *suq* of his home town. This is an ambition he rarely achieves. His more usual fate is to die young, especially if he be also a pearl diver. Pearling from Kuwait and Bahrein is carried on during the season of the hard southwest monsoon in the Indian Ocean, when the big dhows are laid up and there is no ocean sailing. It is therefore possible for the same men to carry on both callings, though in these days the seaman is becoming a little too enlightened to go off cheerfully to the purgatory of pearling.

The seaman is also helped by his religion, by his interest in the seafaring life (which has a great appeal of its own) and the fine camaraderie about it, and in many cases by the delights of night life in such ports as Zanzibar and Bombay. If he has no harem of his own back in Kuwait, he is certainly no celibate at Zanzibar. He generally seems to manage a small home in Kuwait after a few voyages, depending upon his own business acumen and the general success of the dhow he serves in. Many *nakhodas* appear to maintain several.

In addition to the merchants, *nakhodas,* and seamen, there is another class of importance in the dhow trade. These are the mates, the experienced officers who, never able to become *nakhodas* themselves because of an unacceptable financial status, very often have more to do with the actual sailing of the dhow than the *nakhoda*. Each big dhow carries at least one such experienced man. Sometimes he is of Iranian origin, and has been sailing since he could walk. Sometimes he is a Negro, member of a trusted ex-slave family, who lives with the *nakhoda* at home or has been brought up in his courtyard.

He is always an able mariner, but he is not often trusted to trade. It is not at all uncommon for a *nakhoda*, on the usual East African voyage—which always begins with a long haul and long-winded peddling of dates round the coasts of Southern Arabia, and to Berbera and perhaps Djibouti—to leave the ship for considerable portions of the passage at sea, while he looks after her business interests ashore. For example, in one Kuwait dhow in which I had the good fortune to sail for some eight months, the *nakhoda* cheerfully left the ship at Aden and went on to Mukalla by steamer, to steal a march on the other shipmasters and scoop the cream—he hoped—from the passenger market. Again, he left the ship at Zanzibar, and his mate took her down to the delta of the Rufiji, hauled her out on the beach at Kwale Island south of Dar es Salaam, loaded her with mangrove poles, and brought her back to Zanzibar again, where the *nakhoda* had ostensibly been trying to assemble passengers and extra cargo for the return to Arabia but in fact had been enjoying a new harem.

Mates are paid by shares, and are, in my opinion, an oppressed class. They carry their own ventures, engage in smuggling on a small scale—haberdashery, currency, and so forth—and generally keep the ship's books. They may become *nakhodas* of small *booms*, running to the Basra river; but it is unusual for a man from the more dignified deep-sea trades to descend to this. There is no social status about the *nakhoda* of a coastwise water dhow.

Ships are built by shipwrights who employ no naval architects. Both builders and riggers' lofts are unknown. The ships are put together entirely by eye and take the traditional form either of the double-ended *boom*, or the carved and embellished *baggala*, which obviously has a considerable ancestry from the Portuguese galleon. *Baggalas*, being both costly to build and unwieldy in

FIG. 9-2 Baggala.

a seaway, are now unfashionable. A *boom* is both cheaper and much easier to build, and carries just as much. Her sharp stern makes her safer in a seaway, though it is no part of her builder's plan that her *nakhodas* will try her qualities in a storm. Their sailing, he hopes, will be confined to sunny seas and more or less favorable winds; therefore the clumsy lateen rig will do.

The lateen is awkward but cheap; it demands a big crew, but these are cheap, too, for they are the sailmakers and riggers as well as mariners, and their only cost is an agreed share in the ship's earnings. The lateen is a grand pulling sail, and the dhows sail handsomely in their own conditions. There is nothing clumsy about them, though their fish-oiled hulls smell abominably and their underwater bodies are preserved by a mixture of tallow and lime, rubbed on by hand and renewed quarterly. The sailors do this work, as well as handle all the cargoes, keep the passengers in order and extol the merits of their ship so that more passengers might sail with her, tow the ship with her own longboat and propel the smaller dhows by sweeps, in calms, and fight for her if need be. The Kuwait dhows today are never armed, though the Suri may be.

III

A brief description of my personal experiences will serve to illustrate a typical East African voyage.[3] I sailed in a Kuwait dhow of the *boom* type, a vessel of 2,000 date-packages capacity —perhaps 150 tons—which had a crew of twenty-eight. She carried something between 120 and 180 passengers, although her hold was full of salt and rice, and her decks were already crowded with a large longboat, a small gig, and a dhow under construction for sale at Lamu.

I joined the vessel at Maʻalla, the native port of Aden. She had already been several months at sea, peddling a full cargo of dates from Fao (by the mouth of the Basra river) around the coast of the Hadhramaut, and to Berbera. When I joined her, she had been hauled out on the beach at Maʻalla and her bottom repayed, and already was loaded with her cargo of salt and rice in sacks, and some mysterious parcels on deck for the Sultan of Mukalla. All her crew had their sea chests filled with trade goods from the cheap *suq* in the Crater at Aden; her carpenter was at work on a 40-foot dhow for sale on the voyage; and she had shipped several Suri and Omani merchants, from Aden, bound on a general trading voyage on their own account, wherever the dhow might take them.

We sailed first to Mukalla and Shihr, where we embarked passengers (the fare was eight rupees regardless of destination, the passengers providing their own food and looking after themselves entirely) and some further cargo. This consisted mainly of a parcel of condemned dates which it was hoped to sell to the Somali (or failing that, to feed to the Swahili labor in the Rufiji Delta,

[3] The voyage here summarized is described in detail in the author's *Sons of Sinbad* (New York, 1940).

when loading mangrove poles), some dried shark which smelled high even aboard the dhow, some cooking stones, and a considerable quantity of basketware.

With this lot aboard, and the *nakhoda* pessimistic and depressed at the small number of passengers, though his dhow appeared crowded, we sailed first to Haifun, a salt port on the northeastern coast of Italian Somaliland. There we anchored among a fleet of dhows, and did nothing at all for some time. Finally, some rice was sold, some haberdashery smuggled into boats which the local Somali brought alongside, and lot of fish caught and dried. Then we went on to Mogadishu, running down the coast with the northeast monsoon. At Haifun another Kuwait ship was caught smuggling and heavily fined; and all the Kuwaiti in the harbour contributed to pay the fine. At Mogadishu, it was hoped to land a hundred or so passengers, but the Italians would not permit them to disembark. Trade there was extremely difficult, and little could be done. Some of the merchants left, as far as I could gather, to try to collect debts owing to them from previous voyages. Some smuggling went on (I saw a lovely carpet change hands), some of our passengers melted away and their places were taken by others, equally undocumented.

After a week or ten days we passed on down the coast to Lamu. Here more passengers landed and there was a determined attempt to sell the new dhow which the carpenter had completed. She was a lovely little vessel which could carry some fifteen tons. The price asked was 1,000 East African shillings, or about $240. At that price, there was no buyer; she finally changed hands at 700 shillings. Lamu was a mangrove-pole port, but I gathered the trade was rather too well regulated for our *nakhoda's* taste, and we bought nothing.

Next came Mombasa, a port with a large dhow trade. Some figures I saw in the *Report of the General Manager on the Administration of the Railways and Harbours (Kenya and Uganda)* showed that the dhow trade was increasing, rather than diminishing. The latest returns I saw, for the year ended December 31, 1937, showed that 1,427 dhows had arrived at Mombasa, an increase of ten percent on the previous year. These 1,427 dhows were computed to register—if they had been registered—nearly 40,000 tons. Many were Swahili, from Lamu and Zanzibar, but a

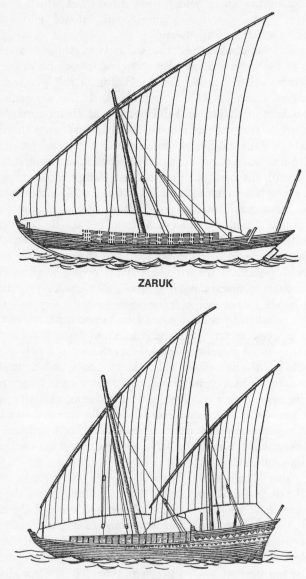

ZARUK

SAMBUK

FIG. 9-3 Zaruk and Sambuk.

large proportion was Arab. There was a native harbor set aside for them, and here we sold salt, landing it in our own longboat. We got rid of our surviving passengers, gave feasts to merchants and officials of the native harbor (these were a great feature of the voyage, and were always accompanied by much monotonous singing and dancing), gathered tidings from brother *nakhodas* from Kuwait and Sur about trade prospects further south, collected debts, and finally departed toward Zanzibar.

There were three Indian and one Iranian deep-sea dhows in the port at Mombasa. The Iranian was an enormous vessel of over 400 tons—the largest dhow I saw anywhere. She was a *boom* and had been built at Kuwait, but the Kuwaiti sold her because they found such large vessels uneconomic, in bad times, for the mere reason of their too great capacity. They brought too much to sell, when the market was depressed, and they could not wait indefinitely to dispose of their cargoes because their overhead was too high, despite the fact that everything possible was done to keep down building costs, even to the sending of Kuwaiti shipwrights to the Malabar coast to build big vessels there, rather than carry the timber to Kuwait.

Zanzibar, at that season of the year, was an even busier Arab port than Mombasa. In the first month of the northeast season, over a hundred ocean-going dhows had arrived at Zanzibar, most of them Arab. I noticed in the registry office of the Customs building that some were entered as Somali, and a few were registered in the Hadhramaut. No longer did they bring down picturesque cargoes of myrrh and frankincense (if they ever did) or ship out slaves and ivory, ambergris and hippopotamus teeth. They brought salt and dried fish; and when they came, the quantities of hashish and other drugs in the town showed a significant increase. They loaded little at Zanzibar for the homeward voyage, but went on down to the coast of Tanganyika.

We completed the discharge of our outward goods at Zanzibar, and the crew busied itself for weeks selling Hadhramaut basketware and Aden haberdashery—port of origin, Yokohama. When we sailed, leaving our *nakhoda* behind, our only cargo was the parcel of condemned dates, which the Somali would not have. We passed on down to the delta of the Rufiji River, a place given up to mosquitoes, malignant malaria fever, monkeys, sad Swahili, rain, and the best mangrove poles in the world. Here we lay six weeks, while a cargo of some 142 score of poles was laboriously cut and loaded. For this work, Swahili were engaged to help our crew, and at last the bad dates found consumers. The mangrove poles were ferried out in the dhow's longboat, and paid for in silver shillings to a white supervisor. There were some twenty dhows loading in the Rufiji delta at the time, all for the Persian Gulf.

It struck me as strange that the dhow should spend so much time embarking a cargo in which the total investment was less than $500, for no matter how I tried to figure things out, I did not see how it could possibly be worth her while to haul such a paltry cargo so long a distance, or how she could make enough from it to show a reasonable profit on the voyage. There was certainly something mysterious about this mangrove pole business, and the white supervisor, energetic as he was, by no means knew all that went on. I noticed later, when we sold our cargo to King Ibn Saud's agents at Bahrein for use in a new palace at Riyadh, that the Arab receipt was for 295 score, and the price paid, over 4,000 rupees, approximated $1,200.

There was some attempt in Zanzibar to regulate the dhow traffic, and precautions were taken to see that there was no slaving, under any guise. A local act requires that evidence be shown that any new crew members in Arab ships joined voluntarily; vessels must not be overmanned, and crew and passenger lists must be provided and in order; ships must be surveyed, and kept seaworthy; and *nakhodas* must be certificated. As for the last, the port officials conduct examinations, and the general principle seems to be that if a man is capable enough to bring a dhow down to Zanzibar, certificate or no certificate, he can also be trusted to sail her away again. But the fee for examination is fifteen shillings, and the Arabs complain about it.

We touched at Zanzibar again after loading in the Rufiji, re-embarked our *nakhoda* and took aboard a few Swahili school-teachers as passengers (they proposed to hire an automobile at Kuwait to take them to Mecca), filled the decks with coconuts and cases of soap and vermicelli, and departed toward the Persian Gulf again with the first of the broken weather at the end of the northeast season. We did not await the coming of the true southwest monsoons, for it sets in hard; we sailed direct to Muscat, in twenty-six days.

Muscat was depressed and there was no trade there, not even smuggling. All that changed hands, as far as I could see, was a box of Maria Theresa thalers, enormous Austrian coins minted in London for the Omani and available in Zanzibar at a price less than the exchange rate in Muscat. The Arabs turned everything to profit and were prepared to sell anything, even the ship. The sailors' pastime in the Rufiji was buying lemons—a thousand for a shilling—and converting them into sherbet, which they hawked in the *suq* at Kuwait throughout the summer.

Our cargo of mangrove poles sold at Bahrein, the ship returned to Kuwait, to lay up inside a coral breakwater until the new season's Iraqi dates ripened and it was time to go out again. At Kuwait, when all her people were returned—several relations of the *nakhoda* had dispersed from Zanzibar back to Lamu and Mogadishu to collect debts—a general balance sheet of the whole round voyage was struck, the profits computed carefully, and divided by a system of shares arranged traditionally. It was not a straightforward statement of income and expenditure; I never saw or heard of any piece of Arab seafaring business which was as simple as that. It was all complicated by prior advances, debts, odd earnings not shared and even odder earnings which were shared, and mysterious complicated procedures, some of which I never did fathom, for the war came, and stopped my investigations.

The son of the merchant family which owned our dhow, however, told me that her gross profit on the nine-month round voyage was 11,000 rupees, not including the proceeds of the crews' and officers' private ventures. But I think he exaggerated, for the total investment in the dhow was little more than that. But at any rate, the dhow's people were well satisfied and they all, save one, went back to sea with her. The *nakhoda* grew fat throughout the summer, and took a new wife, and a new *boom* for his brother at a cost of 10,500 rupees; and I heard no complaints from the merchants.

As far as I was able to discover, half the gross earnings went to the ship; this was the merchant's share. The cost of the food for the round voyage (which was not much, for all hands lived

very simply and fishing lines were the most important equipment
in what passed for her storeroom) was deducted from the other
half, and the remainder was then divided by shares arranged
strictly in accordance with the accepted value of each man's rat-
ing aboard. The sailor's share on the voyage which I made was
reported to be 135 rupees (about $40), whereof 35 rupees had
been advanced. This was little enough for such a long voyage,
and though they worked hard at all sorts of things and were
ready for any kind of business, I doubt whether a sailor's earnings
from other sources amounted to more than 20 or 30 rupees, clear.

I heard of dhows from Kuwait that season which were distributing less than 100 rupees; according to the Kuwaiti, who
had no high opinion of them, the Suri rarely paid out more than
fifty. To a sailor whose only home was the sand of the *suq* and
his bed the cloak around him, whose wants were few and whose
paradise was assured, even 50 rupees may be a vast sum of
money. There was, at any rate, contentment throughout the Arab
shipping industry as I knew it, and the quiet philosophy I learned
among the simple seamen was of great help to me in the days of
the long-drawn war which was soon to follow.

FRANCISCO BENET

10. Explosive Markets: The Berber Highlands

The place occupied by the market in society has usually been investigated in regard to societies characterized by a normal functioning of government. It has become almost an obsession to associate the development of markets with peaceable communities.* At the back of such a preconception there lurk unrealistic ideologies concerning the institutional character of what we are wont to call the peace of the market. The fact [is] that in non-centralized societies, where no power structure links the segments, especially where blood feud and tribal clashes are prevalent, markets do exist, but in the absence of government they must rely for the peace of the market on the political device of intergroup truces. With nomadic desert dwellers these truces are usually made to coincide with the seasonal periods so as to make the most of the chances offered for trading. But this would, of course, by no means suffice for the needs of sedentary highland tribes. Regular markets for fresh food are to them a matter of life and death. Where they have to fall back for their provisions on mutual exchanges these have to be continuous, not merely occasional.

This throws into relief the sociological paradox of everyday markets under conditions of near-anarchy. Such markets are bedevilled by the ambiguities of neutral jurisdictions in the midst of the complexities of intertribal relations. Yet the peace of the

Permission to reprint this chapter is granted by the Macmillan Company from *Trade and Markets in the Early Empires* by Karl Polanyi *et al.* Copyright by the Free Press, 1957.

* The author is indebted to Professor Arensberg for suggesting the possibilities inherent in the Berber material.

market must rely on the balance of forces between the hostile groups.

The sociologist of economic institutions has cause to explore societies such as these for the enlightenment they offer on the functioning of markets in a labile societal context. Offhand, he will find these societies only in the regions of the world where we meet with highland peoples whose general attitude is one of militant refusal to accept the rule of the governments of the plains below. The political institutions of these peoples reflect a spirit of utter independence. The groups which compose these societies, though they may not altogether fail to fuse are scattered in mosaic fashion. Each group stands to the other very nearly in the same relation of a hostile sovereignty, in which the highland society as a whole relates to the society of the plain. These societies are composed of a mere juxtaposition of segments each of which possesses an acute consciousness of its own singularity and solidarity.

The salient feature is, of course, the complete absence of centralizing institutions. Unified government is exceptional. Only occasionally is it brought about through the ire of all the groups against "interference" by the government of the plains. The ambition of outstanding individuals may for a while break the straitjacket of clan or tribal affiliations and set up its iron rule. But when the self-made chieftain fails, things once more lapse into their previous state of a segmented anarchy.

The signal success of such societies in resisting imposition of the forms of government of the plains springs from the endurance of sturdy patterns of decentralization. Within a mountain ecology isolation is traditional and a thin scattering of groups living in widely separated valleys keeps the centralizing forces at low ebb, be they acting from within or the outside.

In our inquiry the economic process is best discussed in terms of integration. It may then be found that in a society lacking political centralization the economy would be without redistributive forms of integration; that the political tension that is permanent between the segments of such a society would prevent economic reciprocity to develop between the villages, clans or tribes; that in absence of redistributive relations as well as of outgroup reciprocity market exchanges usually gain great significance and, indeed, play an integrative role that may transcend the economic sphere itself.

SIBA AND MAKHZEN

The conditions described above are nowhere found with more striking clarity than in the highland societies of North West Africa. The Berbers of the Atlas exist politically as a loose aggregate of social segments without reference to a common center. The reluctance of these societies to accept the patterns of the world below has resulted in a complete severance of ties between the society of the plains and that of the mountains.

C. S. Coon pointedly uses the Moroccan name *Bled el Makhzen* —literally, "The Land of Government"—to denote the area of the lowland urban centers and those villages which recognize the authority of a central government. The word *Makhzen* comes from the Arabic *khazana,* "to lock up," "to hoard."[1] The word was synonymous with "government" and, more especially, with the treasury department. The word is certainly expressive of a government based on the redistribution of staples.[2] From the word *makhzen* comes the French *magasin,* the German *Magazin,* and the Spanish *almacén.* It is a graphic term for what might be described as a polity based on a storage and tax-levying economy in kind.

In opposition to it, the independent mountain societies are known as the *Bled es Siba,* the Land of Independence (literally "insolence"). We shall use these two terms abridged as *Siba* and *Makhzen* to denote the two different societies.[3]

The Siba is untouched by forcible centralization, and may be compared with the manner of existence of annulated worms consisting of rings and capable of easy fission. Even the tribes are but an aggregate of a few of the cells which are the units of society.

---

[1] The word is believed to have been first used in North Africa as an official term in the 2nd century A.H., applied to an iron chest in which Ibrahim i. al Aghlab, emir of Ifriqiya, kept the collected taxes.

[2] Cf. E. Michaux-Bellaire, article "Makhzen," *Encyclopedia of Islam.*

[3] For a discussion of the typicalities of these two worlds cf. C. S. Coon, *Caravan,* pp. 263 ff.

These segments are the cantons (*taqbilt*), expanses of some 8 or
10 kms. across, inhabited by a few hundred families in a dozen
or so of scattered hamlets or three or four bigger villages, and
forming for all practical purposes minute independent states. Beyond the cantons the feeling of attachment fades, so that the
tribes—a group of cantons, from three to twelve—are hardly more
than a name, a definite territory and some commonly shared traditions. Their unity appears only in times of danger and, in between, it dissolves into a vague sentiment of brotherhood
between tribesmen which may be rationalized in terms of an
assumed common descent.

Not so the cantons. These are vital organisms. Small though
they be they have to be considered for all practical purposes as
true states. The feeling of attachment to the canton is narrowly
territorial and is enhanced by the fact that in a mountain area
there inevitably must be, if only for military reasons, some adjustment of the size of each social unit to the natural dimensions of
hills and valleys. Nevertheless, as Robert Montagne discovered,
the cantonal territories proper tend to be of fairly equal size
throughout the Berber lands. For the limits of the canton do not
quite coincide with the natural boundaries of these mountain
habitats, but may fall short of them, a canton occupying only the
space it actually requires, ignoring the more generous expanse
offered by nature.[4] This standard size of the cantons is due to
organizational reasons. The cantons are ruled by assemblies
(*djema'a*) of notables (*inflas*) or heads of the extended families,
who are supposed to meet regularly. A day's walk over hilly terrain is therefore the canton's natural radius.

Rule by representative assemblies (*djema'a*) is, as this feature
strikingly shows, typical of Berber society. It is a form of republi-
can democracy suitable to a society of equals. There is a *djema'a*
of the village, of the canton (composed of the notables of all the
villages of the canton), of the tribe (composed of the notables of
the diverse cantons of the tribe). In certain regions the chiefs of
powerful families may overthrow the democratic process and
start out on an authoritarian rule. Such personalities are called
amghar, chiefs of war, and as the term indicates, their origin may

[4] R. Montagne, *Berbères et Makhzen*, p. 153.

lie in the custom of appointing chiefs to rule the cantons when war was declared. The local regulations of the codes of village law are called *qanun*—from the Greek *canon*. Within the village regulations are enforced and the *djema'a* sees to it that fines are imposed on infractors. A harsher punishment is exile, applied when feuds between families threaten the existence of the township or canton.

Internal dissensions might mean that neighboring cantons would take advantage of a weak moment and make war. This danger was parried in an unusual, but most effective way. The cantons of a whole region were affiliated to either the one or the other of two political parties which formed in this way intercantonal alliances. Of these "political parties" there were, as we said, but two, so that if we plot on the map the territories of the cantons and color them according to the party (*leff*) they belong to, the result is something like a checkerboard. The fractions which compose a tribe are exactly divided among the *leffs*, so that an equilibrium is achieved inside the tribe. When a canton was attacked by another canton of the opposite hue, it could call to its aid its *leff* allies. A war involving a vast range of mountains would thus be provoked over night, a possibility which alone would be enough to make the two original contenders come to their senses. In this way the division of the cantons of a tribe between two opposite parties becomes a guarantee for the survival of the cantons. Equilibrium is maintained in spite of the wars; permanently balanced opposite parties (*leff*) contribute to this result as much as either common markets or common shrines. Local wars remain innocuous even inside the smaller tribes, so neatly are the hostile forces balanced within.[5] In Kabylia, a region of large villages, the townships are divided into two parties called *soffs*. The village is here the equivalent of the canton, and the *soff* plays a part comparable to the *leff* of the mountain regions.

We have here, in effect, the very reverse of a system of centralized authority. Instead of a pinnacle of power at the center there is balance of power where opposite forces check one another and conflicts are resolved not by decision from summit but

[5] *Ibid.*, pp. 162–63.

by agreement, or, if no agreement is reached, the efforts to limit warfare to local bounds.

Under these singular conditions the market or *suq* is a preeminent organ of the formation of public (larger than canton) opinion, directing common effort and integrating otherwise disparate forces.

The usual and, indeed, obvious rendering of the Arabic term *suq* as market leaves much unsaid. Both the bazaar and the *suq* are markets, yet they differ very much, not only from one another but also from the Western concept of market. Nowhere perhaps is this truer than in the Berber mountain region, where the market forms also locationally a counterpart to the village. In effect in the *suq* we are confronted with a complex legal, social, political and often even religious institution which serves primarily economic ends. Important *suqs* are of historical origin. In no case does the mere frequency of random exchanges taking place in it make an open space a *suq*. Only under the auspices of authority, after proclamation has been made and a table of fines posted in a customary or appointed spot, does a gathering over a definite stretch of time assume the character of a *suq*. The complex criteria that make for a *suq* raise even the most modest *suq* onto the institutional level of the Champagne fairs of the thirteenth century. It is not the externalities that matter. A *suq* may be installed in an elaborately fitted walled area, furnished with important public buildings; other *suqs*—and these are the great majority— are held at a desert site with hardly a trace to indicate their whereabouts when the *suq* is over. Just as a Parliament building should not be confused with the political institution known as Parliament, a market place does not amount to a *suq*. Though market place and *suq* may be here used interchangeably, it is always the specific, *sui generis* institution that is meant.

Certain Kabyle laws fine those who, under the pretext of having nothing to buy or sell, do not attend the market.[6] To attend

---

[6] Cf. Robin, "Fetna Meriem," *Revue Africaine,* XVIII, no. 105 (mai-juin 1874) 173; cf. E. Doutte, *Merrakech,* p. 141; also, H. Basset, *Literature des Berbères,* p. 94, where he says: "En Kabylie plus souvent qu'ailleurs il arrive que la coûtume reconnaisse, à côté des individus, l'ensemble en tant qu'état. . . . Un citoyen n'a pas le droit de ne pas assister au marché, n'eût-il rien à scheter ni à vendre."

the market of the tribe is at least in certain cases an obligation even though otherwise the villager may also attend other markets. When a tribe in Kabylia establishes a new market the tribesmen are compelled to frequent it to the exclusion of any other.[7]

Observers are unanimous in their insistence on the unique significance of the *suq* for the existence of the Berber polity. Earlier and later writers are equally emphatic on this point. Robin, in 1874, wrote: "The markets are the forums of the tribe. Ideas and business affairs are dealt with here once a week between individuals who live at a considerable distance. It is here that collective sentiments form and manifest themselves. Villages and families fuse their emotions into that often entirely different product which grows from mass contacts. The market creates that external individuality of the group often so dissimilar from the feelings of the individuals composing it. The egotism of the tribe or the *douar* [village] takes the place of the egotism of the individuals."[8] E. Doutts, a generation later, could still confirm his statement. "The market," he attests, "is a factor of highest importance in Arab [read Berber] life; it is no exaggeration to say that the life of the tribe almost in its entirety happens in the market. It is the place where the natives meet; not only do they provide for their daily needs through sales in the market but it is also the spot where ideas are exchanged, political information is passed on, the announcements of the authorities are made and the reaction to these are formed, where decisions about peace and war are taken, political conspiracies started, public outcries raised, broadminded proposals mooted and crimes hatched."[9] De Segonzac sums up its political function with brevity and precision. "Markets," he writes, "have here a dual significance, which is not less political than economic, for they are the source of news, the place where people assemble, discussion takes place and decisions fall."[10]

[7] Hanoteau et Letourneux, *Kabylie*, III, 65.
[8] Robin, *loc. cit.*
[9] E. Doutte, *Merrakech*, p. 144.
[10] De Segonzac, *Au coeur de l'Atlas*, p. 162.

THE MARKET IN THE SIBA

The market could, of course, never have attained to the political importance it is universally credited with but for the part that fell to it in the everyday life of the highland Berber. The economic organization of the Makhzen and the Siba is of interest in this order of things.

The heart of the Makhzen is the level country with its urban agglomerations. The storage economy of a central government forms the material backbone of the army and civil service, maintained by a taxation system comprising all classes of the population. The Siba is the hill country which, though lacking towns, has nevertheless a sedentary population of farmers, living in settled fortified villages. They tend their flocks in the temperate season around the scattered crude shelters right in the middle of the individual holdings, and on the hillocks in winter. Each hilltop is crested by an *agadir,* as the squat stone quadrangles are called, solid structures of military value, along the four walls of which small storage rooms are located within. Under lock and key the grain of the householders is hoarded in these cells. The *agadir* is the mainstay of the political and military independence of the village or perhaps of a whole canton. Yet in spite of the common defence based on the *agadir,* the householders keep their grain in the *agadir* stored in strictly separate cells—a remarkable demonstration of economic individualism.

Within this economic frame the market played an essential part in sustaining the livelihood of the people of the Siba. Their isolated villages had no shops or inns; no regular trade reached them; there were no grocers' shops where meat, butter, eggs, fowl, vegetables or other fresh food could be procured. Apart from some spices there was a lack of imported household goods like coffee, tea, sugar, or salt. The highland markets which provided these were a vital necessity.

The mountain markets are primarily places for the purchase of fresh foodstuffs. They offer the possibility of buying cuts of meat which are certainly the most important item in these transactions. ". . . Early in the afternoon the men begin the trek back to their villages. . . . Most of them will be carrying some meat on a string or have it tied to the saddle of the donkey. Market day is often the only time the Kabyle has meat. . . ."[11]

Butter may well come next in importance. In retail markets it is sold in small jars "and it is up to the buyer to judge whether the price demanded corresponds to the weight offered."[12] However in markets that specialize in the wholesaling of butter—as, e.g., in the Suq el-had of the Ulad Jellul, it is sold by weight.

Thus, the markets of the Siba amounted to externally located grocery stores and butcher shops where foodstuffs were retailed and taken home. Indeed, the waste incurred in killing a sheep for each day the family wants meat at their meals would be prohibitive. These markets have come to supersede the collective customs by facilitating individual isolated consumption.

This does not mean that the Berber markets are places where cooked food can be purchased, in contrast to the Makhzen where such markets are the rule. To give an example, in the small Makhzen town of Agadir the market is sure to offer fresh meat at every hour of the day and bread fresh from the oven.[13] Very little meat is bought at the butcher's. Instead it is purchased cooked, seasoned and prepared to be eaten.

The feeding of the poorer subjects, clients or followers of a chief or sovereign is an unavoidable necessity which is sometimes resolved in the cooked-food markets. A chief, *qaid* or *sayyid* keeps "maison et table ouvertes,"[14] especially when on the rise to power. At other times he may try to ensure a cheap supply of staples which may be directly distributed, e.g., at the "gates."

Generally speaking the Bled es Siba has no such proletariat because it has not suffered detribalization, and division of labor remains primitive. The need to feed the poor is absent in a society over which no sovereign rules and where everyone is the equal of everyone else. The appearance of an internal proletariat in the Siba is a sure sign that it is developing an oligarchic tyranny of local character and a Makhzen of its own.

Reciprocity produces an important form of assistance in the

[11] G. Wysner, *The Kabyle People*, pp. 131–32.
[12] E. Michaux-Bellaire, *Le Gharb*, p. 229.
[13] Ch. de Foucauld, *Reconnaissance au Maroc*, p. 126.
[14] This applies both to organized political states and to tribal societies.

muna,[15] a dole of food given to a needy stranger or neighbor, taking place in a public reunion, usually at night so that the occasion is called "the night of succor" (*laila el muna*). In its ancient Arabic form the *muna* was simply a gift of food to the hungry or, rather, a first-fruit of alms owed to the needy or to God. A Berber who desires the benefit of a *muna* appeals to the chief of the notables of the group in the bustle of a market day. The following night, as soon as the group has returned home, food is collected from the households and served to the needy person and his family. The *muna* obliges the other villagers to do likewise.

The village itself is devoid of shops. Everything that is not domestically produced has, therefore, to be obtained from the market, through market transactions, and no exchanges or commercial activities of any kind are attempted outside of these times and places. The market place has a monopoly of exchange transactions.

Itinerant traders, again, do not visit the villages, but only the markets. This does not, of course, apply to travelling craftsmen who repair saddles, ploughs, or other bulky objects which cannot be taken to the distant market, nor to the doctor (*tubíb al-muslimín*) who pays irregular visits and carries and sells his own drugs and medicines. Nor does it apply, by a remarkable exception, to a class of peddlers who visit the villages when the men are away, for the women are their only clients. In return for the foodstuffs, spices, small manufactured articles, jewelry, cosmetics, charms or whatever their all-purpose bags may contain, they receive eggs, wool rags or fleeces or small quantities of oil filched by the housewives from home supplies. This uncommercial form of trade is undisputed women's prerogative; no money is used, barter is the governing principle. In the face of such an exception, restriction of all other commerce to the *suq* is all the more striking.

The physical equipment of the market may be simple enough. It is held on a flat surface, sandy where possible, so as to avoid dust in summer and mud in winter. Essential to a market site is a

[15] For the *muna* cf. R. Maunier, *Coûtumes Algeriennes,* pp. 65–66; also E. Daumas, *La vie arabe et la société musulmane,* pp. 449–57.

good source of water, often connected with a shrine, so that at least in the big places of pilgrimage (*mussem*) marketing is combined with religious practices and ritual bathing. At the shrine oaths are taken in litigation cases. The shrines possess a holy perimeter (*haran*), serving as a refuge in case of need, and where people in danger (blood-feud, etc.) may take shelter. All this contributes to the security conferred on this turbulent area by the covenant of the market. The correlation between shrines and markets is too close to be of very recent origin. If the shrine of the spring or of the mosque is a famed one (*siyyid*) the yearly pilgrimage will most likely coincide with an increase of the merchandise offered in the market.[16]

According to the volume of business transacted in the markets and the number of persons who attend, we may divide *suqs* into two classes. The first kind are small and held in the territory of a mountain canton or at the boundary limits of two or three cantons; some crude removable shelters forming shops (*tahanout*) provide room for the few dozen persons who visit the market (a hundred at the most). The notables of the place will run such a market without receiving any remuneration. The large kind of *suq* occurs at crossroads or strategic locations, or other important points of communication, as at the foot of mountains, on the borderline between ecological regions. In some instances such markets may be surrounded by a wall, especially if market dues are collected. They may contain hundreds of shops, like cells in a beehive, made of mud and stone, each the stall of a merchant. Within the enclosure we find permanent buildings (storehouses, coffee shops, a mosque, etc.). Such markets may be frequented by all the tribes of the region and several thousand persons may gather in them every week.

Suqs as just described are typical of rural North Africa, whether Arab or Berber. With the single exception of the desert areas they form a system of weekly markets held alternately within walking distance of the villages. This method is not only advantageous for the farmer who gets a larger choice of products,

[16] W. Fogg, "A Moroccan Tribal Shrine and its relation to a near-by Tribal Market." Also *Folklore*, Vol. 51 (June, 1940). In the market of Sidi el Yemani (Djebala) after the wheat harvest there is every year an important *mussem* at this shrine. The grain is disposed of.

but also necessary in nonpoliced countries where no towns are in reach. It is made possible by the villages being close together, not in a line, but rather radially. Indeed, the system is at home throughout the Middle East, for the products of the countryside appear in the city bazaars on appointed days. But nowhere is the system as elaborately perfected as in North Africa.[17] The markets are there named for the day of the week in which they are held followed by the name of the tribe to which they belong, and the market days are so allotted between neighboring market places that it is always possible to make weekly rounds of markets, returning home for the night. The whole area could be plotted in this way: as clusters of markets of which it is possible to make weekly rounds, their clustering offering pointers to the student of the geography of economic units. Each village school has its free day on the allotted market day.[18]

Such a distribution of markets must have been reached in each region by a method of trial and error. Rivalries were bound to arise if two neighboring markets were held on the same day. In Kabylia, when a tribe wanted to establish a new market it had to obtain the consent of the neighboring tribes and select a day which would not infringe their rights.[19]

Thus, decision by decision, always with the general interest in mind—the nearer and more frequent the markets, the better—the mesh came to be knit. Eventually, on appointed days persons protected by their particular day's safe conducts, flowed from all directions into the paths leading to definite markets. Such a piecemeal method of evolution did not favor a national development. While in pre-Muhammedan nomadic Arabia the time allotted to trading was a specific season of the year (the *maswin* or monsoon months), when blood feuds and tribal feuds would be dropped,

[17] This cyclic organization has been studied by E. Michaux-Bellaire, "Le Gharb"; L. Massignon for Fez, *Enquête sur les corporations musulmanes,* pp. 97–98, and the Dukkala, *Le Maroc au XVIe siècle d'après Léon l'Africaine,* p. 116; for the Djebala and Anjera regions of Spanish Morocco by Walter Fogg, "Tribal markets in Spanish Morocco," *Journal of the Royal Asiatic Society* (July, 1939), pp. 322–26, and "The importance of tribal markets in the commercial life of the countryside of Northwestern Morocco," *Africa,* XI, 4 (1938).

[18] G. Wysner, *op. cit.,* p. 130.

[19] Hanoteau et Letourneux, *op. cit.,* II, 65.

the sedentary population of North Africa seemed to have been prevented by its own devices for continuous trading from achieving a common period of truce which could have acted as an amalgamating factor on a national scale.

More often than not the market places are located in the valleys halfway between opposite *leffs* occupying parallel mountain ranges. They are thus fully exposed to the consequences of that peculiar system of power vacua which is at the heart of the Berber polity.

In these nonpoliced and politically split areas, attendance at the markets as well as travel between territories is achieved under agreements providing for neutrality. The Berber *ánaia* or safe conduct is granted either by the tribes themselves or by individual tribesmen who are, of course, supposedly backed by the full force of the tribe to which they belong. Anyone can grant his *ánaia* on his own responsibility and expect his tribesmen to respect it. Thus a person going to the market finds himself the balanced focus of opposite forces and entrusts life and limb to the recognized guarantees that protect the market place.

SAFE CONDUCT

To secure this peace of the market is one of the supreme aims of the highland polity. This is indeed a dominant theme of Berber life. The markets are the places for "external" contacts, where the narrow in-group solidarity of village life gives way to a "freer" behavior that results from the intercourse with individuals who belong to other groups. Cantonal isolation thus finds its counterpoise and its outlet in the market habit.

Psychologically as well as physically market places stand on the "fringes" of the in-groups. Here the world of the villager comes into contact with similar outside groups. The *villages*, centers of life and habitation of the in-groups, and the *markets*, centers of commerce of the out-groups, are completely dissociated in the physical sense. The *suq* stands locationally apart from and in contrast to the village. It is situated well outside of the settled centers, in low-lying and deserted spots, far from the plowed fields. After the market ends, the merchants and shop keepers pack their stands away and the market place remains deserted, unmarked—almost indistinguishable in the landscape. These places resemble in fact no man's lands assigned to the weekly truces of commerce.

There are important exceptions. In all regions travelling traders may be stopped and asked to sell the merchandise they carry —compulsory trade—in the villages or in the middle of the road.[20] In certain areas, indeed, the markets stand just on the outskirts of the village. Finally, in the specialized towns of the oases (*qsar*) the market place is in the middle of the town itself which is in fact to be considered as a "market-town" servicing both the visiting nomads and the cultivators of the place. Yet though these last "markets" are "towns" they also carry the imprint of the neutrality that goes with the noninhabited market place. The *qsars* are generally under the protection of nomadic groups that rent buildings in the town as storehouses. If the *qsar* is central to different nomadic tribes, its independence may be even more complete. Indeed, the situation of the *qsar* of the oases seems in many respects to approach that of the "port of trade." Desert and sea are akin.

The physical separation of village and market makes possible the co-existence of two well-developed forms of integration in the same society—market exchange and in-group reciprocity. Though at certain times of the year a full tenth of the Kabyle population is engaged in itinerant commerce (mostly of the peddling and barter type described above), in the villages themselves there is a striking absence of professional merchants.[21] Nevertheless, apart from some transactions on real estate, sale of trees, or the crops, etc., which may be prepared at the villages and concluded in the market, the extent of the transactions made in the villages is very limited, probably no more than a fraction of the volume of business done in the market. Further, payment in kind, services, barter, etc., prevail in the villages whereas cash payment is the invariable rule at the market.

Over and above the *ánaias* and related conventions which

20 Cf. for instance de Segonzac, *Au coeur de l'Atlas,* pp. 68–69.
21 Hanoteau et Letourneux, *op. cit.,* II, 77.

made a safe access to markets possible, the groups which "owned" a market delegated authority to certain individuals or certain bodies. The regime of the market which resulted might vary from district to district, but, as we shall see, there were only a few methods available for delegating the administration and the policing of the markets.

When the market was truly intertribal, "owned" by different groups, their representatives would obviously sit together and deal with all cases either by common decision or separately, i.e., each representative settling the disputes of his own tribesmen. There is a limit to this method. In the Rif, for instance, the markets are occasions for the concluding of tribal alliances (*ribat*). In such reunions the chiefs may have to decide litigations that arise in assemblies composed of crowds of armed warriors.[22] The market of Tarqist, for instance, situated at a crossroads of the High-Ghis region, was under the control of three *amghars* appointed by the three interested tribes, the Beni Mesdwi, Tarqist and Zerquet.[23] Thus the system of intertribal markets is prevalent in districts belonging to the Makhzen, where the tribes tend to be at peace with one another, and stand moreover under the jurisdiction of the central government.

When, on the contrary, a single tribe or village owned the market, the *djema'a* of one tribe alone could not very well exercise control over the market, for this would have been equivalent to applying local jurisdiction to an interlocal affair. Also, it might not be convenient for a single *djema'a* to handle the administration of a market place where great distances were involved. Authority over the market would therefore have to be delegated.

Now, the simplest solution in the areas where religious personages played an important role in the Berber parts of Kabylia and Northern Morocco consisted in turning control over to a holy man (*murabit*) or a family of *murabits*. Such markets under murabitic authority, we are told, while exempt of all specific regulations, offer a picture of general harmony.

To the same type belong in the tribal areas of the Makhzen the markets of religious teachers (*tolba*). Their origin is ancient; in

[22] R. Montagne, *op. cit.*, p. 252.
[23] *Ibid.*, p. 253.

olden times in these places of reunion young men or students would get together to discuss professional questions. Merchants, attracted by the periodic congregations, put up shops and stalls and started a market. Examples are the Kjouma'a Tolba, the Thenin Tolba, where the religious teachers themselves sell all kinds of foodstuffs. The *tolba* rule and police these markets which have no master, neither *qaid* nor *khalifa*. Only to watch over judicial matters does a judge (*qadi*) turn up from a nearby center.[24] These *tolba* markets seem very independent of Makhzen authority. Towards 1898 the market of Thenin de Smid el-Ma was suppressed at the demand of the lease-holders of the tolls in the neighboring town of El-Ksar. They had complained of unfair competition exerted by the unofficial *tolba* market which diverted many goods. But the inhabitants of the countryside continued to visit the market in spite of prohibition by the Makhzen, and the religious men managed without any representatives of authority.[25]

The *murabits* to whom the market had been entrusted could be long dead. The market place then would continue as a shrine and there remained only the malediction (*tagat*) of the saint venerated in the sanctuary to punish troublemakers. Since oaths were taken at the shrine, the notables were spared the trouble of intervening in litigations. In particular the great autumn fairs were of this type. "Such fairs," we learn, "attract the populations of whole countrysides of several days distance. The crowds that meet here are rent by lifelong feuds and no chief, no committee of notables can be expected to overawe them. Nothing less than a formidable saint and the awful penalties dispensed by him will suffice."[26]

In the regions where these religious institutions could not insure neutrality, private individuals were entrusted with the policing of the market. Offhand, it would seem as if this was only a secular variant of murabitic control. But the purpose of this method was rather the opposite, namely, to hand the police of the market not to a superauthority, but to a nonauthority, so as to make it more palatable to visiting aliens by offering the chance

[24] Michaux-Bellaire et G. Salmon, "Les tribus arabas de la vallée du Lekkous," *Archives Marocaines,* VI (1906), 257–58.
[25] *Ibid.,* pp. 261–62.
[26] R. Montagne, *op. cit.,* p. 261.

of a neutral jurisdiction. Nevertheless the person had to be rich and well connected, able to depend on his *soff* or *leff* for allegiance. These persons, a sort of *custodes nundinarum*, were known as "masters of the market." Actually their semi-official status was only the result of the abstention of the group from applying its territorial jurisdiction over the market. Hanoteau and Letourneux rightly affirmed that the "masters of the market" were, in Kabylia, the only office-holders comparable to our magistrates.[27] The practice was an old one. Robert Montagne has traced it, perhaps stretching it too fine, to Roman Africa, where rich gentlemen farmers would establish native markets to their great profit.[28]

An alternative to the appointment of some local notable was the procedure of farming out the market to individuals by auction. Markets were auctioned for a fixed period of time, generally one year, to the highest bidder, who recouped himself through the collection of market dues. Since the taxes were to be paid over to the Makhzen in full, the tax farmer had to increase their amount, in order to pay the taxes to the government and still retain a profit for himself. It became an open invitation to abuse, sparing only the European and other influential persons who should not be antagonized.

Such farmed markets seem in general to run smoothly. The collectors are regarded as individuals who make an investment and therefore can expect a return. Moreover, the policing functions are also auctioned, so that fines are imposed with alacrity by the market constables. In auctioned markets, furthermore, there is a virtual separation of the administrative from the judiciary apparatus, resulting in a better functioning of the whole.

The method of farming out the markets, widespread in the Makhzen tribal areas, is almost absent from the Siba. It was a useful method for collecting central government taxes from outlying areas by auctioning them out to local persons. We cannot expect to find such a feature in the Siba regions. Payment of taxes to the Makhzen or the *qaids* is here not known and, in general, there is a disinclination to tax the goods which enter the

[27] Hanoteau et Letourneux, *op. cit.*, III, 47.
[28] Boissier, *Afrique Romaine*, p. 149; quoted by Montagne, *Berbères et Makhzen*, p. 231.

market. Nevertheless the men of the Siba accepted this innovation like many other economic or social practices reaching them from the Makhzen.

By and large, command of the market is a stepping stone to power. The mere growth of the market entrusted or farmed to the authority of an individual seems to help in the development of his personal power. In the regions of rampant chieftainship, it is in "commanding over the market" that an *amghar* shows best his prestige and ability.[29] This may open the door to a Makhzen development. A very close dependence upon markets, especially in the High Atlas, follows in the wake of the destruction of the old democratic and co-operative ways, the true home of in-group reciprocity. Sociologically, we have here a set of interacting factors where markets can hardly function without successful oligarchs or prominent chiefs, and the development of chieftainship leads to a further growth in the size of the market. The process may be cumulative and become overwhelming: the *amghars* or chiefs (later *qaids*) come to be more and more dependent on Jewish money-lenders, and complicated financial operations begin to take place; the old tribal law is replaced by the religious *shari'a*, and the local market regulations traditional to the Siba are absorbed by those of the Makhzen.

But this is only the latest stage of a line of evolution. In the regions where the oligarchy did not rise to the status of a social class, representative assemblymen (*inflas*) continued to administer the markets. In Kabylia, where chieftainship has not made any strides at all though an oligarchy did establish itself as a class, markets are administered by prominent members of the oligarchy appointed as masters of the market. The dangerous combination of expanding market exchanges and self-aggrandizing personal authority was averted by increasing the number of the markets while keeping their size as small as before. This, in conjunction with the *soff* or *leff* mechanisms, themselves the greatest obstacle to the emergence of despotism, kept the traditional social structure intact, and chieftainship did not develop.

[29] R. Montagne, *op. cit.*, p. 253.

EXPLOSIVE MARKETS

The different types of control—whether of the supernatural, conventional or administrative order—would normally appear sufficient to ensure the peace of the market place. But not under the extreme conditions obtaining in these traditionally feuding party-ridden areas. Here markets are powder kegs which may go off at the slightest shock. There is a customary name for the sudden, panicky "snapping" which breaks the peace of the *suq:* the *nefra'a.*

These markets, it must be remembered, are supposedly[30] neutral ground, and tribesmen of hostile groups are able to meet each other, even if a merciless intertribal war is raging during the other days of the week. The situation is overloaded with latent conflict and the precarious truce may dissolve in mutual violence.

The *nefra'a* is naturally more common in large intertribal markets, and rather rare in the small markets of the mountain cantons, for these gather too few people to give rise to such a phenomenon of mass psychology as is the *nefra'a.* The larger intertribal markets are the place where members of opposite tribes, *leffs,* or *soffs* meet squarely with each other. Where blood feud is the immemorial right of the families even the best controls emanating from neutrality, *ánaias* and covenants cannot replace a common positive authority. The *nefra'as* thus are not exceptional phenomena; a *nefra'a* can be intentionally provoked by rogues out for pillage, but generally it is a spillover from a simple dissension between two individuals, ending in a brawl in which all take sides. In 1880, in the Sunday *suq* of El Had Berriada, one Ait Boudvar tribesman and one Ait Wasif tribesman argued about a kidskin worth no more than thirty cents. Two factions took part in the dispute and came to fight each other for the whole day, using small stones, hatchets and knives. Firearms were prohibited in this *suq;* everyone was carrying his own dagger. At the end of the day 300 men were lying dead or

[30] To a lesser extent the cults and pilgrimages of religion function likewise, of course.

wounded.[31] In the *suq* of the Ak'bil a man of the Ait el Arba
(Ait Yenne) argued with a debtor of his of the Ait Hikhem (Ait
Yahyia). The debt was in the amount of forty-five cents. A tribal
war ensued.[32]

Most of these market battles, and the bloodiest ones, are
fought in Kabylia. This is a region of large villages, as we saw,
divided into *soffs* which readily organize into *leff*-type alliances. Also, Kabylia is a country of important markets where the
tribesmen act as tradesmen and itinerant merchants, mixing
freely in the territories of foreign tribes. If the chiefs and constables of the market, as so often happens, are unable to separate
the contenders, only exhaustion puts an end to the fray.

The very tenseness of the crowd in the market place sometimes
acts as a mechanism of control. The people in a market may take
terrifyingly swift measures to stop an imminent *nefra'a* through a
sort of lynch-law. The lightning action of the crowd and the
ferocity of the punishment inflicted is the true measure of the
instability of these meetings.

Often the prohibition of arms was observed in so far as long
arms were concerned, but the practice of carrying concealed
guns was widespread. In the Sunday *suq* of the Ait Iraten, Said
Naid Ahmed of the village of Ait el Arba (Ait Yenne tribe) was
in blood-feud with the clan of Kassi-ou Mrad, an old headman
of the Taguemiont Ihedden (*soff* of the Ait Irsten). Said
wanted to kill Kassi, and following the old man to a corner of the
market, he cocked the gun he was carrying under his burnous.
The noise betrayed him; someone uttered a cry, and only min-
utes later he lay dead under the pile of stones with which he
had been lapidated. Such piles covering a dead body may be left
untouched to serve as a reminder.

Nothing but brutal preventive behavior can ensure the neutrality of the market place. The Berber social structure permits a
chain-reaction of ever larger conflicts. In this politically cleft
society it is more important to isolate trouble spots than to punish
merely because there was breach of the law. The *qanuns* chastise
threats as heavily as completed acts. To unsheath a yatagan in
the *suq* is as bad as to stab someone. And no meddler in a dis-

[31] Hanoteau et Letourneux, *op. cit.*, III, 303.
[32] *Ibid.*

pute not his own can get away without a fine. He who fires a gun at the *suq* of Massat, though nobody is injured, pays as much as the murderer of a man on nonmarket days. To our ears: "Be bold and quick. Give to your act all the marks of the inevitable. Don't fumble."

It is not surprising that the *nefra'a* breeds xenophobia. Strangers and foreigners are sometimes inclined to take the law in their own hands,[33] they have no part in the policing of the market and do not suffer from the long-range consequences of a *nefra'a*. *Nefra'as* will discredit a *suq* and people will stop coming to it. Besides, if a murder has been committed in the *suq* the market is closed for a period of purification, generally one year.[34]

Lynch law and draconic legislation is thus an outstanding feature of the Berber highland market. Under conditions of anarchy only extreme rigor of the law and its ruthless application can ensure an area of peace and freedom such as these markets broadly represent.

Incidentally, women play an important part in maintaining the peace of the market. This sociologically well-grounded fact may also account for the tradition that all through history the Moghreb women were conciliators and messengers of peace in wars and private quarrels. Among the Arabs this mediating function of women derives from the marriage alliance (*çihr*) which acts to unite two social groups. In many tribes the woman who marries a foreigner becomes a citizen of both tribes. The Ait Mesruh and their neighbors admit also that foreign women married in the tribes become automatically Mesruiah. The Talsint only grant citizenship, however, when the woman gives birth to a male child.[35] The *ánaia* of women is the strongest kind of *ánaia*, a cloak of immunity and protection that involves a group's honor. Moreover, as housewives, women are eager for their market supplies and market earnings. Their presence in the market place is a matter of course. To the women belong exclusively two fields of economic activity, namely, poultry and

[33] *Ibid.*, p. 79.
[34] I. Biarnay, *op. cit.*, p. 221.
[35] M. Morand, *Études de droit Musulman et de droit coutumier Berbère*, pp. 314–15.

eggs, pottery, as well as within limits, the sale of wool, charcoal and henna. They keep their gains for themselves so that the market is a source of feminine private income. The cash they obtain in these exchanges they keep as ornament money, or convert it into jewels, perfumes, dresses, etc. Many breaches of market peace are avoided by their presence and others are restored by their intervention.

RIGOR OF MARKET LAW

Islam itself has never developed special codes for commerce, since religious law encompasses all activities. Subject to this limitation, the Berbers have tables of fines for villages and tables of fines for markets.

Characteristically, the market, as such, is little mentioned in the *qanuns* of the villages; out of the 25 complete *qanuns* and 29 incomplete ones examined, the author has been able to collect only a dozen references to the market (though some *qanuns* count up to 50 and even up to 150 articles). Almost none exist in regard to the regulation of the markets themselves. In the few cases when the village *qanun* mentions a specific market it does so to enact penalties that are harsher in the market than elsewhere.

The market is *the* danger spot in the social structure. The full rigor of the law is applied there with intent. Of this we have a confirmation in the *qanun* of Massat. This tribe of recent constitution in the Moroccan south was studied by Robert Montagne.[36] The physical center which held together the newly formed Massat confederation was the market. We can follow step by step its body of laws as it developed, for in the *qanuns* the regulations appear as added year by year.

The climax of this progression is provided by the penalties for thieving in the market. In the final articles—180 and 181—enacted a few years after 1880, we read:

[36] R. Montagne, "Une tribu berbère su Sud-Marocain, Massat"; also, M. Ben Daoud, "Recueil du droit coûtumier de Massat." Montagne et Ben Daoud, "Documents pour servier a l'histoire due droit coûtumier du Sud-Marocain."

The Suq et Tetla being transferred to its old site to the N. of Touba, the Tribe of the Ida u Mont has decided that all adults in full possession of their faculties guilty of stealing in the aforementioned market, will pay 110 mitqals. If one such refuses to pay, or if his means of fortune do not permit him to do so, he will be blinded by gouging out his two eyes, if he cannot manage to obtain the pardon of the *inflas.* Such is the debt to society of the transgressors of the law.

And article 182:

The ancient custom by virtue of which fines could be paid for the culprit by the seven nearest kinsmen's houses is hereby abolished, for it was an arbitrary measure which was not according to the Shar'ia [Moslem religious law] nor the *orf* [Berber customary law]. Only the wife of the thief, or his father, or both together, can help in the payment of the fine, if there has been between them no separation of their property. Otherwise, the transgressor alone is responsible for his act.

These two articles reinforced each other. The abrogation of the customary principle of extended family responsibility stands here alongside of the till then harshest law against thievery.

What was especially meant by the "neutrality" of the markets was their insulation from all conflicts arising out of other contexts. In the *qanun* of Massat (article 113) it is forbidden to bring into the market place any litigation of cases except the local commercial ones. Conversely, local commercial transactions have to be executed and completed on one and the same market day, and incompleted ones cannot be left over for the next market day. In Kabylia, for instance,

Anyone quitting the market and leaving behind him a debt of more than 1 real is fined ½ real.[37]

Such provisions would necessarily prevent the emergence of a system of markets, i.e., a linking of markets with one another.

[37] *Qanun* of the tribe of the Ait b. Youcef (village of Taourirt Amran), Hanoteau et Letourneux, *op. cit.,* III, 429, art. 8.

No credit system can develop; no price arbitrage can be practiced. The road leading to market trade is blocked. Even finance and business evolve outside of these markets. Not markets, but trade and government are their founts.

The Berbers never fully accepted the usury laws of orthodox Islam. It was traditional of the earlier French writers of the conquest to contrast Berbers and Arabs in this respect.

In a typical year during the second half of the nineteenth century the French issued 8,000 to 10,000 passports to traders in the circle of Fort National. Considering that the population there numbered only 76,616 inhabitants, at least one-eighth of the total population was, off and on, actively engaged in trade. Three-fourths of these passports were issued to itinerant peddlers, or "perfumers." In payment for their cosmetics, ribbons, charms, kerchiefs and other trifles of female attire, they took some handfuls of flour, or raisins, some wool rags, or oil, whatever the household could dispense with. If these peddlers never asked for money, neither did they spend any. Successful begging was one of the marks of a thriving peddler. When he had gathered enough by barter and begging, he went to town to sell. An Ait Yenne who started with a capital of 25 fr. allegedly made 1,000 by the end of the season. Another Ait Yenne who invested all his capital, amounting to 10 frs. in cheap wares netted 500 frs. These peddlers carry their cheap merchandise in bags, and they are called "traders of the bag" to distinguish them from "traders of the tent," who have pack animals, tents and servants. The bags weigh sometimes 35 or 40 kgs., and when the poorer Kabyle comes home after one of these ventures, he has deep scars on his back.[38]

SEGMENTAL ANARCHY AND "FREE" PRICES

We have to take up finally the question of price formation in these markets.[39] Very broadly we may say that Makhzen and

[38] *Ibid.*, I, 564 ff. Ch. de Segonzac, *Voyages au Maroc*, p. 221.

[39] Market exchanges at set rates (equivalencies) were also known in North Africa, but only in the desert regions. It seems to be proper only with the Arab nomadic tribes. The equivalency of barley against dates, for instance, would alter progressively travelling from North to South.

Siba markets were organized along different lines. Markets in the Makhzen were strictly controlled; prices were fixed by authority and publicly announced; such control permitted fluctuations from month to month, week to week, or even day to day, according to proclamations. In the Siba, on the contrary, evidence points to a much greater freedom of transactions with prices at least to some extent the result of the bargaining of the parties.[40]

Unfortunately, the evidence is one-sided. The Makhzen is fully documented; price lists are available over long periods of time and even the organization of trade is fairly well known. In regard to the Siba we are almost completely in the dark. Our authors offer merely vague statements; not a single detailed description of activities in a typical Siba market is in evidence.

In the Makhzen cities the prices of goods—especially foodstuffs, necessities, textiles, etc.—are set by proclamation of an official delegated by the central authority, the *muhtasib*. His rates are decided upon after consultation with wholesalers and taking into account the prices paid by these to the producers. Once the official rates are proclaimed, nobody is allowed to sell at a higher price although underselling is allowed. The Makhzen prices remain therefore partly a function of the prices paid in the wholesale markets. In these markets, rural and regional, the prices were arrived at by free transactions and by auctioning. Lower prices were obtained whenever wholesale transactions were concluded through long-term operations, the brokers buying up the crops in advance.

The Siba markets resented the presence of such rural wholesale markets in the making, since they themselves were often supply markets for the towns. Further, the complicated organization which in the Makhzen was responsible for the setting of prices, and which involved consultations with wholesalers, examinations of the merchandise, punishments for the infractors, and a minute policing of the market places, could hardly be expected from the fickle and transitory political equilibrium of the Siba markets, which moreover lacked the specific adminis-

[40] R. Maunier, *Loi Française et ûtume indigène en Algérie*, pp. 137-38; *Kabylie, op. cit.*, III, 397.

trative machineries of control.[41] Thus, if some of the Siba markets served, as we have said, as supply markets for the towns, yet wholesaling of crops by the Berber peasants to the town brokers did not set the latter's prices, for the wholesale operations and the urban retail sales belonged to two different orders of things. It happened often, then, that although the rural markets supplied the towns, their own subsequent retail prices rose higher than in the Makhzen cities.

Speculation by manipulating the supply was not an unknown phenomenon in the Morocco of pre-Protectorate days. Its effects were, however, not much felt. In the cities and towns of the Makhzen, the organization was based on a policy of protecting the consumers by fixing the retail price of foodstuffs and other necessities. Wherever such organization was lacking, as in the Siba, speculation could not be controlled to the same extent; but there the consequences of hoarding and of manipulating the supplies of necessities were, in the nature of things, much less grave for most consumers were also producers of the same necessities. However, even in the Siba the possibility of speculation appeared in some cases as potentially dangerous. The Kabyles, for one, were ready to cope with this problem, and there is no reason why we should exclude similar restrictive measures in many other of the socially compact tribes or districts of North Africa. Temporary scarcity was met by rationing. As Hanoteau and Letourneux put it, "Trade is almost always free. In wartime when communications are interrupted or inadequate, the *djema'a* fixes the ration of grain that any person may buy at any one time. Similar measures are taken if the roads are blocked by snowfall or there is a failure of crops; in this latter case ablebodied adults must wait their turn until the sick, expectant or recently confined women have been provided for."[42]

The implications of such *ad hoc* rationing are far-reaching. It presupposes a high measure of market discipline on the part of the general public; also it establishes a strong presumption in

[41] It is a pity that most travellers have not given more attention to prices. It is understandable that they were unable to record the index of fluctuation of the market prices from market day to market day, for their weekly nature made it difficult for travellers to attend these markets more than once.

[42] Hanoteau et Letourneux, *op. cit.*, III, p. 268.

favor of a practice of set prices for the staple and interchangeable necessities of life.

Abuses of the freedom of transactions were punished. To dissuade competitors from buying, either by gifts or promises, is not an offense in itself among the Kabyles, but "he who runs down the merchandise out of malice, or with intent of purchasing himself at a cheaper rate, is fined 5 duros if it turns out that the merchandise did not suffer from the shortcomings he had asserted."[43] From this interesting provision it is further evident that norms of fair bargaining were obtained.

In the matter of prices, then, we cannot say that the evidence is very satisfactory. We do not possess any exact details of the bargained prices and of the specific price-mechanisms which functioned in the Siba. Yet there are sufficient indications which point to the fact that these were mostly of the "free" type, and that spontaneous price fluctuations were a widespread feature. Nevertheless the limitation of business ventures to those of the peddler-trade type carried on through barter indicates that profit was taken more on the side of trade, i.e., carrying, than on price differentials in the market itself. The Berber mountain markets, however, remain in economic anthropology one of the rare cases which may approach to bargained market prices for daily necessities. The extent to which they do this may well be related to the fact that attitudes in markets were formed in an implicit system of cultural and social conventions wherein freedom could manifest itself in a pattern of action.

CONCLUSIONS

In-group reciprocity and out-group market exchanges are the two most obvious forms of integration which obtain in this society.[44] Their co-existence seems to go hand in hand with the communal, individualistic and segmented traits of a culture of

[43] *Qanun* of the Ait Frawsen, art. 94, Hanoteau et Letourneux, *op. cit.*, III, 393.

[44] It can be argued that householding is the most important form of integration in this society, but as it always applies to a group smaller than society, it does not encompass all the systems of relationship found there.

which Hanoteau and Letourneux said that "nowhere else could we find such a combination which is nearer equality and farther from communism."[45] The reciprocal exchanges, to be sure, bolster the communal feelings of interdependency in a community.[46] Planting or harvesting are often done communally, especially if a family is short of hands for the occasion. The solicited help received is returned in kind; also he who receives help is host to all who worked for him. The resulting scheme of reciprocally co-operative interaction comprises the whole community. Such work-bees do not exhaust the forms of interpersonal relations of Berber society. The individual is by no means submerged in the group and occasionally he can be the sole beneficiary of reciprocative communal behavior.[47] Nevertheless the large field of Berber market exchanges is the ground for the expression of individualistic tendencies.

The Berber combination of in-group reciprocity and individualism is made possible because the society is "free" in the sense that the groups which compose it are not related except "freely" to one another. No higher center enforces the unity of the whole —this most basic feature of Berber society, its absence of any political, urban or social center and its lack of any centralization, is so fraught with consequences that we have to stop for a moment in their analysis. The idea of centralization has penetrated our thought to the point that whenever we find a society where it is absent, we are prone to interpret that society incorrectly and to misjudge it for living in a chaos. As E. Masqueray said of the Berbers: ". . . des populations qui n'ont aucune idée, *aucun sentiment, qui ne soit l'inverse des nôtres,* ne doivent pas être étudiés avec des idée préconçues."[48]

[45] Hanoteau et Letourneux, *op. cit.,* II, 468.
[46] We have briefly described customs such as the *muna* and *usa.* The *twiza* is bee-work and it is so fundamental that it almost makes unnecessary the existence of a labor market. For the *twiza* cf. E. Laoust, *Mots et choses Berbères,* p. 322 ff.; J. Bourrilly, *Éléments d'ethnographie Marocaine,* p. 153 ff.; E. Richardot, *Notes sur la touiza: essay d'utilisation de la touiza dans un but mutualiste;* R. Richardot, *La mutualité agricole des indigènes de l'Algérie;* R. Maunier, *La construction collective de la maison en Kablie,* etc.
[47] Cf. the *tawsa* rituals, a sort of gift-exchange by which the individual obtains cash at certain specific occasions (weddings, births, etc.) at high interest and in mutualistic fashion.
[48] E. Masqueray, *Comparaison des dialectes,* Introduction, p. 5.

The only comparison which comes to mind for Berber society is one of the utopian anarchist schemes of a Proudhon, Bakunin or Kropotkin. Even there, given the relationships of which the social philosopher is aware, the utopian, like the modern social scientist, is always inclined to confuse organization with central authority. He is likely to assume, for instance, that a change in population density or numbers necessarily means a complete change in the constitution or structure of society. Bakunin himself—even if it was in the temporary need of launching the revolution—thought it necessary to combine a system of federations of workingmen forming, in the language of the time, free pacts with one another, with a central executive revolutionary body which controlled them. This has been the traditional set-up of the anarchist movements down to the present, deeply affecting the doctrine.

Nevertheless, empirically, when centralization is truly absent or only exists in embryo, as is the case here, a change in numbers, for instance, will not readily change the quality of social organization. Society may also develop—as the ethnographic record best shows—along the lines which this very lack of centrality permits. This is the case of Berber society which, like the phoenix, is reborn. The absence of a center makes for a system of balances which can regenerate, and in fact has often done so. Sporadically centralization has taken on importance among the Berbers. Nevertheless, every time these new sovereignties were destroyed, decentralized and locally autonomous institutions regained their force as if nothing had happened. They emerged once again, as before, into a wide cultural integration through their inherent system of out-group balances and in-group reciprocities. And alongside them, the economic constitution which fitted that decentralization and balanced integration reappeared. Market exchanges revived and eventually the closed fabric of village and cantonal life was counterbalanced. If markets were wiped out, maybe as a result of warfare, the balance would tip over to the other side, and in-group reciprocities in village, kinship and canton would be strengthened.

All this, in the last resort, is possible because, due to the lack of centrality, there is an interplay of two types of behavior which can alternate and find a natural setting in the in-group vs.

out-group dichotomy. This society has a double *facies*, an alternance of reciprocative forms and of free individualizing forms. The social anthropologist may be at pains to work out the two faces presented in village and market. To the economist this duality appears in a greatly simplified form: whenever the first *facies*, that of the village, comes to the fore, economic behavior is reciprocative; when the second *facies* comes up, in out-group customs of pilgrimages, safe-conducts, travel and trade, exchange and market dominate the economic scene. If the individual ventures out of the district, he is safeguarded only by the customs which govern markets and market places and he himself acts individually—an economic man of market mentality. His personality is limited by the nature of his "free" pacts with the other members of his group in this society and by the contexts, the one reciprocative and bound, the other individualizing and free, which his society and culture provide. Note that no allowance is made at the villages for a disrupting bargaining behavior. It is only at the markets that legislation favors individual action. That both these contexts of Berber life are institutionalized into physically separate places of action, village and markets, is important indeed. If they were not, these contraries would come to a head-on collision.

If we look again at the market as we saw it, this situation has curious consequences. First, there was the lack of specific administrative stipulations of internal control of price, motive, or marketing action. It was the context itself, the market peace, which had to be safeguarded and explicitly rigged. Secondly, in the absence of such internal controls, the markets, one would assume, may be on the way to becoming free markets with free and fluctuating prices. This happens, however, only to a point, for essentially they are still merely places where supplies are in fact exchanged by producers against supplies fitted for consumption. They are, in other words, transformation centers which do not acquire an acting power of their own, and where therefore marketing continues to be limited. Thus the markets may threaten the communal fabric of the society, but only within bounds, which again ensures the permanence of the duality of village and market. With this crucial reservation, markets are here external places for exchanges between individuals who are shedding the corporate personality of which they were a part within township and village. One may wonder if this combination of individual behavior and marginal intergroup location is not, where it occurs, a compound which tends to result out of the working of the market institution.

11. Saints of the Atlas[1]

This paper will describe the politico-religious structure of the central High Atlas range of Morocco. In the wider context of comparative Mediterranean studies, this may illuminate the following issues:

1) Marginal or dissident tribalism.
2) The role both of wider and of local religion in rural life.

In a recent public lecture on the anthropological study of the Middle East, delivered in London, Dr. Fredrik Barth stressed the fact that tribal and village life in the Middle East does not always fit notions developed by anthropologists earlier, and perhaps suitable in other areas, such as 'real' ('black') Africa. The features he mentioned included: the fact that small social units in the Middle East cannot easily be taken to be representative samples of the larger aggregates of small units, and the fact that social relations can extend over large, socially unhomogeneous areas.

There is one particular feature which seems to me to differentiate the Middle East, and perhaps the Mediterranean, from other areas which have influenced and formed the anthropol-

Permission to reprint this selection is granted by the author and the publishers, Mouton & Co., The Hague, Maison des Sciences de l'Homme, from *Mediterranean Countrymen* (ed. J. Pitt-Rivers), Paris, 1963.

[1] I am greatly indebted to Paul Stirling for guidance in this research, and to David Hart for the generosity and enthusiasm with which he supplied me with stimulating ideas and information about other parts of Morocco. In the field my greatest debt was to my wife and to my assistant, Youssef ben Lahien, himself an Ahansal from Amzrai, now of Marrakesh.

ogist's vocabulary: namely, the meaning which can be attached to the term *tribe*.

Tribes elsewhere can be conceived (I do not know how rightly) as a kind of final political unit; in terms of Professor Evans-Pritchard's well-known definition, as the largest unit within which it is held appropriate to resort to mediation in case of conflict.

Consider the difficulties which would arise if one wished to apply this definition literally to the Middle East or North Africa: its corollary might well be that the whole region is one tribe.

This would, of course, deprive the word of any good use. It seems to me far better to say: Middle Eastern or Maghrebin tribes are generally marginal or dissident groups within a wider cultural and moral continuum, which embraces both other tribes and non-tribal, urban groups. Tribal groups are groups which have, through choice, armed resistance, geographical isolation, or subterfuge, or by tacit agreement, or in other ways, opted out of the political system of a wider world; and yet, at the same time they understand the concepts and systems of that world and even, on many occasions, acknowledge its moral if not its effective authority.

Perhaps tribalism, where it exists or has for a long time existed around the Mediterranean, has in the main been of this kind—a partial opting out of a system which at the same time was not wholly disavowed. Of such dissident areas, the uplands of Morocco are perhaps the largest and most characteristic example. Moroccans employ a concept, *siba*, which, though it is often translated as anarchy, really amounts to *institutionalised dissidence*. The boundaries of the land of dissidence were unstable as well as ill-defined: and it can be argued, as it is in a recent Moroccan study of constitutional history,[2] that the tribes at the border were presented with a kind of Social Contract situation, a choice, at least in part, between the respective ills and boons of government and anarchy.

The consideration of the land of dissidence naturally brings

[2] Mohammed Lahbabi, *Le Gouvernement Marocain à l'Aube du XXe Siècle*. Rabat 1958. See also my discussion in *The Middle East Journal*, Winter 1961.

up the question of how and to what extent, order was maintained in it. The main answers fall into a number of parts:

1) The usual mechanisms of unilineal segmentary societies, the balancing of opposing segments.
2) The legal decision procedure of collective oath.
3) The influence of *igurramen*, (singular: *agurram*) of members of holy lineages.

I doubt whether I have anything substantially original to say in connection with (1), a well-explored subject. I have discussed the general principles which seem to me to underlie (2) elsewhere.[3] At present I shall concentrate on the manner in which (3), holy lineages, supplement the other two mechanisms.

Before discussing the role of holy lineages in the political balance of Atlas tribes, it may be best to indicate their relevance to the second general issue raised—that of rural religion.

Tribal and rural societies which are incorporated in a wider cultural and political area which they recognise, are liable to experience two forms of religion—one related to local needs, and one expressing the unity of the wider society. The wider society includes and is dominated by literate towns; its religion is a religion of the Book, mediated or guarded by literate, properly qualified, academically selected learned men.

The local or tribal religion serves a predominantly illiterate population, and the needs it serves are those arising from agriculture, the maintenance of cohesion of local groups and the maintenance of peace between them. Illiteracy calls for personal mediation with stress on the person rather than the Book; local conceptualisations of groups require a specialised lineage rather than an academic elite; specific and local symbols are required, and so on. And yet, at the same time, the universal religion of the Book is not disavowed, indeed it is highly respected and there exists a passionate identification with it.

But the latent tension or incompatibility between the local and the universal religion, between, so to speak, the Shrine and the Book, can characteristically be resolved by the *marabout*.[4]

[3] *The Listener,* Easter number 1958 (3.4.1958).
[4] I use this term which, in this form, has virtually become a French word.

The most characteristic religious forms of North Africa are indeed such compromises between the religious needs of rural life and of Islam. There is a sharp contrast between the Muslim southern shore of the Mediterranean, and the non-Islamic northern shore. The dominant form of official Christianity incorporates rural shrines, etc., in its system, and provides specialised religious personnel. Protestantism, an egalitarian and literate cult of the Book, is a *deviant* and segmented tradition. In Islam, all this is reversed: 'Protestantism', i.e. rigorous impersonal urban religion, respectful of the Book, has remained at the centre of orthodoxy, and the hierarchical and personal religion of the shrine, on the other hand, is the local, regional, segmented deviant heterodoxy.

In those cases when concentrations of simple *political* power crystallised in the lands of dissidence, (which did *not* occur in 'our' region), it was often as a result of some local notable successfully playing off local groupings against central power, setting up as defender of local independence to the locals and as an upholder of order to central authority: in consequence, he might emerge as a kind of Lord of the Marches.[5] Similarly, however, the marabouts, the 'saints' of the rural Maghreb, (whose role *was* very marked in this region) may be seen as kinds of *spiritual Lords of the Marches:* they both incarnate the general religion and at the same time serve local needs in a way in which a genuine representative of it could not.

The official religion of the Book is *also* represented in this region, as in the rest of Morocco. Each village has its (more or less) literate *fquih.* Generally a stranger, always a Berber, most often from South of the Atlas, he is an annually appointed scribe and teacher of boys, paid by a levy on each household. The significant thing for this analysis is that he is of no local political importance whatever. He has no local lineage to support him. He can easily be sacked, and often is.

This paper aims at presenting a sketch, of the Saints (and not the *fquih*), of a North African hagiarchy, its structure and its decline. To do this is, in effect, to describe the main features of the political and religious life of the region: it is to analyse the

[5] *Cf.* Robert Montagne: *Les Berbères, et le Makhzen dans le Sud du Maroc,* Paris, 1930. Also *La Vie Sociale et la Vie Politique des Berbères,* Paris, 1931.

hagiarchy, or 'rule' by hereditary saints, in the maraboutic state or quasi-state, which was to be found there, and whose final decline is a matter of the very recent past or even the present.

The region in question is the central High Atlas. (Geographical terminology seems somewhat unsettled on whether or not this is a part of the Great Atlas.) This region is virtually at the centre of Morocco, and is the area where the main chain of the High Atlas, and the range of the Middle Atlas, begin to separate.

The direction of line of the main Atlantic-Sahara watershed is roughly from the South-West to the North-East. Locally, it is customary to refer to the areas to the South-Eastward of the main as the 'East'. I refer to it as the South.

The part of the Atlantic plain nearest to the hills is called the Tadla. The hills rise from the Tadla plain suddenly and sharply, in a striking wall. On the Atlantic or northern side, the area can be considered delimited by this wall. The linguistic Arab-Berber boundary also roughly corresponds to it, although Berber-speakers tend to overspill slightly into the plain. This was also, roughly, the boundary of dissidence.

On the southern, Sahara-ward side, the region has no sharp boundary. The hills slope off towards a kind of high arid valley, through which there wind rivers fed by the Atlas snows, creating a kind of thin sausage-shaped oasis, in which irrigation agriculture takes place. To the South of the valley the hills rise again: this is the Jebel Saghro (which can be considered an eastward extension of the Anti-Atlas). The Jebel Saghro is considerably less high than the Atlas and correspondingly more arid. Beyond it there is the Sahara.

Though Arabic speaking populations do exist South of the Atlas, the region adjoining ours to the South is predominantly Berber. Going southeastwards from our region towards the Sahara, there is no cultural boundary at any point.

The region itself is, essentially, a high plateau riven by deep gorges, particularly on the northern side. On the northern slopes, there is also a good deal of forest. (On the southern side, there is none). The valleys are sometimes wide enough to have accumulated relatively broad and rich alluvial plains which lend themselves to intensive irrigated agriculture. More often, the valleys are narrow and only allow discontinuous strips of irrigation. There is also a good deal of rain cultivation in higher places. There are, however, some areas inherently well suited for agriculture which remain uncultivated because they are reserved for pasture; and finally, there are extensive areas only suitable for pasture.

The general principles of social organisation are of a familiar kind. The Berber tribes are patrilineal and segmentary, with a strong tendency to endogamy and with preferred marriage with father's brother's daughter, or more distant patrilateral parallel cousins. Actual genealogical knowledge, (except in the case of some holy lineages), does not generally extend beyond knowledge of one's grandfather's name. But between the actual family grouping, consisting of father-and-sons or a set of undivided brothers, and the ultimate acknowledged ancestor, there tend to be about four or more further genealogical steps, corresponding to the 'little clan' inside the village, the village unit (measured in hundreds of people, say 300), the wider clan and finally the tribal unit, measured in thousands or tens of thousands, and which in some cases is too large to act as an effective group.

The genealogies are what I call 'Occamist' in type: ancestors are not multiplied beyond necessity. Remembered (or invented) ancestors are those corresponding to existing social groups (except of course in the case of the Saints, whose genealogies are very rich).

The actual number of steps varies from tribe to tribe. In the case of the highly sedentarised intensive agriculturalists of the broader valleys, the name of both the village segment and of the ultimate tribe may be place names, without genealogical fiction.

When employing the term 'ultimate tribe' I mean merely the largest group with which the individual can identify himself and for which a name exists (short of, of course, 'Muslim', or *possibly* terms such as 'Moroccan' or 'Berber'). North African tribes are not, and were not, ultimate political units in the sense that they presented the limit within which appeal to arbitration was held desirable. On the contrary, they were parts of a kind of cultural continuum within which this condition is always satisfied. The

political horizons of individuals and groups form a kind of series
of overlapping circles: in any area there will be a multiplicity of
shrines, saints, markets and so on; and if, for instance, one were
to move from shrine to shrine or market to market, accompanied
only by muleteers who already have affiliations of some kind
with the area (and in disturbed times, this tends to be the condition on which one can get a muleteer), one could still, by a
kind of relay, move from one end of North Africa to the other.

THE POLITICAL ORGANISATION OF THE MARABOUTIC STATE

The areas or tribal groupings falling under the influence of the
igurramen, holy men, marabouts, of Ahansal origin with whom
we are concerned are only loosely circumscribed: given the patterns of transhumance, some tribal groupings come under their
influence for a part of the year only. Others would acknowledge
their influence and their role in arbitration with regard to disputes with some other tribes but not all. In one particular part of
the Central High Atlas the Ihansalen have a near monopoly of
sanctity. This is 'their' region.

Within this area, there would fall a number of 'ultimate' tribal
groupings, (though most of them not exhaustively so), each of
them, of course, internally segmented.

Leadership within these tribes tended to follow the following
rules (which will be explained): annual re-appointment of
leader; rotation of eligibility; cross-election; supervision of election by *igurramen* and its synchronisation with presentation of
ziara (religious donation) to them.

The functions of a chief of a segment were to assist in the
pacific settlement of disputes, to impose fines for offences, supervise observation of rules such as non-entry into reserved pastures
prior to agreed opening-day, etc. He was elected for a year only.
It is said that re-election was possible but not usual. If it did not
occur, the next chief had to be elected from a next segment, and
so on, so that each clan provided a chief for one year, by rotation.

The election took place at the *zawiya* (lodge, village) of the *igurramen,* usually in autumn, when the 'men of the tribe' had assembled there and brought the annual donation. The election is made by all the clans minus the one *from* whose number the chief is to be chosen (cross-election). The *igurramen* are present. The men of the clan-of-the-year, so to speak, are outside the assembly. No fixed rule governs the exact number of representatives of each clan. Having chosen the man, the men of the 'clan of the year' (including the future chief) sit in an inward facing circle; the electors circle around them and finally place a tuft of green grass—so that the year be fertile—on the turban of the chosen man.

The principle of rotation and cross election is liable to operate at all the levels of size: for the whole area under Ahansal influence; at the level of total tribe or large segment; and at the level of minor segment (groups of villages, or single village, clan, measured in hundreds). In consequence, the lay, non-maraboutic part of the maraboutic 'state' may be conceived as a set of rotating wheels within wheels. The real system is not quite as neat and symmetrical as this. A number of qualifications is called for:

The largest wheel or rotation of leadership is only called into being at times when joint action is called for. This was the case at the time of the French advance into the region (from the First War till 1933), an advance which incidentally was very slow.

The segmentation for purposes of election (i.e. for providing a chief) need not always correspond exactly to the segmentation conceived genealogically nor correspond to size. For instance, a certain large segment may in some tribe be held to be particularly propitious—i.e. if chiefs are chosen from it, the harvest will be good. Then each of its sub-segments will provide a chief for one year, and the whole of the rest of the tribe will count as one election unit (i.e. will get one year during which the chief is chosen from it). This will have as its further consequence that in that year, the principle of cross-election cannot operate: as one does not know from which subclan the chief will come, one cannot exclude his subclan from electing.

A further complication arises from the relationship of leaders at various 'levels' to each other. This matter remains obscure, and I shall not discuss it in this paper.

THE IGURRAMEN

Within this general area, settlements of Ihansalen, or descendants of Sidi Said Ahansal, settlements varying in size from village
(c. 300 people) to hamlet or even solitary household, are dispersed. They have a near-monopoly of 'sanctity' in it. In their
dispersion already they differ from the more characteristically
continuous areas of other tribes.

The families and clans of Ihansalen share the general principles
of organisation with the surrounding tribes. For instance, they
share the rules of inheritance which, in effect, divide the deceased
man's property equally amongst his sons (who may, of course,
postpone division and frequently do).

But their major asset, that of being an *agurram*, of possessing
baraka,[6] is not so easily divisible, for its excessive diffusion would
make it worthless. At the same time, there are no clear formal
rules, such as primogeniture or selection by father, for transmit-
ting it. How many of a *baraka*-endowed father's sons inherit it,
and which one if one only, is left unclear—and this ambiguity is
inherent in the social situation.

Igurramen are locally said to be such in virtue of their descent
from Sidi Said Ahansal and further back, from the Prophet. This
explanation, which is the one first given, is not however logical,
for not all descendants of Sidi Said, not all Ihansalan, are actually
effective igurramen. The differentia which separate what I call
effective from what I call latent *igurramen* is not clearly conceptualised. Only a minority of the alleged descendants of Sidi
Said Ahansal actually act and are treated as *igurramen;* everyone
knows how to distinguish them from those who are merely latent
igurramen; and yet, the only theoretical reason that can be given
for *why* the effective ones are effective is their descent, which, at
the same time, they are acknowledged to share with the merely
latent ones . . .

The supply of *igurramen* is greater than the demand. A kind
of Malthusian principle operates: *igurramen* multiply geometri-

[6] Blessing, good omen, the power to bless, to bring prosperity, to mediate
with God.

cally, but are usable by the surrounding society only in a stable or at most a slowly progressing ratio.

Thus of the descendants of Sidi Said who can claim *agurram*-hood, only a few are or can be full, respected *igurramen;* the rest provide a kind of spectrum which ends in pious beggary. The poorest *agurram* lives at a standard probably lower than the average for the surrounding population.

This 'fall-off' of effectiveness corresponds to something like the demand curve for *igurramen*—what the market will take. *Igurramen* have a sharply diminishing marginal utility. The supply being almost free, it is the demand which determines the reward. The peculiar nature of the demand is such that *some* must be well rewarded however great the supply. An *agurram* can only do his job if singled out and respected—and rewarded. The impoverished marginal *agurram* is the one who has tried, or whose forebear tried, to be an effective one, and has failed. Latent *igurramen,* inhabitants of an effective lodge, tend to be clients of the effective *igurramen,* sometimes rather poor clients. (It should be noted that lodges practise agriculture as ordinary villages do; the wages of *agurram*hood are an extra.) The question which arises is this: what determines success in the struggle to be a fully effective and recognised *agurram?*

The first consideration is descent. As a rule, only the offspring of effective *igurramen* stand a good chance of being such themselves. There is a qualification: the possibility exists of reactivating *agurram*hood in families where it has been latent for some time. However, the importance of birth in the transmission of *agurram*hood has a corollary in the moment of succession which becomes crucial when more than one son wishes to succeed. There is no strict rule either of primogeniture nor of selection by the father, nor that only one son may succeed, but there is a vague predisposition in favour of such principles. The rules of this struggle are hidden or obscure ones. They cannot be elicited directly, for they are not overtly conceptualised. They can only be inferred from observing what happens and from interpreting suggestive legends.

In the end, an *agurram* is he who is held to be such by the surrounding lay tribes. 'God decides': but in a very real sense here *vox populi* is *vox Dei.*

What we are faced with is a slow, generation-by-generation game of musical chairs; or rather, a variant on musical chairs where the number of chairs remains constant but the would-be occupants multiply. (The chairs are allocated, ultimately, by the tacit consent of the lay tribes who are clients of the Saints . . .). As it is desirable to stay as near the centre as possible, two (at least) alternative strategies are open to *agurram* lineages.

Firstly, they may go lay, become latent rather than effective. To abandon active *agurram* pretensions in good time may be preferable to becoming a marginal *agurram*, whose standing and income may be lower than that of an average lay Berber. There are other advantages; giving up *agurram* pretensions allows one to give up *agurram* ideology, including seclusion of women (costly) and pacifism (dangerous unless one *is* a highly respected *agurram*).

But the most interesting possibility open to an *agurram* who is none too sure of coming out top at home, is to *migrate* and resettle. Here Mohamed's progeny does indeed go to the mountain.

After all, the thing which locally puts a limit to the number of acceptable full *igurramen* is a kind of saturation of the market: the kind of services performed by *igurramen*—arbitration, mediation—can be performed, at any one place, by a small number of people, even by one man. (And it is useful to *concentrate* this role. Diffusion weakens its efficacy.) But they cannot conveniently be performed by the same people or the same man at some distance.

Hence *igurramen* tend to disperse far more than lay tribes. They are dispersed over the whole region.

One should add that even lay Ihansalen, latent *igurramen*, are comparatively dispersed. The explanation of this is that even they find it easier to settle amongst other tribes, without arousing their fear and hostility, than would a segment of a large lay tribe. Furthermore, having done so, they have more motive for remembering their origins rather than gradually coming to count themselves as members of the local groupings. Or, indeed, Ahansal origins may sometimes be 'remembered' without having been true in the first place.

If we now locate the positions of the effective *agurram* settlements, of the *zawiyas,* on the map of the segmentation of the large lay tribal groups, we shall find the effective *zawiyas* at the important boundaries. Not surprisingly, for mediation and arbitration is their main function. Effective ones arise 1) on a boundary, and 2) not near an already existing effective one. The seed is dispersed and these are the conditions of its bearing *distinctive* fruit.

Thus the 'maraboutic state'—if we dignify it by that name—consists of the superimposition, within the same territory, of two kinds of kinship groups, similar in their basic structure but dissimilar in leadership pattern. Amongst the lay tribes, everything is organised so as to prevent the emergence of power: the balancing of groups, the rotation of eligibility, the manner of election—all are designed to limit the duration and hence the effectiveness of power. Everything is transient. Amongst the *igurramen,* on the other hand, the achievement of position is, in principle, for keeps. There is concentration, not diffusion, of power: though the concentration is not absolute. The game is one of slow elimination, the victor remaining (in theory) in permanent possession, as opposed to the lay game of each taking his turn and passing on: the musical chairs and the merry-go-round.

The important thing about the two systems is of course their mutual relationship: the fact that they make each other possible. The fact that the land of Ahansal has been spared those characteristic sudden and disastrous crystallisations of secular power which appear in other Berber regions has presumably been due to the fact that chiefs are so reliably available for deposition after a year's tenure, and this in turn has been possible because *igurramen,* and not chiefs, provide the required minimum of stability and continuity. The fact that the rule or influence of the Ahansali lineages has been so relatively stable (which it was) has in turn been due to their neutrality, their position outside the system. (If foreigners do not exist, they have to be invented. Ihansalen are artificial foreigners amongst the Berbers.) These features of Ahansal-land, the absence of powerful secular chiefs, the stability of such power as there is and the religious foundation of this power, distinguish it from characteristic patterns of Berber society elsewhere (and notably from the analysis provided by Robert Montagne in *Les Berbères et le Makhzen* or by Jacques Berque in *Les Structures Sociales du Haut Atlas*).

The complementary of *igurramen* and their clients can be further clarified by stating the ideology of *agurram*hood. That *igurramen* are the witnesses of elections and oaths has already been stated. Furthermore: *igurramen* are 'sherifian' and thus the local embodiment of the Prophet's progeny and thus of Islam. When appealed to as a court of appeal in important cases—one would not bother them with triviality—they would, it was believed by them and others, adjudicate according to the *Shra'a*, Koranic law, and not according to local custom as lay tribesmen and chiefs would. Moreover: *igurramen* should not dance (an immoral, un-Islamic practice in the local view), they seclude their wives, they do not give away their daughters in marriage to lay tribesmen, they do not fight (and hence, by extension they also do not litigate). They possess magical powers. They should be scrupulously pious Muslims.

All these things call for important qualification. In fact, what the *igurramen* called Koranic law was local custom. Thus both ends were achieved: the tribesmen had both their own custom, *and* identification with Islam. Some *igurramen*—i.e. those very secure—*do* in fact dance. Many are lax in other ways. The pacificism is not a matter which bears careful looking into.

Nevertheless, there is something in the claim to pacificism (and the others). The exceptions to it of which I am aware were either cases of *agurram* fighting *agurram*, or *igurramen* being involved in the war of pacification by the French, or they followed extreme provocation (the murder of one of their own number). On the whole, however, *igurramen* do abstain from military action and alliance. They could hardly perform their role of neutral arbiters otherwise.

Government by *agurram* is a case of the one-eyed leading the blind: a nearly acephalous segmentary system (but one endowed with a kind of inner *grading* of personnel) provides leadership or indirect rule and judicial service and a permanent framework for one which is wholly devoid of permanent leadership.

The existence, however, of a number of still-fully-effective *agurram* lineages within the same *zawiya*, and the existence of a multiplicity of *zawiyas*, presents tribesmen with alternative *agurram* leadership; they can take their allegiance elsewhere—all the more easily as multiple allegiance is perfectly permissible and common. It is not always all that easy, but it is feasible, to transfer loyalty. (*Igurramen* are rivals to each other. Between lodges, hostility may be open. *Within* a lodge, it is kept within *some* bounds . . .)

In the maraboutic state there have been no wars of succession; the lineages do not control their clients sufficiently to be able to engage them in a civil war. But there is a kind of permanent, slow, long-drawn-out competition between the marabouts.

The maraboutic 'state' does present a remarkable instance of the division of powers, of a separation of the secular and the spiritual (which is normally said to be alien to Islam . . .); neutral, pacific, sherifian arbitrators, a kind of diffused hagiarchy, constitutionally approving a changing series of secular, impermanent, removable chiefs . . .

The major agent of social change in this century has of course been the French penetration. The French arrived on the verge of the region just before the first World War; they made some minor advances after it and in the early twenties, and then more or less halted; and they completed the occupation only in 1933.

The comportment of the *igurramen* during the crisis of the French advance illustrates a number of our themes.[7]

The first advance provoked an activation of the largest circle, the election of a secular war-chief under *agurram* supervision and ultimate authority.

However, various considerations, notably experience of French technical power in the form of a motorcar and of the need to find allies against the Glawi, the Pasha of Marrakesh, who tried also (and failed) to subdue the region, convinced the top *agurram* of the need to come to terms with the French.

This led to a triple direction of fragmented *agurram* power:

1) One *zawiya* was a genuine leader of anti-French resistance.

[7] *Cf.* Georges Drague: *Esquisse d'Histoire Religieuse du Maroc.* Paris, 1951 (Part II, chapter III).

2) One, the main and founding centre, was a spurious leader of resistants, attempting to lead them over slowly to a pacific submission in covert co-operation with the third.

3) One, newly set up in subdued territory, provided a local authority for the French to work through.

Zawiyas (2) and (3) were in fact one unit—genealogically though not in location—and in terms of their political action: but covertly.

In other words, the *igurramen* adapted their old technique of border arbitrators to the French-against-dissidents conflict. But in the past, they would have set up a *zawiya* at the border of the two hostile sides and received donations from both. This was now impracticable, and the French did not know the rules of this game, or anyway were unwilling to play it in its literal form. So, instead, what was in effect one and the same *zawiya* had to have two geographical locations, one in the land of dissidence and one in subdued territory.

However, those lay tribes which emphatically and unambiguously wished to continue the struggle could transfer their full allegiance to the *zawiya* (1) which was genuinely dissident. In fact of course the major determinant of the desire to continue resistance was itself geographical position.

Whilst the *igurramen* knew how to deal with the French advance to their own best advantage, they were, in the long run, less successful in dealing with the conditions arising after the final French victory in 1933. The genuinely dissident *igurramen* were then deprived of power and artificially incorporated, for purposes of the newly instituted indirect rule, in the segmentary system of the lay tribes surrounding them.

The allies of the French—covert and avowed—were rewarded by permanent chieftainships on the native side of the double system of authority set up by the Protectorate. (To be more precise, three such positions were created and filled by leading *igurramen*.) This arrangement doubly violated the traditional pattern: by making chiefs *permanent*, and by turning *igurramen* from indirect rulers into *direct* ones. They themselves—or those selected for the posts—were keen on this transformation: the short run advantages were obvious, in terms of authority, in new kinds of possibility of enforcement and in a new kind of remuneration. It was however barely compatible with their *agurram* status, and in the long run cost them their influence. Even before the final dismantling of the Protectorate in 1955/56, they lost some of the areas originally attributed to them; their unpopularity sometimes made it preferable, even from the viewpoint of French authority, to rule without their aid through lay chiefs or even annually changeable ones (a reversal to local tradition).

The victory of the Nationalists over the French accelerated the decline of the *igurramen*. For one thing, in the ideology of North African nationalism there is incorporated the anti-maraboutic, 'Protestant' teaching of the Reform movement.[8] For another thing, the independent Moroccan state was primarily concerned with maintaining the organisational structure built up by the French and re-staffing it with its own nationals, and not with maintaining pre-Protectorate local political structures.[9] The *igurramen* were ill-qualified, being generally illiterate, to occupy posts of the modern kind. Nor did they have the skill and understanding to exploit the political crisis of 1953–56 as they had done that of the twenties and early thirties during the French conquest . . .

Their influence and revenue as *igurramen*, weakened and transformed under the Protectorate, is small today. However, the past is still written into the group boundaries and other features of the present. The *igurramen* were heavily represented amongst the functionaries of the two or three political parties (one is in the process of fission) operating in the region in 1959. But their role in the rural 'communes' which are intended to replace tribal groupings, and in the long postponed local elections, is a matter for the future. They did very well in the first modern-type elections [of] 'rural councils' in 1960.

[8] On the nature and impact of this ideology, I am greatly indebted to Mr. Thomas Hodgkin. It is to be hoped that his study of it will soon be available in printed form.

[9] *Cf.* my 'Independence in the Central High Atlas', *Middle East Journal*, Summer 1957.

12. Aspects of the Legal Status of Women Among Awlad 'Ali[1]

The group of men who gathered near the public water faucet were obviously discussing something very important. They were shouting and arguing. No one could hear what they were saying because all of them were talking at the same time. One thing was clear, however; what they were discussing had something to do with the newspaper that one of them was holding in his hand. A man riding his donkey stopped and greeted the gathering, who suddenly stopped shouting. He was Sheikh Suliman,[2] a respectable man and the 'Omda (mayor) of one of the tribal segments in the area. He must have asked about something, because everybody started shouting again and pointing to the newspaper. Then Sheikh Suliman began to talk and everybody listened: "I know you are angry for what she had told the newsmen about us. . . . I agree with you that she did wrong by describing us as ignorant and hostile to strangers,[3] especially after we have opened our homes to her and treated her like one of us. . . . But you are forgetting that, after all, she is a woman. . . . True she is edu-

Reprinted, with minor revisions by the author, by permission of the author and publisher from *Anthropological Quarterly* 40:153–66 (1967). This paper was originally read at a conference on the economic and political status of women in Mediterranean societies at State University of New York at Binghamton, June 2–3, 1967.

[1] Materials presented in this paper were collected during my field work in the Egyptian Western Desert in the period October, 1965, to August, 1966.

[2] Names used in the paper are not the actual names of the persons indicated. Strict transliteration of Arabic is not used.

[3] Reference here is made to an article in a national newspaper about my field work among Awlad 'Ali in which the reporter had misquoted me in an attempt to give a colorful and more stimulating account of the study. For weeks this article was the main subject of discussions and argument among the people in the area.

cated . . . she went to schools like men and probably knows more than you and I . . . but educated or not, a woman is a woman and the prophet—God's prayers and peace on him—had said that women are lacking in mind and religion. . . ."

Everybody seemed to be convinced, at least for the time being. What Sheikh Suliman had pointed out was the common view of women among Awlad 'Ali of the Western Desert of Egypt. The idea that women are mentally inferior to men and that God has preferred men over them in matters of correct judgement and good counsel is common among Awlad 'Ali as it is among other Moslem groups. This idea has its support in certain passages of the Qur'an which have been interpreted by some to mean that women are inadequate creatures unfit for public duties and that God confined prophecy, leadership, testimony in courts of law, duties of holy war, and other public functions to men. (Ibn Khaldun, 1858)

It seems that Awlad 'Ali have taken this interpretation literally. With the exception of a few holy women from the Murabiteen tribes, who may be considered as performing certain public functions, women are, as a rule, excluded from participating in public duties. Leadership on all levels is confined to men; so is mediation in dispute settlements. Their testimony is not accepted in legal cases except where they are a party in the dispute, neither can they take the legal oath—a cornerstone in the tribal judicial process. They do not share in the payment of the bloodmoney, and the bloodmoney for a woman is half that for a man.

But participation in the public affairs of the society is only one index of the political position of an individual or a group. An individual or a group may be related to politics in two different, yet related ways. First, he may be related to politics as a policy maker. Here his position is determined by the amount of his participation in ". . . determining and implementing public goals . . ." (Swartz, 1967, p. 7). Second, he may be related to politics as subject to political decisions and activities. One area in which such decisions and activities are manifested is the domain of legal rights. Here, one's position is defined in terms of the number and nature of the legal rights he is given in a particular system and the guarantees he has for such rights. Needless to say that the two domains, that of political participation and that

222 Peoples and Cultures of the Middle East

of legal rights, are closely related, and the person's position in
one is likely to influence his position in the other. This is especially true in a society such as that of Awlad 'Ali where the domain of politics is not separate from that of law, and where the
legislative, judicial, and executive functions are undertaken by
the same set of individuals. Yet the two areas are distinct, and the
individual's position in one is not always a reflection of his position in the other.

Within the area of legal rights we find a picture of Awlad 'Ali
women which is quite different from the one given above. For
the customary law gives them rights and privileges some of which
are not given to women by the modern legal system of the state.
And although they are not given full legal status in all matters
and in many cases are put under the guardianship of their male
relatives, yet this guardianship usually works to guarantee rather
than to limit these rights, and gives women in certain respects
a position equal to that of men.

Not denying women any role in the first of these domains, this
paper will focus on the position of women viewed from the other
end of the political action. Analysis of some of the legal rights
given to women by the customary law of Awlad 'Ali, especially
in the area of marriage and the family and of the guarantees they
have for such rights, may give us insight into the position of
women not only in the legal system of Awlad 'Ali but in their
society as a whole.

I

Awlad 'Ali are a number of Arabic-speaking, semi-nomadic
tribes of sheep and goat herders who inhabit the northern part
of the Western Desert of Egypt.[4] In addition to the Arab Awlad
'Ali (Sa'adi) who were driven out of their home in Cyrenaica
after their defeat in one of the tribal wars, the name covers a
number of client tribes of Murabiteen (holy men) of Berber origin who occupy an inferior political position.

The economy of Awlad 'Ali is based on livestock husbandry,

[4] Part of Awlad 'Ali live in the Delta as settled agriculturalists.

supplemented by occasional cultivation of barley. Owing largely to variation in the amount of rainfall, the source of food in the area has the characteristic that the place and quantities of its occurrence are unpredictable. Throughout most of the area the tribal populations are concerned predominantly with warding off shortage in food supply by moving with their flocks from one place to another, or by sending their flocks to areas where grazing lands are available. While Awlad 'Ali keep a variety of domestic animals, the most important are sheep and goats. Their whole economy is based on the utilization of the products of these two animals. Milk and its products constitute the basic element in the people's diet. Wool is either sold or spun and woven into rugs, male lambs are sold in the market and the money is used to buy the necessary supply of food, clothes, and utensils. These items are usually obtained from shops in the settled communities in the area, although some of the major items are obtained from the larger urban centers.

The basic unit of production and consumption among Awlad 'Ali is the household. It is usually based on an elementary family of a man, his wife or wives and their children. Authority is vested in the male head who is the property owner. Division of labor within the household is based mainly on age and sex: women and girls do the domestic tasks and care for the children, men tend the animals, buy household needs, visit the market, meet strangers and represent the household in all matters of a public nature. Herding is often done by paid shepherds. The activities of men take them away from the households quite frequently. This gives the wife a chance to participate effectively in the decision-making activities for production and consumption, disciplining the children and other aspects of household activities. The ultimate authority, however, remains in the hands of the father.

II

As a girl in her father's household, the woman is under the direct authority of her father who is responsible for her. When the father dies, this responsibility, as well as the authority, goes to her brother or her closest male kin. At marriage the girl usually moves to live with her husband and this subjects her to his control and, sometimes, to that of his parents if the couple lives with them. But the authority of the husband over his wife remains secondary to that of her father. The woman's membership in her father's household does not cease upon marriage and the strength of her relations to her kin is maintained by their frequent visits to her new residence and by her occasional visits to them. This right of visitation cannot be denied by the husband who not only has to allow such visits, but is also required to treat members of his wife's family, especially her father, with great respect and hospitality. If the husband fails to do so the wife's father can order her to leave her husband and go back with him to his household. The case of Meftah illustrates this point.

> ". . . I was not there but my wife was. She received her father with the customary respect and made the duty in my absence. When I came back from the market late that evening I slaughtered a lamb in his honor and invited our neighbors. After supper he wanted to sleep. . . . It was summer and the night was hot, so I brought him a rug and spread it outside the tent in the cool air, then I went inside the tent to spend the night. In the morning he was angry . . . very angry . . . and ordered my wife to prepare her things because she was going to leave with him. He wouldn't talk to me . . . he later said that I had insulted him by spending the night inside the tent with my wife while he was visiting us. I couldn't prevent her from going with him. He is her father and has the right to take her whenever he wishes. I had to pay £. E. 10 and 'thebeha' (a goat) before he let me bring her back. . . ."

While the right of the father to take his daughter away from the husband constitutes a check on the authority of the latter and insures her good treatment by her in-laws, yet this right has been frequently misused to force the husband or members of his family to obey the father's wishes in matters that have nothing to do with the welfare of the wife. In one case the right was invoked to pressure the husband's father into approving the marriage of one of his daughters to a friend of the wife's father. In another case the brother took his sister in order to force her husband to drop his claim in a land dispute.

The woman, on the other hand, cannot refuse to go with her father, for this means that she is disobeying him. A woman who disobeys her father is not worthy of his name. He can cut her off from the family which means that she is left without any support or protection. A woman who is cut off from her family is left vulnerable to her husband and to society. She will have nobody to defend her or to be responsible for her actions. The responsibility for the woman's behavior is not transferred by marriage to the husband. If the woman kills or assaults someone or causes damage to property for which compensation is required, her male kin pays the bloodmoney or the compensation on her behalf. It is sometimes stated that if the woman has grown sons, they, and not her family, pay for her. Since the children belong to their father's family, it may seem like transferring the responsibility for the woman's actions to her husband's family. However in all the cases where this happened, the woman was quite old, her father was dead and her brothers were either dead or had moved outside and cut off all relations with the area. In such cases the sons pay because they are the woman's closest male kin.

On the other hand, if the woman is the victim of murder or assault for which bloodmoney or compensation is to be paid, the husband is the one to benefit from the situation. To understand why this happens we have to consider the contractual nature of marriage among Awlad 'Ali. Before the marriage is final, the prospective husband or his father pays the woman's father a certain amount of money[5] called *mahr*. In exchange for his money, the husband expects his future father-in-law to outfit his daughter with such items as rugs, blankets, and [a] few other household items. These items become the private property of the wife, but the husband has the right to use them. In addition, the man expects to gain certain rights to the woman herself. The customary law of Awlad 'Ali gives the husband three basic rights over his wife: the right to her sexual services (which includes the right to bear him children); the right to labor in domestic activities; and the right to her obedience. Of the three rights the

[5] In the past, the mahr used to be paid in sheep, goats, or camels. In certain areas in the present time, part of the mahr is still paid in sheep.

first is the most exclusive. Not only does the husband have a complete monopoly over his wife's present sexual services, but he
also has the right, if the girl had never been married before, to
be the first to use such services. If he discovers that she is not a
virgin he can send her back to her father and get back his mahr.

The other two rights are not as exclusive. The husband's right
to his wife's domestic labor does not prevent her from occasionally helping out in her father's or brother's household, especially
if they live nearby. Finally, the husband's right to be obeyed by
his wife is always subordinated to that of her father who retains
the ultimate authority over his daughter.

If the woman is killed or injured the husband is deprived, depending on the seriousness and the permanency of the injury,
from all or some of her services and, therefore, is entitled to
compensation. The right of avenging the woman's murder remains, however, that of her family since she is still a member of
that family.

The contractual nature of marriage is most clearly manifested
in the case of the wife's adultery. Since the woman belongs to her
agnatic group, her behavior has direct effect on the honor of that
group. It is, therefore, the responsibility of her closest kin to keep
an eye on her. If the woman commits adultery, it is her father or
her male kin who are supposed to avenge the honor of the family by taking drastic actions, including killing, against the
adulteress and/or her partner. But marriage usually takes the
woman away from the close watch of her family and puts her
under the supervision of her husband who becomes entrusted
with the duty of guarding her, and therefore, partially responsible
for her actions. His responsibility is enhanced by the fact that
although the wife's behavior does not affect him or his family,
yet it has definite effect on the honor and reputation of his children (Abou-Zeid, 1965).

The responsibility for retaliation in the case of adultery, then,
is divided between the woman's nearest kinsman and her husband. This gives both sides vague and undetermined right of
revenge. This division of the right of revenge explains the infre-
quency of drastic actions taken in cases of adultery. Of the fourteen cases of adultery that I examined during my field work,
none resulted in the killing of the adulteress and only three re-

sulted in the murder of her partner. In all three cases where the adulterer was killed the avenger was the husband, and in all three cases the husband had to pay the bloodmoney to the murdered man's kin group. His payment of the bloodmoney, among other things, may indicate that the right of the husband to kill the adulterer is not completely accepted among Awlad 'Ali. All agree, however, that such killings never result in blood feuds because of the shameful circumstances in which the victim dies.

But while the right to retaliate for the shameful action of an adulterous wife is vague and diffused, the right of the husband for compensation from the adulterer remains clear and undisputed. In this respect, adultery is treated very much like theft; the adulterer has stolen the husband's exclusive right to his wife's sexual activities. The compensation for this offense is estimated at £. E. 20, in addition to the mahr if the husband decides to divorce the wife as a result of her adultery.

Marriage does not deprive the woman of some rights of her own. The customary law gives the wife three basic rights corresponding to those of the husband's sexual services, domestic work and obedience. Corresponding to the first of these, the wife has the right to have a normal sexual life with her husband. This right, however, is not an exclusive one since the husband can marry more than one wife. A woman can be divorced from her husband without having to return the mahr if she claims that the husband is unable to perform his sexual duties. In such cases the marriage is usually dissolved quietly. In certain rare instances the husband may deny his wife's accusations. If both insist on their stand, one or both may ask to be submitted to *bait el-shana'a* or "house of the dreadful deeds." Reports are extremely vague about the exact procedures involved in such a case. Some informants stated that the married couple would live in a tent without sidewalls so that everybody can see what goes on inside it. Most informants, however, insist that it merely means that the couple move their tent near to that of a respectable man whose word is believed and honored. This man is supposed to keep a close watch on the couple's activities, by listening or looking through the holes in the tent. His verdict determines the future of the marriage. If the wife is justified in her claim the husband is forced to divorce her and to forfeit his mahr. If, on the other hand, the verdict is for the husband he not only can divorce his wife and get the mahr back, but he is also entitled to *kabara* or compensation for his injured pride. There was no case of bait el-shana'a in the area during the time of the field work, and most people insist that this practice is something of the past when the mahr was relatively high and was paid in livestock, in which case its return to the husband would have caused great financial inconvenience for the wife's family.

Corresponding to the second right, the husband's right to his wife's domestic work, is the wife's right of maintenance. The husband has to support his wife. This includes providing her and her children with adequate food and proper clothing. If the husband fails to do so because of poverty, sickness, crop failure or unexpected disaster, the wife's father or brother provides her and her children with necessary food and clothing. If the husband's failure to fulfill his duties is due to neglect the wife can leave him and go to her father or brother who talks the matter over with the husband who in turn, either agrees to their demands or has to divorce his wife and forfeits his mahr.

> An example is the case of Mabruka who married a member of her tribe. When he married her he was very poor. He did not have sheep or goats and lived by selling tomatoes in the market of the nearby town. Her father helped them out whenever he could. He sent food and clothes to his daughter and her child. Then the husband worked in smuggling goods and became rich. He bought sheep and goats, but he never provided for his wife and child and he told her, if she kept bothering him, he would marry another wife. The wife took her child and went to her father. She stayed there two months. When the husband did not come to take her back, her father had him divorce her.

Finally, corresponding to the husband's right to his wife's obedience is the wife's right to fair treatment by her husband. There are a number of ways in which the wife is mistreated. One is excessive punishment; although the right of the husband to punish his wife is provided in the Qur'an, yet the punishment must not be excessive or severe. Awlad 'Ali draw a line between acceptable and severe punishment. A punishment is severe if it results in something that other people can see or hear. If the husband insults his wife or her family and others overhear it, or if he beats her and this results in visible traces, then the punishment is severe.

A wife also considers herself mistreated if the husband, when married to more than one, treats any of the other wives better than he treats her. Although the wife cannot deny her husband the right to have addditional wives, yet he must give them all equal treatment. This includes providing them with the same kind and amount of food and clothing.[6] It also includes dividing his time equally between them, spending one night in each wife's tent. The first wife, being the chief, has certain privileges: her tent is the guest house, food is brought first to her residence and she is the one to divide it among the other wives, and her house is the place for the husband to stay if he becomes sick and unable to move every night from one tent to another. Other than the exception made for the first wife, the husband has to treat all his wives equally.

Normally such cases of mistreatment do not result in divorce unless they are persistent. In most cases, if the wife is mistreated, she goes to her father's or brother's house, or sends for them to come and take her. For the husband to bring her back, he must pay her *nasafa*. This is a gift given by the husband to his wife as an acknowledgement of guilt and as a from of apology for not giving her a fair treatment. In some cases the nasafa is equal to what the husband paid originally as mahr.

III

These are some of the rights that marriage gives both men and women in the tribal society of Awlad 'Ali. These rights, however, are useless unless they are backed by certain means of enforcing them. The husband's rights are guaranteed by his ability to dissolve the marriage at will. According to Islamic law, a man can divorce his wife by simply pronouncing the sentence, "I

[6] In proportion to the number of children of the wives respectively.

divorce you," in the presence of credible witnesses. No justification for divorce is demanded from the husband according to the Qur'an. No such privilege is given to the wife by the Qur'an. She can obtain divorce only under specific circumstances in the absence of which the husband can force her to live with him. Following the Qur'anic rules, Awlad 'Ali give men the right to dissolve the marriage at will and without any necessary justification. However, they differentiate between cases where divorce is justified and those in which it is not. In a case of justifiable divorce, the husband can take back the mahr and possibly all other marriage expenses. In the case of unjustifiable divorce the husband forfeits his right to regain the mahr. Divorce is justified whenever one or more of the husband's rights are violated by the wife or members of her family. Not all degrees of violation are considered as justification for divorce however. Only intolerable violations can be considered as such. In deciding whether or not an act constitutes an intolerable violation, Awlad 'Ali judge it against the standard of the reasonable man, and what he customarily would have tolerated in a similar situation.

Although women among Awlad 'Ali are not given the same legal right of divorcing the husband by pronouncing the "dismissal formula," yet they are given the right of certain customary procedure which in practice gives them equal facilities for dissolving the marriage. This is known as the right of the woman to "throw herself." According to this procedure, a woman who does not desire to continue living with her husband, can go to a respectable man in the community and "throw herself" over him. By throwing herself, this man becomes obliged to give refuge to the woman and to start negotiating with her husband to divorce her. Owing to the prestige of the man usually selected, the husband cannot object to the divorce although he may demand the mahr back. In this case the negotiator tries to persuade the woman's father or her nearest kin to return the mahr to the husband. If this fails, the negotiator may find himself in a position where he has to pay the husband from his own money. Due to the nature of his role in mediating, the woman must be careful in selecting the man over whom she throws herself. These considerations are manifested in the following case taken from my field notes:

Hadia was forced by her father to marry a man from the same tribe who paid her father £. E. 100 as mahr. She did not want to marry him because she was in love with someone else of whom her father did not approve. One month after she was married, she left her tent and never came back. Later, she appeared in the house of 'Omda 'Ali, the chief of another tribe, and everybody knew that she had thrown herself on him. She later told me why she had selected 'Omda 'Ali and not the 'Omda of her own tribe. ". . . because my husband works for the 'Omda of my tribe and I thought he would be biased. Of course I couldn't have gone to my father, he was the one who forced me to marry that man. 'Omda 'Ali is very respected and can protect me . . . he is also rich and is known for releasing wives from their husbands." 'Omda 'Ali called the husband in and asked him to divorce his wife. The husband agreed but insisted that she pay him £. E. 300 (this includes the mahr and all marriage expenses). The 'Omda tried to reduce the amount but could not. He then tried to get the father to pay, but the father refused. He had to pay the husband £. E. 200 of his own money and promised that the rest would be paid when the woman remarried (it would be paid from the mahr). The husband divorced Hadia.

Another example:

Sabha was forced by her father to marry her cousin. She could not live with him so she threw herself on one of the holy men in the area. This holy man convinced the husband to divorce Sabha, and then went to her father and convinced him to pay back the mahr to the husband, and the case was settled. People say that both the husband and the father agreed to the demands of the holy man because they were afraid of his supernatural curse.

It is obvious from these and similar cases that the success or failure of the procedure depends on the careful selection of the man on whom a woman throws herself. It is also apparent from the above examples that this right of refuge is resorted to only in the cases where a woman cannot go to her father or her closest kin to help her get a divorce, because they are either unable or unwilling to help her. A father is unable to help his daughter if the husband is powerful or if he is the woman's *ibn 'amm* (father's brother's son) who has, according to the tribal law, the undisputed right to marry his *bint 'amm* (father's brother's daughter). The father is usually unwilling to help his daughter if he is the one who has forced her to marry the husband, or if she was cut off from the family for some reason or other.

From the frequency of women using that right in the area, it seems that no social disapproval is associated with it, nor is there a social stigma attached to women who throw themselves. It certainly liberates the woman from the tyranny of the husband and offers her a considerable guarantee to her marital rights. It also gives her, so far as the ability to dissolve the marriage is concerned, a status close to that of her husband. This relative equality is reflected in the lack of stigma associated with the divorce in the Western Desert, and in the fact that the women usually have no difficulty in finding another husband.

While the right of "throwing herself" offers the wife some guarantees of her rights, her main guarantee is derived from the security she gets from retaining her membership in her father's family. After the death of the father, the woman's claims extend to the households of her brothers. She acquires in them the same rights she had in her father's household, and the brothers take the responsibility of their father in protecting and defending their sister. The woman achieves this continuation of support partially through forfeiting her rights of inheritance to her brothers.

Awlad 'Ali recognize the right of the daughters to inherit their father's estate. They accept the system of inheritance specified in the Qur'an which gives the woman half the share of her brother. In practice, this is usually side-stepped. Only sons inherit their father's property. The justification given for the non-inheritance by women is that the main items of inheritance in the Western Desert, livestock and the right of land use, require certain protection and care which are beyond the natural ability of women. Women, however, are supposed to be compensated by their brothers for their share. But very few would normally ask their brothers for such compensation. In forfeiting her rights of inheritance a woman secures for herself the continuous security and protection of her kin-family, and the protection of her rights. This security applies to herself and to her children. A child is always welcomed in his *khāl's* (mother's brother's) house, and the relationship between the child and his khāl is always a warm one among the Awlad 'Ali. As an informant put it:

> . . . the khāl is always too kind. We say here, 'if you are crying go to your *'amm* but if you are hungry go to your *khāl*' . . . the ''amm is like the father, you go to if you need support in a fight, but the khāl is like the mother . . . kind and considerate.' Last year I went to visit khāli (my khāl) in Libya. I was in debt but I said nothing about it. He looked at me and told me that I looked troubled and asked me what was wrong. I told him about my debt. Without saying a word he left the house. I don't know where he went. He was away for two days. When he came back, he had eighty pounds. It was a bad year and he did not have the money so he went and borrowed it . . . I don't know from whom. I told him that I needed only seventy pounds, but he insisted that I take it all . . . he told me to buy something for my wife and children from Libya.

In conclusion, women among Awlad 'Ali enjoy a number of significant rights. But, it is only through their forfeiting certain of these rights that they are able to maintain the others. It is basically through blind obedience to her father or closest kinsman that the woman secures the protection and the backing of her kin-family which is the major guarantee of her marital rights. And it is mainly through forfeiting her rights of inheritance that she is able to maintain such protection. Theoretically, at least, a woman has the choice of which rights to sacrifice and which to maintain. And although most women follow the pattern described above, some have found the right of inheritance more important than that of protection and claimed their share in their father's property, and others have found their security in marrying the man of their choice rather than in the submissive membership in their father's household.

PART III

Rural Peoples of the Middle East: Nomadic Pastoralists

Editor's Note: Nomadic pastoralists of the Middle East have attracted attention and study that seem to some to be out of proportion to their proportional representation in the total populations of the area. Yet both the theoretical problems for cultural ecology and the practical problems of their dominance over vast areas warrants this interest, not to mention their historical significance. The selections here draw from classic and new studies, and omit some materials widely available in reprint.

13. *Peace in the Desert*

Upon a morrow, when there was a great coffee-drinking at
Zeyd's, one cries over his cup, *bahhir*! "Look there!—who come
riding yonder?" All shadowing with their hands, and fixing the
eyes, it was answered, "Are they not tradesmen of Teyma, that
ride to sell calico; or some that would take up well camels; or
the sheukh perhaps, that ride to Hâyil?" The Beduw make no
common proof that I can find of extraordinary vision. True it is,
that as they sit the day long in the open tents, their sight is ever
indolently wavering in the wide horizon before them, where any
stirring or strangeness in the wonted aspect of the desert must
suspend their wandering cogitation. But the Arabs also suffer
more of eye diseases than any nation. It was not long before the
weak-eyed Arabs discovered the comers, by their frank riding,
to be Beduins; but only a little before they alighted, the company knew them to be their own skeykh Motlog and his son, and
a tribesman with them. Motlog had mounted very early from
the other camp. Our company, of nigh fifty persons, rose to welcome their chief sheykhs; Motlog re-entered cordially amongst
them, with a stately modesty; and every man came forward in
his place, to salute them as kinsmen returning from an absence,
with *gowwak ya Motlog*, 'The Lord strengthen thee.' *Answer:
Ullah gowwîk*, 'May He give thee strength:' so, falling upon
each other's necks, they kiss gravely together, upon this and
upon the other cheek. Room now is made for them in the highest

Reprinted by permission of the Executors of the Charles M. Doughty Estate and the publishers, Jonathan Cape Ltd., London, from *Travels in Arabia
Deserta* (chap. XII), 1936.

place, where they sit down, smiling easily; and the Fukara
sheukh, noblemen born, of somewhat an effeminate countenance,
excel, as said, in specious and amiable mejlis manners: yet their
Asiatic hearts are full of corruption inwardly, and iniquity. Roasting anew and braying and boiling are taken in hand, to make
them coffee; and Zeyd, as an host, brings them forth a bowl of
his musty dates to breakfast, (he would spend for none better
at Teyma,) and another of butter-milk, and those in small measure;—it was Hirfa and Zeyd's known illiberality, for which cause,
there alighted almost no guest at Zeyd's beyt in the round year.
This is the goodly custom in the wilderness, that somewhat be
served immediately, (however early it be,) to the guest alighting from his journey. The sheykhs consented to join our camps
from the next ráhla, and we should remove further into the Bishr
country.

Bishr is a main partition of the Annezy nation, and certain of
their great kindreds, as the *W. Sleymàn* in Nejd, might be compared with whole tribes. High sheykh of all the Nejd Bishr, is
a warlike man of my later acquaintance, *Misshel* (called after his
fendy) *el-Auájy*; and entitled, Sheykh of the seven Kabâil (tribes,
Kabîlies). Their kinships or fendies are, said Zeyd:

W. Sleymàn.	*Khumsha.*
Sweylmát.	*Sìllimat.*
Jiâfera.	*Hósenny.*
el-Aly.	*Sbá.*
Gathowra.	*Feddân.*
S'goor.	*Ammarát.*
Shemlán.	

Zeyd seemed to reckon the Ruwàlla Annezy with Bishr. They
inhabit by the Nefûd, under Jauf, and westwards toward Syria;
they are Beduins of raw and simple manners. Their kindreds
are: *Aarab Ibn Muzzeyed, el-Hósenny, el-Musellîkh.* Incorporate
of old with the Ruwàlla, are the ancient Annezy Aarab, *el-Jellàs*;
of whom a wady of Kheybar, their former possession long forsaken by them, is yet named. Their kindreds are:

el-Nussîr; Noàsera.	*Deraan.*
Shalân.	*Unseir.*
Ribshàn.	*Belais.*
Sualma.	*B'dûr.*
Ferujja.	*Aarab Ibn Mahjil sheykh el-Esshàjir.*
Koatcheba.	*Aarab Ibn Jíndal sheykh es-Suàlma.*
Gaaja.	*Aarab Ibn Umjeyd sheykh Abdillah.*
Dogmàn.	*Kleyfát.*

As our Aarab were pitched together again, there arrived a principal sheykh of Teyma, *Abd el-Azîz er-Román,* riding round to the Aarab, to buy well camels. The price is two or three camel-loads of dates or a load of corn, *aysh,* for a good nâga. He alighted at Motlog's, and I went down to the coffee meeting, to hear the country news. Motlog welcomed me graciously, and called, "Bring a shidàd for Khalíl." The Teyma sheykh was a well clad, comely, stirring man, in the favour of Ibn Rashîd, collector of the prince's revenue in his oasis; presumptuous, penetrating-malicious, and, "as all the Teyâmena," in the opinion of the no-mads, *jàhil,* of a certain broken-headed ineptitude, and rusticity. In the nomad-like village, he had not learned letters: Motlog, among Beduins, was the friend of his youth. As we sat on, Abd el-Azîz, turning abruptly, demanded of me, 'What did I there in the wilderness, and wherefore had I banished myself from all world's good,' (that is, from the shadow by day, bread and dates sure, and water enough, and the stable dwelling). "I take the air." —"If this be all, thou mightest as good take the air upon yonder top of Irnàn." His rafîk enquired in his ear, yet so that I heard it, "Is not this a Yahûdy?"—"Jew, there is no doubt (answered Abd el-Azîz), or what they tell me Nasrâny, a difference in the names only." The other then, with a ghastly look, as if he be-held a limb of Sheytân, "Lord, for thy mercy! and is this—akhs! —Yahûdy? Ullah confound all the kuffâr." Abd el Azîz, when I came again to Teyma, had put on a new courtesy, since he heard the stranger had publicly pronounced him, "Ignorant ass, and skeykh of all the Yahûd of Teyma:" for the Arabs, who covet to be praised, are tender as vain women of men's opinions. They brought tidings of a disaster at home, the Haddàj was fallen! yet he looked merrily upon it, because his two or three draw-wheels and the side which belonged to his own sûk, were yet standing; the loss was not of his faction.

The knavish Beduins heard unmoved of the mischance of the Teyâmena; those merchants of dates and corn, that beguile, they think, their uncunning with false measures. Of some who came later from the oasis, we heard that the townspeople and fanatics laid all to the charge of the Masrâny. 'The Haddàj fell only few days after my being there, I had overthrown it with mine eye;' but the graver sort said, 'it was not fallen but by the permission of Ullah.' I asked a plain worthy man of the town, "How could I have cast down your well?" And he: "Khalîl, I believe not it was thy doing; (he added darkly,) I think rather it was of Ibn Rashîd!" The prince and his riders (perhaps three hundred men), returning from the raid upon W. Aly, had encamped without Teyma walls a day or twain. He added, "The multitude of them was as the sand, *ouff!*"—Was it the tread of their waterers about the Haddàj?"—"Not this, but *el-âyn*, the eye!" The evil eye is part of the Semitic superstition. The darling of the body is the eye, the window of the soul, and they imagine her malign influence to stream forth thereat. Fanatical nomads, from that day, looked upon me as a yet more perilous 'God's adversary.'

One of these evenings there rode into our encampment a main ghrazzu, eighty men of Bishr, that had mounted to go set upon their foemen W. Aly; they passed this night as guests of the Fukara, in their own dîra. They were friendly entertained, and heard after their suppers the latest advice of the W. Aly's being pitched about the wells *Mogeyra*; about eighty miles from hence, at the haj road, a journey below el-Héjr. I enquired of Zeyd, Would they not send this night to warn their cousins of the sister tribe? *Answer:* "Ha, no! but let them all be taken, for us." Months later, being with some W. Aly tribesmen I heard them censure this treacherous malice of the Fukara; and yet being full of the like themselves, which in truth is the natural condition of Beduins. Of the Annezy nation, into which all these tribes belong, and that is greatest of all ashîrats in the Peninsula, it is spoken in proverb, "God increased Annezy, and He has appointed divisions among them:" there is no time when some of the kindreds are not *gôm*, or robber enemies, of some other.

The Annezy have been compared with B. Israel; they are not without resemblance. The seat of this people, in the first Mohammedan ages, was, according to their tradition, the dîra lying a little north of Medina, which is now of the W. Aly. Then they conquered Kheybar, whose feverish palm valleys became their patrimony to this day.

It happened strangely that whilst Bishr was out against them a main ghrazzu of the Wélad Aly had mounted to go and set upon Bishr. These hostile squadrons by a new adventure met with each other in the wilderness. An hundred thelûl riders cover the ground of a regiment. It is a brave sight, as they come on with a song, bowing in the tall saddles, upon the necks of their gaunt stalking beasts, with a martial shining of arms. The foemen in sight, the sheukh descend with the long lances upon their led horses; and every sheykh's backrider, *radîf*, who is also his gun-bearer, now rides in the thelûl saddle. Those thelûl riders, upon the slower sheep-like beasts, are in comparison of their few light horsemen, like a kind of heavy infantry of matchlock men. The nomad cavalier, sitting loosely upon a pad without stirrups, can carry no long and heavy firearm, which he could not reload. Only few amongst these southern sheykhs are possessors of some old flint horse-pistols, which abandoned in our grandsires' time, have been sold away from Europe. Their hope is in the romhh or shelfa, the Beduin lance: the beam, made of a light reed of the rivers of Mesopotamia, is nearly two of their short horse-lengths; they charge them above their heads. Agîd or conductor of the W. Aly part, was a beardless and raw young man, *Fáhd*, their great sheykh's son; and *Askar* of the other, son of *Misshel*, the great sheykh above mentioned: these young hostile Annezy leaders were sisters' sons. Fáhd, tilting impetuously, pierced his cousin Askar; but, overborne by strong men's hands, he was himself taken alive. The W. Aly, glorious and confident in the tents, were seized with panic terror in the field, in presence of the warlike Auájy, the most big of bone and resolute of that country Beduins; in each of whom they looked for an avenger of the blood slain before Kheybar. They cried out therefore that they were brethren! and those W. Aly, which were one hundred and twenty riders with arms in their hands, submitted to the eighty lion-like men of Bishr; every one pitifully

intreating his spoiler, "*akhyey, ya akhyey,* ah, little brother
mine! take thou then my thelûl, have here my arms, and even
my mantle; take all, only let me go alive." No more than a few
sheykhs of them, who were horsemen, escaped that day upon
their mares. Yet of the thelûl riders there broke away three hardy
men, mountaineers; they were Moahîb, that had ridden with
them in hope to divide the spoils of the common enemy.—Before
the year was out, the Moahîb by the same Bishr were miserably
bereaved, in one day, of all their cattle. The sheykhs upon all
sides were, at some time, of my acquaintance; and I had this tale
among them.

The Bishr received their *dakhîls* to quarter; they would not,
only remembering the vengeance, make a butchery of their kinsmen; and, as the southern Aarab use not to take human lives to
ransom, they let their enemies go, in their shirts, to ride home
to their wives, upon their bare feet. It is contrary to the Arabian
conscience to extinguish a kabîla. There are tribes of neighbours,
cruel gomânies since their granddames' days, as the Fejîr and
B. Atîeh, that have never met in general battles, when, in a day,
they might void so long controversies, by the destruction of one
of them. Even the Beduins' old cruel rancours are often less than
the golden piety of the wilderness. The danger past, they can
think of the defeated foemen with kindness; having compassion
of an Arab lineage of common ancestry with themselves. When
men fall down wounded in a foray the enemies which had the
upper hand will often send again far back, and bear them to
their menzil: and there they nourish their languishing foemen,
until they be whole again; when they give to each a water-skin
and say to him *ruhh,* "depart," without taking promises, putting
only their trust in Ullah to obtain the like at need for themselves.
But Fáhd was led away with the Bishr, since he must answer
for the life of Askar: if his cousin died he must die for his death,
unless the next of kin should consent to receive the blood ransom; he would be entertained in the meanwhile in his hostile
kinsmen's tents. Askar recovered slowly, in the next months. I
asked, "When those shearers of W. Aly came home shorn, with
what dances and lullilooing will the hareem sally forth to meet
them!" It was answered, "Ay billah, they had merited the wom-
en's derision!" "But how, being one hundred and twenty strong,

had they submitted to the fewer in number?" *Answer:* "Are they
not W. Aly? and this is the manner of them." They are unwar-
like, but the Fejîr, the sister tribe, were never contemned by
their enemies, which are all those strong free tribes behind them,
B. Atîeh, Howeytát, Bíllî, Jeheyna.

The clouds of the second locust brood which the Aarab call
am'dàn, 'pillars' [it is the word we read in Exodus—the *ammud*
of cloud and fire], wreathing and flickering as motes in the sun-
beam, flew over us for some days, thick as rain, from near the
soil to great height in the atmosphere. They alight as birds, letting down their long shanks to the ground; these invaded the
booths, and for blind hunger, even bit our shins, as we sat at
coffee. They are borne feebly flying at the wind's list, as in the
Psalms, "I am tossed up and down as the locust." There fell of
them every moment upon the earth, and were dashed upon the
stones. After this we saw them drifted to the southward: and
the Aarab, knowing they must now devour Kheybar, where
their dates would be lost, came forth, and stood to gaze after
them with a fatal indifference; and with *aha!* they went in to
sit down again, leaving their lot in the hands of Ullah, who they
say is Bountiful. And oftener than no, the Arabs will smile in
such mishaps, over their own broken hopes, with a kind of godly
melancholy. The children bring in gathered locusts, broached
upon a twig, and the nomads toast them on the coals; then pluck-
ing the scorched members, they break away the head, and the
insect body which remains is good meat; but not of these latter
swarms, born in time of the dried-up herbage. A young man at
our fire breaking the toasted body of the first, there fell out a
worm, and he cast it from him with loathing; and cried, 'akhs!
Wellah this cured him of all locust eating.' Yet women went out
to gather them; they were of some poor households. The coffee-
drinkers asked of me, "Eat you the locusts in your béled, Khalîl;
tell us, be they wholesome?" (We read in Leviticus that the children of Jacob might eat the kinds of locust.) Nearly every
seventh year, in the Arabians' opinion, is a season of locusts.—
This year was remembered for the locust swarms and for the
great summer heat. The male insect is yellow, spotted brown,
the female somewhat greater and of a leaden colour. The pair of
glassy wings are spotted, the inner pair are wide and folded

under. Her length to the end of the closed wing is nearly three
inches. The Beduins say, "This is not the eye which appears such,
in the head, but that clear spot under the short first legs." I took a
pen and made the outline of a locust, and upon the next leaf was
another of Abu Zeyd: all the Arabs came to see these two pictures. "Very well, Khalîl," said the simple gazers, "and ha! his
image Wellah, without any difference!" And one smutched the
lines of the locust with his fingers, seldom washed, to know if this
lay even upon the smooth paper, and *yeteyr* quoth he, "it will rise
and fly!" And ever as there came coffee-bibbers to Zeyd's menzil,
they asked for Khalîl, and "Let him show us Abu Zeyd and his
book of pictures;" these were a few prints in my book of medicine. Then they wondered to look through my telescope, in
which, levelling at any camel a mile distant, they saw her as it
were pasturing before their faces. Nevertheless, as a thing which
passed their minds, they did not learn to covet it; and yet to
sharpen their vision the best sighted of them, seeing as falcons,
would needs essay all my eye-washes; for there is no endowment
of nature so profitable to them in this life of the open wilderness.

Only the starveling hounds of the menzils, in these days, greedily swallowing up locusts, seemed to be in better plight, running
gaily in the encampment, sleeping with their fills, and now sul-
lenly careless of the Aarab. Their hounds, say the nomads, "bite
the wolf:" they waken all night whilst the Aarab slumber. With
the Fejîr, Beduins of a "camel dîra," the "wolf-eaters" are not
many, and those of currish kind, nearly like the street dogs of
Syria. The best I have seen with any Aarab, were the great
shagged dogs of Bíllî, in the Tehárma. The common nomad hound
is yellowish, shaped as the fox; the like is seen over most wild
parts of the world. A few Beduins have their greyhounds, light
with hunger, and very swift to course the hare; and by these the
gazelle fawn is taken. The common barkers of every Beduin village (for they go not out with the flocks), in tribes where the
house-mothers have little or no milk to give them, are carrion
lean, and in hunger-times they receive no sustenance of man's
hand but a little water: it were hard to say of what uncleanness
they then live. Only for a few days once in the long year they are
well refreshed: these are in the date-gathering at Kheybar, when
the fruit abounding in the Beduins' not improvident hands

(above that they may carry,) they give to the camels and asses their fill of dates, and fling also to their wretched hounds largely.

The hounds for their jealous service have never a good word. It is the only life mishandled at home by the gentle Aarab, who with spurns and blows cast out these profane creatures from the beyt, and never touch them (unless it be the unweaned whelps) with their hands. If any dog be an house-thief, a robber of human food, he is chased with hue and cry, and will be most cruelly beaten; the men swear great oaths 'he shall be dead, he has it well deserved.' This makes that the parasite creature, in these countries, is of more diffident behaviour, towards his masters: only to the nomad greyhound is granted, as of noble kind, to lie down in the booth. The hounds watch all day in the menzil, every one by his household, *ahlahu.* They follow in the ráhla with the baggage-train and their mistress; pacing, with a half reasonable gait, in the shadows of the lofty moving camels: impatient of heat and the sand burning under their paws, where they spy any shelter of crag or bush, there they will go in to pant awhile. At the alighting, the booth-cloth is hardly raised, when (if suffered—this is in the sheep-keeper tribes) they creep into the shadow and scrabble the hot sand, and dig with their paws under them, to make their lair upon the cool soil beneath. A dog strayed at the menzil, and running by strange tents, is hooted—*ahl-ak, ahl-ak!* 'to thy household, sirra!' The loud nomad dogs, worrying about the heels of all strange comers, are a sort of police of the nomad encampment. A few of them are perilous snatchers with their teeth; a man may come by, skirmishing with his camel-stick behind him, and the people call off their dogs. But if there be only hareem at home, which do but look on with a feminine malice, a stranger must beat them off with stone-casts. Some woman may then cry, "Oh! oh! wherefore dost thou stone our dog?" And he, "The accursed would have eaten me."—"But, O thou! cast not at him."—"Then call him in thou foolish woman and that quickly, or with this block now, I may happen to kill him."—"Eigh me! do not so, this eats the wolf, he watches for the enemy, he is the guard of our beyt and the ghrannem; I pray thee, no, not another stone."—"Mad woman, before he eat me I will break all the bones in his skin, and cursed be thy tongue! with less breath thou canst call him off!" In such case, I have not spared for stones, and the silly wife thought herself wronged; but the men answered, "It was well enough." The hareem, as to whom little is attributed, are naturally of infirmer reason, and liker children in the sentiment of honour; so there are tents, where the passing guest may not greatly trust them nor their children.

The sharp-set nomad hounds fall upon aught they may find abroad, as the baggage (when sometimes it is left without the booth) of any stranger guest: then they rend up all with their eager teeth and sharp claws; therefore to carry in the guests' bags is accounted a charitable deed. Men who are pilferers of others' provision, are often called "hounds" by the Beduins. Hirfa called one of these mornings at my tent door, "Where art thou, Khalîl? I go abroad, and wilt thou the while mind my household?"—"And whither will my hostess to-day?"—"I go to buy us yarn: Khalîl, open the eyes and beware, that there come no dogs to my beyt." When she returned some hours after, Hirfa came to chide me, "Ha! careless Khalîl, the dogs have been here! why hast thou not kept my beyt? and did I not bid thee?"—"I have watched for thee, Hirfa, every moment, by thy life! sitting before the booth in the sun, and not a hair of any dog has entered."—"Alas, Khalîl does not understand that 'the dogs' are men; tell me, Khalîl, who has been here whilst I was out?"—"There came two men, and when I saw them sheltering in thy apartment, I guessed them to be of kindred and acquaintance; could I suppose there would any tribesman steal from a tribesman's beyt?"—"But these have stolen, said she, a peck of dates, and all by thy fault." In the popular sort of nomads is little or no conscience to rob food (only); they holding it as common, kheyr Ullah.

The cheerful summer nights are cool from the sunset in these dry uplands. As they have supped, men wander forth to talk with neighbours, coffee drinkers seek the evening cup: in the mejlis coffee company, the Aarab gossip till midnight. Often in our men-zil only the herdsman remains at home, who wakens to his rough song the grave chord of the rabeyby.

Some moonlight evenings the children hied by us: boys and girls troop together from the mothers' beyts, and over the sand they leap to play at horses, till they find where they may climb upon some sand-hillock or rock. A chorus of the elder girls as-

semble hither, that with hand-clapping chant the same and ever
the same refrain, of a single verse. Little wild boys stripping off
their tunics, and flinging down kerchiefs, or that have left all in
the mothers' beyts, run out naked; there being only the *haggu*
wound about their slender loins: this is the plaited leathern rib-
bon, which is worn, and never left, by all the right Arabians, both
men and hareem. Every boy-horse has chosen a make, his *fáras*
or mare; they course hand in hand together, and away, away,
every pair skipping after other and are held themselves in chase
in the moonlight wilderness. He kicks back to the horses which
chevy after them so fast, and escapes again neighing. And this
pastime of Aarab children, of pure race, is without strife of en-
vious hearts, an angry voice is not heard, a blow is not struck
among them. The nomads are never brutal. This may last for an
hour or two: the younger men will sometimes draw to the merry-
make where the young maidens be: they frolic like great camels
amongst the small ghrannem; but not unclad, nor save with the
eyes approach they to that chanting bevy of young damsels; an
ill-blooded nature appearing in any young man, he shall have the
less estimation among them. After the child's age, these indolent
Arabians have not any kind of manly pastime among them. Of
Ahl Gibly, or southern nomads, I have not seen horsemen so
much as exercise themselves upon their mares. Child's play it
were in their eyes, to weary themselves, and be never the better.
They have none other sport than to fire off their matchlocks in
any household festivals. Herdsmen, they are naturally of the con-
templative life: weakly fed, there can be little flushing of gross
sanguine spirits in their veins, which might move them to manly
games; very rarely is any Beduin robust. Southward of Hâyil I
did not see any young woman with the rose blood in her cheeks;
even they are of the summer's drought, and palled at their fresh-
est age.

Now in the mild summer is the season of *muzayyins*, the nomad children's circumcision feasts: the mother's booth is set out
with beggarly fringes of scarlet shreds, tufts of mewed ostrich
feathers, and such gay gauds as they may borrow or find. Hither
a chorus assembles of slender daughters of their neighbours, that
should chant at this festival in their best array. A fresh kerchief
binds about every damsel's forehead with a feather; she has ear-

rings great as bracelets, and wears to-day her nose-ring, *zmèyem*: they are jewels in silver; and a few, as said, from old time are fine gold metal, *thahab el-asfr*. These are ornaments of the Beduin women, hardly seen at other times (in the pierced nostril, they wear for every day a head of cloves), and she has bracelets of beads and metal finger-rings. The thin black tresses loosed to-day and not long, hang down upon their slight shoulders, and shine in the sun, freshly combed out with camel urine. The lasses have borrowed new cloaks, which are the same for man or woman. Making a fairy ring apart, they begin, clapping the palms of their little hands, to trip it round together, chanting ever the same cadence of few words, which is a single verse. Hungered young faces, you might take them, for some gipsy daughters; wayward not seldom in their mother's households, now they go playing before men's eyes, with downcast looks and a virginal timidity. But the Aarab raillery is never long silent, and often the young men, in this daylight feast, stand jesting about them. Some even pluck roughly at the feathers of the lasses, their own near cousins, in the dance, which durst answer them nothing, but only with reproachful eyes: or laughing loud the weleds have bye and bye divided this gentle bevy among them for their wives; and if a stranger be there, they will bid him choose which one he would marry among them. "Heigh-ho! what thinkest thou of these maidens of ours, and her, and her, be they not fair-faced?" But the virgins smile not, and if any look up, their wild eyes are seen estranged and pensive. They are like children under the rod, they should keep here a studied demeanour; and for all this they are not Sirens. In that male tyranny of the Mohammedan religion regard is had to a distant maidenly behaviour of the young daughters; and here they dance as the tender candidates for happy marriage, and the blessed motherhood of sons. May their morrow approach! which shall be as this joyful day, whose hap they now sing, wherein a man-child is joined to the religion of Islam; it is better than the day of his birth. The nomad son is circumcised being come to the strength of three full years; and then as the season may serve without any superstition of days, and as the mother shall be able to provide corn or rice enough for her guests' supper. They sometimes put off the surgery till the morrow, in any rough windy weather, or because of the Aarab's ráhla.

The friends of the father will come in to be his guests: some of them have adorned themselves with the gunner's belt and gay baldric, rattling with the many little steel chains and brass powder-cases; and they bear upon their shoulders the long matchlocks. Therewith they would prove their hand to shoot, at the sheep's skull, which the child's *babbu* has sacrificed to 'the hospitality.' Every man kills his sacrifice, as in the ancient world, with his own hands, and the carcase is flayed and brittled with the Arabs' expedition. Nomads are all expert fleshers; the quarters hang now upon some bush or boughs, which wandering in an open wilderness, they have sought perhaps upon a far mountain side. As the sun goes low the meat is cast into the caldron, jidda. The great inwards remain suspended upon their trophy bush. After the flesh, a mess is cooked in the broth of such grain as they have. The sun setting, the maidens of the ring-dance disperse: the men now draw apart to their prayers, and in this time the cattle of every household are driven in. The men risen from their prayers, the supper is served in the tent: often thirty men's meat is in that shield-wide wooden platter which is set before them. A little later some will come hither of the young herdsmen returning boisterous from the field; they draw to the merry noise of the muzayyin that feel a lightness in their knees to the dance. A-row, every one his arm upon the next one's shoulder, these laughing weleds stand, full of good humour; and with a shout they foot it forth, reeling and wavering, advancing, recoiling in their chorus together; the while they hoarsely chant the ballad of a single verse. The housewives at the booth clap their palms, and one rising with a rod in her hand, as the dancing men advance, she dances out to meet them; it is the mother by likelihood, and joyously she answers them in her song; whilst they come on bending and tottering a-row together, with their perpetual refrain. They advancing upon her, she dances backward, feinting defence with the rod; her face is turned towards them, who maintain themselves, with that chanted verse of their manly throats, as it were pursuing and pressing upon her.—The nomads imagine even the necessity of circumcision: graziers, they will allege the examples of all cattle, that only in the son of Adam may be found this manner of impediment. When they questioned me I have said, "You can amend then the work of Ullah!"—"Of that we speak not, they answered, but only of the expediency." Questioned, What be the duties of a Moslem? they responded "That a man fast in the month, and recite his daily prayers;"—making no mention of the circumcision, which they call "purification."

The 15th of April, after a morning wind, blustering cold from the north-eastward, I found early in the afternoon, with still air and sunshine, the altitude being 4000 feet, 95 deg. F. in the booth's shelter. The drooping herb withered, the summer drought entering, the wilderness changed colour; the spring was ended. The Beduins removed and lodged in their desolate camps: upon a morrow, when the camels had been driven forth an hour, an alarm was given from the front, of gôm. A herdsman came riding in, who had escaped, upon a thelûl, and told it in the mejlis, "*él-'bil*, the camel-herds are taken." The sheukh rose from the hearth and left their cups with grave startled looks: all went hardily out, and hastily, to find their mares. Hovering haramîyeh had been seen yesterday, and now every man hied to take arms. The people ran, like angry wasps, from the booths: some were matchlock men, some had spears, all were afoot, save the horsemen sheykhs, and hastened forth to require their enemies, which could not be seen in that short desert horizon: bye and bye only the housewives, children and a few sick and old men were left in the encampment. Some asked me would I not ride to set upon the thieves: for Zeyd's talk had been that Khalîl would foray with them. "Khalîl (cried the housewives), look for us in your wise books; canst thou not prophesy by them (*shûf fil ghraib*): read thou and tell us what seest thou in them of these gomânies.—A punishment fall upon them! they certainly espied the people's watch-fires here this last night, and have been lurking behind yonder mountain until the camels were driven out."—The long morning passed over us, in the cold incertitude of this misadventure.

Motlog had ridden days before to Hâyil to treat with the emir, and left Rahŷel to govern the tribe; a man of perplexed mind in this sudden kind of conjuncture. The armed tribesmen returning

after midday, we went to sit in the mejlis and talk over this mis-
hap. I heard no word spoken yet of pursuing; and enquiring of
my neighbour, "Ay, they would mount their thelûls, said he, so
soon as the 'bil were come home at evening;" for all the great
cattle were not taken, but those which had been driven forth
from the north side of the menzil. Celerity is double strokes in
warfare, but these Beduins sat still the long day and let the robbers run, to wonder what they were; they all said, "some Aarab
of the North," for they had seen them armed with pistols. They
reasoned whether those should be Sherarát or Howeytát Ibn
Jàsy (Beduins from about Maan); or else of the Ruwàlla. "Hear
me, and I shall make it known to you, said Zeyd (who had this
vanity among them), what they were. I say then, *es-Sokhûr*,
and ye shall find it true." The few words which had fallen from
the foemen's lips were now curiously examined. They had challenged the camel herds, "What Aarab be ye—ha! the Fejîr?" but
this could not suffice to distinguish the *loghrat* of a tribe. The
gôm were thirteen horsemen, and twenty riders upon thelûls. In
driving off the booty a mare broke loose from them, and she was
led into the encampment, but of that nothing could be learned,
the nomad sheykhs not using to brand their horses with the tribe's
cattlemark. This mare, by the third day, perished of thirst! that
none would pour out to her of their little water. If a tribesman's
goat stray among them, and her owner be not known, none will
water her. In the time when I was with them, I saved the lives of
a strayed beast or two, persuading some of my patients to give
them drink.

They now reckoned in the mejlis the number of camels taken,
saying over the owners' names: Zeyd kept count, scoring a new
line for every ten in the sand; so he told them and found six
score and seven camels—the value of £600 or more. All this
tribe's camels were not so many as 2000, nor I think fully 1500;
and the whole fortune of the Fukara Beduins in the field, two
hundred households, their great and small cattle with the booths
and utensils, I suppose, not to exceed £17,000. Besides which is
their landed patrimony at Kheybar, that may be worth £7000
more. A household of these poor southern Beduins may thus, I
think, possess the capital value of £120 sterling; and much like
to them are their nomad neighbours about. In the same small

tribe there are nobles and commons, the sufficient livelihood, and
the pittance, and abject misery. The great sheykh Motlog, possessing more than other men, had not so many of his own as
twenty-five camels. There is difference also between tribe and
tribe: the great tribes of the north, as the Annezy in Syria, and
the northern Shammar upon Mesopotamia, wandering in plente-
ous country, are rich in cattle and horses: so also may be reckoned Kahtân and *Ateyby* of the southern tribes, (their dîras we
shall see are watered by the yearly monsoon;) but these middle
tribes of nomads, in a rainless land, are "weaker." Those at the
haj road which receive a surra, are the most coffee-lazing, beggarly and pithless minded of them all. The Fejîr sheukh divided
between them, every year, I think about £600 of these payments! whereof almost an hundred pounds fell to Zeyd, who received his father's surra, and £160 to Motlog: besides some
changes of clothing, grain, and certain allowances for their tents,
and utensils; yet poor they all were, and never the better. Motlog's halàl, or 'lawful own' of cattle, his mare, and his tent and
household gear together, were worth, I think, not £300: add to
this for his funded property at Kheybar, and we may find he
possessed hardly above £500.

The Aarab trifled time which could never be theirs again; the
housewives made some provision ready for those that should
mount at evening. This mounting is at every man's free will, and
yet the possessor of a thelûl cannot shun the common service
and keep his honest name. Rahŷel led the pursuit. Some as they
sat boasted, "This night or towards morning, when the haramîyeh
think themselves come in security, and are first reposing, we
shall be suddenly upon them, and recover our own, if the Lord
will, and take their beasts from under them." As camels are driven
off in a foray, the robbers chase them all that day at a run before
them, hoping to outgo the pursuit; and now as the sun was setting, these might be gotten almost fifty miles in advance. The last
words were, as they rose, "Please God, every camel of those taken
shall be couched again, to-morrow about this time, before the
booth of his household:" and with this good augury the company
dispersed, going to their suppers, and afterward the riders would
take their thelûls, the sheykhs (for a long pursuit) not leading
their mares with them. Zeyd sat still at home; he had two thelûls,

he said "they were ailing." Khálaf sat also close in his booth, a man who, though vaunting his mare's worth at so many camels and himself of the principal W. Aly sheykhs, had not a beast to mount. A weak reason is found too light in the balance of public estimation; and Zeyd all the next day sitting melancholy, sipping much coffee, vehemently protested to be ever since sorry, by Ullah, that he was not ridden along with them.

His camels were saved that day, feeding on the other side of the desert; but a calamity as this is general, and to be borne by the tribe. None which had lost their cattle to-day would be left destitute; but the governing sheykh taxing all the tribesmen, the like would be rendered to them, out of the common contribution, in a day or two. He will send some round as assessors to the menzils, where every man's state being known, the computation is made of the cattle of every household. There was levied of Zeyd the next day, of less than twenty that he had, a camel, and the value of certain head of small cattle. The nomad tribes we have seen to be commonwealths of brethren, ruled by their sheykhs with an equitable moderation. They divide each others' losses, and even in such there is community between whole tribes. Mischief is never far from them, an evil day may chance which has not befallen them in many years, when a tribe is stripped at a stroke, of nearly all its cattle, as later in my knowledge, the Moahîb.—And what then? The next Bílli of free-will gave them, of their own, much cattle.

If cattle be robbed of any strangers dwelling in the tribe, the tribesmen are not bound, as neither upon those should fall any contribution for the losses of their hosts: yet there are magnanimous tribes, (I have heard it told of Shammar,) that will give somewhat, of free-will, to him who has long time lived in fellowship amongst them, in his afflicted case. If any villager has entrusted beasts to a nomad, to graze with his own cattle, and they are reaved by the tribe's enemies, the villager will demand his own, and scurvily attach the Beduwy, as his debtor, if he may take him again in his village: but the Beduwy, whose law does not bind him to such restitutions, will be ware, and no more adventure thither. These controversies are long-lived, and often the old grudges are inherited among them, to the third generation.—The law of Israel is for the villager in this case, and enjoins the grazier's restitution of the entrusted cattle. There is also amongst Beduins a loss without remedy, when a man's beasts are taken and the sheykhs in the mejlis find that the loss is his own, and not in the public adventure of the tribe. The unhappy tribesman bitterly calls his sheykhs unjust, he is bare and they will not repair his undoing out of the public stock: I have known some such, sad men for life. I have known also well-faring Beduins suddenly come to poverty, when their camels had all died of a murrain. As in the whole world, so among this poor folk, it is much, in the evil day, to be well befriended. At the good and liberal man's need, every one of his fellowship will bring him a head of the flock in his hand; so may he come to a little strength again.

Their ghrazzus and counter-ghrazzus are the destruction of the Aarab. Reaving and bereaved they may never thrive; in the end of every tide it is but an ill exchange of cattle. So in the eyes of nomads, the camel troops of the Fukara were all "mingled" cattle and uneven, that is, not home-born-like, but showing to be robbed beasts out of several dîras. Motlog's son said to me, he who should be great sheykh after him, "Ay, wellah! all our camels are harrâm, (of prey taken in the forays,) and not our lawful own." The Fejîr were impoverished of late years, by their neighbours' incursions: Bishr, and after them the W. Aly, had taken their flocks; but they lost most by a murrain, in these hot sandy marches, a kind of colic, in which there had died nearly all the remnant of their small cattle. A year before, Zeyd had a great mixed herd of goats and sheep, so that Hirfa, the last spring time, made a camel load and a half (as much as £18 worth) of samn. Now I saw but an ewe and two milch goats left to them, which yielded in the day but a short bowl of milk, and, discouraged, he would not buy more. Zeyd had inherited of his father, who was the former great sheykh's brother, a large landed patrimony of palm-stems at Kheybar: the half fruit being to the negro husbandmen, his own rent was, he told me, nearly 200 reals. Thus Zeyd, with his surra, had spending silver for every day, in good years, of nearly two reals, the value of a goat, which is much money in the khála: yet the man was miserable, and loving to defer payments, he was always behind the hand with old usury. Sheykhs of the B. Wáhab lay up their money, *tháhab*, (spared from the haj surra,) at el-Ally; out of this, one who is low will increase his "halàl" silently, and may sometime go to the bottom of his bag to purchase him a new mare.

Rahŷel's pursuing party was three nights out. The men left in camp being now very few, they came continually together to drink coffee. The affectionate housewives sat abroad all day watching: at mid-afternoon, the fourth after, we heard the hareem's jubilee, *lullilu!*—but the merry note died away in their throats when, the longer they looked, they saw those that came riding in the horizon were leading nothing home with them. The men rose together, and going forth, they gazed fixedly. "What, said they, means this cry of the hareem? for look, they arrive empty-handed, and every man is riding apart to alight at his own household!" so returning to their fatal indolence, they re-entered as men that are losers, and sat down again. "Some of them, they said, will presently bring us tidings." Rahŷel soon after dismounted at his tent, pitched near behind us.—The house-wife comes forth as her husband makes his thelûl kneel; she receives him in silence, unsaddles the beast, and carries in his gear. The man does not often salute her openly, nor, if he would to the mejlis, will he speak to his wife yet; so Rahŷel, without entering his booth, stepped over to us.—"Peace be with you!" said he from a dry throat, and seating himself with the sigh of a weary man, in some sadness, he told us, 'that in the second day, following the enemy upon the Nefûd, they came where a wind had blown out the prints,' and said he, "So Ullah willed it!" They turned then their beasts' heads,—they had no list to cast further about, to come again upon the robbers' traces. "Ha well! God would have it so!" responded the indolent Aarab. A weak enemy they thus faintly let slip through their fingers, for a little wind, though these were driving with them nearly a tithe of all their camels. But Rahŷel, to knit up his sorry tale with a good ending, exclaimed, "Wellah, they had found water at the wells el-Hŷza in the Nefûd; and as they came again by Teyma, he heard word that some of the gôm had touched there, and they were of the Sherarát:"—Rahŷel, with his troop, had ridden nearly two hundred idle miles. "Bye and bye we shall know (said the Beduins) which tribesmen robbed our camels; then will we *ghrazzy* upon them, and God willing, take as many of them again." But the ghrazzus often return empty: a party of Fukara, "twenty *rikáb*" or warfaring thelûls, which rode lately upon the Beny Atîeh, had taken nothing.

Every man leans upon his own hand in the open desert, and there will none for naught take upon him a public service. The sheykh may persuade, he cannot compel any man; and if the malcontent will go apart, he cannot detain them. The common body is weak, of members so loosely knit together, and there befalls them many an evil hap, which by a public policy might have been avoided.—"Why send you not out scouts, (thus I reasoned with Zeyd,) which might explore the khála in advance of your pasturing cattle? or cannot you set some to watch in the tops of the rocks, for the appearing of an enemy! Why commit yourselves thus to wild hazard, who are living openly in the midst of danger?" When Zeyd gravely repeated my words in the mejlis, the sheykh's son answered readily, "Ay, and that were very well, if we might put it in practice; but know, Khalîl, there are none of the Beduw will thus adventure themselves by twos or threes together, for fear of the habalîs, we cannot tell where they lie until thou hearest from behind a crag or bush *deh*! and the shot strikes thee."

Later in the week Motlog came again from Hâyil: he had not before been thither, nor his companions; but they crossed an hundred miles over the open khála guided by sight only of the mountain landmarks, which they had enquired beforehand. We had shifted ground many times in his absence; and it was strange for me to see them ride in, without having erred, to our menzil. As the journeys of the tribesmen are determined beforehand, they might reckon within a day's distance, where riding they should fall upon our traces, which finding they will follow the fresh footing of our late ráhla; and climbing on all heights as they come, they look for the black booths of their Aarab. Thus these land-navigators arrive bye and bye at the unstable village port of their voyage. All the tribesmen which were not abroad herding, assembled to parliament, where they heard Motlog was gone down, to his brother Rahŷel's tent, to hear their sheykh give account of his embassy to the emir, which imported so much to the policy of their little desert nation.—Every man had armed his hand with the tobacco pipe, and, said each one arriving, "Strengthen thee, O Motlog!" and to the great sheykh he handed up his galliûn. Motlog sat freshly before them, in his new apparel, the accustomed gift of the emir, and he filled all their pipe-heads benignly, with the aromatic tittun *el-Hameydy* of Mesopotamia; of which he had brought with him a few weeks' cheer, from the village capital. The coffee was slowly served round, to so great an assembly. Burdensome was that day's heat, and now the mid-day's sun overhead, yet there was none who thought of going to his slumber, or even to eat; such was all the people's expectation to hear the mind of the terrible emir. They sat this day out, no man moving from his place, and yet fasting, except only from coffee and tittun, till the evening.—The prince licensed them to return, without fear, into their own dîra.

The vassals of Ibn Rashîd receive, after the audience, a change of clothing; besides, the emir bestowed sixty silver reals upon Motlog, and gave ten pieces to each of his way-fellows. These are arts of the Arabian governors, to retain, with a pretended bounty, the slippery wills of the wild Beduw; and well sown is the emir's penny, if he should reap, in the next years, ten-fold. Motlog was sheykh of one of the tributary tribes, a little wide of his reach. The tax upon the nomads is light, and otherwise it could never be gathered; a crown piece is payment for every five camels, or for thirty head of small cattle. Of the Fukara was levied thus but four hundred reals, which is somewhat as eight or nine shillings for every household: yet the free-born, forlorn and predatory Beduw grimly fret their hearts under these small burdens; the emir's custom is ever untimely, the exaction, they think, of a stronger, and plain tyranny: yet yielding this tribute, they become of the prince's federation, and are sheltered from all hostility of the Aarab in front. Motlog was a prudent man of reach and sight; but he could not see through sixty reals. This was a pleasant policy of the emir, and by the like the wisest man's heart is touched; and the nomad sheykh brought back, in his new-smelling clothes, a favourable opinion for the while, of the flattering prince, and Hâyil government; and thought in his heart, to be the prince's liegeman, for the present, of whom he had received so gentle entertainment. But the haughty Mo-

hammed Ibn Rashîd, who paid the scot, had another opinion of
him; the emir afterward told me, with his own mouth, that he
misliked this Motlog.

Blithe were the Fukara to return to their home marches, and
better to them than all this high desolate country, which (said
they) is 'ghror, a land wherein is nothing good, for man nor cattle.' Also, they think that dîra better, by which the derb el-haj
passes; they say, "We have a kella," that is a house of call, and
store-chambers, the caravan market is held there, and their
sheukh receive surra. On the morrow we marched; and the Beduins henceforth removed every day by short journeys; now their
face was homeward. Behind us we left J. Misma, then some
mountain which I heard named *Roaf*: the third day we came
to drink upon the upland, at a wide standing water, in a gravel
bed, which in winter is a lake-plash, of the ponded rain, *Therrai*.

We marched then in a sandstone country, where, for crags,
thick as loaves in a baker's oven, we could not see the next riders
about us. From the fifth march, we alighted again under Birrd,
to water, in the natural deep chaps of the precipitous sandstone
mountain: the herdsmen, digging shallow pits with their hands
in the fetid sand, took up in buckets, with their waterer's song, a
sandy foul water. We removed now daily, loading before dawn,
and alighting at high noon. In another march we came, under the
flaming sun, over the high open plain, a barren floor of gravel,
towards a great watering place and summer station of the tribe,
el-Erudda. These uplands are mostly without growth of the desert
acacia trees: woe is therefore the housewife, for any tent-peg
lost in the ráhla. Yet now appeared a long line of acacias, and a
white swelling country, these are the landmarks of el-Erudda;
and here, at the midst of their dîra, is a *mákbara*, or common
burying-place of the tribe, with few barren plants of wild palms.
It is hardly a journey from hence to el-Héjr: the Beduins would
be here umjemmîn, for many days.

Camels strayed the next night from Zeyd's menzil; the owners
scoured the country, hoping to have sight of them, for where all
the soil was trodden down with innumerable footprints of the
tribe's cattle, they could not distinguish the traces. It was not
that they feared their beasts, losing themselves, must in few days
perish with thirst: the great dull and sheeplike cattle have a per-

fect conscience of all watering places of their home dîra; though, for all their long necks, in but very few of them might they attain to drink. Three years before, when the Fukara were in Syria, some camels of theirs, frayed and lost near the Hauran, had been recovered by tribesmen returning later in the year from Medina, who, crossing their own dîra, found those beasts feeding about a watering, in the border of the Hejâz. The men knew them, by the brand, to be some of their tribe's cattle, and brought up again those fugitive camels, which had fled to their native marches, over seven geographical degrees.

We had no more notice of the haramîyeh.—Then, by a Solubby family which arrived from over the Harra, there came uncertain tidings, that their cattle had been retaken by the Moahîb: a small Moahîb foray riding in the north had crossed the robbers; (hostile ghrazzus, meeting in the wilderness, hail each other, *ya gôm!* "ho! ye enemies,") but not able to overtake the main body of them, they had cut off but fifteen camels. The custom of one real salvage, for a head, is paid between friendly tribes, and they are restored to the owners.

At length we understood that the robbers, as Zeyd foretold, had been a party of Beny Sókhr, who from their tents in Syria, to the place where they met with us had ridden out not less than four hundred miles; and in their company there rode a few men of the Sherarát nomads who are part friends, part "not well" with the Fejîr. As for the Sokhûr, our Beduins reckoned them hitherto neither friends nor enemies; yet certain Fukara households, of the northern migration, were wandering with that tribe to this day. A ragged rout of B. Sókhr, carriers to the Haj, must every year pass, with the caravan, through the Fukara country.—On behalf of the Fejîr, a young sheykh, *Mijwel*, was sent after this to the North, to treat peaceably with the B. Sókhr for the restitution of his tribe's camels. The elders of B. Sókhr responded in the mejlis, "They that had reaved the Fukara cattle were a company of ignorant young men; but their ignorance to be less blameworthy because they found the Fejîr wandering out of their own dîra." The sheykhs promised that good part of the cattle should be brought again with the Haj; the rest they would have conceded to the turbulent young men, "which must be appeased, with somewhat for their pains, and that for an end of

strife." More might not Mijwel obtain: and this is as much justice
as may commonly be had in the world.

Now, arrived at el-Erudda, my mind was to forsake the Beduin
life and pass by el-Ally to the sea coast at el-Wejh. My friends
bade me speak with Motlog in the matter of my camel. Why did
not Zeyd obey the pasha's injunction?—and then this mischief
had not chanced. I had not the price of another camel,—hard must
be my adventure henceforth in land of Arabia. The custom of the
desert is that of Moses, 'If any man's beast hurt the beast of another man, the loss shall be divided.' Frolic in the succulent spring
herbage, the great unwieldy brutes rise in the night with full cuds
to play their whale-sports together; some camel then, as the Beduins held, had fallen upon the neck of my gaping young camel:
whether it happened then, or in the camels' bouncing forth to
their morning pasture, it was among Zeyd's troop of camels. I
must bring witnesses: but who would give testimony against a
sheykh of his tribe, for the Nasrâny? Amongst Mohammedans,
and though they be the Beduins of the wilderness, there is equity
only between themselves. I found Motlog in his tent, who with
a woollen thread was stitching in his mare's saddle-pad. "A pity,
said the sheykh, that any controversy should grow betwixt Khalîl
and Zeyd, who were brethren, but the Pasha's words ought to
have been observed." Zeyd was disappointed in me of his greedy
hopes; fortune had given us both checkmate since the hope of
my vaccination had failed; there remained only my saddle-bags,
and his eyes daily devoured them. Great they were, and stuffed
to a fault, in a land where passengers ride without baggage.
Heavy Zeyd found their draught, and he felt in them elbow-deep
day by day, which was contrary to the honourable dealing of an
host;—besides my apprehension that he might thus light upon my
pistol and instruments, which lay hidden at the bottom in our
menzils.

For these displeasures, in a last ráhla I had forsaken Zeyd, and
came on walking over the waste gravel, under the scalding sun
many miles till the Aarab alighted. Zeyd found in his heart that
he had done me wrong, I had not deceived him, and he respected
my person: I also heedfullly avoided to rake up the wild unknown
depths of their Mohammedan resentment. I entered Motlog's
tent, the sheykhly man sat playing with his children, he was a

very affectionate father. Thither came Zeyd soon and sat down
to drink coffee; then raising his portentous voice said he, "If I
had not intended to devour him, wellah, I had not received the
Nasrâny; I would not have suffered him to accompany the Aarab,
no not in a ráhla. The Nasrâny gave sixty reals (a fable) to Mohammed Aly, and I require the like to be paid me in this hour."
"No, (Motlog answered from behind the women's curtain, whither
he was gone for somewhat,) this is not in thy hand, O Zeyd."
Zeyd, complaining that my being in his menzil was an expense
to him, I proved that Zeyd had received of me certain reals, and
besides a little milk I had taken of him nothing: but his meaning
was that I brought too many coffee guests, who all came thither
to see the stranger. Zeyd had bought two reals worth in the haj
market. "Here (I said) is that money, and let Zeyd trust further
to my friendly possibility. Zeyd complains of me with little cause;
I might complain with reason; should one treat his guest's baggage as thing which is taken in the ghrazzu? he seeks even in
my purse for money, and in my belt, and ransacks my bags."—
"Ha! how does Zeyd?" said some sheykh's voice. I answered, in
my haste, "Billah, like an hablûs." Motlog shrank at the word,
which had been better unsaid; the Beduins doubted if they heard
Khalîl aright: the worst was that Zeyd in all his life came so near
to merit this reproachful word, which uttered thus in the mejlis,
must cleave to him in the malicious memory of his enemies. He
rose as he had sipped the cup and left us. In our evening mirth
the hinds often called to each other, hablûs! hablûs! which
hearing, and I must needs learn their speech of the Arabs, I had
not supposed it amiss: but Zeyd vaunted himself sherîf. When
he was gone out some said, so had Zeyd done to such and such
other, Zeyd was a bad man; (the Beduw easily blame each
other). Said Motlog, 'in the question of the camel I must bring
witnesses, but he would defend me from all wrongful demands
of Zeyd.'

As we sat, one came in who but then returned from an absence;
as the custom is he would first declare his tidings in the mejlis,
and afterward go home to his own household. He sat down on
his knee, but was so poor a man, there was none in the sheykhly
company that rose to kiss him: with a solemn look he stayed him
a moment on his camel-stick, and then pointing gravely with it

to every man, one after other, he saluted him with an hollow voice, by his name, saying, "The Lord strengthen thee!" A poor old Beduin wife, when she heard that her son was come again, had followed him over the hot sand hither; now she stood to await him, faintly leaning upon a stake of the beyt a little without, since it is not for any woman to enter where the men's mejlis is sitting. His tidings told, he stepped abroad to greet his mother, who ran, and cast her weak arms about his manly neck, trembling for age and tenderness, to see him alive again and sound; and kissing him she could not speak, but uttered little cries. Some of the coffee-drinkers laughed roughly, and mocked her drivelling, but Motlog said, "Wherefore laugh? is not this the love of a mother?"

Selím came soon to call me from his father; "Well, go with Selím, said Motlog, and be reconciled to Zeyd; and see that neither require aught of the other." Zeyd invited me into his wife's closed apartment, where we sat down, and Hirfa with us, to eat again the bread and salt together. Zeyd soon returned from these rubs, when he could not find his 'brother' in fault, to the Beduin good humour, and leaning on his elbow he would reach over, pledge of our friendship, the peaceable sebîl, I should 'drink' with him tobacco:—and such are the nomads. Our late contention was no more mentioned, but it was long after branded in Zeyd's mind, that Khalîl had called him hablûs. In the autumn of this year, when the Fukara lay encamped at el-Héjr, and I was again with them, as I passed by Zeyd's menzil, he called me from the beyt, "*ya Khalîl taal!* come hither," I greeted him, and also the housewife behind the curtain "*gowwich Hirfa*, the Lord strengthen thee."—Zeyd answered, "It is the voice of Khalîl, and the words of a Beduwy;" and he rose to bring me in to eat a bowl of rice with him, which was then ready. After meat, "he was glad to see me, he said, once more here in his beyt, it was like the old times;" then a little casting down his eyes he added, "but after our friendship I was wounded, Khalîl, when you named me hablûs, and that before the sheukh."—"Because you had threatened and displeased me; but, Zeyd, let not this trouble thee; how could I know all the words of you Beduins? Seest thou these black worsted tents? Are they not all booths of hablûses?" We walked

down to the mejlis, where Zeyd related, smiling, that my meaning
had been but to name him "thou Beduwy."

—When I reasoned with Zeyd, "Why didst thou not do as the
Pasha commanded?" cried he, "Who commands me! *henna* (we
are) *el-Beduw*: what is Pasha, or what is the Dowla here? save
only that they pay us our surra, and else we would take it by
force."—"What is your force? were an hundred of you, with club-
sticks, lances, and old matchlocks, worth ten of the haj soldiery?"
—"We would shoot down upon them in the boghrazát." "And
how far may your old rusty irons shoot?" Zeyd answered, between jest and solemnity, "*Arbaa saa,*" to four hours distance:
Saat is with the Aarab 'a stound,' a second or third space between
the times of prayer. Often they asked me, "How many hours be
there in the day? We know not well *saa.*" Their partitions of the
daylight are *el-féjr*, the dawning before the sun; *el-gaila*, the sun
rising towards noon; *eth-thóhr*, the sun in the mid-day height;
el-assr, the sun descended to mid-afternoon; *ghraibat es-shems*,
the sun going down to the setting—*mághrib* is a strange town
speaking in their ears.

The nomads' summer station at el-Erudda was now as an un-
cheerful village. In the time of wandering since the Haj, the
sheykhs had spent their slender stores of coffee; and "where no
coffee is, there is not merry company," say the Aarab. Their coffee
hearths now cold, every man sat drooping and dull, *fi ahlahu*,
in his own household. Said Zeyd, "This was the life of the old
nomads in the days before coffee." The sheukh would soon send
down for more coffee of theirs which was stored at Medáin; and
Zeyd must go thither to fetch up a sack of rice, which he had
also deposited in the kella: I would then ride with him, intend-
ing to pass by el-Ally to the Red Sea coast. The wilderness
fainted before the sunny drought; the harvest was past, and I
desired to be gone. The Aarab languished lying in the tents; we
seemed to breathe flames. All day I gasped and hardly remained
alive, since I was breathless, and could not eat. I had sometimes
a thought in the long days to teach Selím letters: but when his
son had learned the alphabet Zeyd would no more, lest the child
should take of me some faulty utterance; my tongue he said was
not yet "loosed." Having a vocabulary in my hand, now and

then I read out a page or two to the company. Certainly I could
not err much in the utterance of many words that were before
well known to me; but no small part of these town and bookish
terms were quite unknown to all my nomad hearers! of some it
seemed they had not the roots, of many they use other forms.
They wondered themselves, and as Arabs will (who have so
much feeling in their language and leisure to be eloquent) considered word after word with a patient attention. Thus when
simple tribesmen come sometime in their lives to enter any good
town in the border-lands, the city speech sounds wonderfully
quaint in their hearing, 'they wot hardly, they complain, what
these townspeople should mean.' The bookish speech is raised
upon the old koran Arabic, which was a lowland language, and
never perhaps the tongue of the upland Aarab.

The evening before our departure, Mehsan had sacrificed a
sheep, the year's-mind of his father here lying buried, and
brought us of his cooked meat; he was Zeyd's brother-in-law, and
we were a homely company. I made them sweet tea; and distributed presents of the things which I had. As we sat I asked
these Beduins if my *gaûd* (young camel) with the broken mouth
could carry me a hundred and fifty miles to el-Wejh? One sitting
with us proffered, so I would give him ten reals, to exchange his
own nâga for mine. Zeyd and Mehsan approving, I gave the
money; but the meditations of the Arabs are always of treachery.
The poor man's wife and children also playing the weepers, I
gave them besides all that I might spare of clothing, of which
they have so much need in the desert; but after other days I saw
my things put to sale at Teyma. I bought thus upon their trust, a
dizzy camel, old, and nearly past labour and, having lost her
front teeth, that was of no more value, in the sight of the nomads,
than my wounded camel. I was new in their skill; the camels are
known and valued after their teeth, and with regard to the hump.
They are named by the teeth till the coming of the canines in
this manner: the calf of one year, *howwar*; of two, *libny*; the
third, *hej*; the fourth, *jitha*; the fifth, *thènny*; the sixth, *ròbba*; the
seventh, *siddes*; and the eighth, *shâgg en-naba, wafîat, mùfter*.

LOUISE E. SWEET

14. Camel Raiding of North Arabian Bedouin: A Mechanism of Ecological Adaptation[1]

I. INTRODUCTION

The Bedouin camel breeding peoples of Arabia are among the most conspicuous in the public tradition of romanticized warrior nomads, but among the least used in current ethnological theory. Yet they inhabit a desert zone marked by varying and extreme geographical conditions for human survival and display in their modes of adaptation a wealth of features useful for developing cultural ecological theory. Moreover, their contiguity with regions occupied over millennia by complex states provides a host of problems of intercultural adaptations. Most prominent among these, perhaps, has been the persistence and elaboration of kinship as the organizing basis of these desert societies. This paper is concerned with examining some of the features and adaptive functions of one of the core mechanisms of Bedouin socio-cultural systems, institutionalized raiding, as a major factor in the persistence of such kin-based societies.[2]

Reprinted by permission of the American Anthropological Association from the American Anthropologist, Vol. 67, pp. 1132–50 (1965).
[1] The original version of this paper was read at the Northeastern Anthropological Conference, April 13–15, 1962, at the University of Toronto, Toronto, Canada. I am indebted to the following colleagues for comments and criticisms of the original paper: Drs. Robert Carneiro, Leon J. Goldstein, Anthony Leeds, Peter Kunstadter, and Stephen A. Vayda. Contributing data from field work in Kuwait was gathered during 1958–59, supported by a grant from the Social Science Research Council and facilitated by the hospitality of the State of Kuwait and the Kuwait Oil Company.

[2] No cultural anthropologist as such has made a participant observation study of a camel breeding Bedouin tribe of North Arabia. The material that is available comes from the exploratory work of commercial or political agents, Orientalists, historical or human geographers, and "adventurers." The line of descent for this paper begins with the little read work of John

Raiding is variously regarded as a sport, a passion, an industry by Western writers; it has been labelled brigandage, feuding, and warfare, and has been denounced and deplored, and rarely admired. But few serious students of Bedouin life have failed to appreciate its significance for the Bedouin, regardless of the moral or political stand from which the writers might evaluate it. Burckhardt, for example commented upon the precariousness of wealth in camel herds among the Bedouin, the rapid changes of individual fortunes as parties of men raided and counterraided each other's encampments. But he also calculated in monetary terms the cost of living as a Bedouin camel pastoralist. He concluded:

> It may almost be said, that the Arabs are obliged to rob and pillage. Most families of the Anezes are unable to defray the annual expenses from the profits on their cattle, and few Arabs would sell a cattle to purchase provisions: he knows, from experience, that to continue long in a state of peace, diminishes the wealth of an individual; war and plunder therefore become necessary. The sheikh is obliged to lead his Arabs against the enemy, if there be one; if not it can easily be contrived to make one (Burckhardt 1831:I, 71–72).

Likewise, Charles Doughty, one of the very few Westerners who lived with Bedouin, noted an economic aspect of raiding:

Lewis Burckhardt (1831) who travelled in the area and talked to many informants between 1820 and 1830, and continues through the Italian agent Guarmani (1938) who moved through the desert to Anaiza, central Arabia, in 1851, the Blunts (1896), Charles Doughty (1936) and others, mostly British. The early twentieth century work of the Czech historical geographer, Alois Musil, although easily available, is not easy to use, but it is far more fruitful and informative than that of many of the others. Musil (1926, 1927, 1928a, 1928b) and the French human geographers (DeBoucheman 1934; Montagne 1932, 1935, 1947; and Müller 1931) and Dickson (1949, 1956) are the last and latest reliable sources on traditional Bedouin culture.

The time span of recurrent, if diverse, observation stretches from about 1825 to about 1930, with few first-hand accounts after that. The writer was able in 1958–59 in Kuwait, to interview a number of pastoral Arab tribesmen. Some of the scant material on raiding customs from one informant, a man of Dawsiri-Ajman descent, is part of the background stimuli for this paper, but it was second-hand material and referred essentially to how the informant would have expected to act "in the older times" when raiding was a chief concern of tribal chiefdom, clan, and man.

"Their ghrazzus ["raids"] and counter-ghrazzus are the destruction of the Arab. Reaving and bereaved they may never thrive; in the end of every tide it is but an ill exchange of cattle. So in the eyes of nomads, the camel troops of the Fukara were all 'mingled' cattle and uneven, that is not home-born-like, but showing to be robbed beasts out of several diras [tribal chiefdom territories]" (Doughty 1936:I, 391).

Western writers, especially those following Doughty, have tended to emphasize the military aspects, the piracy and pillaging traits, the all-consuming preoccupation with "loot," the chivalry toward women. But Palgrave, who moved in caravan as a townsman through Bedouin territories in 1862–63, contributes from the earlier writers a comment upon raiding which completes the list of general features, a list which has only been added to in detail by others. Palgrave's comment on the raiding of Bedouin tribes is as follows:

> Their feuds are continual, but at little cost of life; the main object of a raid is booty, not slaughter; and the Bedouin, though a terrible braggart, has at heart little inclination for killing or being killed. . . . His only object in War is the temporary occupation of some bit of miserable pasture-land or the use of a brackish well; perhaps the desire to get such a one's horse or camel into his possession—all objects which imply little animosity, and, if not attained in the campaign can easily be made up for in other ways, nor entail the bitterness and cruelty that attend or follow civil and religious strife (Palgrave 1871:23).

Palgrave did not understand tribal chiefdom structure and its consequent values and loyalties; he did explain the peculiarly non-lethal character of these "feuds" by the lack of national loyalties,—the Bedouin had "no home" to fight for, "no country," "no honor," "no religion."

Apart from the biases or special interests of Burckhardt, Palgrave and Doughty, expressed in these three quotations, salient features of Bedouin raiding are set forth which still await explanation. In brief, these are: (1) raids by the tribes are a continual practice; (2) raids are mutually prosecuted among the tribes, as well as made against settled communities and caravans of merchants or pilgrims; (3) raids are predatory preeminently for camels, avoid destruction of human life, and do not seize territory permanently; (4) raids exchange or circulate camels widely among the tribes; and (5) raids are necessary in an economic sense and perhaps in other senses for Bedouin survival. These aspects of Bedouin raiding, long recognized but not further explored, suggest that the warlike reputations and practices of nomadic pastoral peoples are inadequately understood if they are explained as predatory or political mechanisms alone. The tales of great and remunerative raids against distant tribes form, says Müller, the history of the tribe for the tribesman (1931:158). But there is much more to be said.

II. THE NORTH ARABIAN CULTURAL "ECOSYSTEM"

The northern third of the Arabian peninsula was dominated for perhaps 3000 years (roughly 1200 B.C. to 1900 A.D.) by a congeries of nomadic pastoral societies specializing in camel breeding. Most prominent among these in recent centuries have been the Anazah group of tribes of the Hamad and Syrian Desert, the Shammar tribes of the northern Nejd, and such others as the Mutair and Ajman of the east near Kuwait and Al Hasa and the Beni Sakhr to the west (Jordan). They are among the *'asiil* ("noble") Arabs; that is, they have positions in the great traditional scheme of Arabian tribal genealogies which effectively distinguish them from non-*'asiil* Arabs, particularly in their range of dominance, and which contribute to their elite position in the desert.[3] These, following their own definition, I designate specifically as the Bedouin. It is, however, the integration of the institutions of Bedouin camel pastoralism and tribal chiefdom structures of ranked lineages, united by the ideology of common and exclusive descent, in a system effecting dominance which sets these peoples apart from other societies in the same region. The primary use-

[3] The genealogies are, in fact, recorded; they formed in medieval times a branch of Islamic Arab scholarship. At present, according to my Dawsiri informant in Kuwait, the authoritative records are in Riyadh and no longer open to inspection.

fulness of raiding in sustaining this dominance is the subject of this paper; but the function of genealogical identity in reflecting and regulating forms of raiding needs also to be recognized and will be indicated below. It does not define the Bedouin so much as it identifies in the desert who are in fact dominant. It expresses not only the position of the Bedouin tribes relative to others whom they dominate and are therefore not noble or *'asiil,* but it also expresses the mutual relations of the camel breeders as corporate groups to each other. It reinforces, in fact, the kinds of predatory and other relations that hold among the communities in North Arabia. A tribal chiefdom that loses its strength and is forced to pay tribute to another becomes suspect as not really *'asiil* (Musil 1928a:8), and occasionally a powerful group such as the Howeitat who have been known, on the other hand, to fluctuate between cultivating and desert pastoralism are not acknowledged to be *'asiil.*

The camel pastoralists or Bedouin of North Arabia control primarily desert pasturages and wells, routes crossing their territories, the smaller oases, and, occasionally, the major oases. As is well known from the abundant literature, shepherd tribes on the peripheries or in the vicinity of oases, bands of hunters, weak tribes—such "serf" or ignoble peoples as the Shararat, Hutaym, and Awaazim, whose animals are primarily sheep and goats and whose camel wealth is small, and the Sa'na or blacksmiths—are among the desert people who are subservient to the camel Bedouin, who pay tribute or provide services for security.

While agriculturally based states have continuously occupied the fertile lands north and northeast of the Bedouin zone, tribal chiefdom organization prevails in the desert. But the Bedouin chiefdoms have never developed more complex political structure than ephemeral confederations without access to considerable resources other than their own pastoral base. From time to time the chiefdoms have given support to desert emirates centered upon the major oases and holding control of the major caravan routes and resting points. Among such in recent centuries has been the Rashidi Emirate of the 19th century located at Hayl, supported primarily by the Shammar chiefdoms.

The noble Bedouin of North Arabia are not, however, an aristocratic class supported primarily by the productive labor of subor-

dinate classes, in the sense of stratified agrarian societies. They
remain independent camel breeding societies, and their status,
power, and prestige depend upon their great camel herds and
means of maintaining them at full strength. Their relations to
other societies in the desert, with the possible exception of those
oasis cultivators who are their tenants and slaves, are managed
in terms of mechanisms of interchiefdom relations, not mechanisms of state apparatus. And the Bedouin themselves remain
autonomous, segmented societies of kinsmen. It is necessary,
therefore, to focus briefly upon salient ethnographic features of
the camel breeders and upon the role of camels in the position
of the Bedouin as the dominant human societies in the biological
and cultural "ecosystem" of the North Arabian desert.

THE BEDOUIN TRIBAL CHIEFDOMS

In the briefest summary, each Bedouin tribal chiefdom comprises a group of patrilineally related, corporate segments or clan
sections which cohere only on rare occasions in communal movement at the maximum tribal chiefdom level and which can fission
down the subunits of lineages to the level of the family unit according to the conditions of life in the desert. Conditions enforce
fissioning more often than massing. The minimal camping unit,
however, is the section, often called the "clan" (Sweet 1965).
This unit is comprised of a group of patrilineages claiming common descent. They regularly camp and nomadize together, mark
their camels with a common brand of the "clan," are closely concerned with mutual aid and defense of the camel herds, and
organize and prosecute raids. One lineage of the section or clan
ranks above others as the chiefly lineage, and the chief is chosen
from among its men. Within the other lineages a component sub-
lineage or family will also hold a ranking position and the leader
of the unit is chosen from that family by consensus of the members of the unit. The role of chief, at any level within the
chiefdom, is fundamentally a coordinating position, a locus of
redistribution in the typical sense of chiefdom structure (Service
1962:143–77), and a role of intermediary and negotiator with all
persons, societies, and other units external to the members of the
unit of the particular chief. The chiefs of clan "sections" are usu-

ally the most influential men of the chiefdom, and the paramount "tribal" chief among them is scarcely more than a peer among peers.

The desert regime of climate of North Arabia enforces people and herds to congregate in summer near permanent sources of water, well fields which are often claimed permanently by the clan sections. In autumn, shortly before the advent of the rains, the clan sections leave the wells and move out into their customary grazing circuits. Throughout this period of dispersed movement the chiefs maintain constant communication with each other by messengers and the whereabouts of every family, and its herds, is generally well known throughout the desert. The great circuit of the winter-spring-early-summer grazing takes herds and people into reaches of the deserts remote from settled areas and often over a range of several hundred miles; here water is usually available only from rain pools or shallow seasonal wells, and each year's rainfall pattern determines both the location and condition of pasturage and the location of water. The nomadic movement rarely stops in one locale of abundance for more than a week, and from time to time forced marches must be made of several days duration across drought-barren stretches to the next available source of pasture and water.

Years of drought in one chiefdom territory may require families, sections, or the whole group to seek grazing permission with another chiefdom, ordinarily the closest, both geographically and genealogically. On the other hand, a sequence of good years for both pasturage and breeding may swell a chiefdom's herds beyond the carrying capacity of its customary range, and again it may peaceably or by threat of force seek grazing in a wider zone (Blunt 1896:64). The chiefdom *dira* is not a strictly bounded and exclusively occupied territory, but rather a customary one wherein only the permanent wells and oasis communities are specifically claimed by the clan sections, and into which others may come freely once agreement is made between the chiefs.

The daily life of the moving sections of families is not one merely of minding their herds of camels. Much of the husbandry with the animals is performed by herdsmen. These may be the younger brothers in the family unit, poor men of the clan or some other clan of the chiefdom, refugees, or poor men from other

chiefdoms, or men of the "serf" or subordinate tribes. The herdsmen as a group are distinct from the guards and are non-
combatants during raids. The guards patrol the grazing vicinity
and form the band of "warriors" who ride together during migration between encampments. There is no explicit evidence, but
it appears from the events attending the first raid in which a
youth participates, at twelve or a little older, that only those who
have raided and comported themselves well ride among the warriors (Musil 1928b:508). From this band the guards of the special
clan herd are designated by the chief; from it scouts are selected
to precede the clan section as it moves, to serve as messengers
to ride between chiefs, and as escorts and retinue of the chief.
The two groups are not necessarily mutually exclusive in membership, however, for a man working as a herdsman may join
raiding parties in the hopes of acquiring enough camels to become self-sufficient more rapidly than he could hope to do by ac-
cumulating only the annual recompense in kind of a herdsman.[4]
A man of the clan is normally bound to demonstrate his membership by participation in defense and raids; other clients and
servants are welcomed as additional strength. Thus the main occupations of a majority of the men in a Bedouin chiefdom or clan
section have to do with keeping and guarding the camels and
particularly with prosecuting raiding expeditions. The security of
the family, lineage, clan section and chiefdom rests in the possession of adequate numbers and kinds of camels.

THE CAMEL

As a resource of food, wool, leather and other products, and as
a means of freight and personnel transport, the camel, in one
species, provides all these for the Bedouin on a scale that no
other domestic animal or combination of animals in this area can
rival. As highly specialized a desert animal as the camel is, it is
a multipurpose and generalized beast in Bedouin economy. It is
the primary source of nutrients for the Bedouin, both directly

[4] My Dawsiri informant in Kuwait said that the general "estimate" was
that a man would have enough camels to form his own family unit after
seven years of service as a herdsman, an ancient formal contract period of
the area, but he did not seem to be aware of it as conventional.

and indirectly. As a direct source, camel milk is the staff of Bedouin life and is available eleven or more months of the year. No other milk animal in Arabia can compare to this since sheep, goats, and cows lactate only during the season of moist and abundant forage and ample water—about five months in all. As a source of meat, although it is not a staple and generally slaughtered only for sacrifice and ceremony, the mature camel is considered equal to seven sheep (Jaussen 1948:273). As an indirect source, the camel transports Bedouin to such resources in wild desert plants as natural fields of the *samh,* the seed of which provides a source of flour. Further, as a means of transport, the camel enables the movement of the whole social unit together, carrying, as well as men, the women and children, the sick, infant animals, the dwelling tent and its furnishings, and in great leather bags of camel hides, water from distant wells. The forage requirements of a large ruminant like the camel and its capacity to go without water longer than humans, or to drink unpotable brackish water and convert it to a nutritious liquid for man, permit penetration of desert pasturages far beyond the range of sheep and goats. With adequate herds to support them, then, Bedouin society is enabled to flourish at a more complex level of organization in larger local population units—the sections or clans varying from 50 to many hundred tents—than, by contrast, the small bands of Salubba hunters who coexist in the same ranges, and by further contrast with the shepherd peoples, over a much wider and a continuous range of territory.

In the essentials of subsistence, then, the Bedouin-camel-desert-forage and water distribution chain of relationships seems to form a close-knit system in which any cultural mechanism which maximizes the camel herds, maximizes Bedouin survival. There are many such mechanisms, perhaps, but why raiding for camels among the Bedouin should be so prominent among such mechanisms can bear examination.

Camels serve also as an article of exchange between the Bedouin and the settled societies, by means of which the grain supplies, hardware, and textile needs in clothing and tent cloth of the Bedouin are purchased. But only certain types of beasts—males, old or sterile females, are sold to itinerant merchants or in town markets for cash. North Arabia has been the source of camels used in Egypt, the Levant, and Iraq since antiquity, and this external demand is certainly an added pressure on breeding and husbandry.

Within Bedouin society, however, camels are not bought and sold, and this is a point which cannot be overemphasized. Within Bedouin society camels are distributed by kinship mechanisms, and never by commercial mechanisms. The bridal gift, blood vengeance compensation, the *zakat* or tribesman's contribution to the chief, recompense in kind to herdsmen at the end of a year's work, incidental gifts to kinsmen and friends, inheritance, sharing by proportional assessment one's animals with a fellow tribesman who has lost his herd through raid or other misfortune, chiefly exercise of customs of hospitality and generosity—these are the means by which camels are circulated within a Bedouin chiefdom, clan, lineage, or family. Between tribes or chiefdoms of equal status thievery and raid are the only means of circulation or distribution. For one polity to send camels to another tribe or to an emir, or as taxes to the bordering state is acknowledgement of subordinate status or alliance to a greater power. But this does not seem, in itself, sufficient reason for elaborate mutual raiding to be of greater advantage than commercial methods to effect circulation and distribution of camels through the region.

Secondary to primary subsistence usages, but also essential in achieving dominance and full exploitation of North Arabia is military use of the camel. Apparently the chief fame of the camel is that it is the basis of Bedouin mobility and striking power over great distances and in considerable numbers in unilateral raiding and conflict with other communities. Until machine transport systems entered the area in this century, the ability to mount all men between 16 and 40 on special riding camels gave the camel specialists the clear advantage over other communities.

All these specialized uses of the camel place a premium upon herd building and the herds are thus diversified in composition according to the several functions they serve. Milking and breeding camels are the heart of the herd and are never sold to the merchants; baggage and marketed camels are generally males or sterile females; riding camels in North Arabia are customarily females selected for their build and pace, and types bred by some tribes are so highly regarded that raids to secure them may involve great distances. In all these respects the pressure to maintain as large herds as possible is clear. The camel breeding economy in North Arabia is thus not a subsistence economy, but demands an additional supply of animals of non-subsistence types that are used both for economic and social security. This margin of security is in camels only, however; no other resource or form of wealth can be substituted. Bedouin culture and society is thus a unique and highly specialized adaptation to a desert habitat and a domestic animal of unusual capacities.

Consequently, the continuous practice of raiding for camels suggests that in part, at least, not enough camels are available in any one tribal chiefdom or local camp at any one time to satisfy all the needs to which camels are or could be put by the members of that unit. But certain features of the camel and of the ecology of camel pastoralism contribute to making it difficult to maintain large, diversified, self-increasing herds at a local level of self-sufficient, exclusive chiefdom units. These are, first, the primary limiting features of the camel and of desert grazing hazards. Secondly, isolation of Bedouin social units in their territories is not possible; the camel itself makes the desert open to all who possess it, and it can be particularly commanded by those who are not encumbered by sessile economic activities. But access to a market, to water supplies in summer, and to cultivators' surpluses of dates and wheat are also essential ecological relations of camel pastoralists, and the major chiefdoms secure them by force or by proprietary holdings of the chiefly lineages of date gardens in the oasis settlements, whose harvests are collected once a year. These two aspects of desert cultural ecology suggest why such a vast and open region as North Arabia has been exploited and, in fact, administered by a tribal chiefdom system of dominant camel breeding specialists. Such dominance is most efficiently achieved by mobile units whose relations with each other are flexible and generally egalitarian rather than competitive, so that camel husbandry, on the one hand, successfully supports human societies throughout the range, and, on the other hand, supports them also in dominant relations to fellow desert peoples. These latter live within the same range but are dispersed, often fixed in location, and are also dependent upon regu-

lar trade with the camel nomads and with the external centers
of goods and supplies beyond the deserts.

To consider the limiting features of camel and habitat further,
the work of breeding camels and so building herds requires a
time span of three or more years. While it is an advantage for
human survival in the desert that the female camel gives milk for
11 to 15 months, the gestation period is 11 of 12 months, and a
camel produces one offspring only once every two years. New-
born males are often slaughtered, but female offspring are not
and must nurse for the entire first year. Thus only the camels
which have borne males are milked wholly for people. In North
Arabia females are not bred the first time until their fifth year.
The ecology of the nomadic grazing regime in the Arabian desert
is likewise an obstacle to easy and productive husbandry. Extreme fluctuations between years of abundant pasturages and
years of extended droughts are characteristic of the region, not
only in the cyclic patterns over years, but every year in geographical distribution. While the peoples of one tribal *dira* may be
enjoying abundant pasturages, those neighboring them or beyond may be losing camels heavily through drought and disease.
The temporally and geographically uneven distributions of grazing and water resources for the camel herds take an annual toll
that cannot be restored quickly after a poor season. The device
and regular custom of raiding for full grown animals can be an
effective measure for recovering herd strength in local groups
and, like the fissioning trait of Bedouin social structure which I
have discussed elsewhere, is in part, perhaps, an adaptive response to these habitat conditions of camel pastoralism (Sweet:
1965; cf. Doughty 1936:I, 357).

But reciprocality of raiding among the Bedouin tribal chiefdoms serves also to maintain, by continuous movement of aggressive raiding parties, the active dominance of the camel
breeding tribes in North Arabia. While raiders set out with an
objective in mind they are easily deflected, to action against any
passing parties who cannot claim promptly the protection of a
chief with whom the raid party is on friendly relations. As Musil
experienced over and over in his many years of exploration in
North Arabia, shrewd use of the rules of intertribal relations was
a greater security than firearms, when confrontation with a raid-

ing party was inescapable. Such incidents of competition for the means of survival among several variants of desert economies, reinforce respect for the capacity of cultural sanctions to overrule human behavior in the interests of a wider scale of social survival than the individual or local advantage. They also suggest that Bedouin raiding functions as an institution of supra-tribal significance in the desert. It is in this context that it is discussed below.

III. THE RAIDING MECHANISM

Camel raiding has its own name in Bedouin Arabic, *ghazw*, and as such is distinguished from fighting for territory (*harb*, war), to subordinate another tribe or settled community, and also from pillaging expeditions against non-Bedouin, or from plain thievery against fellow Bedouin. Burckhardt found that his informants distinguished between mounted looting expeditions of larger parties and smaller parties of robbers and thieves who went on foot, hoping to return to their camps on captured mounts (1831:I, 133–48, 157–76). Thus raids for booty (i.e. camels) occur in several contexts and at several scales of organization in the desert: when a leader such as Ibn Rashid of the Shammar established himself as an emir and began the development of a putative state centered upon Hayl in the North central Nejd, he used raids to capture booty with which to pay his mercenaries, and, at the same time, to extend by threat his loose hegemony over tribes and chiefdoms beyond the Shammar territories. In similar fashion but at a more modest scale, Nawwaf, son of the Rwala chief, captured the oasis of Jauf from the Rashidi dynasty and began, through raids, the process of acquiring booty with which to reward his warrior kinsmen (Musil 1927, *passim*). Clearly, also, the Shammar and the Anazah confederations or groups of tribal chiefdoms form two major enclaves of camel specialists of the desert pressing against each other for occupation dominance; bit by bit, over the past two centuries the Shammar have given way, and segments of them have crossed the Euphrates into the Syrian Jazira where they have gradually converted to shepherding (Montagne 1935, 1947). When Nuri, chief

of the Rwala, decided to support his son's effort to contest Ibn
Rashid for the Jauf oasis, he began to "step up the pressure"
against the Shammar by encouraging the incidence of raids
against them. This mutual raid may well have erosive action against fellow camel breeding tribes, but it is not a means of
overt conquest. Its use in such contexts as above is, perhaps, at
one end point of a scale of relations between the chiefdoms which
moves from small scale incidents of thievery to repeated raiding
under declared hostilities, but only rarely accompanies competitive warfare for permanent occupation of new territory.

While the term *ghazw* may thus be used in the desert as
loosely as the word *raid* is in English, there is a core institution
in Bedouin culture to which it applies specifically and which is
unlike predations against non-Bedouin tribes or communities.
These last may be called "unilateral raiding" to distinguish them
from the mutual or "reciprocal" raiding discussed here. Unilateral
raiding against non-*'asiil* pastoral tribes, peasant villages, caravans, and oasis communities may be made unless a tribute or
protection contribution is sent annually to the Bedouin tribes.
Most shepherd tribes of the borders of the cultivated zone secure
their relations to the nearest Bedouin in this fashion, but of course
are vulnerable to raiders from distant Bedouin. My Dawsiri-
Ajman informant in Kuwait described the relation between the
Ajman Bedouin and their "clients," the Awaazim, as one in which
the Ajman could raid the Awaazim, but not vice versa. The Awaazim were thus famous for their stubborn defense capacity, but
they were not regarded as "aggressive," that is, they did not practice reciprocal raiding as did the Bedouin tribes (Dickson
1949:572). Such lower caste or non-*'asiil* tribes of the northwest
exchanged raiding with the Bedouin, but the formalities and
etiquette which regulate Bedouin mutual raiding are not evident
in engagements with these latter.

The objective of raids against other Bedouin is the capture of
camels. Most valued are the milking camels or fine riding mounts;
of secondary value are baggage camels. Very young animals will
be separated from the captured animals and driven back toward
their owners' camp since they cannot move at the pace successful
escape demands. Horses and mares taken in the course of a raid
bring great prestige, but raiding for horses is not an objective as

such. Occasionally in an all-out successful raid the raiders will also make away with some tents and furnishings, and in particular, weapons. Neither small livestock, such as sheep or goats, if present, nor persons such as slaves, nor the chiefly emblems, are vulnerable.

The reciprocal *ghazw* or camel raid is well known for the rules and etiquette which govern its prosecution against clans of a fellow Bedouin chiefdom, predatory though its objective may be, and dangerous to life as the clashes may be that can result.[5] The raids are formally organized expeditions. Composition may vary, with men of several lineages or even different tribal chiefdoms participating. The leader or leaders hold unquestioned authority according to some, the only time such power is recognized. Apparently the larger and more important raids are usually organized and led by aspiring young men of the chiefly lineages. Agreement is reached beforehand by the participants on the division of captured animals according to several customary modes. It is not surprising that prosecution of raids is also surrounded with lucky and unlucky days, good and bad omens.

Reciprocal raids are directed by the Bedouin only against herds of the clan encampments of a tribal chiefdom with whom the raiders' group stands in a relation of formally declared hostilities. The relations governing raiding between the chiefdoms are always clearly known by all members and there are apparently two major modes: (1) of truce and peace with raiding forbidden but with small thieving parties probably in action; (2) clearly defined hostility and mutual raiding in force. I think there is reason to believe that such formalized relations of truce or mutual raid are usually negotiated *only* between chiefs of the *'asiil* tribal chiefdoms and that they commit all clan sections of the tribal chiefdom to the terms of peace or raid; thus the exclusive lines of demonstrated kinship emphasize the Bedouin as a widespread "caste" of warrior societies of the desert.

At any one time a Bedouin chiefdom is on hostile relations with several others, and on truce relations with still others. Each tribal

---

[5] The pattern has changed and danger to life has increased since the introduction of modern firearms into North Arabia, replacing lances, swords, and other equipment formerly used in case of actual combat contact (Müller 1931:158).

chiefdom makes its own arrangements through its paramount chief with others and without regard to the plans of its genealogical cousins. Thus the Sba' and Rwala may be on hostile footings with each other, though both are of the Anazah group, and the Rwala may be on hostile footing with all Shammar tribes, while the Sba' are not. By mutual agreement and the rules of desert hospitality, a raiding party may even pass safely through the territory of a chiefdom with whom they are at peace, and enjoy hospitality in its encampments, to raid the next chiefdom beyond; on their return journey, if they have been successful, they leave some of their booty (i.e., camels) with the people who allowed them passage, a chiefdom that may be on truce status with the one raided (Müller 1931:156). Genealogical connections between the tribe of the raiders and that of their hosts as well as careful negotiations may be effective in such cases.

Musil says that the more distant geographically tribes are from each other, the more prolonged will be their hostile relations with each other (1928b:504). Other writers speak of "traditional enemies" as opposed to "traditional allies" and in such cases not only is distance a factor, but genealogical position. Tribal chiefdoms that are *'ibn 'amm* (descendants of brothers, i.e. first cousins) to each other may engage in mutual raiding, but not for prolonged periods; or when a third force of some sort, such as a threat from the settled areas, appears against either, they may join forces. Moreover, as most writers note, adjacent chiefdoms are frequently "allies" in the interest of sharing pasturages in drought years.

Musil's account indicates that tribal chiefdoms at peace, a temporary state at best, move into one of mutual hostility when the men of one group put pressure upon their seemingly reluctant paramount chief to make the formal declaration required. The men complain that they are tired of persistent thievery in small scale incidents by members of the other chiefdom. They believe the other group is harboring camels stolen from them. And this in fact may be the cue which sets off a period of formalized reciprocal raiding between two tribes. The reasoning seems to be a simple analogy of the "retaliation" of vengeance rules which, in theory at least, equalizes the kin groups affected. Reciprocal raids, with all their attendant conventions, are made between equals. There seems to be no other statement in the literature which indicates how or why truce is overtly broken and raiding resumed between two tribal chiefdoms. One might infer a "felt shortage" of camels (or otherwise recognize as a Shammar saying does—"Raids are our agriculture" [Musil 1928a:10]). Economic pressures *may* be immediately involved, but this does not fit with the evidence for reciprocal raiding as a continuously employed mechanism of intertribal exchange of camels.

For raiding is a continuous practice of the Bedouin, year round, and not a simple, direct customary response to particular and temporary economic fluctuations—losses through drought, disease, or other factors. Raiding is rather the major occupation of the tribesmen, taking up much of their time. It is an institutionalized, regular activity. Musil says of the Shammar that during the winter season of cold and rains small parties of 15 to 40 men make their expeditions; during the spring when pastures and water are plentiful, major expeditions are made and an annual one is led by the paramount chief as a ceremony, "with banners flying"; and during the summer, when water is scarce and the herds of all Bedouin are often pastured at a distance of two or three days march from the encampments on the wells, the raiders go out in bands of a hundred men on 50 camels (Musil 1928a:10).

Since in any one year a tribe is on hostile footing with several tribes as well as at peace with others, sources from which to raid animals and friends, in case of need for sharing pasturage or alliance, are thus ensured. There are, however, no examples given which clearly illustrate this total complex of relations of one tribe with others. From the scattered evidence of Musil's accounts of the Rwala in the winter-spring season of 1908-9, the Rwala were on reciprocal raiding status with most, but not all, of the Shammar tribes and with the Dahamsha; separate Rwala clans were striking in unilateral raids against the low caste Shararat although their paramount chief was not on a hostile footing with the Shararat. Peaceful relations were in order between the Rwala and the Weld Sleyman, the Weld 'Ali, and probably also the distant 'Amarat; they were also peacefully oriented toward the powerful but non-*'asiil* Howeitat (Musil 1927:*passim*). This example covers only a few of the North Arabian tribes but no more detailed information is available.

Raiding ceases between two Bedouin chiefdoms only upon formal truce negotiations which in no way subordinates one to the other. Both the elaborate declarations of hostility and truce are phrased in terms of the honor and fair name of the people, and the truce messages revive the ideology of kinship and its obligations (Musil 1928:570–71).

Thus there is clearly a conventional sequence of forms of raid-truce relations between one tribal chiefdom and another. Without regard to other factors such as distance or season we may arbitrarily arrange them thus, with an initial letter to signify in the diagrams below: P = peace or truce; t = thievery; / = declaration of hostilities or truce; r = small mounted raiding parties, up to 40 men; R = large mounted raiding parties; CR = annual ceremonialized raid led by chief. With each letter set in a box to represent a span of time, such as a season or year, the sequence reads in abbreviation:

P	t	/r	R	CR	/P

If we plot this, then, against the background of information about Bedouin life, social structure, and raiding presented here, we can draw out two further diagrams which suggest that raiding is not merely a simple response to particular local crises in camel supply, but rather a system-sustaining mechanism which functions throughout the Bedouin niche of North Arabia.

The next diagram allows for the development of the sequence by the intensification, through repetition of episodes of mutual thievery leading to declaration of formal raiding.[6] Formal raiding takes up the time and energies of more men and camels, and it may be supposed that even a very large and powerful chiefdom reaches a limit beyond which it cannot prosecute major raids continuously against all possible objectives, even if other factors do not enter in. But again, arbitrarily, we may represent accumu-

---

[6] This sequence moves, in fact, from less to greater social control of participants in camel raiding. Following Norbeck's recent analysis of African customs violating common practice, it provides an interesting example of increasingly formalized control of incidents that might otherwise lead to disruptive hostilities (Norbeck 1963).

lation of small scale thieving episodes to the point of formaliza-
tion, followed by prosecution of large scale raids, and climaxed
by the major raid, with subsequent return to truce relations, in
the following diagram:

P	t	tt	ttt	/r	rR	RR	CR	R	/P

Now, if we return once more to the real patterns of relations
that hold among the tribal chiefdoms, it will be recalled that any
one unit will be on different footings with all the other units in
the region. Theoretically, therefore, Chiefdom A may be in any
one of the phases of the sequence set forth above in its relations
with Chiefdom B, C, D, etc. Hence it is possible to construct a
partial paradigm of the relations of Chiefdom A with several
others:

RAID-TRUCE RELATIONS OF CHIEFDOM A

With Unit	at arbitrary time units								
B	P	t	tt	ttt	/r	rR	RR	CR	R	/P
C	t	t	ttt	/r	rR	RR	CR	R	/P	P
D	ttt	/r	rR	RR	CR	R	/P	P	t	tt
E	/r	rR	RR	CR	R	/P	P	t	tt	ttt
F	etc.									

Such an extrapolation, unhistorical though it may be, allows
us to see reciprocal raiding as an ongoing process distributing
camels through a wide area, since all chiefdoms may be assumed
to be acting as in a field with the same diversity of relations with
others as is set forth for Chiefdom A above. If we substitute camels for letters in the paradigm, this will become quite obvious,
letting t = ten camels, r = 20 camels, and R = 40 camels. If men
are then substituted, it can also be seen that a chiefdom will
reach the limits of its raiding power when all available men are
involved, and presumably a truce with the chiefdom against

which the sequence is at its climax releases the largest number of men to redirect their energies to other and possibly more productive objectives.

Such arbitrary treatment of meager data ignores the rich cultural context of reciprocal raiding. It is on extremely tenuous grounds that such a "self-organizing" system is submitted here, but it seems to help to relate the essentially "Non-lethal" and only rudimentarily competitive nature of Bedouin mutual raiding in regard to territorial control to the ecological problems of survival as camel pastoralists dominating the whole desert region.

The prosecution of mutual raids between *'asiil* tribal chiefdoms is hedged about with rules and an etiquette which clearly function to prevent the wiping out of raided encampments and even of their total resources in herds. Such niceties do not hold in unilateral raids. For example, the clan section encampment of a chiefdom which stands in close genealogical relation to the raiding party (as *'ibn 'amm*) may not be attacked after midnight or before dawn: they must have an honorable opportunity to mobilize defense of their herds and camps. When a camp is successfully attacked—camels are regularly couched at night directly before the tent of their owner—and the men defending it flee, a variety of rules and customs ensure that women and children are left with enough camels, food, and equipment to get to their nearest kinsmen, normally another section of the chiefdom not too distant. Dickson observes that men will defend their camp if they see a fair chance of routing the raiders; but if they are clearly outnumbered they retire rather than make a suicidal stand. Life is, ultimately, more important than property, and their opportunity to retaliate will come another day (Dickson 1949:341).

Every large encampment of the more powerful tribal chiefdoms includes numerous non-combatants or non-participants: merchants, blacksmiths, visiting friends or even kinsmen of the raiders. The camels and other possessions of these are secure and must be restored if they are seized by mistake. Kinsmen of the raiders who may be working as herdsmen for tribesmen of the raided encampment are also supposed to be left with three of their patrons' milking camels. These and many other details easily located in the literature attest that reciprocal raiding is not warfare, either of subjugation of another society, or of competition

for territory, or of seizure of the total resources of another society of similar subsistence base.

As in other aspects, conventionalization is displayed in the tac-
tics of a raid. Whether directed against an encampment at times
when the herds are just leaving or returning from daily grazing,
or whether at herds located at some distance from the camp,
raiders follow a customary pattern of approach, cutting out of
animals, and retreat, with protection of the line of retreat by
reserves. Defense and counter-attack, if the raiders have gotten
through the outposts of guards undetected, is equally patterned
in its mobilization and movement. All involved know what to
expect, and luck, swiftness of movement, surprise, and superior
strength at the moment of encounter are the chief factors of success or failure. The pastoralists' pattern of movement on migration, by more or less dispersed clan sections of the whole mobile
chiefdom organization, always organized for defense as well as
efficient handling of multiple herds of the component families,
makes any raid a minor depredation in terms of the total resources in camels. The accounts of Doughty, Musil, and Dickson
do not indicate that *all* the camels are ever successfully driven
away by raiders except when very small encampments are raided.

While raiders are feared and guarded against by all Bedouin,
and counter-attack and pursuit vigorously prosecuted, the institution presents a record in the literature of consistent success. A
group of tales taken down by Musil from a Sba' tribesman of the
Anazah group describes 12 successful expeditions in which he
participated out of a total of 14. By custom, the leaders of the
expeditions received more of the booty than the rank and file of
raiders, but Musil's informant mentions several times that four to
six animals were the shares of members like himself (1928b:641–
61).

Once successful raiding parties have returned to their home
encampments with their captured animals, the distribution of animals continues. Musil writes that the raider may give away all
that he has taken. There is ample indication in the literature that
within the local unit of Bedouin life, the clan or section, the "redistribution" of camels and other booty, particularly those gained
on raids, follows patterns that reflect not only the tribal scale of
Bedouin organization, but the means by which key economic re-

sources of Bedouin life are disseminated to achieve non-economic objectives.

As a central institution of the "cultural core" of Bedouin society, camel raiding, whether reciprocal or unilateral, small scale or large scale, thus feeds into other central institutions which organize and sustain some human societies in the Bedouin "niche." Many examples are to be found in Musil's accounts, but one in particular can be outlined briefly here because of its importance. Participation in a raid is a prime means to gain prestige and influence in the chiefdom. A bold and ambitious man seeks to become a successful raider and especially to gain a reputation as a leader of many successful raids. The largess of booty animals that he can distribute adds further prestige to that gained through demonstration of his capacities as a leader. Such a man, if he is not already a member of a chiefly lineage, may well be adopted by his chief or his loyalty be secured by receiving a daughter of the chief as wife. As Musil indicates, the rise of such leaders, always members of lineages themselves and hence, by their successes, furthering the influence of incipiently powerful sub-lineages of the clan or section, presents a threat or challenge to the incumbent chiefly lineage. Such a situation calls into play all the means by which a chiefly lineage maintains its ranking position, or a new one displaces it (Musil 1928b:507).

IV. SUMMARY

We may now sum up and briefly discuss the adaptive and sustaining mechanism of camel raiding in Bedouin culture and its significance for the position of the Bedouin tribal chiefdoms in North Arabia. I have suggested here that the core of all raiding practices are those reciprocal ones carried out only among the "noble" tribal chiefdoms themselves and which are governed by sanctions and obligations which maximize the security of human life in Bedouin society. Less conventionalized by conserving rules and more so by ruthless predatory and exploitative practices are the unilateral raids against communities which are socially more distant from the Bedouin by virtue of their own ecological specialization (oasis cultivators; border farming villages; shepherd peoples), but which are economically symbiotic with them. Both kinds of raiding are, of course, equally adaptive practices which serve to ensure Bedouin survival. Unilateral raids very clearly bring into the Bedouin encampment booty or tribute goods useful to the economy. But reciprocal raiding, operating with prime effect in direct relation to problems of camel husbandry in the desert and also integrating significantly with other core institutions in Bedouin society, is the more dependable of these two mechanisms of expending energy to harness energy; it is a continuously operating system of camel exchange, while unilateral raiding falls more nearly in the category of windfall sources of energy. Reciprocal raiding clearly solves fundamental ecological problems of survival of the camel herds in the desert.

The primary ecological problems of Bedouin camel husbandry are set by geographical factors, the recurrent (if short term) and localized fluctuations of necessary pasturages and water resources between severe drought and relative abundance, which characterize the desert. To these must be added those diseases which may periodically reduce herds. Important cultural factors of the field of ecological pressures are contributed by such traits as selective slaughtering customs and the demand for diversified herds in usage; we may suppose this demand to have become increasingly intensified and elaborated as the use of the camel spreads rapidly beyond the pastoralists' own economy. Reciprocal camel raiding, as a continuous practice, operating at both long and short distances between tribal breeding areas, maintains a circulation of camels and of camel husbandry over the maximum physical range for camels and the societies which specialize in their breeding and depend upon them. The continual exchange by mutual raids serves thus to recoup local losses owed to failures of pasturage and water, or disease.[7]

But raiding further contributes to relative stability of the position of the great camel tribes of the North Arabian desert, first in relation to each other and secondly in relation to other communities within the region. Through the reciprocal raids, continuous communication and negotiation go on among the desert

[7] Raiding may also be offered as a selective factor in the development of the camel as the desert mount par excellence, selecting for the combination of traits of strength, endurance, and speed which are necessary to desert life.

tribes, reinforced by ideological devices such as the genealogical traditions. A continuity of discrete chiefdom-structured societies of camel breeders is thus enabled to occupy the whole zone. The ongoing processes of making and breaking of raid or truce relations and other alliances holds the chiefdoms of the area within a rather narrow range of levels of integration—that is, between the minimally organized field of chiefdoms operating relatively independently of each other in terms of variable relations of raid or truce to each other, and the maximally organized field of confederated action of freely associating chiefdoms supporting an oasis-based emirate. Throughout this narrow continuum of the scales of Bedouin political cohesion, the fundamental ecological units and economic bases are preserved; the Bedouin remain camel pastoralists deploying their herds over the annual grazing regime in their customary territories.

Secondly, by the extension of raiding or the threat of raiding to its unilateral aspect, the Bedouin chiefdoms exercise control over lesser communities by their superior mobility and specialization at desert raiding, in addition to the other mechanisms of symbiotic relations. Raid threat is the effective sanction of power.

If we can consider the institution of reciprocal camel raiding as an example, it adds its weight to previous studies which suggest that some predatory activities of human societies may be more fully understood as ecological adaptations supporting particular subsistence patterns at their widest range, and at the maximum advantage for the human societies dependent upon them (Leeds 1963; Sahlins 1961; Suttles 1960; Vayda 1961, 1962). While other factors in North Arabia play reinforcing and elaborating roles—the preservation of dominance over neighboring but distinct ecological types, for example—fundamental service of the reciprocal raid is to sustain a general balance of camel pastoral economies spatially through an extended region which is relatively uniform in geographical imperatives. But the economic aspect is not alone supported; the whole network of social and ideological relations of Bedouin life is supported. Raiding emerges therefore as an integral mechanism of Bedouin culture. It is generalized in its multi-functional advantages to a kinship based society; it probably developed as the Bedouin pastoral economy acquired more culturally instigated needs for its basic resource animal. And it effectively met both external pressures and the localized habitat hazards without conflicting with the internal kin-based social relations of Bedouin society. The two or three thousand year time span which we can allot to Bedouin occupation of the North Arabian desert as camel breeding specialists seems to demonstrate quite adequately the success of this system.

The past half century, however, has seen marked changes in the cultural sector of the desert environment. Encroachment into the area by industrial weaponry, tools, transport and other technology has surely altered not only the demand for camels but also the distribution of water resources. The emergence of such political features as national boundaries, frontier garrisons, and permanent forces of policy and armies has presumably inhibited the nomadic and raiding movements of the Bedouin. The development of an increasingly powerful state structure in Arabia has further altered drastically the prosecution of raiding. Traditionally a powerful emirate reduced unilateral raiding, especially against caravans, but the present state seems also to have suppressed reciprocal raiding. Were more than anecdotal information available on the present sizes of camel herds, of encampments, of kin groups, on the range and viability of camel husbandry, and on the present status of Bedouin societies in relation to the other peoples within the desert and in relation to the state, the system supporting functions of the raiding mechanism proposed here could be, in a measure, tested.

15. Social Distance and the Veil [Tuareg]¹

> The company scatters, the lights go out, the song dies, the guitars grow silent, as they approach the habitations of man. Put on your masks; you are again among your brothers.
>
> José Rizal in *Noli Me Tangere*

This is an essay on the means by which man promotes the establishment of social relationships and the maintenance of social interaction through aloofness, removal, and reserve. It attempts, on one level, to present a functional interpretation of a curious Tuareg custom, but, in a more general sense, the paper undertakes an exposition of certain dialectical processes in social life.

The question I have asked of a body of field data is very simply: why do Tuareg males cover their faces so completely that only areas around the eyes and nose may be seen? We will come back to this matter in greater detail, but, for introductory purposes, my answer is that by doing so, they are symbolically introducing a form of distance between their selves and their social others. The veil, though providing neither isolation nor anonymity, bestows facelessness and the idiom of privacy upon its wearer and allows him to stand somewhat aloof from the perils of social interaction while remaining a part of it.

Reproduced by permission of the author and the American Anthropological Association from the *American Anthropologist*, Vol. 66, pp. 1257–74 (Dec. 1964).

¹ This article emerges from fieldwork carried out among the Tuareg during 1959–60. The research was supported by a Foreign Area Training Fellowship, granted by the Ford Foundation, and by the Social Science Research Council, which awarded me a Faculty Research Fellowship for the period 1957–60. I wish to acknowledge my gratitude to these organizations and to the Research Committee and the Institute of Social Sciences of the University of California, Berkeley, for their generous support. Several colleagues have been of assistance to me in the formulation of this paper, but I am particularly indebted to Dr. Erving Goffman for his stimulation and criticism.

SOCIAL DISTANCE

It is not my purpose to become involved in a general exegesis on the subject of social distance, privacy and reserve, and I wish in these prefatory comments only to inform the reader of the theoretical framework within which I am operating. This study rests heavily on ideas first advanced by Georg Simmel, especially upon his delineation of self-revelation and self-restraint as necessary qualities of all social relationships, rather than as mutually exclusive categories applying to some relationships as opposed to others. For Simmel, distance was inversely related to the amount of knowledge of each other available to actors. This knowledge can never approximate completeness, however, for he stresses that the sphere of knowledge is determined by the type of relationship and, more important, that the actor's self-revelations are filtered to produce what he calls "a teleologically determined non-knowledge of one another" (1950:312). An area of privacy, then, is maintained by all, and reserve and restraint are common, though not constant, factors in all social relationships. Society could not perdure if people knew too much of one another, and one may also ask, following Simmel, if the individual could endure as a social person under the burden of complete self-awareness.

Further writing on the subject of social distance rests only on a part of Simmel's work and has tended to emphasize distance as an inverse function of affect. Shibutani, in a recent work, sees social distance to lie along an axis between "sentiments" and "conventional norms" (1961:382), a usage closely related to Bogardus' criterion of "the degrees of sympathetic understandings" that obtain between persons or groups (1938:462). Distance scaling using these standards has been extensively applied to certain problems in modern industrial society, and generations of undergraduates have answered questionnaires oriented towards data on rate and kind of interaction between groups and on preferences of propinquity. Of central concern is the axis between antipathy and affection, as expressed in marriage, residence, and other choices. Norms regulating interaction between groups in our own society may thus be ascertained, but the social anthropologist would be hard put to derive comparable results by asking a Tiv if he would live next to his mother's brother. Or marry a father's brother's daughter. I would suggest that recent sociological writing on social distance has often departed from Simmel's original work and is more reflective of Western society than interpretative of Society. Knowledge of the other does not necessarily involve sentiment, nor is the expression of sentiment always based upon knowledge. Quite the opposite is often the case in ordinary life, and to Simmel knowledge was more closely related to penetration of the identity and intrusion into closed areas.

Since Simmel, the requirement of privacy in society has been discussed by such writers as Park and Burgess (1924:231) and more recently by Merton in his treatment of role segregation (Merton 1957:374–76). Merton notes the dilemma imposed by the assumption of multiple roles and the fact that the members of the actor's various role sets have differing and sometimes contradictory expectations of him. He then proceeds to the self-evident proposition that, if these expectations are to be maintained and conformity to the role model assured, the actor must insulate these various activities and sometimes the role sets and sub-sets themselves. In short, if social interaction is to be made possible, a public life must be at one and the same time a private life.

In many types of role, this separation is assured by a restriction of information within the confines of the role set. The doctor takes care to give minimal information about his profession to the patient (and often minimal information on the patient's ailment), and the husband-wife set guards its intimacies with jealousy. This imposition of distance on the parameters of the role set does more than make other roles possible, for it promotes the solidarity of the relationship itself. In this sense, many role sets are effective secret societies. Just as the impersonator of a god must wear a mask to erase his other *roles*—for everybody surely knows who he *is*—the actor in the profane situation must stylize his impersonation of the moment in such a way that he can be at some future moment one of the many other persons he is thought to be.

The above discussion takes us finally to the problem of the individual identity and the concept of the self. Goffman (1956) has written eloquently on the person as a sacred object, a bearer of demeanor and a recipient of deference, and argues that the individual's sense of worth and significance is threatened by his vulnerability and penetrability. These sources of weakness arise, of course, out of the fact that we are of necessity social beings and, of equal necessity, require some stable definition of ourselves if we are to effectively interact with social others. Beyond this, the self is the object of our own attachment, and identity is by its nature conservative. One of the great human dilemmas, following George Herbert Mead (1934), derives from the premise that the concept of the self is bestowed upon us by society and through social interaction. But these very processes are at one and the same time testing this identity and working to change it; senescence and altered circumstance, then, conspire in an erosion of, and sometimes assault upon, the ego. Interaction is threatening by definition, and reserve, here seen as an aspect of distance, serves to provide partial and temporary protection to the self.

Beyond the above strictures on identity, the expression of distance in one form or another promotes autonomy of action (cf. Merton 1957:375). That the privacy obtained makes other roles more viable has already been discussed, but reserve in the playing of one particular role is also an essential ingredient of interaction. Here the actor allows the other enough cues so that the game may go on, but withholds sufficient stimuli so that his further course of action cannot be fully predicted. This not only gives him flexibility, but by decreasing the show of emotional attachment to the means and also the end of action he is not trapped into commitment. More simply, and elegantly, this is what is known as "playing it cool."

Of central importance in this paper, the display of distance in social relationships is crucial in settings of ambivalence and ambiguity. Here flexibility and autonomy are essential because the outcome of the transaction cannot be predicted, because contrary interests are involved or because of some special indeterminancy in the situation. We joke with the person who is in the midst of radical status change, just as many peoples do with a cross-cousin. A senior affine may not always be avoided, but he is generally accorded some patterned and stylized treatment. And the person about whom we know little is treated with constraint and reserve if absence of embarrassment is to be assured; this is the converse of Simmel's measure of distance by knowledge of the other.

It would follow from the above that the expression of distance would occur just as commonly, if not more so, in our intimate associations as in our more marginal ones. Where knowledge of the other is minimal, the actor need know only that he is dealing with the butcher, the baker, or some *other* social *thing*. The actor gives socially and personally nothing more than the situation requires for accomplishment of a task. On the other hand, as the sphere of knowledge increases, the defenses about certain residual private spheres must be correspondingly strengthened. It is these intimate relationships, commonly the most affect-laden and central to the life of the individual, most difficult to maintain, and most ambivalent, which are most demanding of expressions of distance, however elusive and subtle these may be. This was best expressed by Simmel in the concluding lines of his famous discussion of marriage (1950:329):

> The fertile depth of relations suspects and honors something even more ultimate behind every ultimateness revealed; it daily challenges us to reconquer even secure possessions. But this depth is only the reward for that tenderness and self-discipline which, even in the most intimate relation that comprises the total individual, respects his inner private property, and allows the right to question to be limited by the right to secrecy.

This is the real meaning of Simmel's use of knowledge as a measure of distance, for he understood well that familiarity, carried too far, breeds threat as well as contempt.

In summary, social distance is here viewed as a pervasive factor in human relationships and the necessary corollary of association. The more common usage of the term sees it as a spacing between individuals and groups, determinative of rate of interaction and reinforced by consciously felt attitudes. This gross, structural sense of the term is but one expression of the general phenomenon of distance, however, and I have briefly noted its manifestation as privacy and reserve in small scale interaction settings, as well as its relevance for the sociology of identity.

The intensity and form of distance, as well as its areas of occurrence, are variant and a function of social systems. It is inadequate to comment merely that distance mechanisms are found in society, and we must also inquire into the symbolic means of its expressions and the relationship of these symbols to other cultural factors. And given my, by no means original (cf. Radcliffe-Brown 1952:90–116), hypothesis that distance may be found pronouncedly in ambivalent relationships, we must search out those sectors of the social system and analyze the function of distance in maintaining the social order. Finally, just as the territorial requirements of different species of animals vary, it might be that human spacing, accomplished by symbolic, cultural means, is similarly different from one society to another. We will pursue this inquiry and seek the structural reasons for such variation.

THE TUAREG

Even in the eyes of the experienced and well-traveled anthropologist, the Tuareg are a strange and exotic people. The French appellation of "les hommes bleus" is most appropriate, for in their finest robes of indigo-dyed cotton, and with blue veils falling from the bridge of the nose to below the chin, little shows of them except hands, feet and the area around their eyes. Even the small exposed sections of skin have a blue tinge, the result of the dye rubbing off the cloth, and the overall impression given by one of the fully armed warriors is almost awesome. No accurate census exists for the Tuareg but their numbers are estimated at about a quarter of a million. Their language is one of the Hamitic group, and it is closely related to the Berber of the Mediterranean littoral. This is their genetic affinity also, and the Tuareg are basically a Caucasoid people of Mediterranean type, though there has been a good deal of admixture, especially among the Sudanese and Sahelian Tuareg, with the Negroid peoples who live in their midst and to the south. There is no single, unified

Tuareg tribe, and when we speak of them as an entity it is only
to signify a people having common characteristics of race, language, and custom, as distinguished from their neighbors. There
are deep and lasting enmities between different political federations of Tuareg, and, as should be expected, there are significant
differences in dialect and culture throughout their vast territory.
This area covers a large section of the Territoire des Oases in
southern Algeria, and the northern parts of Mali and Niger. There
is a slight extension of Tuareg into Libya, and their caravans
reach Haute Volta, Nigeria, Chad, Morocco and other African
countries. Though some Tuareg are sedentarized in Saharan
oases or in farming communities of the northern Sudan, most are
nomadic pastoralists, tending flocks of camels, sheep, goats, and
in their southern extension, cattle. They are usually identified as
dwellers of the Sahara desert, but the large majority of the population lives outside this forbidding and impoverished zone, tending their flocks in the richer pastures of the northern Sudan and
the Sahel, the belt of savannah between the Sudan and the true
desert.

The southeastern Tuareg of the Tanout and Agades districts,
among whom I worked, are aligned in a number of major tribal
confederations based on regional contiguity and traditional
amity. These functioned mainly in time of war and today have
diminished political significance. The component tribes of these
federations are territory holding units under a chief whose powers
are limited by traditional Tuareg egalitarianism and the coun-
tervailing power of the notables of the tribe. These tribes are
commonly further divided into subtribes, each of which is under
the leadership of a lesser chief and has a territorial locus. Both
tribe and subtribe are conceived to be descent groups, the members of which acknowledge a common ancestry, but the mutual
kinship of their members is putative and no genealogies of any
depth or comprehensiveness are kept except in chiefly lines. Below the subtribe is the fundamental unit of Tuareg society, the
iriwan, or house, which consists of some 50 to several hundred
people who reside about a well to which they hold rights and
who pasture their herds in the surrounding land. The name of
each iriwan is taken from the name of its leader, who is acknowledged as the most notable member of the group, and as at the

levels of segmentation of tribe and subtribe, it is a local-political-kin group. Kin ties are demonstrably closer in the iriwan than at higher levels, however, and its members feel themselves to share close bonds of consanguinity and, as we will see, affinity.

In addition to the differentiation of the population along tribal lines, Tuareg society is divided into three distinct and endogamic classes. The true Tuareg consist of the politically dominant noble tribes, or *imajaren,* and their vassals, or *imrad.* Each noble tribe exacts tribute and fealty from one or more vassal tribes, both noble and vassal tribes acting as corporate entities in their inter-relations. The members of each class hold property individually in slaves, or *iklen,* who act as herdsmen and servants for their masters. The slaves are of Saharan and Sudanese Negroid origin, but most cannot trace their ancestry beyond slave status among the Tuareg. In language and in most aspects of their culture they are much like their masters, despite certain differences which are not the subject of this paper. Tuareg stratification has broken down in recent years, for French colonial rule loosened the po-litical hold of the nobles over their vassal tribes, and many mem-bers of the slave class have been manumitted in accordance with government policy. But even where the traditional ties have been severed, the classes remain distinct as status groups, and mem-bership in one class or another is the single most important cri-terion of a Tuareg's worth and standing.

The Tuareg, like their neighbors on all sides, are Moslem. They are noted, however, as infamous and unregenerate back-sliders who observe neither proper law nor custom, who misperform the ritual postures in prayer, fail to make ablutions, eat and drink during the fasting days of Ramadan, and who have few of the wise and holy in their ranks. Despite the best Tuareg efforts to simulate orthodoxy in the presence of their censorious neighbors, these charges are substantially true.

One of their most obvious points of heterodoxy is in the treat-ment of their women. The Tuareg woman enjoys privileges un-known to her sex in most Moslem societies. She is not kept in seclusion nor is she diffident about expressing her opinions pub-licly, though positions of formal leadership are in the hands of the men. Frequently beautiful and commonly mercurial in tem-perament, she places little value upon pre-marital chastity, stoutly defends the institution of monogamy after marriage, maintains the right to continue to see her male friends, and secures a divorce merely by demanding it—and she is allowed to keep the children. The shock of early Arab travelers at this state of affairs is understandable and was aggravated by the fact that the men were veiled and the women were not.

The high status of the Tuareg woman is linked to their traditional matrilineality. Among many Tuareg tribes, especially those in the southern part of the territory, matrilineality has disappeared or become severely attenuated and has been replaced by a patrilineal mode of descent or a bilateral one. In the traditional system, still in force in many tribes, group membership is determined matrilineally and office passes through the male sibling group and then to the eldest son of the eldest sister. Tuareg matrilineality is, however, a curious institution and should not be equated with the rule as we usually know it. Most rules of unilineal descent are, of course, associated with a corresponding rule that marriage is exogamic to the descent group, but among the Tuareg the group is endogamic. There is a decided preference among the Tuareg for cousin marriage of all types. In addition to the Koranic preference for the daughter of the father's brother, it is considered good to marry the daughter of the mother's brother or sister, and the father's sister's daughter also is an acceptable partner.[2] Despite these preferences, marriages are usually not between first cousins, and the ideal of cousin marriage should be looked on as the ultimate idiom of a more general preference for endogamy. This pertains first to the local-political-kin group, or iriwan, which is an in-marrying unit as well as the most close-knit aggregation of kinsmen. After the iriwan, marriage is preferentially endogamic in the subtribe, the tribe, and the tribal confederation, in that order. Tuareg marriage

[2] Briggs (1960:128) states that among the northern Tuareg of the Hoggar massif marriage is prohibited with first cousins and with members of the same "camp community or fraction," which I assume to be the iriwan. This may well be an area difference, but my informants expressed a normative preference for such unions, and actual genealogies and censuses showed large numbers of marriages within the iriwan. On the other hand, only a small percentage of marriages were with actual first cousins, though they did occur. To pursue these points would carry us into a full analysis of Tuareg marriage and kinship, which is beyond the scope of the present essay and the subject of a future article.

preferences should be borne closely in mind because they are highly pertinent to our discussion of veiling practices. For present purposes, however, it should be noted that endogamy vitiates the rule of descent by making it an academic point in an in-marriage, inasmuch as both mother and father belong to the same group and so also will the children. And, more important, the setting of the boundaries of the kin group by endogamy rather than exogamy makes the Tuareg social system unique and typologically different from most other systems of kinship. The veiling of the men is a most strange custom, but it occurs in a most strange and baffling society. We will now turn to our attempt to impose rationality upon the bizarre.

THE SOCIAL USES OF THE VEIL

The Tuareg veil, or *tegelmoust* in the Air Tuareg dialect, is the distinguishing characteristic of dress of this people. The standard Tuareg raiment consists of an underrobe and a flowing outer garment that extends from shoulders to ankles. The underrobe is sleeveless, but the outer garb has loose wide sleeves ideal for carrying the long daggers that are worn in sheaths strapped to the arm. These robes are either blue or white; some Tuareg affect a blue outer garment and a white inner one, while others adopt the opposite mode. Still others wear either all blue or all white. The more expensive cloth is the blue, and it is quite common for a man to wear various mixtures of blue and white for ordinary dress but to reserve an all blue ensemble for festive occasions. The most expensive item of dress, however, is the blue turban and veil, a long bolt of cloth that is made up of narrow strips of cloth sewn together. This special cloth is made and dyed in Nigeria and a good specimen may cost well over twenty-five dollars, a large sum of money to most Tuareg. A Tuareg who cannot afford this price, or who simply wishes a veil for everyday use, will generally use a bolt of ordinary white or blue cloth, but it is worn in much the same manner as the expensive kind. The art of putting on the veil is not easily mastered but, quite simply, the cloth is wrapped about the head to form a low turban and the end is then brought across the face, the top of the cloth falling across the nose and the bottom hanging well below the chin. The resultant effect is that the only part of the face showing is the area across the plane of the eyes. Raised to its extreme height, only a narrow slit is left open and even the eyes can barely be seen. There are situational differences in the actual attitude of the veil and the amount of face that the wearer exposes, but this is a key part of my analysis and will be discussed more fully below.

Whatever may be the precise position of the veil in different social settings, the most striking fact is that it is worn almost continually. The veil is worn when at home or traveling, during the evening or the day, when eating and smoking, and some even sleep veiled. That this is not simply a casual mode of costume is manifest when one watches a group of Tuareg men eating. Whether using spoons or their fingers, or drinking milk from a calabash, the veil is not lowered for the food to be passed to the mouth; rather, the proper Tuareg carefully raises the veil enough to enable him to eat but not far enough for his mouth to be seen. The occasional Tuareg who lowers his veil to eat reveals his low status as either a slave or a member of a vassal tribe—a member of a noble tribe does not expose his mouth. The veil has even inhibited the diffusion of that most pervasive habit, smoking. An occasional Tuareg would accept a proffered cigarette and proceed to smoke it by holding it gingerly under the veil—it was suspenseful to watch them light it. Most, however, take tobacco mixed with lime, and pack this mixture in their cheek or behind the lower lip, thus eliminating the obvious dangers of smoking. The constancy of veil wearing was once impressed upon me when I encountered in Kano, Nigeria, a rather deviant and renegade young Tuareg who was flamboyantly dressed in yellow plastic shoes, blue shorts, a checked sport shirt—and the turban and veil. It is not only the hallmark of the Tuareg but their most unchanging item of clothing.

Such a unique custom has not been without its interpreters, and I will give and discuss a few of the more common, and obvious, reasons advanced for veiling. Most explanations have been of the 'origin' type, though my prefatory remarks indicate that mine is quite clearly of a structural and functional kind. Even these origin theories, however, indicate that the custom persists for the same obvious utility that it had in its incipience, and it is worthwhile and pertinent to consider them. The first, of course, is that the veil keeps out the sand and dust of the desert and steppes. It does indeed do this, and during the dry season Kanuri, Hausa, Teda and other traders commonly wrap the ends of their turbans across their mouths and noses while on caravan, much in the manner of the American cowboy driving a herd to market. But the Tuareg also wear their veils during the rainy season when there is little dust, and when sitting within the confines of their huts. Moreover, the veil is not worn until a youth approaches the manly state, at about the age of seventeen, and it is exactly the unveiled youths, and slaves, who do much of the dusty work of herding. It should also be remembered that the women go unveiled whatever the atmospheric condition; in fact, women only pull their shawls across the lower parts of their faces when expressing reserve and modesty.

The French explorer, Henri Duveyrier, noted and refuted this argument in 1864 and raised also the question of whether the veil disguised the Tuareg from their enemies (Duveyrier 1864: 391–92). The ethnographer can only agree with his observation that the Tuareg recognize each other despite the veils and that this explanation is beside the point. I might add, however, that the Tuareg wear the veil highest and conceal their faces most completely when among many of those who are closest to them and know quite well who they are; they are sometimes most lax in the wearing of the veil when among non-Tuareg, exactly those from whom they could conceal their identity most successfully by veiling.

The Tuareg can probably recognize others among their range of acquaintances as rapidly and at as great a distance as Europeans, for they use a broad range of means of identification other than the face. First, every Tuareg affects a slightly different style of dress by varying the colors of the various items of apparel and individualizing the mode of wearing them. Second, the Tuareg are even more sensitized to the common criteria of identity given by stature and body set than are we, and they use a series of other cues from the exposed parts of the body. One Tuareg claimed that, though he had left home as an unveiled boy and returned five years later veiled, his sister recognized him by his feet. Even the non-Tuareg accustoms himself to these forms of recog-

nition, as was forceably brought home to me on one occasion
when a Tuareg friend approached me for the first time unveiled
and I failed to recognize him. The source of my confusion is
evident; he had disguised himself by adding facial cues rather
than subtracting them.

The question of identification raises a series of interesting problems, for face reading and mouthwork are virtually absent among
the Tuareg as media of communication. The first months of field
ethnography among a totally unfamiliar people are disturbing to
the anthropologist because of his inability to accurately assay
the meaning of both verbal and non-verbal responses from his
subjects. Among the Tuareg, these difficulties are aggravated by
the fact that entire zones around the nose, mouth, chin and
throat, from which he is so accustomed to make inferences about
the subjective state of the other, are concealed to him. He notes
that the Tuareg is not a mouth-watcher, but rather an eye-
watcher and that during interaction his eyes are fixed by the
steady stare of his respondent. On one occasion, I countered this
by wearing dark glasses, but my Tuareg friends retaliated by the
same technique and succeeded in totally effacing themselves.
Everything is watched and used as a cue. The position of the
eyelids, the lines and wrinkles of the eyes and nose, the set of
the body and the tone of voice are all part of the Tuareg's gestalt
of the situation, and the outsider must adapt himself to this and
learn to control these stimuli in himself and observe them in the
other if he is to correctly interpret the behavior of his subjects.
It would be a mistake then to assume that the veiling practice,
among a people who are accustomed to the continual wearing of
the veil, *totally* conceals the disposition of the actor to a certain
course of action: quite clearly, this would be the negation of
social interaction. Rather, this curious article of apparel cuts
down the total range of stimuli that can be emitted and received
and makes for a diffuseness of Ego's behavioral stance. Beyond
this, and perhaps of greater importance, by concealing the primary communication zone of the mouth region the Tuareg decreases his vulnerability to others by *symbolically* removing
himself from the interaction; he becomes less labile before the
world. It is their quality of remoteness that strikes the outside

observer, and it is congruent with the Tuareg's own expressed feelings of exposure and defenselessness when he is unveiled.

It is exactly the feeling of openness and the corresponding sentiment of shame expressed by the Tuareg as their reason for wearing the veil which is our principal clue to an understanding of the custom. When asked to explain the usage, the Tuareg informant will simply say that it would be shameful to show his mouth among his people. This sense of shame suggests that the veil is connected with privacy and withdrawal, and these sentiments are consistent with the comments at the outset of this article upon the nature of social distance. It suggests also that the exposure of the mouth is a violation of the moral order, a transgression that lowers the prestige of the offender and his own self-esteem. The restrictions surrounding the use of the veil are rigid and highly formalized, and we can well infer that they impinge upon vital areas of social life.

The place of the veil in the social system is best seen in its specific, situational uses, and variation in style according to the mood and situation of the wearer is vividly described by Henri Lhote (1955:308–9):

> The style of wearing the veil, of placing the different parts about the head, may vary from one tribe to another and some individuals give their preference, according to personal taste, to certain local styles. . . . But beside these different fashions, there is also the turn, the knack which makes it more or less elegant. Similarly there is a psychology of the veil; by the way in which it is set, one can gain an idea of the mood of the wearer just as among us the angle of the cap or hat permits analogous deductions. There is the reserved and modest style used when one enters a camp where there are women, the elegant and *recherchée* style for going to courting parties, the haughty manner of warriors conscious of their own importance, like the whimsy of the blustering vassal or slave. There is also the detached and lax fashion of the jovial fellow, the good chap, or the disordered one of the unstable man of irritable character. The veil may also express a transient sentiment. For example, *it is brought up to the eyes before women or prestigeful persons, while it is a*

sign of familiarity when it is lowered. To laugh from delight
with a joke, the Tuareg will lift up the lower part of his veil
very high on his nose, and, in case of irritation, will tighten
it like a chin strap to conceal his anger (Italics mine).

The veil, then, is not a fixed article of clothing to be worn either
uniformly or relaxedly. Most Tuareg are continually adjusting
and readjusting the veil, changing the height at which it is worn,
tugging on the lower part of it, tightening its ends beneath the
turban and straightening its folds. The observer soon notes that,
though there is a certain element of random primping involved,
the different individuals in a group will readjust their veils as the
tone of relationships subtly shifts or persons enter or leave the
setting.

The Tuareg are notable for their haughty and arrogant demeanor. They walk with a long swagger and hold their heads
high with dignity and aloofness; even when mounted atop a
camel they hardly deign to incline their heads to a pedestrian.
The veils promote this atmosphere of mystery and apartness,
and the Tuareg whether in town or in his native desert has often
been remarked upon for his penchant for appearing the master
of all he surveys. That the cold, long look through a slit of cloth
impresses the foreigner is indisputable and is used to this end,
but it is exactly when in the presence of the outsider with whom
he is on familiar terms that the Tuareg is most relaxed in his veiling. This was most manifest when I encountered them in Nigeria,
well outside of their proper territory. In these circumstances,
they would frequently allow the veil to fall below the nose, but
still covering the mouth, and others would occasionally allow
their mouths to show. The first reaction of our little children to
the veils was, of course, to pull them down, which provoked only
indulgent laughter from the Tuareg. Despite the strictures on
covering the mouth, it evidently mattered least when in our
house and especially before little children, who, after all, hardly
have social identities. Distance requirements were not so rig-
orously observed in our case because we were outside the social
system, nor were those familiar with us attempting to impress us
with the haughty bearing that they often assume toward the
sedentary Sudanese populations. Besides, differences of custom

and language were already so great that we could not intrude too closely upon their identities.

Many of those who were most lax in their veiling were members of the inferior vassal tribes or of the slave class. The slaves also go veiled, but through a kind of implicit sumptuary restriction on dress, they are much more slack about the position of the veil than are the Caucasoid nobles and vassals. Slaves commonly go about their work with their veils below their chins or at least across the chin. On other occasions, a slave may wear his veil under the nose but covering the mouth and, even when placed across the nose it generally rides well below the bridge. Vassals, as a rule, wear their veils much above the level of the slaves but do not take quite the care that the nobles do. The occasional vassal who affects the high and tight veil is usually attempting to improve his status.

Among all segments of the Tuareg population, the veil is worn higher when confronting a person of power and influence. The Tuareg do not prostrate themselves before a chief, as is the custom among their Hausa neighbors, but they do elevate their veils to the bridge of the nose. The person of higher status will usually keep his veil at a somewhat lower level, though its actual height depends much on the amount of deference due the other. On the other hand, veils may be worn at the level of the tip of the nose or below it by a companionable group of young men, especially when they are outside of camp precincts.

Variations in veiling usage are found not only at fixed positions within the status hierarchy but at relative ones such as in the dyadic relationships given within the kinship system. This is most clearly seen, and the distance setting usage of the veil best demonstrated, in affinal relationships (cf. Nicolaisen 1961:114). The Tuareg speak of proper decorum toward the parents of the wife and, to a lesser extent, the siblings of the latter as being based on the observation of both shame (*tekeraki*) and respect (*isimrarak*). A man shows this, among other ways, through avoidance of the name of his father-in-law, which he generally accomplishes by calling him *amrar*, or 'leader,' in reference to the father-in-law's position as head of his own household, or through teknonymy. The latter usage is most commonly expressed by addressing the father-in-law as the father of one of his sons, as for

example "aba 'n Ibrahim." The mother-in-law's name is also ta-
boo, but the Tuareg generally refrains from addressing her by a
title, inasmuch as he commonly does not have as much contact
with her as he does with the wife's father. There is some tribal
variation in the extension of these taboos to the siblings of the
father-in-law and mother-in-law, but such avoidance pertains in
most of the southeastern Tuareg tribes.

Conduct toward the senior affines is characterized by general
restraint and self-effacement. During the courtship period, the
Tuareg does not take food or drink when visiting in the house of
the intended or possible bride, for commensality among the
Tuareg, as among most peoples, symbolizes the closing of distance and the establishment of solidary bonds. This form of
avoidance is maintained even after marriage, though the groom
has more frequent occasion to contact his father-in-law on matters of business. Similarly, the bride observes greater avoidance
of the father-in-law, but here there is a further normative component to the relationship, for the bride commonly will draw her
shawl over her head and across the lower part of her face when in
his presence. Thus the female has occasion to approximate the
veiling practice when observing distance in a highly specific and
intensive form. This, I might mention, is the nearest any Tuareg
woman comes to the Near Eastern purdah, one aspect of which
entails the veiling of the woman's face in compliance with Sura 4
of the Koran, which says of good women: "They guard their un-
seen parts because Allah has guarded them."

It is, then, all the more interesting to observe that the Tuareg
men are most strict with their veils when in the presence of the
father-in-law or the mother-in-law, for, in addition to other signs
of respect and avoidance, the son-in-law is careful to adjust the
veil so that only a very narrow aperture is left open, and the eyes
are hooded and left in shadow. At this point, we are no longer
dealing with an analytic statement of the relationship of veiling
to social distance, but with a concrete, conscious motivation, for
the Tuareg state that reserve and shame are the essence of conduct toward the senior affine and that they partially express this
with the veil. Beyond the aspect of ceremonial avoidance, it
would seem that there is another component closely related to
this symbolism, that of maintenance of the dignity of the actor—

by his symbolic withdrawal from the threatening situation vis-à-vis the superordinate, Ego is also furthering the maintenance of his self image. This is manifest in the fact that the veil is also worn high when courting, and very special care is given at the formalized courting sessions, or *ahals*. On the latter occasions, the young suitors conduct themselves with great dignity; the veils are worn very high and close and a full retinue of retainers accompany the young men, if they are sufficiently wealthy. But avoidance, in the physical sense, could hardly be the function, either latent or manifest, of the veil at such times, for Tuareg courting frequently culminates in sexual activity. Rather, the young man attempts to communicate to the girl his own worth and standing and, concomitantly, through standing somewhat aloof, maintains his command over a rather critical situation in which the prognosis of success is never certain.[3]

The above data suggest that there are two aspects to distance: the external dialogue and the internal dialogue; the actor maintaining the interaction situation and Ego maintaining ego. Perhaps this is best illustrated by the fact that the veil is not worn by men at two phases in the life cycle—when they have no status, as in the case of minors, and when they have too much status, as in the case of the *hajji*. The latter is the honorific term applied by most Moslems to persons who have made the pilgrimage to Mecca, and this status signifies that the occupant of it has gained religious merit and, with it, secular prestige. But beyond this the *hajji* is a person who has partaken of the sacred and by so doing has absorbed it as part of his identity. Among the southeastern Tuareg it is quite common for such men—and they are relatively few in number—to permanently divest themselves of the veil, for dignity and esteem are theirs by right. Moreover, a Pilgrim need show no shame or respect before others: his very status is adequate to guarantee him distance. It will be remembered, how-

[3] Nicolaisen, in his important paper on Tuareg magic and religion (1961), also recognizes that a proper understanding of the veil must be sought in the social system. He notes that the veil is always worn in a high position when confronting a stranger, especially a female, a status that must be distinguished from that of the friend or acquaintance who is but marginally involved in the society. This is consistent with my previous remarks on the function of social distance, here expressed in hauteur and reserve, in situations that are not readily definable nor their outcomes easily predictable.

ever, that even very powerful chiefs wear the veil, suggesting
that there is a further quality to the divestment of the veil than
that of sheer prestige. What then is this difference between the
Pilgrim and the Chief? It is simply this: though the latter may
have more power and influence than the former, the status of the
chief is secular and that of the pilgrim is sacred. The symbolism
of the veil, then, belongs to the realm of the sacred in social relations, and I would suggest that this is why the secular chief continues to wear it while the holder of the status of pilgrim does
not. That the veil is best understood in terms of Durkheim's
concept of the sacred and that its use conforms to ritual has
already been suggested by the form and protocol surrounding it.
I will develop this point further in the conclusion of this essay.

SOCIAL STRUCTURE AND THE VEIL

It would perhaps belabor the point to inquire further into the
functions of the veil as a maker of symbolic distance, and I wish
to turn to its structural setting. Granted the premise that the
Tuareg veil is a distance setting device, why do the Tuareg need
such a device? If distance is a component of all social relations
and is essentially a part of sociation, as was maintained at the outset of this article, then why do not all peoples wear veils?
Granted that all humans present a facade of sorts to society, the
proper question is why do the Tuareg go to such extremes? After
all, these people *really* wear veils. To answer this question, we
must return to the subject of Tuareg social structure and explore
certain aspects of it in some detail, for the veil has been seen to
be a part of the ritual apparatus of the society and must have a
meaning within the social system itself.

It will be remembered that the Tuareg social units are preferentially endogamic, from the local groups settled about the
wells to larger tribal aggregations, and that the boundaries of
these groups are set by in-marriage and not by exogamy as is
common in most societies having extended kin groupings. Among
the Tuareg this yields a rather distinct spatial juxtaposition of
role players. Almost every type of residence possibility is known
among the Tuareg. Though couples are not normally neolocal, it

is not unknown for a family to move to residence among a group in which they have no close kinsmen but where certain concrete advantages await them. Duolocality also occurs, at least among the Kel Oui tribes south of the Air massif, and the couple in the early years of their marriage resorts periodically to life with the families of both bride and groom. Most Tuareg, however, profess to a norm of patrilocality, though they admit freely that the alternative of matrilocal residence, especially in the initial phase of marriage, is also common. To summarize, despite the professed patrilocality, there is considerable variation in residence alternatives, and no local-political-kin group yields a uniform composition in terms of types of kin. It should, however, be reemphasized that the rule of endogamy does determine a majority of marriages—and to the extent that marriages are endogamic the above residence choices become an academic matter. A Tuareg may well state that he resides with his own kin, but further questions will reveal that his wife's relatives indeed reside in the same group. Under conditions of residence near the affines, however, it is common to observe avoidance through placing the hut at some distance from that of the wife's parents. In a humorous mood, one said to me: "We don't want them to hear the noises we make at night." Wherever they camp, the fact remains that life among one's consanguines is quite commonly life among the affines, and, further, they are the same people.

This takes us to a very real, and sometimes overlooked, aspect of most societies having unilineal descent: rules of group and local exogamy function primarily to define the boundaries between the conceptually antithetical, and complementary, principles of incorporation and alliance and the social groups based upon these principles. This segregation is impossible in a society such as Tuareg, for one's in-laws are at one and the same time members of one's kin group. This situation is compounded by the fact that, despite the nominal matrilineality discussed above, the Tuareg actually reckon their ties of kinship bilaterally; in this way they differ from the Arab Bedouin who also practice kin and local group endogamy but suppress the resulting diffuseness of cross-cutting relationships through a formal ideology of patrilineality. Lacking such an ideology, the Tuareg recognize and trace ties through both lines and further insist upon regarding all mem-

bers of local-political aggregations at whatever level as co-
descendants from some common ancestor. This, combined with
endogamy, results in a multitude of ties through which any two
people in one of the iriwan groups can trace relationship in several ways. In most of the Tuareg groupings the shallowness of
genealogies allows kin ties to remain diffuse and unspecified except with very close relatives, thus giving some protection from
the possible role conflicts inherent in the cross-cutting ties. But
these relationships remain ambivalent for this very reason, and
bonds of incorporation and solidarity within the social units are
charged also with the antithesis and opposition of affinality and
alliance.

My thesis, then, is that given this ambiguity and ambivalence
of relationships, this immanence of role conflict, the Tuareg veil
functions to maintain a diffuse and generalized kind of distance
between the actor and those who surround him socially and physically. By the symbolic removal of a portion of his identity from
the interaction situation, the Tuareg is allowed to act in the presence of conflicting interests and uncertainty. The social distance
set in some societies by joking and respect or avoidance behavior towards certain specific categories of relatives is accomplished here through the veil. It is, however, difficult to maintain
specific differentiation of kin roles given their dual character,
and the expression of distance is generalized in varying degree
to all one's fellows. It is, therefore, for sound structural reasons
that the Tuareg is most mindful of the attitude of his veil exactly
when he is among his own.

That women do not wear veils is another manifestation of the
very simple and universal fact that the differences between the
sexes go beyond biology, a cause for wonder to those who, for
example, point out that father's sister's child marriage is quite
common in patrilineal societies (with asymmetrical cross-cousin
marriage)—for women. The Tuareg woman is also placed in a
situation of ambiguity vis-à-vis her kin, but, despite her rather
high prestige in this society, she is not a public figure and does
not operate in as wide a social context as does the man. The
quality of her social relationships is not so instrumental as that
of the man. It is repetitive to stress that kinship relations are

political relations in a society of this kind, and the Tuareg woman is not a significant political actor in the formal sense.

CONCLUSIONS

In this paper, I have taken the single item of the Tuareg veil, and through an analysis of its operation in the social system, I have attempted to say something general on the subject of social distance. I have argued, following Simmel, that social distance pervades all social relationships though it may be found in varying degrees in different relationships and in different societies. I take this as axiomatic, for inasmuch as social conduct implies limitations upon range of expectable behavior and closures upon other relations and behavior, the actor must insulate large portions of his social existence. This is done through withholding knowledge of his course and commitment in the action situation, and it is concretely accomplished through distance setting mechanisms—the privacy and withdrawal of the social person is a quality of life in society. That he withholds himself while communicating and communicates through removal is not a contradiction in terms but a quality of all social interaction.

Pursuing the well-established premise that distance is to be found most strongly in those relationships that are most difficult but which must be perpetuated, I have examined the custom of veiling among the Tuareg and have concluded that it functions to maintain a generalized distance. This is manifest in the specific use of the veil, as for example in association with senior affines, and we have seen that the more delicate of social interaction situations requires the greatest distance and removal of the actors. Further, the use of the veil has been interpreted as being ritualistic in nature, not only because of the protocol and punctiliousness surrounding its use but because it concerns itself with something "sacred." The sense of the sacred is seen here in the sentiments of shame and pollution that surround the hidden region of the mouth and derives, I believe, from the very delicacy of Tuareg social relations, from the fact that maintenance of the social system is deeply connected with the maintenance of a high degree of social distance. Though this sacred quality is found suffused through all societies and all social action, and though all social *conduct* is in a sense ritual, certain characteristics of the Tuareg social order cause it to be more pronounced here. I found this quality to lie in some aspects of marriage, descent, and residence practices, one result of which is that there is no segregation of bonds of locality, affinality, and kin group membership. From this there proceeds an ambiguity of role complementarity that is partially resolved by the maintenance of diffuse distance towards all others. Beyond this, there is a complete overlap, both in the real situation and in the formal, jural sense, of ties of descent and the antithetical relations of alliance. While it would be incorrect to say that the Tuareg solves the potentiality of role conflict by physical avoidance, he certainly promotes this resolution by distance. In so doing, two things are accomplished. First, the setting of distance in relations with a broad range of others removes the actor from the interaction situation sufficiently that he diminishes his commitment to a specific course of action. This allows for flexibility and viability in social situations that are not highly defined by the kinship system. Second, given the particularly threatening quality of the interaction situation, the actor is enabled to maintain autonomy and self-esteem. In a very real sense, he is in hiding.

The above analysis is directed to the question raised earlier as to whether distance, in general, varies from one society to another, and, if so, what are the structural concomitants of this distance. Briefly, I find the answer to lie in the immanence of role conflict. I also queried the forms of symbolism that are involved in distance maintenance, and I deem this to be the more difficult problem. Though I do not wish to go into the psychological bases of the symbolism, I would call the attention of the reader to the fact that distance setting techniques are quite commonly associated with the eyes and the mouth. The extreme case of this is perhaps the masked ball, which, in its more earthy traditional form, allowed maximum latitude and freedom of behavior by totally effacing at least the area of the eyes. Other examples that come to mind from our own culture are the averted eyes of the Victorian maiden, who also was wont to demurely cover her mouth with a fan. That this is not simply a rather passé European trait was brought home to me when doing research in an Amazonian Indian group in which the definition of a wanton woman is one who looks directly at men and laughs openly without placing her hand over her mouth (Murphy 1962:50). In contemporary society such a means of defense and withdrawal is often achieved by wearing dark glasses. Sun glasses and tinted glasses are almost badges of office among West African emirs and Near Eastern potentates, and they have also become items of prestige in other parts of the world. They are commonly used in Latin America, where, indoors and out, heavily tinted glasses are the hallmark of the prestigeful as well as those aspiring to status, for they bestow the aloofness and distance that has always been the prerogative of the high in these lands.

The literature of Freudian psychology gives extensive documentation to the female symbolism of the mouth, its vulnerability to penetration, and to the unconscious association between the eyes and the male generative powers; it is not surprising to find that it is these areas that are defended most often in social interaction. Beyond this, these are the areas of the body by which we most actively communicate with others and from which we emit the cues that guide those with whom we interact. But there is more to social distance than the simple symbolism involved in the non-use of the eye and mouth regions. It is well established that distance of a kind can also be set by the use of humor and that there may be involved heavy and expressive use of the eyes and mouth for communication on these occasions. I would state that the single binding and unifying characteristic of all distance techniques is constancy of demeanor. This may take the form of a constant kind of behavior in a specific social situation, be it joking with one's cross-cousin, the showing of respect to one's father-in-law, or the even observance of business etiquette. The actor achieves a refuge by submergence in his social identity and, through uniformity of behavior, discloses the least of himself, while maintaining his social relationships.

The kind of social distance that is best known to us, be it under the rubric of joking, reserve, avoidance, or antipathy, is that which obtains between certain categories of role players and which is part of expected behavior in specific interaction settings. This I would term *role specific distance,* as opposed to the kind of diffuse social distance connected with the Tuareg veil. The

latter I classify as *generalized distance*, for it is not only characteristic of a series of specific relationships but tends to pervade
social interaction in its entirety. Often identified as a basic personality trait and attributed to ontogeny, it is seen here as a requirement of the social system as a whole. Role specific distance is
manifested at certain nodal points in any social system, but generalized distance varies from one society to another depending
upon the total configuration of the social system. It can be seen
in the husband who treats his wife with the same polite consideration and affection which he accords to all ladies, and it can be
seen in the Tuareg behind his veil. I will conclude by reminding
the reader that it was a novelist, and not the social scientist, who
told us that the uniform affability and the evenly distributed
backslapping of the middle-class American were the loneliest of
all gestures. But this aloneness is not the tragedy and dilemma
of our place and time only, for alienation is the natural condition
of social man.

16. Camp and Surra [Baggara Arabs]

As a group of neighbouring tents is associated with an extended family, so a camp (*ferig*) is associated with a lineage of the kind known as 'surra'. One or more camps constitute a mobile physical framework for accommodating surra members. Humr regard the surra as the ideal camping, migrating, and cattle-herding unit, as well as the limit of intimate and undifferentiated brotherhood. A camp should, in ideal circumstances, consist of the males of a surra and those dependent on them; they should camp together, move together, look after their herds together, and share together the burdens of hospitality; they should make up a named unit exhibiting complete solidarity. In practice, however, this ideal is continually thwarted by economic necessity and the changing relations of surra members.

COMPOSITION AND RESIDENCE OF 'IYAL GANIṢ

The surra of 'Iyal Ganiṣ takes its name from Muḥammad[1] Ganiṣ, 'Muḥammad the Hunter', who is said to have been alive when the Humr moved east from Wadai. Seven generations are counted; the supposed date of the migration, 1775, makes it possible that no telescoping has taken place.

Fig. 16-1 shows how the founders of the extended families of

Reprinted by permission of the author and publisher from Ian Cunnison, *Baggara Arabs: Power and the Lineage in a Sudanese Nomad Tribe,* Chapter 5, pp. 55–85 (The Clarendon Press: Oxford, 1966).

[1] I write 'Muḥammad' in the recognizable form, but Humr say 'Meḥimmed'. Many other names have unusual pronunciations, as, for example, 'Abd el Raḥman, which becomes 'Adderḥaman.

'Iyal Ganiṣ are related to one another. The diagram is not a complete representation of the higher generations of the lineage: I
have omitted from it those men who produced only daughters,
or who were childless; the question of the extended families of
ex-slaves is deferred to a later section. The most recent men
shown are those from whom the present extended families take
their names. Ganiṣ is said to have had five sons, all of whom can

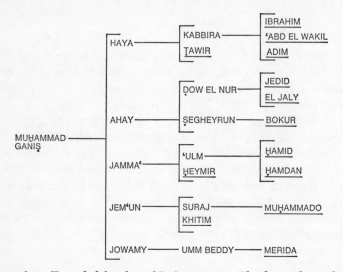

FIG. 16-1   Extended families of I. Ganiṣ, 1954. The figure shows their
relationships to one another and their descent from Muḥammad Ganiṣ
through males. Names underlined are founders of extended families
now recognized as such. In each case the founder was dead and his
sons were alive, except for I. Ḥamdan, whose founder was still alive.
Note: the order of the five sons of Muḥammad Ganiṣ is not remembered.

be linked by patrilineal descent with living people. But the order
of the sons is not remembered; accordingly 'Iyal Ganiṣ have no
notion of senior and junior lines, and all extended families are of
equal status if their founders were of the same generation.[2]

[2] The extended families deriving from Ṭawir, Ḥeymir, and Khitim are a
generation older than the others. The eldest man in these extended families,
El Khatim Ḥeymir, had the honorific title of *judul*, 'tree-stump', which is

With the exception of Ḥamdan, all the founders of extended families were dead. Their sons were alive, and, with 'Iyal Merida, some granddaughters and a grandson already had children. But mostly one extended family consisted of the adult sons (with their young offspring) of a dead man after whom it was named. Ḥamdan was an old man, so weakened with age that he had practically stopped migrating and lived at the granaries for most of the year.

Although the surra itself had clear agnatic segments, those intermediate between the surra and the extended family were not named. Thus the descendants of Ibrahim, 'Abd el Wakil, and Adim, were never mentioned together as forming a group called 'Iyal Kabbira; similarly, the descendants of Kabbira and Ṭawir together were never mentioned as forming a group called 'Iyal Haya.

It is consistent with this that the members of one extended family cohere more than the members of closely related extended families. During most of my fieldwork the members of 'Iyal Ganiṣ resided mainly in two camps. The main camp, which was under its leader Ḥurgaṣ, contained most members of 'Iyal Merida, 'Iyal Jedid, 'Iyal Bokur, 'Iyal Adim, and 'Iyal Ḥamid, as well as some ex-slaves and their descendants. The splinter camp consisted of 'Iyal Ḥamdan, 'Iyal Ṭawir, and 'Iyal Ḥeymir. Thus the descendants of 'Ulm were split: 'Iyal Ḥamid were in the main camp, while 'Iyal Ḥamdan were in the splinter camp. The descendants of Kabbira were also split: 'Iyal Adim lived in the main camp, while 'Iyal Ibrahim and 'Iyal 'Abd el Wakil lived in various other places. As among the larger segments of the tribe, alliances are formed within the surra which cut across those lines of cleavage which agnatic descent provides.[3] This is a feature of segmentation at all levels.

given to the living man of the surra who is closest to its source. He was accorded no special respect, and I did not notice that the possession of this title made any difference to the way people behaved towards him.

[3] In some respects, the intermediate groups between surra and extended family have statuses relating to their varying depths in a system of agnatic lineages. Examples: a claim to marry a girl of the surra can be upheld only if no closer agnatic cousin wishes to marry her; residual rights in property accrue to the closest surviving agnatic group; guardianship rights revert in the same way.

The last chapter* gave some details of households and extended families in the main camp. I show now where the other members of 'Iyal Ganiṣ were residing. The splinter camp existed under the name and the leading spirit of the old man Ḥamdan, although he himself lived in it only when it was near Muglad. The focal person around whom the other members of the splinter camp gathered was Ḥamdan's old widowed sister, Ḥamidy (Fig. 16-2). She had six daughters, who had been married; these were by her marriage to Muḥammado, the founder of one of the extended families; and through these marriages, she held cattle in trust for her daughter's children. The fact that she had these cattle in hand allowed her to move with 'Iyal Ganiṣ independently. Her only son, Kabbashy, now lived with his wife from 'Iyal Ganiṣ in another surra; if Ḥamidy had been poor, she would have lived with him. Although she was the daughter of 'Ulm, she was considered as belonging to the extended family of '*Iyal Ḥamdan*, named after her brother. Amongst 'Iyal Ḥamdan, the

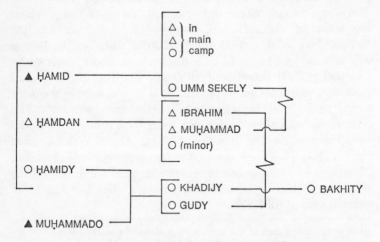

FIG. 16-2   The nucleus of the splinter camp of I. Ganiṣ.

elder son had married a daughter of Ḥamidy and Muḥammado, and the other was a bachelor, who was later to become engaged

* [Not reprinted here. Ed.]

to El Neimy (tent 8, main camp). Another daughter of Ḥamidy was the mother of El Hunna (tent 4) by Ḥurgaṣ's brother.

'Iyal Ḥeymir also lived here. El Khatim, the only son, was an oldish man with some dozen head of cattle. He had previously married a daughter of Ṭawir, but this had ended in divorce, with no children. He then married a woman from another surra, and their children were not yet married. Finally, *'Iyal Ṭawir* were present; the group consisted of Mas'ud, who had a wife from another surra; his brother Mulah, who was married to a woman of 'Iyal Ibrahim; and the bachelors El Hireyky and Bashir, who contributed in various ways to the upkeep of Mas'ud's household, and lived with him.

Some of the extended families were not represented in either of these two camps. Among *'Iyal Ibrahim,* one man worked as a policeman in Muglad and lived there with his wife from the Jubarat omodiya; another married a woman of the Kelabna lineage of Awlad Kamil and lived with his affines. Two of the daughters of Ibrahim had married out; a third was working in Muglad cooking at the girls' school, and the youngest was the wife of Bakora (of *'Iyal Khitim*), a cotton grower, who spent his spare time bringing hides from Dinka. From *'Iyal 'Abd el Wakil,* Ḥasan had married a woman of 'Iyal Ḥamdan; a hunter, he spent most of his time on the Bahr. His brother Adim, and his wife from another lineage, lived with him. El Medir was a bachelor who went from place to place engaging in trade in a small way. Of the daughters, one was married to Kabbashy Muḥammado and never lived with 'Iyal Ganiṣ, and another was married out. The only son of *'Iyal el Jaly* had married into 'Iyal Belebbo surra, with whom he lived; his sister had married into another surra. There were two senile half-brothers of Jedid and El Jaly, whose mothers had been Dinka. One was a frequent visitor at the main camp, where he lived on tent 8; the other lived with a married daughter. *'Iyal Khitim* seldom visited either of the camps. The eldest of the sons had died, leaving a daughter married in 'Iyal Belebbo surra. The other three were alive: Rashid herded sheep in the camp of his Awlad Mumin affines; his brother Timan, who had previously been married to a daughter of Ḥurgaṣ, was often with him. The other was Bakora, mentioned above.

At this time 'Iyal Ganiṣ had thirty-four males of what I took to be marriageable age (about twenty years) and over. Of these, eighteen were married, eleven divorced, and five had never been married. Thirteen were in the main camp, seven in the splinter camp, and fourteen elsewhere (four of these were at their wives' camps; three, all of them old men, were living with daughters or sisters who had married out; three were wandering merchants; two spent their whole year on the Bahr cultivating cotton and hunting; one was a policeman in Muglad; one lived with his wife, also from 'Iyal Ganiṣ, in another surra; and one bachelor lived with his brother and his wife in another surra). Thus twenty men resided in the two camps of 'Iyal Ganiṣ; and three others lived in different surras of Awlad Salamy; this meant that two-thirds of the men of 'Iyal Ganiṣ were usually within easy reach of their own leader in an emergency. Those staying with female relatives were old men; those away as merchants and cotton cultivators had no cattle and were trying to get capital. The temporary shortage of cattle in the surra had, I think, led to a greater dispersal of males than was normal. But there was still a strong nucleus of 'Iyal Ganiṣ men available, and when, a few months later, an attack was made on Ḥurgaṣ in his capacity as omda, all the males of 'Iyal Ganiṣ gathered in Muglad, where the conflict was staged, except the merchants who were out of the country.

At this same period there were forty-seven women of marriageable age (which I took to be about sixteen) and over. Of these, thirty-one were married, seven were widowed, six were divorcees, and three had never been married. Twelve were in the main camp and four in the splinter camp. Twenty-three lived with their husbands in other camps. Four widows were living away with their grown-up sons in their late husbands' camps; three middle-aged women were working for wages in Muglad and Abyei; and one girl had run off to Nahud. The dispersal of women is thus marked in comparison with that of men. Humr say their women are like water-melons,[4] because they spread far from their roots. Nevertheless, the extended family of birth always remains the focus for divorced or widowed women, unless it happens that they have grown-up sons to look after them in the camps of their affines. The surra is where the family of origin is, and where they make appeal in times of difficulty.

[4] *El 'ayyin biṭṭeykh.*

THE CAMP: PHYSICAL

Quite obviously 'Iyal Ganiṣ did not achieve the ideal association of camp and surra. I doubt if any surra does so permanently.
The last section showed the residence of members of this surra at
one point of time. Different seasons would show different residence patterns; different material conditions within the surra
would also lead to different residence patterns over a longer
period. Yet we are not left with a situation completely without
form, because a camp, although its membership changes, yet
retains an identity through its association with a surra. No camp
consists of males of more than one surra in regular co-residence.
A camp's identity, and such stability as it has, derives from this
asociation. The problem now turns on the relation between surra
and camp. I discuss this in general terms before considering 'Iyal
Ganiṣ in more detail.

A camp has four named parts: the ring of tents, the inner area
where the livestock are kraaled, the tree under which the men
sit in the daytime, and the hearth where men sit in the mornings
and evenings and where bachelors sleep.[5]

Tents of a camp are pitched as evenly as possible in a ring
which varies in diameter with the number of tents to be accommodated and the number of cattle to be kraaled.[6] The various
sites differ in the roughness of ground, the disposition of shady
trees, and the position of anthills, and these account for any difference there may be in the distances between the tents. When
the man directing a caravan has chosen the camp site, he indicates to the first woman who arrives where she should unload

[5] The camp is *ferig* (the word implies a unit of residence; it refers also to
the tents of one extended family, i.e. to an arc of the camp's circle). The
livestock enclosure is *dor*; the tree is *shejera*, or more fully *shejerat el juma'a*,
'tree of the group'; and the hearth is *ḍarra*.

[6] While the camp is usually circular in shape, when it is pitched beside a
watercourse or meadow in the Bahr region it is semicircular. The open side
faces the water or grazing, to which the cattle have free access at night. A
semicircular camp does not have its circumference cut at any particular place,
but the tents associated with one extended family always remain adjacent.
Bad ground sometimes leads to camps on the Bahr being pitched in a straight
line, or a gentle curve.

her bull and the direction in which her tent should face. The women following behind know what position to occupy with reference to the first. No member of camp, not even the leader, has any prerogative in regard to the position or the orientation of his tent.

The point in the camp circle at which a woman should pitch depends on two things: first, the recognized position in camp of the extended family to which she is attached, and second, her own place within the extended family. Although tents belong to women, the pattern of residence is based on the kinship relations of men. A father's tent is pitched with those of his sons in descending order on its right, and the position of the father's tent is determined in turn by the position which he occupied, in relation to his extended family, at the time he first established a household, and so on. Thus not only are the positions of fathers and sons established but also the relative positions of extended families, all deriving from the application of the same rules over past generations.

As the camp consists ideally of all the extended families of the surra, so each surra has a plan according to which all of its extended families can be accommodated in the same camp. But as all of the extended families, and all of the associated tents of each extended family, are seldom at the same camp at the same time, the circle is adjusted accordingly. Those members and their dependants who happen to be camping together form an even ring of tents; if some other members and their dependants form a second camp, they also form an even ring. In each case the relative order of pitching is determined by the ideal plan, but the gaps in the circle left by those who are absent are filled up to give the impression of a complete and undifferentiated unit. At any time other surra members or their dependants may be living away with relatives, or absent for some reason of economic need; such may be cultivators, merchants, or hunters, or those seeking wage labour. The camp is thus divided into arcs, each composed of some or all of the tents associated with one extended family. Those tents which do not belong to wives of camp members are those of divorced or widowed members of the surra, of widows whose sons are members, or of temporary visitors.

These women pitch their tents in the arc associated with the extended family to which they are related, and beside the tent of the closest married male.

Inside the ring of tents the livestock sleep at night and are milked morning and evening. Tethering ropes or small thorn enclosures are placed there for calves and small stock. If lions are about, the whole area inside the tents is enclosed with a thorn fence (*zariba*); a similar fence is built when a camp is near standing grain. Inside the circle, log fires are set at night among the cattle to provide smoke to keep off insects. Here, too, the camp's drum is slung over the limb of a convenient tree.

The general situation of a camp is chosen so as to be within convenient reach of water and grazing. Its actual site is selected so as to be within about a hundred yards of a tree which provides good shade. At this tree the men of the camp and their guests spend the hours from nine to five, roughly, if they are in camp at all. The angereybs are brought out; the men sit, pray, feed, rest, and work during the daytime and guests are received at the tree. It is the centre of the men's social life.

When the cattle are brought back from grazing in the late afternoon the men move from the tree to the hearth, which is normally situated on the camp's circumference close to the tree. This hearth is the equivalent of the tree for the mornings and evenings. At it the men have their evening meal and bachelors sleep. The less important guests also sleep here, but those accorded special respect are not brought in among the cattle; they sleep at the tree. Men congregate at the hearth at dawn for prayers and early morning milk and tea, and move out to the tree only when the cattle have gone to graze, or the sun becomes too hot to sit without shade.

There used to be another integral part of the camp. Domestic slaves built their shelters in an outer circle immediately behind the tents of their owners. Today those Humr (few by comparison with former slave-owners) who have Dinka servants or herders place them in the positions which slaves formerly occupied.

CO-OPERATION IN CATTLE MANAGEMENT

Of the two main economic activities, millet cultivation involves
co-operation on the basis of the household and cattle husbandry
involves co-operation on the basis of the camp. Cattle husbandry
has to go on all the time, and thus seasonally the household is
faced with the problem of simultaneously herding and cultivating, while those households which grow cotton have work in
yet a third place. Cattle herding invites large-scale co-operation,
and in some circumstances a few members of a camp have a joint
responsibility for all the cattle. At all times the members of one
camp recognize general responsibility for all their cattle.

When cultivation is not in progress the daily grazing is organized by means of a camp roster of herders. Each cattle owner,
or two or three together, in turn provides a youth (or sometimes
a girl or an adult) to go out with a grazing herd.[7] In the camp in
which I stayed, each cattle owner provided a youth who herded
five successive days and then rested. The owner of no, or very
few, cattle is not normally asked to provide a herder; if the owner
of a large herd is temporarily without herders this is no matter:
the duties are still carried out. Adults herd the cattle if the terrain is difficult or if the grazing itself is scarce or distant. Sometimes the cattle of a father and those of a son are counted, for
the purposes of the roster, as one unit. Arrangements vary widely
from camp to camp. A rich man may employ a Dinka to herd
his cattle for a year in exchange for food and clothing and a nominal wage. Ex-slaves of a family, or their descendants, or other
dependants of a rich man, may act as herders and receive in
return gifts or loans of cattle. A gift or loan in the past compels
a poor man to serve in any capacity: even if he does not go
herding, he assists in milking, in fetching logs, and in general
supervision of the cattle at night.

[7] By a 'grazing herd' I mean not the cattle of one man but a group of cattle
that normally go out to graze together. It may consist of the cattle of more
than one owner; or it may consist of part of one man's herd. The cattle of one
camp are sometimes formed into one grazing herd, but two or three can exist
in one camp. The criterion is usually numerical: see next section.

Thus it often happens that the grazing duties are undertaken by youths of one household on behalf of the cattle of all camp members. A different herding system is used in the special circumstances of the planting and harvesting seasons. It is used also at other times when, for various reasons, it is advisable to remove the cattle from the main camp: for the sake of mobility if the grazing is scarce and sporadic, or to ensure that women will not take milk that calves should be drinking, an important precaution in hot seasons when there is little greenery. This arrangement involves the division of the camp into two parts, the one being the cattle camp, and the other consisting of those people who stay behind with the heavy baggage.[8] On these occasions the cattle go off under the charge of youths and girls, with occasionally one or two adults for general supervision and a woman to do a little cooking. Those who stay behind in the main camp retain a few cows to provide some milk. Here again, each owner does not need to supply a youth for the cattle camp; if he can spare no one, he still knows that his cows will be properly tended.

During the short periods before planting and after harvest when cattle are set to manure the gardens, the camps themselves break up into single tents or into small groups. Those of the same surra who happen in any year to be gardening near one another herd their cattle together, and have them spend the nights in successive gardens.

With these various arrangements a man can have his cattle tended at all times, be he rich or poor, with or without family, with or without interests elsewhere. In particular, they allow of prolonged absence on the part of individual members of the camp for the sake of activities such as marketing, trading ventures, fetching grain from distant granaries, giraffe-hunting, wage labour, and so forth. Any member can go away and be sure that his cattle will be herded and that his camp mates will keep a watchful eye on his beasts.

A grazing herd is much more stable than a camp of men and women. Cattle get to know their herds, and stay with them.

---

[8] Respectively, *'azzaba*, from *'azab* and *'azaba*, bachelor and spinster, for those who go with the cattle are usually youngsters; and *tegeliya*, from *tagil*, meaning heavy.

Beasts which are moved to another grazing herd always cause
trouble for a few days: when grazing, they wander off after the
herd they have left. Changes are avoided as much as possible.
Men and women, on the other hand, are continually on the move
for a variety of reasons: a man may visit his in-laws for a brief
spell, or go to another camp until a grudge wears off, or go away
to contract business or take a job. When he does so he leaves his
cattle in their original camp and grazing herd. To take his cattle
away would be a sign of acute difference with his camp mates.
If he leaves his cattle he implies that he intends to return soon,
and also that he has not lost faith with his kinsmen to the extent
that he fears they will neglect his animals during his absence.

THE INFLUENCE OF CATTLE NUMBERS ON SURRA ORGANIZATION

The way a surra is organized depends to some extent on the
number of cattle the members own and the distribution of this
ownership. A surra with few cattle may have all its beasts as a
single grazing herd. A surra with many cattle may divide them
into two, three, or more grazing herds, and if they are so divided
the divisions tend to be permanent while the cattle numbers
remain constant. Brothers, or a father and his sons, usually have
their cattle in the same grazing herd, but within the surra close
cousins are no more likely than distant cousins to have their
cattle together.

Humr recognize an optimum size for a grazing herd. A very
large one becomes unwieldy: the tail end straggles out of sight
through the trees; towards the end of the dry season, when grazing may be scarce, a large grazing herd is bad because the fast
cattle trample over the small patches of good grazing before the
slower cattle arrive. Humr do not enumerate their cattle, but it
appeared to me that about 150 head was the largest convenient
size for a grazing herd that would suit all seasons. If grass is ample, young herders may join their grazing herds together as they
go out so that they can chat and play as the cattle graze; but the
division into herds of this size ensures easy handling in the more

difficult seasons. Watering from wells also limits the useful size of a grazing herd. But herds vary widely in the number of their cattle: the owner of a thousand head, unable to find the hands to deal with six or seven herds, may have to divide his beasts up as conveniently as he can in relation to the labour available; and conversely, many people break away from their main camps and herd their cattle on a very small scale.

If the cattle owned by members of one surra are split into more than one grazing herd, as they usually are, various arrangements are possible. Under one of these, all the cattle are kraaled inside the same camp. Each herd has its own sector of the enclosure; each herd is provided separately with its roster of herders; each herd is provided separately with its own smoke fires; and the small stock and the calves of each herd—or sometimes of each owner—are tied up or enclosed in separate thorn fences. The cattle know the herds to which they belong, and if they leave camp at night of their own accord to go to nearby grazing, they go out and return by herds. This arrangement does not lead to any other differences in the organization of a camp. The men still sit together under the same tree; they entertain guests in common; the tents form an unbroken circle; although the cattle are taken out in different groups, they leave at the same time; the camp has a unified grazing policy, and moves from site to site as a unit.

Under an alternative arrangement, the tents of the owners of different grazing herds are pitched in adjacent circles, and each herd is kraaled in a separate enclosure. Here, the two or more camps still usually have a unified grazing policy, decide together on times of moves and on new sites, and move in a single caravan; and while there may be much intervisiting, each camp has its own tree and its own hearth, and the men do not entertain guests in common.

A third possibility is for the owners of different herds to camp quite separately, perhaps many miles apart. If there is a tendency in this matter, it is that on the Bahr in the dry season the camps are small and scattered and that in the Babanusa in the rains the camps are large. These arrangements are consistent with the situation of water and grazing; and moreover, Humr say that

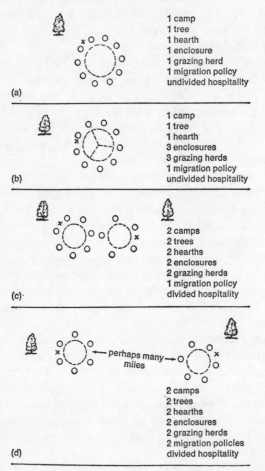

(a)

1 camp
1 tree
1 hearth
1 enclosure
1 grazing herd
1 migration policy
undivided hospitality

(b)

1 camp
1 tree
1 hearth
3 enclosures
3 grazing herds
1 migration policy
undivided hospitality

(c)

2 camps
2 trees
2 hearths
2 enclosures
2 grazing herds
1 migration policy
divided hospitality

(d)

← perhaps many miles →

2 camps
2 trees
2 hearths
2 enclosures
2 grazing herds
2 migration policies
divided hospitality

FIG. 16-3   Some possible types of camp formation.

during the rains, if mosquitoes have penetrated the Babanusa, it is better to have big camps, for they create more smoke.[9]

These alternatives cover the possible cattle-herding arrangements at times when there are no separate cattle camps. Extended families of more than one surra hardly ever join together in a single camp. But when there are separate cattle camps, the cattle of more than one surra may join together in one large enclosure. In the early part of the southward migration, and during the harvest period when cattle are taken to eat the regrowth in the Goz, cattle camps of two or three surras may join together, with many hundreds of head inside the ring of the few rough shelters that the women present may build. Large concentrations are possible and even suitable at these times because the herding can be left to children, and one or two adults are enough to deal with any emergency that may arise. Likewise in the first few weeks in the Babanusa this arrangement is useful; safety in numbers is then sought by the young people, who do most of the herding while elders work in the gardens. The cattle which combine on these occasions usually belong to surras which are closely related, or which at least belong to the same omodiya. There is a strong element of chance in the combinations: cattle camps which happen to find themselves close together may temporarily amalgamate to form a single enclosure. The cattle continue to be taken out in their individual grazing herds.

Whether a surra moves and camps as a single unit or in separate groups, and the lines along which it divides, are thus matters which are to some extent determined by the number of cattle the surra owns and the way in which the ownership is distributed among the surra members. The limiting factor is the convenient size of a grazing herd, but the availability of water and grazing leads to seasonal variations. The arrangements in operation at any time may take account also of the relations of surra members with one another.

[9] When insects are about, camps of many different surras are often pitched close to one another, forming a big encampment called *dukuk*. Smoke from one camp covers others instead of drifting uselessly into the forest.

LEADERSHIP AND SOCIAL CO-OPERATION WITHIN
THE SURRA

The convenience of herding may by itself be an adequate cause for the splitting of a surra into different units for the purpose of cattle husbandry, and the fact that the males of one surra camp in different places does not by itself indicate strained relations. Cattle may be so numerous as to cause a united group to form more than one cattle-herding unit. On the other hand members split up for other reasons, and the few head of cattle of a small surra may be divided into a number of grazing herds in widely separated camps even though it would be quite practicable to graze them all together.

Each surra has a generally accepted leader, who, in this capacity, has no administrative recognition; but he may happen to be an administrative officer such as an omda, or a tribute sheikh, or be known to the administration as a 'notable' of the tribe. The surra has no administrative function as far as the Government is concerned, although its importance to the Humr is great. The man recognized as its leader is called the *reis* (head); he has his position from the fact, usually, that he is the wealthiest of its members in cattle; but a man who is already an omda or sheikh, or is brother or son to a past one, may have the position. Spokesmanship and general diplomatic ability are also good qualifications, but they have to be backed by wealth. In his capacity as leader of a camp rather than leader of a surra he is known as *reis el ferig*. A splinter camp also has its own leader.

The name of a surra usually includes a form of the name of its founder. But Humr may mention instead the name of its leader; thus 'Iyal Ganiṣ could be called *nas Ḥurgaṣ,* Ḥurgaṣ's people. The splinter camp was never referred to as 'the camp of 'Iyal Ganiṣ'; it was usually 'the camp of 'Iyal Ḥamdan', or 'the camp of Ḥamdan', or, very occasionally, 'the camp from among Ḥurgaṣ's people' or 'the camp from among 'Iyal Ganiṣ'.[10] It seems

[10] The phrases used are in the form *ferig 'Iyal Fulan, ferig Fulan, ferig nas Fulan,* and *min nas Fulan.* The use of the word *ferig* followed by the name

to be general that the splinter camp takes the name of its own leader and not the name of the surra leader or the surra founder; this is an implied insult to the surra leader and the founding ancestor.

The ideal behaviour is for members of one surra to show a united front.[11] They should be seen to camp together, and be mentioned together in a phrase linking them to their common ancestor, in the ''Iyal Ganiṣ' form. A large camp is a matter for admiration, and one which has more than about fifteen tents gives rise to approving comment: the leader has many followers, and their relations are harmonious.

But when a surra has divided and a part of it has camped at a distance for reasons not connected with the needs of the cattle, those in the main camp, who still follow their surra leader, speak ill of their kinsmen. There has been a quarrel, but the comment goes beyond the immediate reasons for it, to state that the splinter camp is showing disrespect to the ancestor who founded the surra. To move away is to exhibit undue pride: the name of the leader of the splinter group is mentioned at the expense of that

---

of the splinter-camp leader is in line with the use of the word *ferig* applied to the section of a camp associated with one extended family.

[11] Although it may be split by temporary quarrels, the surra retains a formal unity much clearer than that of lineages of other kinds. Some of the characteristics of this unit are as follows. Its male members should form a single camp with their dependants. Members should give the outside world the impression that they are all brothers of an equal degree of kinship. They should play down to the outside world any cause of shame in their behaviour to one another. Marriage within the surra is preferred. A man does not boast, as he boasts of other exploits, that he has made love to women of the surra or to wives or ex-wives of its members. If he wants to marry the ex-wife of a fellow-member he first seeks the permission of her ex-husband, even though the divorce has been final and irrevocable. If a man leaves his surra and joins another, the surra of his birth still bears important responsibilities if he should inflict death or injury: the surra is a man's blood, which is indivisible. Until recently blood-money could not be claimed against a fellow-member. No claims for damages by cattle to crops are made against fellow-members.

These established rules apart, there are other indications: some surras have a drum beat which is exclusively theirs; some have an exclusive cattle brand; some have an exclusive ear-clip for their stock. Many instances have recently arisen in which those people who are on the books of one sheikh for the purposes of tax-paying are exclusively the members of one surra.

I set these points together here for convenience. Some of them have been discussed; others will be amplified in due course.

of the surra ancestor or the man upon whom his mantle has fallen, the surra leader. Moreover, people who move away impair the notion that their surra is united and undifferentiated.

What Humr find most offensive about a split is connected with the value of generosity. Often those who break away give as an excuse the meanness of the surra leader, who, after all, is usually the wealthiest man in it. But those in the main camp reciprocate with an accusation which is much more devastating: that they are avoiding their obligations of hospitality. For as a general rule Humr treat their guests with a generosity and formality which varies in relation to their social distance. If a man from a closely related surra drops in to see a friend or a relative, he goes straight to the tent concerned and has the freedom of the camp. People from distant surras are received at the tree. Those who are not very close kinsmen come as guests not of a single person but of the whole camp. A traveller looking for a place to spend the night inquires in the locality and goes to the camp of the man in the neighbourhood with the best reputation for hospitality. I lived in the camp of an omda whose generosity was a tribal byword, and hardly a night passed without the obligation to feed and accommodate guests. The arrival of a guest is an immediate excuse for a party. It is the duty of each extended family to produce tea, milk, sour milk, and a grain dish. A ram can be seized from anyone's flock for the entertainment of the visitor. The men of the camp serve the guest in addition by feeding, watering, and tying his horse, supplying water for ritual ablutions, and providing an angereyb and comfortable bedding for his sole use to sit on by day and to sleep on by night. A traveller seeks out a renowned leader of a surra, and his visit affects all those in the same camp. Those who camp separately from the leader of the surra attract fewer guests. Accordingly those who leave, and pitch camp apart, are accused of conserving their resources at the expense of their kinsmen. The visitor sees less food prepared in his honour, and sees a smaller camp, than he would do if the surra camped in one circle.

CO-OPERATIVE ASPECTS OF CULTIVATION

Although the household is the main unit of co-operation in agriculture, some activities connected with it involve a wider group. We have seen how, for sociability and if convenient, owners of nearby gardens may camp together at sowing and harvest, and how they use their cattle together for manuring. In the use of garden land, the protection of stored grain, and to some extent its transport, groups larger than the household share common interests.

Humr have communal grazing rights over the whole of their country but they own garden land as individuals: whereas in a broad sense grazing land is abundant, land suitable for cultivation was in the past comparatively scarce.[12] Individual ownership gives garden land a special meaning: more than any other place, the Humrawi nomad looks upon his garden land as his 'home'. Members of an extended family often cultivate close to one another, and together they regard the site as their home. The same is to some extent true of the surra. For 'Iyal Ganiṣ the rain-pool called El Bieyṭy was the main cultivation area of the leading extended family, 'Iyal Merida, and had much the same relation to the surra as the Muglad had to the whole tribe: it was, so to speak, their *dar*. But each person has various places which he goes to and cultivates. A single garden may retain its fertility for five years or so; a move is then made to another garden which may be some miles away, and this may be cultivated for another five years and in turn may be regarded as 'home'. Most surras have two or three blocks of land where most members have gardens, but these blocks are not exploited in a unified fashion: some gardens are depleted sooner than others; families sometimes move away out of dudgeon with their fellows, and so on.

[12] The recent deep bores in the Babanusa supply dry-season water for those wishing to open gardens there. When Humr first settled their present country the question of defence encouraged the concentration of gardens and granaries in the single area of the Muglad. The cultivable area in the Muglad is much smaller than the Muglad itself, since the staple bulrush millet is grown only on the sand ridges.

Yet the association of individual, extended family, and surra with particular pieces of land persists, and indeed the only even semi-permanent structures of Humr nomads are the granaries which serve groups of neighbouring gardens and which persist so long as anyone is cultivating them.

The gardens lie for the most part near the migration trails of their owners. The millet gardens of the Mezaghna omodiya are nearly all inside a strip, about twenty-five miles long and about three miles across, running north and south through the Muglad. Within this area, there are gardens belonging to other omodiyas as well and to Muglad townsmen; gardens of Awlad Kamil, Fadliya, and Jubarat are intermingled with pockets of Mezaghna.

Most of the garden land in the cultivable areas of the Muglad and along the Wadi el Ghalla has long been exploited and blocks of it are associated with particular surras. This association derives from the method of opening up garden land, which follows the sequence of events I witnessed when a member of 'Iyal Ganiṣ found an excellent tract for cotton cultivation on the Bahr. He discovered this land, about half a square mile, when he was out herding. He mentioned it on his return to camp, and next day all the available men of the camp went to see it. They took axes and cut a sign like the cattle brand of 'Iyal Ganiṣ on the tree trunks. In this way they reserved it against all comers: any one might graze there during times when it was not planted, but as far as cultivation was concerned it was Ganiṣ land. The discoverer divided it unasked among the other members of the surra who had gone with him and who wanted to add to their cultivations. When men from closely related surras begged him for shares, he refused.[13]

Thus tracts of garden land came to be associated with surras; within the blocks the ownership of sites is personal, and is handed down from father to son. Individual ownership is strictly recognized, but there is very free give-and-take among members of one surra, who use one another's land with permission. In any year all or most of the surra's land which is in a cultivable

[13] I. Ganiṣ have an exclusive cattle brand, but even if they share a brand the discovering surra owns the cultivation rights. I. Ganiṣ had not used it by the time I left the field, but the rights in it are theirs so long as the signs remain visible on the trees.

state is put to the most convenient use. Once land has lain fallow for some time it is readily loaned to members of other surras, who do not, however, gain title to it.

Thus, despite this association, in any year the worked gardens of one surra are dispersed; no one block is used in its entirety at one time. And the blocks of one surra are interspersed with gardens belonging to members of other surras and even other omodiyas.

Small groups of tents form at sowing and again at harvest. The farmers co-operate in manuring the gardens, and in making thorn enclosures to contain millet heads as they are cut and to keep off livestock; when the cutting is over each household takes its turn to have its grain stamped: children ride bulls round and round over the heads of grain. The crop then has to be stored for the period when the camps are away from the gardens. Those of the same surra who cultivate near one another have a number of granaries, built on stilts, in one place, often enclosed by a thorn fence. Details of the arrangements for storage and protection of grain differ. Each granary site has a guardian, and arrangements vary in relation to the distance between the gardens of one surra, and the number of people who are willing to remain in the Muglad to guard the grain. Thus the crops may be stored in one, two, or more clusters of granaries and guarded by different numbers of people. Those who are willing to remain behind include senile people and those with obligations to care for them; men with no cattle; and ex-slaves, also with no or few cattle, who live in a semi-dependent position upon their former masters. The grain guardians may build a semi-permanent 'village'[14] of grass huts beside the granaries; they usually cultivate intensively themselves; and they have a reward for guarding the grain.[15]

A household takes with it on the southward migration only as much grain as a bull—or perhaps two—will carry. In order to be supplied during the course of the dry season grain caravans called *jangala* leave Bahr camps to go to the granaries, and

---

[14] The Humr call it *hilla*, the usual term for a village of a non-nomadic tribe.

[15] Often a *midd* (about seven pounds) for every bull load (about 210 pounds) removed from the granaries they are guarding.

return laden. The transport is organized sometimes by a single household but more often by a camp, available bulls being sent with available men to bring grain for those households that need it. In some camps there is an arrangement whereby all the grain brought south in one transport is divided equally among the households, even although the household itself may not have grain stored. This has the effect of conserving for the calves the milk which the household would otherwise have to drink.

Cotton demands different patterns of residence and co-operation. Most people cultivate millet, but the recently introduced cotton is a matter of choice. A few people have given up the cultivation of millet entirely, and depend on the proceeds of their cotton crop to buy grain. Where cotton has been longest cultivated, notably among the Salamat near Lake Keylak in the east of the country, most people work at it during the rains after sending cattle camps off northwards. These who remain follow after the weeding, but stay in the north for only a month. The Salamat have what amounts to almost permanent camps, with tents more elaborate than the usual Humr tent. Some cultivate grain in the region of Keylak. But further west only a few members of some surras grow cotton. During the season (May to August for planting and weeding, and November onwards for harvesting and selling) they live in villages, also called *hilla*, of grass huts, or tents if available. At one cotton centre, Seidana, the village consisted of members of half a dozen surras, each group forming their own small circle of tents or huts within the village. Nearly all were Mezaghna in whose summer area the village was situated, but it included a few Faḍliya and Awlad 'Umran. Cotton has thus led to a new form of residential arrangement, to which we may relate the scarcity of suitable high ground in the Bahr region and the fact that very few Humr cultivate cotton and those who do seek the company of their fellows.

MODES OF CO-OPERATION AMONG 'IYAL GANIṢ

The organization of 'Iyal Ganiṣ is to be understood in the light of these general comments on the organization of camp and surra and how they are related. 'Iyal Ganiṣ formed two camps following a dispute over the marriage of one of the women. Ḥurgaṣ, the leader, decided to give his half-sister Umm Una in marriage[16] to an influential middle-aged man of the 'Ariya major lineage of the Mezaghna. In this decision his main antagonist was the old man Ḥamdan 'Ulm, who wanted the girl to go to a youth of 'Iyal Ganiṣ: either to his own son Muḥammad, or else to El Hireyky, son of Ṭawir. The custom is to give preference to someone of the girl's surra, but Ḥurgaṣ, as the wealthiest man and an omda, felt in a position to force the issue. He wanted a marriage into the 'Ariya for political reasons and he arranged it, although he must have guessed the consequences. Nevertheless, the breach was not wide enough to endanger seriously the permanent unity of the surra; the splinter group, without exception, gave him moral support during the later attack upon him.

In 1954 the groups comprising these two camps co-operated in varying degrees. At the end of 1953 all the cattle had made the southern migration together as a single cattle camp, but when the first full camp sites were formed on the Bahr, 'Iyal Hamdan and their followers camped separately. Each group went to four sites independently before they reunited at the end of the dry season: then in March they camped in adjacent semi-circles at the side of the Regeba Angol. The splinter camp began its northward move a day earlier than the main camp; and it was not until their second rains site in the Babanusa that they came together again in adjacent circles. At the return to the Muglad in September they moved separately. Then gardeners went to their gardens and the people of each camp organized their own cattle camp. For the Goz grazing before harvest the cattle of the whole surra reunited, and shared a big kraal with the cattle of a closely related surra and those of a surra of the 'Ariya lineage. Once more they returned to the gardens and split up until the southward migration, when they slowly reunited as chance dictated throughout its course.

It was useful to have arrangements of this kind. The splitting and reuniting of herds answered the practical problems of cattle

---

[16] In fact Sheybun, his young half-brother and full brother to Umm Una, would normally have had control of her destiny. But Sheybun was much younger and had received financial and other assistance from Ḥurgaṣ, and it was difficult for him to go against him.

management and agriculture. In this case the splitting and coming together of cattle tallied with the accepted procedure: concentration of cattle in the Babanusa and in the Goz at harvest time, dispersal on the Bahr. The detailed arrangements were made in the context of a quarrel which had divided the surra. In the course of my fieldwork 'Iyal Ganiş never camped in a single exclusive circle of tents: 'Iyal Ḥamdan and those with them never agreed to share a single tree with the leader of their surra, and so did not help him to entertain his guests. They often visited one another, sometimes for argument, but sometimes out of friendship. The brotherhood of surra fellows is taken for granted, and has the strength to contain a dispute of this nature. While still bitter towards one another the members continued to take responsibility when occasion arose for one another's cattle.

In these camps marital connexions within the surra appeared to add to the value of those ties which already existed through close agnatic kinship. Those who resided in the splinter camp did not have the same kinds of connexions by marriage with Ḥurgaş and his extended family as did 'Iyal Adim, 'Iyal Jedid, and 'Iyal Ḥamid. Those who had such connexions through extant marriages all remained in the main camp. No doubt the wealth and prestige of Ḥurgaş as omda added force to the obligation of his surra in-laws to live with him, although sometimes it was a struggle for them to do so. The case of Abu Dik is one in point. As brother's son to Ḥamdan he was in a delicate position. Although Abu Dik was living in the main camp with his wife, Ḥurgaş's daughter, he struck up a close friendship with his cousin El Hireyky, with whom his sympathies lay in the dispute, and he seldom sat at the omda's tree. A member of the camp commented: 'He cannot be angry, he has eaten the sweets of Ḥurgaş and married his daughter; yet he has to show some anger if his uncle Ḥamdan is not to tax him with neglect simply because Ḥurgaş has given him a wife.'

Another factor affecting the groupings was no doubt the shortage of cattle in the surra at the time. It was because of this shortage that some men were away from both camps earning enough money to start herds. In order to survive, 'Iyal Ganiş were forced to cluster round those with cattle. This clustering arose from economic dependence, but in turn it led to dependence of a more general kind. The biggest owner by far was Ḥurgaṣ himself, although in the main camp El Hunna and ʿAli Jakkak both had about ten head. Likewise the splinter camp clustered around the nucleus of the widow Ḥamidy's cattle and those, rather fewer, of El Khatim Ḥeymir. Ḥamdan could lead this break-away on the practical basis of his sister Ḥamidy's cattle. Most of the other members of these camps had no more than a riding bull for the household and perhaps a cow or two.

These two factors affecting alliances—differential riches and marital links—are themselves closely connected; a poor man, like Abu Dik, has a better chance of marriage within the surra, for a surra wife costs less, and additional allowances for poverty are more likely to be made within the surra than outside it. The marriage itself accordingly creates a sense of indebtedness. There are two consequences: first, the felt indebtedness is repaid by loyalty; and second, the husband knows that in great hardship he can rely—if not on his account, then on account of his wife and her children—on his richer affines.

The distribution of cattle ownership thus affects not only the composition of households, but that of camps also: men with few cattle cluster round those with many; poor people live beside their richer affines; a man who has given or loaned a cow attaches the recipient to him in perpetuity.

NON-ARAB DESCENT

So far I have mentioned only those members of ʿIyal Ganiṣ who are said to be of Arab descent. These include some people whose mothers were Dinka, Nuba, Fur, or other non-Arabs. Humr used to take slave women as concubines; descendants of these unions are as completely 'Arab' as other Humr, and through their fathers they have a firm place in an extended family.

ʿIyal Ganiṣ and most other surras also have attached to them people whose paternal ancestors were not Arabs. They claim to belong to surras, and are accorded membership in various degrees and with some misgivings. They fall into a number of different categories. We have to distinguish between those with a male ancestor who was a Dinka (or less commonly a member of another tribe) who was not a slave; those with a male ancestor who was a freed slave, or who themselves were ceremonially freed; and those of a slave line, of whom none were ceremonially freed.

The Humr dialect does not distinguish between a person who was a slave to a Humrawi and a person who was or is a pagan. The word *'abid* refers alike to domestic slaves and to people who, because they were pagans, could have been appropriately captured and turned into slaves. Nowadays the word applies to any Dinka (and the few Nuba who are in this position)

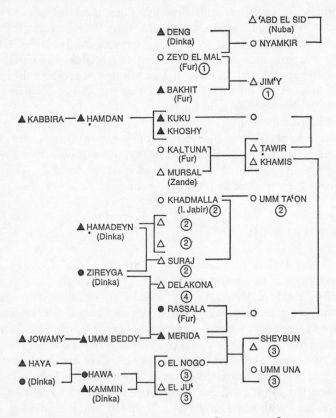

FIG. 16-4   Non-Arab descent in I. Ganiṣ, showing residence in main camp and links with I. Merida, etc.

hired by Humr to herd their cattle and to cultivate, and, more widely, to the southern Sudanese in general. But a 'good' Dinka, one who has adopted Islam, or who follows some Humr customs, or who lives (as a few do) in independence among Humr, may be mentioned more respectfully as Jengayi, or Dinka.

Domestic slavery came under administrative control with the Condominium and was supposed to be abolished finally by 1924. Many of the domestic slaves of 'Iyal Ganiṣ remained with them voluntarily. At any time a slave could be freed by being declared free by his owner. A slave was his owner's 'son'; a freed slave (*'atig*) became a 'brother'. The liberation ceremony, which continued to take place after the official abolition of the system, consisted in a declaration of the owner; the freed man was then ridden on horseback round neighbouring camps and greeted with applause; he would receive presents of money or small stock, some of which he used for a sacrifice. Once liberated, a male slave and his offspring were Arabs and full members of surra and tribe. An unliberated male slave's child was himself a slave and was inherited like his father; a female slave was never liberated, but could be taken as a concubine (*serraya*) by her owner, and her children would then be freeborn; alternatively her owner might marry her off to another slave.

'Iyal Ganiṣ had people belonging to all these categories. In the main camp, tents 1, 2, and 3 consisted largely of people with non-Arab descent in one line or another. To take first tent 3, whose household has already been described in terms of its relationship with Merida: the woman who owned it, El Nogo, and her brother El Ju', were children of a Dinka called Kammin. He was not a slave but a 'good' Dinka who spent much time in the 'Iyal Ganiṣ camps. He married Hawa, who was the daughter of Haya, one of the five sons of Muḥammad Ganiṣ; Hawa's mother was also a Dinka. El Nogo and El Ju' were treated like real Humr, and both were Muslims. El Ju' was no more subservient to Ḥurgaṣ than were others without cattle who depended largely on him. But El Ju' suffered one disability: he belonged to no extended family of the Humr, and he took no part in the payment or receipt of blood-money. On the other hand if he had been injured there is no doubt that 'Iyal Ganiṣ would have put forward a strong case for blood-money on his behalf.

The household of tent 2 was connected through Merida's father, Umm Beddy, to the people of tent 3. Umm Beddy had, amongst others, two Dinka slaves, a woman called Zireyga and a man called Ḥamadeyn. Zireyga as Umm Beddy's concubine bore Delakona, the old man who was still an occasional visitor at tent 4. Then Umm Beddy married Ḥamadeyn off to Zireyga. Ḥamadeyn was ceremonially freed, and their son Suraj later married Khadmalla, a freewoman from 'Iyal Jabir surra, and brought her to live in the camp. The other members of the household were Khadmalla's daughter by a previous marriage, and two young children who were half-brothers of Suraj. Suraj and his child brothers thus constituted an extended family of Humr, *'Iyal Ḥamadeyn,* and they had their part in blood-money transactions. A freed slave receives a formal status higher than that of a 'good' Dinka.

Tent 1 belonged to a woman called Zeyd el Mal; she and her late husband Bakhit had both been slaves of Umm Beddy, and later of Merida. Although Bakhit's character was still highly praised, he had never been freed. Zeyd el Mal and her son Jim'y made up this household. Jim'y was in his late twenties when I knew him. He and his mother had been inherited by Ḥurgaṣ on Merida's death; Ḥurgaṣ then ceremonially freed him. In terms of blood-money the effect, although he was now by courtesy a 'brother' of Ḥurgaṣ, was to give him a position in a separate 'extended family' of which he was the only male member: he would pay and receive a share equal to that of each other extended family of the surra. But outside this formality he had disabilities. Although he was courting, and spending much money on, the step-daughter of Suraj (tent 2), his antecedents made it likely that she would not be allowed to marry him. He was without cattle, and was on Ḥurgaṣ's own roster of cattle herders. His ceremonial freedom created a sense of indebtedness in him, which had been strengthened by loans of animals from time to time.

On Bakhit's death Zeyd el Mal married Deng, another 'good' Dinka. The daughter of this union, Nyamkir, married a slave of Merida called 'Abd el Sid, who was destitute and who now frequently helped Ḥurgaṣ in herding; some years he would stay behind in the Muglad to guard the granaries of 'Iyal Merida. In the same position also was El Siteyb, with his sons; he was the son of a Nuba woman who had been a slave of Umm Beddy, and had married another slave from 'Iyal Belebbo surra. El Siteyb himself married a slave of 'Iyal Jabir surra. None of these were given ceremonial recognition of their freedom; none had cattle, and all had depended upon the omda for their upkeep in one way or another.

Lastly there was a group which did not move with the camps at all, but lived in a permanent village near one of the cultivation areas of the surra. A man called Mursal, who had been a Zande slave of a Ganiṣ man, married a Fur slave woman and had a number of children. On the official ending of slavery the family set up the village. There were two sons, of whom one married a daughter of Merida and a Fur slave woman; the other married the daughter of Kuku Ḥamdan, the brother of Mursal's 'owner', and a free woman. These were close kin to 'Iyal Merida because Kuku was also the father of Ghubeysha's daughters in tent 4.

Umm Beddy and his fellows had other slaves as well, but they had emigrated and I could only get the vaguest information about them. Some lived in Kadugli. But for those ex-slaves still present, it is noticeable that they have become connected by blood ties with the families that owned them. The marriages and concubinages of these people were in the hands of their owners who seem to have made a point of creating these ties. In the event, when the slaves were freed by Government order or were given ceremonial recognition of their freedom, many already had their economic dependence reinforced by kinship with their former owners. The family of Mursal apart, all those mentioned were still dependent on Ḥurgaṣ economically, and served and supported him.

Descendants of slaves, even though ceremonially freed, do not fully enjoy the privileges that Humr do. Personality enters in to some extent, but usually the knowledge of non-Arab descent is enough to make Humr attribute a lower status to slave descendants. There is a contradiction apparent in the difference between descendants of 'good' Dinka, who do not achieve recognition in terms of blood-money, and freed slaves who do, for the offspring of good Dinka seem, in general, to have better standing than the offspring of freed slaves. Thus El Juʿ and El Nogo were hardly distinguishable from Arabs as most freed slaves were. This distinction is further emphasized by the word applied to slave descendants of one surra as a group: *melekiya,* which is connected with the word *melek,* to own. Slave descendants are still *ʿabid* or *melekiya* behind their backs. In general they find difficulty in marrying or courting free-born women.

Within the *melekiya* a distinction exists between those who go with the cattle and those who, like Mursal, are independent, relying on agriculture for their livelihood. Many villages like Mursal's exist in the Muglad and round about, each being called the *melekiya* of the surra, or of the man who would have inherited them had slavery continued. Their way of life is now more akin to that of Berti, Maʾalia, and other settled tribesmen in the area. But they sustain special relations with the surra from which they derive; Mursal said he was a member of ʿIyal Ganiṣ, and most of his family married people with connexions there. Between Ḥurgaṣ and Mursal there was a relationship of a kind in which they emphatically and jokingly emphasized their humility towards one another: at Mursal's for lunch one day, Ḥurgaṣ said he was as nothing and poor, and living on Mursal's generosity; Mursal was the big chief there and Ḥurgaṣ was at his command. Mursal retaliated by bringing the lunch himself, instead of having a woman do so; and brought it, moreover, running. The economic independence of Mursal and his people distinguished them from those who served in the camps, for the latter were in a clear position of subordination to the cattle owners for whom they worked.

THE EXTENSION OF PERSONAL FOLLOWINGS

The way in which I have described the organization of the Humr units, from household to camp and surra, has involved much alternation between social and economic facts. These groups are those which co-operate actively in exploiting the economic resources of a difficult country. There has to be co-operation, and different purposes need co-operation at different levels. Humr who co-operate are kinsmen in the same household or camp or surra. But while everyone is involved in co-operative activity of different kinds, the composition of co-operating groups is very variable. Flexibility arises from the freedom of movement of the individual, who can still rely on his kinsmen to see that his cattle do not suffer. No group of people has to remain in a state of permanent co-operation. The surra is the ideal herding unit, but it can and does split up for various reasons. At any time the camp is the actual herding and residential unit, but the composition of the camp changes with the seasons and its members' personal relations. The freedom to graze one's cattle anywhere in the country and the existence of alternative lands for cultivation allow social strains between kinsmen to be translated into physical distance. Humr suit their residence to their friendships. This is true for political relations at higher levels as well; lack of group rights in specific stretches of land, and the differing weather conditions and the variety of ways in which the land can be exploited from year to year, together make unlikely the exploitation of available resources by permanent large-scale groups.

The existence of cattle as the main form of property gives room for manipulation of alliances, and allows scope for the rich man, through loans, gifts, and marital links, to gather dependants as followers. His primary responsibility is for his nuclear family; responsibility for his extended family runs a close second. Variations in wealth force upon him further responsibilities which can extend readily to embrace people throughout the surra and their dependants. This is his real basis for further political advance; his wealth and generosity are by now proven. Ability to advance beyond this stage does not depend so heavily on economic factors.

17. Seasonal Movements of the Kababish Arabs of Northern Kordofan [Sudan][1]

The purpose of this paper is twofold: to provide a descriptive account of the seasonal movements of the pastoral Kababish, and to stress the rational character of Kababish decisions relating to the utilization of environmental resources.

In recent years many writers have proceeded on the assumption that it is both desirable and inevitable that pastoral nomads be settled.[2] The administrative arguments in favour of this view are often clearer than the economic ones, but in any case my immediate concern here is neither to attack nor to support it. I am concerned rather to show (with special reference to the Kababish) that a pastoral nomadic economy is not necessarily an anachronism, and that the way the Kababish exploit their natural resources is in principle a rational one. To say that the Kababish are rational in the way they exploit their resources does not mean that they do not make mistakes, or that no improvements are possible in their system of resource-use. There is no system anywhere which can claim to be rational in this absolute sense. It means rather that they have certain basic economic aims (which are reasonable), that these aims raise a number

Reprinted by permission of the author and the Editorial Board from *Sudan Notes and Records*, Vol. 45 (1964), pp. 45–58.

[1] I wish to thank the University of Khartoum and Ford Foundation for generous assistance in financing the fieldwork on which this paper is based. I wish to thank, also, Mr. F. Rehfisch who read early drafts of the paper and made useful suggestions for its improvement.

[2] See, for example, Mohd. Awad, "Nomadism in the Arab Lands of the Middle East," *The Problems of the Arid Zones*, UNESCO, 1962; and J. Randell, "The Potential Development of Lands Devoted to Nomadic Pastoralism," *The Effect of Nomadism on the Economic and Social Development of the People of the Sudan*, Philosophical Society of the Sudan, 1962.

of practical problems (which are recognized), and that their pastoral activities and decisions are directed towards the solution of these problems in the light of the knowledge and techniques available to them.

The reason I think this needs to be stressed is that several statements have been made, representing an influential point of view, which imply that pastoral nomadism is essentially an irresponsible mode of existence. These statements range from the dogmatic assertion that "nomadism is not a natural way of life"[3] —which deserves very little comment; to the seemingly objective remark that "nomads use untamed and unimproved natural resources without any contribution to their improvement or perpetuation"[4]—which calls for the following observations:—In the first place the Kababish do contribute to the perpetuation of their natural resources (by alternate use of grazing grounds) for if they did not they could not keep animals in such numbers as they do. Secondly, if the Kababish do not actively contribute to the improvement of their natural resources it is for the simple reason that they have neither the skill nor the means to do so—no more than the traders in Kordofan have for improving the roads they use. Indeed both the individual trader and the individual Kabbashi pastoralist are using extensive communally owned resources whose improvement can only be carried out by a large government or quasi-government agency. Further, if it should prove that the Kababish remain unenthusiastic about improvements imposed from above, which involve de-stocking and restricted grazing, their attitude will be no different basically from that of the owners of any cluster of small traditional industries which are required to submit to rationalization—for the immediate loss to the many individuals is more palpable than the eventual gain in efficiency to the economy as a whole.

[3] Dr. Mihaymid, Ministry of Animal Resources, in "Discussion" following Dr. El Hadi El Nagar and Dr. Taha Baasher, "Psychomedical Aspects of Nomadism in the Sudan," *The Effect of Nomadism of the Economic and Social Development of the People of the Sudan,* Philosophical Society of the Sudan, 1962.

[4] Dr. Mustafa Baasher, "Range and Livestock Problems Facing the Settlement of Nomads," *The Effect of Nomadism on the Economic and Social Development of the People of the Sudan,* Philosophical Society of the Sudan, 1962.

My point is that broad generalizations of the kind I have
quoted above are not only incorrect, but serve also to perpetuate
the misleading impression that pastoral nomadic economy is inherently primitive and destructive, and that it lacks a rational
basis.[5] In fact, as I hope to show, it is nothing of the kind.

The basic economic problem facing Kababish nomads is the
same as that facing individuals in any society: the use of scarce
resources to achieve given ends. How the system of resource-use
can be made more efficient, or different ends substituted for those
now in existence, are subjects for legitimate discussion. But these
things can only be done when the rational character of the system is first understood. And the present system of the Kababish
is rational for the following reasons: (a) by choosing to be
pastoralists herding appropriate kinds of livestock in a marginal environment they make use of resources that might otherwise remain idle, and (b) by organizing the use of unpromising
natural resources for the maintenance of growing herds they are
able to satisfy their needs and produce large numbers of surplus
animals for sale. Both (a) and (b) are connected. The use of
extensive but poor natural resources, and the maintenance of
large herds of animals are only possible because, as we shall see,
the Kababish have a dual cycle of seasonal movements. The
seasonal movements are therefore to be seen as a systematic solution of a number of basic problems which Kababish pastoralism
raises, rather than as an opportunistic and haphazard search for
grazing and water.

The Kababish use the water and grazing at their disposal to
maintain growing herds which constitute their capital. But what
they seek from these herds is the maximum rate of increase in
total animal numbers for enhancing social advantage, rather than
the optimum rate of off-take for maximizing financial advantage.
Their need for cash is limited in part because much of what they

[5] Cf. J. Randell, ". . . the destructive exploitation of the environment . . .
is an almost universal characteristic of (the nomad's) way of life." (op. cit.);
and J. Berque: "Yet under (the nomadic) system, whatever care may be
devoted to supplying the everyday needs of the livestock, there is no direct
and conscious causal relationship between human effort and production." In
Introduction to "Nomads and Nomadism in the Arid Zone," *Int. Soc. Sci.
Bull.*, XI, No. 4, 1959.

consume can be obtained directly from their animals (see p. 352). Their attitude in this matter was once graphically put to me by a Kabbashi in the following words: "A camel has no real price. The buying and selling of camels merely represents a rough equivalent of their value, and it goes on because people need things, not because it represents the true value of camels. One can drink camel's milk, use its hair, make it carry a load—even eat it. And with the blessing of God it multiplies under your hands. But what do you do with the bits of paper the merchant gives you? Put them in your pocket. The Arabs want these bits of paper only because the merchants want them, and the Government wants them."

Money is never used by the Kababish for productive investment. Since land is not individually owned, there is no inducement for individuals to invest in it. And unlike some other pastoral peoples they never buy animals for breeding purposes, although sires are frequently borrowed to improve strains. But to say that the Kababish do not use money for productive investment is not to say, of course, that they do not invest productively. The withholding of animals for the purpose of natural increase is itself a form of investment.

The primary objects of cash expenditure among the Kababish are grain (bulrush millet), tea, sugar, gold and silver ornaments, and animal-tax. The family's consumption of grain (together with milk the staple diet), as well as of tea and sugar is on the whole limited. The purchase of gold and silver ornaments is merely the formation of a kind of unproductive reserve—to be translated back into cash when the need arises. Animals are therefore usually sold only to meet the cash requirements of a relatively stable level of consumption.

In the mobilization of manpower for the care of livestock it is family and kinship ties that are the important factor rather than financial ability to secure wage labour. But the existence of family and kinship ties, though it serves this purpose, has other implications which are equally important for the life of the Kababish, and in the maintenance of these ties livestock are an essential element. Indeed growing herds have considerable advantages for the Kababish other than the purely economic one: thus the more numerous the herds, the greater the measure of prestige, as well as the means of creating useful social links and fulfilling vital social obligations.[6] It is therefore this aim—the maintenance of growing herds of livestock—that provides the underlying motive for the economic life of the Kababish.

II

Most of the pastoral Kababish inhabit the arid belt in northern Kordofan which lies roughly between latitudes 14° and 16° North, and longitudes 21° and 32° East. This area, approximately 48,000 sq. mis. in extent, is administered by Dar Kababish Rural Council with its headquarters at Sodiri. A convenient territorial distinction (but one having no administrative significance) is sometimes made between western and eastern Dar Kababish lying on either side of the great Wadi al Milk. Sharing this area with the Kababish are a number of smaller groups, some pastoral nomads (e.g. Kawahla and Hawawir) and some sedentary cultivators (e.g. Kaja and Northern Nuba). The pastoral nomads number about 113,000 of whom the Kababish alone are about 70,000. The total number of cultivators is about 22,000, and they are scattered in small pockets of a few thousand each mainly in the southern portion of Dar Kababish.

Although by far the greater proportion of the Kababish have their dry season watering centres (*madamir*, sing. *damar*) within the Dar Kababish Rural Council Area, there are considerable numbers who spend the same season at watering centres outside it—to the west, in northern Darfur; to the north-west, in some of the oases in the South Libyan Desert; and to the north-east, along the lower reaches of the Wadi al Milk in Northern Province. Thus when a Kabbashi speaks of Dar Kababish he usually refers to a region larger than that of the Dar Kababish Rural Council Area.

Dar Kababish is a semi-desert region. Although deep shifting sand is not very common, most of the area is covered by loose

[6] Much of what has been described for the Humr of Southern Kordofan concerning the social significance of livestock applies equally to the Kababish. See I. Cunnison, "The Social Role of Cattle," *Sudan Journ. of Vet. Sci. and Animal Husb.*, I, No. 1, 1960.

sand. Bare rocky hills and patches of hard barren ground are also found. Much of the southern portion of the region is cut by innumerable water-courses that are flooded for brief periods during the rainy season. Evidence of erosion is most noticeable in areas with permanently settled cultivators who also keep a few animals.

Mean annual rainfall in the southern portion of Dar Kababish is around 200 mm., and in the northern portion about half this figure. Rainfall is normally confined to the three months July, August and September. It is erratic in its incidence and intensity, especially in the north.

Thorn-trees and bushes (mainly Acacias) abound along the water-courses. Perennial tussock grasses are a common form of vegetation, especially in the vast sandy wastes of the north, and there are also considerable varieties of annual herbs and grasses. Both trees and bushes, wherever found, tend to be stunted.

The Kababish area is not therefore distinguished by an abundance of natural resources. The soil is poor, and both grazing and water are limited. Given that Kababish economy is geared to the maintenance and increase of herds, the problem facing them is how to organize the use of natural resources at their disposal to achieve this purpose. It is worth emphasizing that Kababish economy is not strictly a subsistence one, since they export annually large numbers of animals to the outside world.[7] And this they are able to do not as the result of a mechanical adaptation to their natural environment—since they could conceivably confine themselves to certain selected places and eke out a bare substance by cultivation—but by choosing to make methodical use of scarce resources for the maintenance of livestock.

The Kababish keep camels, sheep, goats, cattle, donkeys, horses, dogs and chickens. Of these, camels, sheep and goats are

[7] Animal statistics on this subject are hard to come by, but some idea of the magnitude of Kababish camel exports alone may be gained by a consideration of the following facts: until the recent official attempts to regularize the camel trade, the Sudan exported camels to the U.A.R. to an average annual value of about £ S.1,000,000. (See *Annual Foreign Trade Reports for 1952–61*, Department of Statistics, Sudan Government.) An official of the Ministry of Commerce estimated that of this total the proportion exported by Kordofan Province alone was about 40%. And in Kordofan Province by far the largest group of camel exporters are the Kababish.

by far the most numerous. Horses and chickens are not very common. Cattle are found mainly in the south; donkeys and dogs everywhere.

The respective advantages of keeping camels, sheep and goats (the major categories of livestock) are clearly distinguished by the Kababish, most of whom try to herd all three varieties. All three, of course, can be sold to obtain cash, although the market for sheep is easily the most secure. Compared with camels both sheep and goats are more prolific, the gestation period for camels being 12 months compared with 6 months for sheep and goats. Goats are good milkers, and because they are generally kept near the household, provide a basic supply of milk for household consumption. In addition they are the readiest and cheapest source of meat on the infrequent occasions when it is eaten. Both camel- and goat-hair are said to be especially suitable for weaving into tents and rugs. But the really indispensable use of camels is of course in transport.

From the point of view of herding, goats (when they are kept separate from sheep) require least atttention. They are generally driven out to pasture before sunrise, and left to graze alone, or with perhaps a child in attendance. By sunset they normally return on their own. Herding sheep is the most difficult in that it requires constant vigilance by day and by night. A considerable portion of the flock may wander off at night, especially if the animals are hungry, and become liable to attack by wild animals. During the breeding season the shepherd has to assist most rams individually to cover the fat-tailed ewes. Lambing also demands the shepherd's help and attention, and during the lambing season supplementary labour may well be required. Herding camels, in comparison, is much less exacting if sometimes more strenuous. While they are grazing, camels are much more dispersed and move more rapidly than any other livestock. When camels get lost, the search usually involves lengthy and tiring journeys. They are also more easily stolen by strangers than either sheep or goats.

The size of herds varies considerably. Technically the herd is a group of animals having its own arrangements for breeding, grazing and watering, usually in the care of two or three herders. The chief herder knows the characteristics, life-history and ancestry of each animal in his herd. For camels the maximum number in a single herd is about 150, and for sheep about 200. Goats, when they are not herded together with sheep, rarely exceed a couple of dozen to a flock.

In their ability to endure thirst camels are of course proverbial. In the hot, dry season Kababish camels are watered about once every nine days; in the winter they need not be watered for several months. Sheep, on the other hand, are watered about once every four days in the hot, dry season, and much less frequently in the winter. Goats can survive without water for longer periods than sheep, but they are normally watered as frequently as the latter, and usually at the same time. Watering in the hot, dry season is hard work in which the normal herders must be assisted by other members of the household (including women) because the water is drawn by hand from wells.[8] In the rainy season it is much easier, and can be done by the normal herders alone as the water is available in open pools.

From the point of view of grazing, goats are least selective (they browse as well as graze), and sheep most selective (they graze only). The advantage of camels in this respect is clearly appreciated by the Kababish: because they are less selective in grazing, they can exploit a given area more efficiently than sheep, but because they are most mobile and most resilient to thirst, they can range much farther from any given water supply, and thus never need to graze a confined area bare.

The availability of water and grazing, which is so crucial in the maintenance of livestock, is subject to seasonal variations in Dar Kababish. There are three main seasons in the year: *khareef* (cool, wet season); *shita* (cold, dry season); and *saif* (hot, dry season). In *saif*, when the animals require water most frequently, the water supply is confined to certain well-centres and consequently the areas available for grazing in Dar Kababish are restricted. In *khareef*, when animals require water less frequently, the water supply is widely scattered in the form of rain-pools and consequently the area available for grazing is extensive. In *shita*, when animals can do without water for considerable periods,

[8] There is a permanent lake in the extreme south-east corner of Dar Kababish used mainly by the Kawahla, but also by the Kababish. In addition, there are five government operated bore-wells in the Rural Council Area used by the Kababish.

limitation to the grazing area available is imposed not by the scarcity of water as such, but by the number of human beings accompanying them who can survive on milk as a substitute.

The problem for the Kababish under these circumstances is to try to keep the maximum number of animals under *saif* conditions in order to utilize *khareef* and *shita* potentialities efficiently. They do this by adopting separate migratory cycles for their main herds and their households—with the former moving over greater stretches of territory than the latter. The main herds, accompanied only by a few herders, have greater mobility. They can thus lighten the pressure on the restricted *saif* grazing grounds by going away early and coming back late; and they can extend the pastures available to them during late *saif* by going south to the early rains grazing in central Kordofan and Darfur, and during *shita* by going north to the desert winter pastures of Northern Province, Darfur, and the Chad Republic. The households, in turn, remain at the well-centres during *saif* to provide the maximum labour when it is needed. During *khareef* they can move a relatively short distance away to the easier sources of water and grazing, thus giving the *saif* pastures a complete rest. And during mid-*khareef* they are able to meet up again with the main herds at a time and place that is advantageous to both.

In the next section I shall give a more detailed account of the seasonal migration of the Kababish which I have here outlined.

III

Towards the close of the hot, dry season in Dar Kababish, but when the rains have fallen in central Kordofan and Darfur (about May), herds of camels and sheep are driven south or south-west to take advantage of the earlier pastures there. This exodus greatly eases the laborious work of watering animals from the wells for the households that remain behind at the *madamir*, and relieves the pressure on *damar* pastures. This southward movement of the main herds is known as *shogara*.

The households are eager to move as soon as the downpours begin in Dar Kababish (about the beginning of July). The urgency in getting away from the *damar* is dictated initially not so much by the need for fresh pastures as by the desire for easy watering which the numerous rain-pools afford. The hot, dry season is the most exhausting and monotonous period of the year and in many places the water-level in the wells sinks uncomfortably low towards the end of this period.

The movement of the households at the start of the rainy season is roughly in a westerly direction. The rule is that in one's migration one should skirt the *damar* lying ahead by a reasonable distance in order not to spoil it for those who usually return there. This rule is generally observed during the outward phase of the migration for the simple reason that there is little point in going through an area that has been intensively grazed throughout the long, dry season. But on the return journey, and especially in bad years, herds are sometime driven through the *damar* grazing around a watering-point at which their owners do not normally settle. However, since neither the watering-point nor the grazing area around it is owned by sections of the tribe, complaints about breaking of the above rule amount to the charge of wilful lack of consideration rather than that of any infringement of legal rights.

The outward movement of the households is fairly rapid. At this stage the families are mainly accompanied by flocks of goats, and sometimes by small numbers of sheep and camels which have not, for one reason or another, been sent south. Information is always obtained, before each move, about the state of water and grazing ahead. The normal practice, on the day camp is struck, is for the animals to be sent ahead early in the morning with the households following on later. The households then overtake the animals on the way and establish themselves at the new site before the latter arrive at sunset. Distances between sites at this stage vary normally between a few hours and a whole day by camel (baggage camels usually travel at between 3 to 4 miles an hour). This outward migration is known as *nashugh*.

By about the middle of the rainy season (August-September) the herds from the south return and meet up with the households in the *khareef* pastures. (News always travels quickly in Dar Kababish; both households and herders make continuous enquiries on their way to enable them to locate one another.) Hitherto the problem of finding suitable grazing and water has not been very pressing. Especially if the rainfall is plentiful, there has been a sense of abundance which has allowed the households to ignore all but the very best places. But with the sudden arrival of large numbers of animals, and the rainy season already half over, the choice of where to move has to be more carefully made. As already mentioned, neither watering-points nor grazing grounds are individually or sectionally owned. Even prior occupation gives no exclusive rights of usufruct. Herds of different owners may and do frequently mingle at the rain-pools and on the grazing grounds. There is, however, the courtesy custom of not allowing one's herd to stray too near someone else's tent.

Herds and households at this stage try to stay together for as long as they possibly can. The need for rapid and extensive moves on the part of the herds does not normally arise yet. This is the period when the milk-yield is highest, so the households have convenient access to the surplus milk which is either drunk or made into clarified butter. In turn, women from the households can contribute towards the extra labour-requirement involved in lambing, milking and separating the lambs from their mothers. And owners, who do not usually accompany their main herds can examine the condition of their animals and discuss herding problems with their herders.

Large groups begin to congregate near the bigger pools, for whom generally speaking longer periods of stay are now possible. But many households make their way to the numerous smaller pools scattered about, thus making it necessary to move rather more frequently as one after another of them gets used up. The choice between frequenting the smaller or larger pools (which is also, on another level, the choice between occupying the more arid North or the less arid South) involves taking into account a number of considerations: the larger pool while giving the assurance of a greater and more prolonged supply of water, and enabling the maintenance of direct contacts with a wider range of friends and relatives, is also more quickly fouled, results in more rapid over-grazing, increases the risk of spread of animal diseases, and is the scene of more quarrels and thefts. Muddy or foul water, incidentally, seems to worry the animals (and especially camels) more than the humans. As the water in the larger pools gets steadily more dirty and depleted, the households that insist on staying have to reconcile themselves to sending most of their animals to drink from other, more satisfactory, sources of water. They are thus separated from their herds sooner, and by greater distances, than those who are willing or able to move frequently with their animals from one place to another.

Many of the large pools used by the Kababish during the rainy season are located in north-east Darfur Province, and this increases the incidence of theft and the possibilities of conflict with such Darfurian tribes as the Meidob, Zeyadia and Berti.

When the rains are over (September-October), the households prepare to make their way back slowly to the *madamir*, and the herds (mainly camels but also sheep) move off further north-west. If the year has been a good one, the camels go far out into the real desert to graze on the succulent grasses and herbs that grow there in the winter. (This vegetation, as well as the area in which it is grazed, are referred to as *jizu*.) The period of sustained or intermittent contact between these herds and the households is now over until well into the next hot, dry season. The return journey to the *damar* is known as *mota*.

Arrival at the *damar* is delayed by the households for as long as they possibly can. More households than ever now collect round the larger pools, some of which have only been completely filled up since the households passed by them during the outward phase of the migration. They stay at these pools for longer periods, sometimes weeks at a stretch. The marked reluctance to get back to the *damar* is determined as much by the desire to put off the arduous but inevitable routine of life during the hot, dry season as it is by the wish to preserve *damar* grazing.

It is when all the water in rain pools is used up that the households hasten back to the *damar*. The last part of the journey usually takes several days, with only overnight pauses. At the *damar* those that depend on impermanent wells (and these are the majority) must re-dig and re-line them—normally several times in the course of the hot, dry season. These wells are owned, sometimes several wells to one household and sometimes one well to several households, depending on the depth of the well

and the amount of water in it in relation to the available manpower and water-requirement of the household. Where the water
is not very plentiful several well-owners may combine their individual wells to form a watering unit for their animals, taking it
in turn to use all the wells together on a given day. The same
procedure is adopted where several households own a single well
in common.

In the few places where permanent brick-lined wells are located water is always plentiful. Although these deep wells belong
to the households that first dug them (they are lined and maintained at the expense of the Rural Council), many others are
allowed to make use of them with the consent of the traditional
owners.

In good years the camels return from the desert grazing
grounds as late as March; in bad years they return several months
earlier. For the herds to return to the *madamir* means that they
are now watered at them. They will therefore be within a reasonable distance from the *damar* watering-point. But this may mean
as much as a four-day journey away for camels, and a two-day
journey away for sheep.

The general pattern of transhumance described above is subject to certain variations. Thus very few of the eastern Kababish
go as far as Darfur Province, their rainy season movements are
normally less extensive and their direction often south-westerly.
They have fewer camels and more cattle than the western Kababish. In the northern more arid portion of west Dar Kababish the
details of rainy season routes vary more from year to year, and
comparatively fewer herds go very far south on the *shogara*
move, although they usually stay longer in the desert pastures
which lie near them. The north is believed to be healthier for
sheep and camels than the south. In the relatively more abundant
south-west, where the Nazir's group has its *damar*, an informal
attempt is made at regulating the main grazing grounds with this
group having a broad priority with respect to rain-pools and
pastures.

Sometimes the households and their main herds (especially
camels) are attached to separate *madamir*. For example in the
south-west many households watering at the deep wells in
Hamrat al-Shaikh have their main herds watered at the bore-

well in Um Sunta about 50 miles west. Because although water from the Hamra wells is free and from the bore-well it is not, if one has exceptionally large herds it is cheaper to pay for the water at the bore-well than to pay for the hire of several people to draw the water from the deep Hamra wells on a daily basis. Watering at the bore-well is of course quicker and less laborious than watering at the deep Hamra wells. On the other hand it suffers from the disadvantage that a mechanical breakdown at the pump may spell disaster, as happened some years ago.

It may also happen that households wishing for one reason or another to spend the hot, dry season at one of the less peripheral centres, are unable to muster enough hands from within the family and unwilling or unable to hire people for the job of watering all their animals there. In such cases they will keep their herds during the hot, dry season at centres where watering is easier, and where preferably there are relatives who are able and willing to help in the watering.

In addition to the transhumance cycle there is another kind of movement in Dar Kababish which may be called migration proper. This occurs mainly, but not only, in bad years and involves the shifting of households from one *damar* to another. Sometimes the usual transhumance cycle is completed, with the household returning to its old *damar*, before the forced march to the new and more attractive *damar* is undertaken. But usually the transhumance route is itself adjusted to end up at the new *damar* (see Table on p. 360).

One of the main factors underlying this kind of movement is of course inadequate rainfall which results in poor *damar* pastures and scanty water-supply in certain areas. But the migration is never haphazard. People normally move to one of a limited number of centres with which they are familiar. The actual choice of where to move is also to some extent determined by kinship links, with households moving to areas where relatives who will be helpful are already established.

The comparatively easy conditions in the south-west means a proportionately smaller amount of migration into and out of this area. Here the existence of deep, lined wells (in which there are personal rights of a kind) exerts a pull on households traditionally based here to return to their *madamir* after the rainy season. But for those who have temporarily come down from the north, the attractions in their traditional area still exist, if

SAIF HOT DRY	KHAREEF COOL WET	DARAD WARM DRY	SHITA COLD DRY
Feb.-June	*July-Sept.*	*October*	*Nov.-Jan.*
HOUSEHOLDS			
At dry season well-centres. Re-digging and relining of wells. Heavy work watering main herds.	Move to West or North-West after first showers. Contact with main herds in mid-*khareef*. Fairly rapid movement between rain pools.	Separation from main herds. Exploitation of larger rain-pools with extended stops.	Digging of shallow water holes. Movement back to dry-season well-centres (speed depending on intensity of *khareef* rainfall). Move to different dry-season well-centres if *khareef* rainfall has been poor.
MAIN HERDS			
Return from North-West in early summer to dry-season well-centres. Circulating in dry-season pastures around well-centres. Move to South or South-West in late summer to exploit early pastures in central Kordofan and Darfur. (Camel herds farther than sheep flocks.)	Rapid move North to exploit *khareef* pastures in Dar Kababish. Contact with households.	Separation from households. Slow move North-West.	Move farther North-West to exploit winter grazing in desert. (Camel herds farther than sheep flocks.)

only because they know the pastures and rain-pools of the north better. And in good years watering is easier from the short wells of the north, and animals are less exposed to contagious diseases there than in the south.

IV

In this paper I have tried to show that the exploitation of their environment by the Kababish is based on rational aims and calculations. I have described, in particular, the separate nomadic cycles of main herds and households by which they seek to achieve their basic economic objectives as efficiently as they are able.

Seen in this light it may in theory be possible to suggest how this resource-use can be made more efficient—although I have not tried to do this here. But to make sweeping generalizations about the alleged primitiveness of pastoral nomad economy as such, or the supposed economic advantage of settling nomads everywhere, does not contribute to clear thinking. In the first place it is necessary to specify whether one is referring to low level of consumption or low rate of production or high degree of wastage of natural resources or some other undesirable feature of the local economy. It may then be possible to calculate, given the natural resources of the region, the capital that can be economically invested in it, and the population to be supported, how these features can best be improved. Whether the answer to this problem lies in the improvement of pastoralism, or the establishment of agriculture or some other new industry, or perhaps in a combination of some or all of these, will depend on various considerations.[9]

In any case, it is quite false to say, as one writer has done, that in the Sudan "taken together, overpopulation of grazing lands and underexploitation of potentially cultivable land, point logically to the necessity of settling nomad populations on cultivable soil."[10] Overpopulation is a relative concept, and may call for greater capital investment rather than an absolute reduction in human numbers. And if the investment required to raise by a given proportion the output of pastoral nomads is less than that required to settle them and enable them to maintain a comparable level of output as cultivators, the supposed economic necessity for settlement is seen to be spurious. But a full discussion of this problem lies beyond the scope of this paper.

What I want to emphasize here is that it seems to me a mistake to regard a system of resource-use such as I have described, as essentially primitive merely because the Kababish are pastoral nomads. Since I take the term "pastoralism" to mean that the economy is based on the rearing of livestock, and the term

[9] For a clear and useful preliminary discussion of this topic in reference to the Sudan, see F. Barth, I. Cunnison, and N. Dyson-Hudson, "The Settlement of Nomads as a Development Policy" (in Arabic), *Sudan Society*, No. 2, 1963.
[10] J. Randell, op. cit.

"nomadism" to mean that the system of resource-use involves the seasonal movement of men and animals, I would maintain that neither pastoralism nor nomadism are necessarily inconsistent with economic progress. As such it is a little difficult to understand the logic that underlies a statement such as the following:

"The course which does not recommend itself either from the view-point of the country as a whole or in view of the long-term interests of nomadic populations themselves is the creation of an artificial environment in which nomadism becomes a more attractive way of life than it is at present. Such measures retard economic, cultural and social progress and have no place in the policy of a country firmly committed to the path of modern civilization."[11]

Surely the intelligent—and humane—policy for a country "firmly committed to the path of modern civilization" is to make the pursuit of rational and productive activities by its inhabitants more attractive as a way of life wherever possible and not less so?

[11] J. Randell, op. cit.

18. The Proliferation of Segments in the Lineage of the Bedouin of Cyrenaica [Libya][1]

In this article I do not propose to discuss the genealogies of the Cyrenaican Bedouin in full, but only such aspects of them as are strictly relevant to an understanding of their process of growth. Many other aspects of these genealogies will be referred to, and indeed, some of the arguments put forward will presume an acceptance of views which cannot be developed adequately in this article. A fuller and more general account of Cyrenaican genealogies is in preparation, and, until this is published, there is no alternative to the somewhat dogmatic statements about them which appear in the introductory part of this article.

The Bedouin of Cyrenaica claim that they are all descendants of a unique ancestress, Sa'ada. Writers in the past (e.g. Robertson-Smith 1903) have considered the occurrence of female names in patrilineal genealogies as evidence of an earlier and matrilineal mode of descent. A more satisfactory explanation of the occurrence of female names is to be found in the combination of two facts: descent in the patriline, whether or

Reprinted by permission of the author and the Council from the *Journal of the Royal Anthropological Institute*, Vol. 90, pp. 29–53, 1960.

[1] My field work among the Cyrenaican Bedouin was made possible by an award from the Emslie Horniman Fund and a later award from the Treasury Committee for Studentships in Oriental Languages and Cultures. I wish here to express my indebtedness to both committees for their generosity. Much of the work I have done on genealogies was included in a thesis presented for the degree of D.Phil. at Oxford University in 1951. The ideas included in this thesis I developed more systematically in a course of lectures on the Bedouin which I gave at Manchester University during the session 1953–54. I subsequently read papers around the problems discussed in this paper at Oxford and Cambridge Universities. I am grateful to Professor Gluckman for reading this article in manuscript, and for the numerous discussions I have had with him on problems relating to lineage organization.

not male names are used, is assumed; and secondly that the
Bedouin are polygamous. If, then, half-brother differentiation
or full sibling unity is to be shown genealogically, the obvious
way in which this can be done is to use a maternal name in the
genealogy. Thus, in the Cyrenaican genealogy, a number of
tribal groups will be shown as sons of a particular father. If differentiation of these groups needs to be shown, this can be effected by clustering the groups round, say, two female names
(the names of the respective mothers) thereby making the two
clusters of groups stand in the relationship of paternal half
brothers. The concept of the 'one womb', of maternal origin, is a
critical one in the context of social cohesion, but it does not deny
patriliny; on the contrary, it serves in a sense to reinforce it.
Female names can be used to show a greater notion of cohesion than the mere use of male names, and the significance
of a female name placed at the apex of the Cyrenaican genealogy is that it is the symbol of full brother unity at the highest
political level.

The founding ancestress Sa'ada is credited with two sons, who
in turn are considered to be the founding ancestors of the two
largest groups of tribes in Cyrenaica. Each of these sons is said
to have begottten two sons, as shown on the accompanying
genealogy. The next generation shows a total of nine names,
and these nine ancestors are considered to be the founding
ancestors of the nine noble tribes of Cyrenaica.[2] Continuing the
line of descent of one of these tribes—the Magharba—the same
pattern of segmentation repeats itself: the tribe is divided into
two primary sections having ar-Ra'aid and ash-Shamakh as the
respective founding ancestors. Ash-Shamakh is said to have had
four sons, and these are the founding ancestors of four secondary
sections. These latter four are credited with a varying number of
sons, as shown in the genealogy (Fig. 18-1).

One feature of the Cyrenaican genealogy immediately stands
out from this brief description: the uniformity in the number of
segments at the various levels of segmentation. Along the line
of descent from Sa'ada to Nasr, the number of sons shown in the

[2] One of these, the 'Ailat Fayid, now only numbers about 150 souls, and
although it is given the structural position of a tribe in the genealogy, it
scarcely merits this distinction in practice.

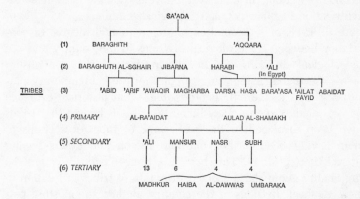

FIG. 18-1 GENEALOGY 1. The names given in this genealogy are the tribal names in use. All are derivatives of personal names of ancestors, like all tribal names, except for some nicknames (e.g. Baraghith means 'the fleas') and a few which refer to a general location (e.g. the Magharba means the 'Westerners').

first four descending generations is two. At the fifth level the number increases to four and finally, at the sixth level there characteristically occurs a marked irregularity in the number of descendants forming the founding ancestors of the tertiary sections.

Another feature of the Cyrenaican genealogy is that its branches show an intimate relationship with ecological areas. Thus, the major division into two branches stemming from Sa'ada represents the eastern and western halves of the country with associated and clear differences in ecology. Continuing the line of descent, the Jibarna and Baraghith groups of tribes occupy plain and mountain foot-hills respectively. The two Jibarna tribes in turn occupy two distinct kinds of plain. Following now the division of the Magharba tribe, its two primary sections are divided by a very conspicuous dry valley. The four secondary divisions of the Aulad ash-Shamakh primary section likewise show a relation to ecological boundaries, albeit on a smaller scale than those previously referred to, but none the less important in this more local context. Finally, the unevenly numbered tertiary sections which are derived from these four secondary sections, in their very unevenness, show a more sensitive relation to more detailed ecological differences.

At all levels of segmentation, therefore, a high degree of consistency between the ecological divisions of the country and the genealogical divisions can be shown. Indeed the relationship is so close that it is tempting to consider the contemporary pattern of things as the only one possible. What historical evidence exists is against such a view being taken. It is known that tribes have been displaced in the past, some of them or sections of them having been pushed out into Egypt, and others having altered their position. This being so, there obviously cannot be any finality about the present distribution of tribes in relation to the ecological divisions of the country. Rather, the existing pattern is one of a number of possible permutations. Again, as the relation between groups of people to their environment becomes progressively sensitive with the decrease in the size and order of the group, then the more unstable will be the relationship between the two. Conversely the greater the size and order of the group the more persistent will be its relationship to the ecology. In other words, the major ecological divisions are more fundamental in their effect on the way of life and the economy of people, whereas the more detailed ecological differences between, say, tertiary sections have a relatively minor effect. The ecological differences between the wooded plateau area with its cow and goat herding economy, and the arid semi-desert area with its camel and sheep herding economy has a much more profound effect on the general way of life, and is a more persistent division, than that which exists between two tertiary sections where the differences may only be in topographical details.

While therefore, the division of people into groups of various sorts is not permanently fixed in relation to ecological divisions, there is always an intimate relationship between the two which is progressively more enduring as the order of the structural segment increases. Yet even this statement of the relationship, guarded as it is, does not suffice, for the pattern and distribution of tribes and their sections at any given moment are not only a function of ecology, but they are also the result of a number of other complex factors which may be operating to reinforce or to complicate the more direct relationship of the distribution of groups of people to the ecology.[3]

The Cyrenaican genealogy, then, is a conceptualization of a hierarchy[4] of ordered territorial segments. The groups stemming from the ancestor at the third order of segmentation are referred to as tribes, and each tribe is the apex of a three-tiered order of segments, which, following customary practice, are referred to as primary, secondary, and tertiary. The latter, the tertiary segment, represents the group of people who, for a period of six to eight months, gather together and live in what, for all intents and purposes, is a single discrete residential group.[5] This tertiary group is also the smallest political group. It has its own homeland, with its water supplies, pastures, and ploughland. In this homeland live most of its members. It is a lineage segment, and most of the agnates of this segment live on their own homeland.[6] It is also the vengeance group, which means that any one of its members can be killed in vengeance for a homicide committed by any other, and that the obligation to exact vengeance falls on all members alike, regardless of relationship to the victim. Likewise, its members pay blood money as a group, and although when they receive it, a bigger portion goes to the nearest agnate of the victim, the remainder is distributed equally among all its members. The number of generations which supervene between the founding ancestor of a tertiary segment and the living is usually four or five, but there is little consistency in this number. Some tertiary

[3] This part of the discussion is necessarily brief, but further amplification will appear in two subsequent articles now in preparation, one of which is concerned with a general treatment of Cyrenaican genealogies, and the other with a discussion of the effects of ecology on the social organization of the Bedouin.

[4] I use the word hierarchy here since, although segments of any order display many like features, the orders represent distinct and progressively more embracing interests, and these differences are of such consequence that to consider one order of groups as a facsimile of a superior or inferior order can only lead to confusion. A tertiary group, that is to say, may possess many of the characteristics of a secondary group, but the one is a fundamentally different sort of group from the other, as I shall show in my forthcoming article on the feud. (cf. Smith, M. G. 1956.)

[5] This statement does not apply to the Darsa and the Hasa tribes, two of the plateau tribes in Cyrenaica. The statements in this article are confined almost exclusively to the camel herders of the semi-desert.

[6] This, admittedly, is too general a statement to make about such an important issue, but I would prefer to leave its documentation and precision for an article on the analysis of the composition of Bedouin camps.

segments show a lineage depth of three generations, while others
show as many as six. No special importance is attached by the
Bedouin to this number, although some writers claim that a depth
of five generations is of particular significance among other Arab
tribes.[7] Normally, in speaking of the vengeance group, the Bedouin refer to the name of the ancestor of a tertiary tribal section.
Any one claiming membership of this group, regardless of his
precise generational relation to the offender or the victim is immediately and equally involved with its other members. When
speaking of the group as such, the Bedouin refer to it as 'those
who have agreed on the blood', and use the phrase *'amara dam*
to refer to it. Blood money does not pass between its members,
and political division does not occur within it.

These small tertiary sections of tribes, then, are small residential groups. Their population varies from one group to another,
but most of them have a total population of 150 to 200 souls.
Successive generations—at least according to the Bedouin view
—add to these numbers, and also increase progressively the
number of generations in their genealogies. Substantial increases
of population would, of course, constitute a pressure on local
resources, on the water available in the particular well of a
group, on the amount of land available for ploughing, and on
the pastures for animals at the end of the rainy season. Again,
if each generation is to be added to the existing genealogy, this
would necessitate a realignment of structural relationships with
each succeeding generation. The discussion that follows is an
examination of the ways in which adjustments are made to
maintain an equilibrium between the population of a group and
the carrying capacity of the land on which its members live, and
of the ways in which the genealogical structure is able to persist
in the face of various contingencies which threaten it.

A beginning might be made by indicating the processes at
work to keep the form of the genealogy fairly fixed when there
is an absence of population pressure on resources. The first problem is the simple one of describing the mechanics of manipula-

[7] e.g. Burkhardt (1831), speaks of the *Khomse,* the five generation group,
as very widespread among Arabs. G. W. Murray also reports the use of the
word *Khomsa* among the Arabs of the Sinai desert to designate the blood-
vengeance group, but the term used by the Aulad 'Ali tribe, the cousins and
Egyptian neighbours of the Cyrenaican Bedouin, he gives as *Awlia'-ed-dam*
(which simply means 'blood kindred').

tion which enable the genealogy to remain constant in length and fixed in form despite its dynamic content.

One of the main processes at work in foreshortening genealogies is that referred to by Evans-Pritchard as telescoping.[8] This process is also a characteristic feature of the Cyrenaican genealogy, although its effects, to be discussed presently, differ conspicuously. The way in which telescoping works in the Cyrenaican genealogy is that several male names come to be omitted in the genealogy below the name of the founding ancestor of the tertiary group. Usually, the form in which this occurs it that the name of a famous tribesman, and particularly his nickname if he has one, is retained along with the personal names of his lineal descendants in successive generations. The example given below is taken from the genealogy of the Haiba tertiary section of the Magharba tribe:

Bu Shliby

|

Yunis

|

Sa'aid (Bu Shliby)

|

Abdul Qadar (Bu Shliby)

|

Yunis (Bu Shliby)

[8] 'It is evident, moreover, that since the minimal lineage consists of four or five actual steps in ascent, there has been telescoping of the agnatic line from the founder of the minimal lineage further up the line of ascent to the founder of the clan, for the founder of the minimal lineage was himself the extremity of another minimal lineage which has, by increase in generations, become the minor lineage, and so on' (Fortes & Evans-Pritchard 1940, p. 199). Since Evans-Pritchard first wrote on the telescoping of genealogies among the Nuer, other anthropologists have discussed the process in various systems. Fortes, Richards, Laura Bohannan, Cunnison, and Mitchell in their writings on the Tallensi, Bemba, the Tiv, the Luapula people, and the Yao respectively are notable examples . . . As the mode of manipulation of Bedouin genealogies is marginal to my present problem, the main comparison is not with these works but with Evans-Pritchard's earlier work on the Nuer, because the Bedouin and Nuer lineage system have more in common than either have with the other systems, excepting possibly the Tiv.

The line shows five male names in all. The eldest surviving members of this line is Sa'aid, who almost invariably is referred to, not by his personal name, but as Bu Shliby,[9] and on the infrequent occasions when his personal name is used it is followed by Bu Shliby and not by his father's name, which is the more common practice. Again, Abdul Qadar, when his father is not about, is called Bu Shliby, and when it is necessary to give him his personal name Bu Shliby is added, except among his more intimate family kindred, when only his personal name would be used. Likewise, his son Yunis carries Bu Shliby in addition to his personal name and is sometimes even referred to as Bu Shliby only. Abdul Qadar had never known his grandfather, was aware however of his existence in the past, but did not feel it necessary to use his name, and whatever obligation he might have felt to keep the memory of his grandfather alive, he fulfilled it when he named his son after him. Many of the older members of the group are also aware of the lineal connexions between Bu Shliby and Yunis, even though they use this knowledge in a genealogical context only, but many of the younger men of the group do not know these details. It is clear that when the boy Yunis grows to old age, three names in this line will have ceased to be used.

This practice of adding to a personal name the name of a deceased ancestor making one the son of the other, is pushed to the extent of carrying forward through the generations a nickname which referred to some peculiar characteristic of the ancestor, but which has little relation to the present bearer. Thus the ancestor whose name has been retained might have been nicknamed 'The Lame One' or 'The Squint-Eyed One' because he suffered either of these personal defects; or he might have been nicknamed 'The Old One' because he lived to a ripe old age. Such nicknames might later be carried by men who are not lame, nor squint-eyed, nor old, while the names of the intervening ancestors are dropped in normal use.

Another process is at work, which needs to be distinguished from telescoping, for although the results in genealogical terms are similar, Bedouin view it in quite a different light. This is the process of fusing names. It is common practice among the Bed-

[9] The prefix *Bu* is used by the Bedouin to mean 'son of.'

ouin—and, for that matter, Arabs in other lands—to name a boy after a deceased relative. Rarely is a boy named after his father, unless the father's death occurs before the boy is born, in which circumstance, the new-born boy would certainly take his father's name. A much more common form of this practice is to name a boy after his grandfather, assuming the latter to be dead. The eldest son usually accepts this responsibility, but it by no means falls invariably to him. There is a number of reasons for this, but they need not concern us here, since they are of no relevance to the general argument. What is of concern at present is that one name in the genealogy might represent the fusion of several other similar names. When circumstances permit, an individual's line might run as follows: Muhammad—'Ali—Muhammad—'Ali—Muhammad. It is true that the man himself and those closely related to him might know full well that there are three men named Muhammad and two named 'Ali, but it would not be considered irregular if only one Muhammad and one 'Ali were given in the genealogy. A mature man, giving his genealogy, omitted his father's name, Ibrahim. When asked about the omission, he insisted that he had given it, and when he was told that the name Ibrahim given by him was intended to refer to his young son, he impatiently dismissed the matter with the observation that having given the name Ibrahim once, it mattered little whether it had been put in the position of his son or father. Pointing to his son he added, 'There is my father, Ibrahim. He has taken my father's position, has he not?'

By the fusion of names, several persons drop out of the genealogy, and by and by, the line comes to be shortened. It also has the effect of giving a person's name a weighting which otherwise it would not possess. In a sense, a young son named after a father is not merely a son but a father and possibly a great-grandfather also. The young boy becomes the contemporary carrier of the personalities of those of similar name who have preceded him, while the behaviour of the living towards him is, in virtue of this, affected in a number of details. A man who had named his son in this way, explained the matter thus: 'He is my son, but also my father because he has his name. I cannot beat him for it would be like beating my father. When he grows up and I grow old, he will look after me as if I were his son.'

Fusion of names appears in another context and for similar reasons. Not only are lineal descendants given the name of deceased ancestors, but a man may be given the name of any deceased agnate of his tertiary section. Usually, this is only done when a man passes on property to another who is not his direct heir. Commonly, this occurs when an agnate is also a mother's brother, as often happens as a result of parallel cousin marriage, and this mother's brother has no sons of his own. If he has a sister's son, who is also his paternal nephew, he is likely to pass on his wealth to this nephew. A father, the Bedouin insist, ought to perform three duties for his sons: attend to their circumcision, and their education in the Koran, and provide bride-wealth when they marry. All fathers attend to the circumcision of all their sons; few provide for the Koranic education of any of their sons; most bear the burden of marrying off at least one of their sons. The performance of the latter duty is what makes the continuance of the deceased's name an obligation, and whoever performs this duty must have his name perpetuated in one male offspring of the union which was brought about with his wealth. Wealth need not take the form of bride-wealth; it can be a legacy willed by a father, maternal uncle of the kind described above, or any other agnate who has died without male issue. Conversely, if a man dies without leaving any property, even his sons might not perpetuate his name, and eventually it will drop out of the genealogy.[10] There are instances of men inheriting the wealth of a number of agnates, using each parcel of wealth to make a new marriage and naming the sons of the various unions after the several dead who had left wealth. The example given below is taken from the genealogy of the Dawwas section of the Magharba tribe. What happened here was that the two lines stemming from Faraj and Sha'aban, after proliferating normally, became extinct. As this happened, Ibrahim, the son of Miftah, began to inherit wealth to which he was not a direct heir; and

[10] To avoid confusion, it ought to be made clear that this is not ghost marriage. As I understand ghost marriages from Evans-Pritchard's (1951) account, two main conditions must be satisfied: (i) that there should be inherited wealth to make a marriage, and (ii) that the wealth remaining after the ghost marriage has been made is inherited by the ghost children only. In Cyrenaica, wealth thus inherited becomes part of a man's total wealth and is not reserved for a ghost marriage and its issue.

as he did so, he entered into a plurality of marriages, begat sons, and replaced those men in the genealogy who had died without heirs. In the following generation the twin process of death and replacement continued. Death removed all the male descendants of Sha'aban and Faraj, and of Ibrahim Bu Miftah's many sons only two, Sharif and Abdallah, were of age to marry at the time of my visits to their camp. Both had enjoyed a plurality of wives, although still young to have done so, and each marriage they contracted took place after the death of one of their kinsmen. The full and intricate details of this interesting genealogy are irrelevant here, since all the example is intended to show is how nine of eleven male names were perpetuated in the genealogy by repeating five of them twice and four of them three times, accounting in all for twenty-two names; and to do this, three men (one of them had died, but the other two were both under forty years of age) married eight wives. All the names in the two lines which have died out have not yet been brought back into the genealogy, but 'Abdallah, the son of Ibrahim, who had already done extremely well in this respect, was confident that soon the obligations towards Musa, Abd al-Rahim, and Sa'ad would be redeemed.

Thus the fusion of names not only ensures that names threatened with extinction are perpetuated, but that one person, in the name he bears, can carry the genealogical burden of several other men of that name.

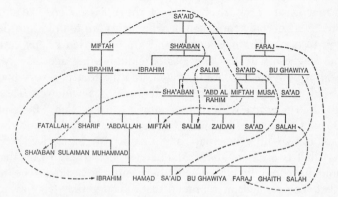

FIG. 18-2   GENEALOGY 2. The names of dead men are underlined.

Telescoping of names, and fusion of names, taken together, can account for the fixity of the genealogy to a large extent. In addition, lines which showed every sign of normal development at one time, have petered out completely, even after they have sometimes assumed the status of tertiary segments. Conditions under which this is likely to happen are not difficult to envisage. If hearsay evidence is correct, disease, when it strikes in the desert, might rage in a camp like wild fire, bringing death to many, but not spreading to other camps, because the camps are so far apart. Even in springtime when men and beasts are together in the pastures, and the larger summer camp has split into four or five smaller ones, the distance between camps may still be a few miles. In summer, when camps are concentrated on the large watering points, the distances between them are considerably more. Disease, therefore, does not spread from camp to camp as rapidly as one might expect in such primitive conditions of living. In 1949 a number of men of a small camp died within a few days of each other. Bedouin opinion attributed these deaths to an allegedly false oath sworn by the deceased a year earlier. Medical opinion ascribed them to filth in a well which the deceased had been cleaning before their illness. In any event, a thriving line of a lineage was wiped off the genealogy. The portion of the Dawwas genealogy shown on this page shows a similar process at work. Again, to give another example, the Nasr section of the Magharba tribe once included six tertiary sections, not four as are now given. Two of these six sections are now represented by only four men of whom two are too old and decrepit to have heirs any longer, and are unmarried in any case; a third, whose wife has long passed child-bearing age, had two sons, but both died before marriage; and the fourth, a very poor and old man, has only one daughter, and is a widower. Three of the four now live with their collateral tribal section, Madhkur, and count themselves members of this group. That they once belonged to two different groups might have passed unnoticed were it not that two elders of the Madhkur section insisted that they should be correctly placed and their entire genealogies be recorded. The younger men argued that although they were aware that the two groups named Farjiani and al-Khadhar at one time existed, it was pointless giving them separate status any longer; they were content to give the three men separate lines of a few

generations, and then to tag them on to Madhkur, the founding ancestor of the segment.

Telescoping, fusion of names, and the extinction of lines are three ways in which the general fixed shape of the genealogy is retained. These three processes are only sufficient, however, in special circumstances, but before discussing these circumstances one further general condition relating to these processes must be made explicit. All three affect the genealogy within the tertiary segments only, and do not affect it at any of the more superior orders of segmentation. There is not a shred of evidence from contemporary Cyrenaican genealogies to show that telescoping or fusion occurs except within the tertiary segment, within that group, in other words, where precise genealogical links are known and can be specified, and within that small group which for most part of the year constitutes a single settlement. It is possible that groups of structurally superior levels to the tertiary have become extinct, in the way that tertiary lines have petered out. There is no definite evidence to support this, and from the analysis of Cyrenaican genealogies in general it seems that when any group is threatened with extinction—and this in turn means that fewer and fewer people will be using the same land and water facilities—there is a definite tendency for the lineage rump to fuse with a collateral lineage (and in so doing fuse their resources with those of the adopting lineage), or for a numerically more powerful lineage group to take it over by force. The number of tertiary segments spanned by a secondary segment, therefore, increases or decreases according to the circumstances; so that a secondary segment, numerically strong in its tertiary segments to-day, may become considerably weaker in future, and the numerically weak secondary section of to-day may proliferate its segments substantially in the future. Short of a significant decline in the total population of a tribe, then, the extinction of lines does not affect any order of segmentation superior to the tertiary. In this respect, the Cyrenaican genealogy differs fundamentally from those collected from the Nuer by Evans-Pritchard. In the quotation from his work on Nuer genealogies (1951), he asserts that telescoping occurs 'from the founder of the minimal lineage further up the line of ascent to the founder of the clan'. This major difference has serious implications for any discussion of lineage proliferation, but these must be left until the conditions under which proliferation is likely to occur have been analysed.

While it is true that the processes discussed are of importance in retaining the general shape of the genealogy, what is assumed so far is that the Cyrenaican population has been stable over long periods. Stability of population is not an unreasonable assumption to make for a people who live on the margin of subsistence in a country where extended periods of drought are not infrequent, though seldom leading, it is true, to actual famine conditions, but producing periodic and local food and water shortages. Disease, following quickly in the trail of shortage, it can be assumed, kept the relationship of total population to the natural resources fairly constant. What evidence there is does not support even this very general assumption, since it is known that there have been large-scale tribal wars in the past, and a certain amount of movement of tribes, some being displaced and others pushed eastwards into Egypt. Unless these shifts were caused by increases in the aggregate population and the consequent pressure on land and water, it is difficult to account for them. This consideration of possible overall increases in population in the past poses interesting problems related to lineage structure which cannot be adequately treated here. For the moment it is proposed to neglect possible increases in the total population during past periods in the history of Cyrenaica. The historical depth of the view now to be discussed is about seventy years, and for this period I have no evidence of any large-scale increases in population. It is reasonable, therefore, to assume a general stability of population for this period. But the vagaries of the Cyrenaican climate are such that, in a given year, one area might be well drenched with rain, giving excellent pastures for animals and good crops, while a nearby territorial strip might suffer a partial drought giving insufficient pastures and poor crops. Good or bad crops, poor or abundant pasture, in turn mean a higher or lower milk yield from the animals and better or worse living conditions for human beings. Such factors as these may well, over a number of years, lead to unevenness in the distribution of population throughout the tertiary sections. Whatever the cause, the genealogies show that the population of the numerous tertiary sections is unequal. Some are numerically so weak that they have to join a collateral section. Others are numerically so strong that their natural resources are insufficient to meet the needs of all their members. It was these latter segments which were in the process of splitting, and which in some cases have already done so. The next task, then, is to demonstrate where, on the genealogy, proliferation is effected.

We have seen that in Nuer genealogies segments proliferate at all orders of segmentation. Here, the process is a continuous one, beginning at any point in time within the minimal lineage and progressing upwards to the apex of lineage bifurcation. As particular names become significant within the minimal segment, they are retained and become a permanent addition to the genealogy. In order to include these successively additional names, names of ascending ancestors are shunted further and further into the genealogical past, until presumably the effect is felt at the topmost limit of the genealogy, when the names here are pushed out of the genealogical framework altogether, and forgotten for ever. More than this, the upward shift in names at each and every point in the genealogical line means also a consequent re-ordering of structural relationships, at all levels in the system. One vital difference between Nuer and Bedouin societies which may partly, at least, account for the different genealogical processes at work among them is that the Nuer, when they were studied by Evans-Pritchard, were expanding territorially, and that continuous proliferation of segments throughout the structure was the mode of dealing with a situation of expansion. The Bedouin, on the other hand, had suffered twenty years of terrible privation at the hands of the Italians, during which period thousands of them died in battle and in concentration camps, were shot up in their camps from the air, or died from want, before I went to live among them. Although I must confess that I now find it difficult to accept Evans-Pritchard's view of genealogical growth and development as stated for the Nuer, it was the view I originally held with regard to Bedouin genealogies. Indeed, thinking in genealogical terms only, it appears inevitable that the addition of successive generations can only mean the lengthening of the genealogy, or, if the length is to remain constant, extrusion of ancestral names must take place at the apex of the genealogy. If this view is to be accepted, several other conclusions must be accepted with it. The genealogy, as far as it goes at least, is an accurate record of descent—some names may have been lopped off at the top, but otherwise the genealogy represents a faithful statement of succession. Again, if successive generations are to be added to the genealogy, then its base must continually expand laterally. From what is known of contemporary Bedouin geneal-ogies, there is no evidence which leads to the supposition that their base is progressively widening. With regard to the authen-ticity of the names in the genealogy, above the point of tertiary segmentation, I hope to show in a subsequent article on Bedouin genealogies in general, that names above the tertiary point of segmentation have remained fixed for very long periods of time, and that they bear slight relation to the passage of generations over the last century at least; moreover, in this article I hope to demonstrate that what manipulation of the genealogy takes place does not affect more than about four or five ascending genera-tions from the living.

Part of the difficulty in a study of this sort lies in the strong temptation to think of the genealogy *per se*, even though it is readily admitted that it has a value in itself for the Bedouin. Yet even in these terms the genealogy must always represent an or-dered grouping of people, and these people live on strips of terri-tory. The starting point of the analysis then ought to begin with the territorial ordering of groups of people. The relation of groups of people to land, moreover, is determined by the carrying capacity of that land, and it is this prerequisite which is the main variable in discussing genealogical manipulation, and not the other way about. The main landmarks of the Cyrenaican ecology are fixed points which cannot be manipulated to fit in with the genealogy; it is the genealogy which must be altered to compre-hend the distribution of people in their ecological setting.

If, moreover, the view of a genealogy as a continually expanding line of descent is to be accepted, it must be accepted also that large structural units, even in conditions of population stability, are to experience a continuous re-ordering of their structural relationships. In practice, what this means is that a tribe of, say 20,000 souls cease to be tribesmen of a named tribe and instead all become members of an almost identical group but with a different name. To take an example from the genealogy given on page 365: the Magharba tribe shown there has a total population of some 13,000 souls. If proliferation affected the topmost limits of this tribe, the apical name disappears and presumably the name of one of the primary sections is to be substituted. That is, half the tribe would have to take on the lineage name of their opposed primary section. The only alternative to the use of the name of a primary segment as a substitute for the abandoned tribal name is the acceptance by 13,000 people of a totally new name, which is most unlikely.

It is reasonable to assume therefore, that the genealogy, in its general form, is fixed for long periods of time at least. This still leaves the problem of how and where adjustments are made to face the contingencies of birth and death, of the succession of generations, and of the irregular increases and decreases of population among the tertiary segments. An important clue lies in the number of segments which appear at the various orders of segmentation. From Sa'ada, the founding ancestress, in the line which runs to Nasr, each ancestor is shown as having a pair of sons for four orders of segmentation. At the fifth generation from Sa'ada—this is now the secondary order of segmentation within the tribe—the number of sons increases to four. Not all tribes will show the same number of sons at each generation as the Magharba—some, for example, might show three instead of two at the primary order—but what is true of all tribes is that there is evident consistency in the number down to and including the fifth generation from Sa'ada; if, that is to say, one of a tribe's primary segments is divided into three secondary sections, the other one or two, as the case may be, will be divided likewise. Throughout the tribes in Cyrenaica, then, segmentation of orders superior to the tertiary segments shows a pronounced consistency in their numbers.

At the next level of segmentation (this now being the tertiary order in any given tribe) the number of segments which appear is conspicuously irregular. For the Magharba tribe, the four secondary segments, 'Ali, Mansur, Subh and Nasr are divided into thirteen, six, four, and four segments respectively. Similar irregularity appears in other tribes.[11] The pattern of the genealogy is always one of regularity in the number of segments at all points in it except for the point of tertiary segmentation where conspicuous irregularity becomes immediately evident. Since these segments constitute the summer camps of the Bedouin, this is not surprising, for these small groups will show greater susceptibility to details of local water supplies, pasturing facilities, ploughland areas, and topographical features than would the numerically larger and structurally superior groups occupying larger areas of territories of greater ecological importance. If we follow the line from Sa'ada to Nasr again, the bifurcation at the first order of segmentation is consistent with the division of the country into the permanently green high altitudes of the plateau, and the extended low-lying plain area of the western half of the country. Between the territory of the Magharba tribe ('The White Plain') and that of its neighbour tribe, the 'Awaqir ('The Red Plain'), there is a major soil difference, which is such a conspicuous feature of the landscape, and so sharply defined, that one is almost aware when one has crossed the tribal boundary. Within the Magharba tribe, a prominent dry river valley cuts the territory in two, the landscape to the west of it being characteristically serrated, making travel in an east-west direction difficult, while to the east the landscape is much more docile and undulating. The four sections of the ash-Shamakh branch again represent four quite distinct areas. The territory of one section is almost conterminous with the narrow belt of sand dunes along the coast; the territory of another is a block of rough and tumbled land in the west; the territory of a third, in the centre, is made up of a few low-lying shallow valleys; and the territory of the fourth,

---

[11] It is necessary here to warn the reader that, brilliant an ethnographer as Agostini undoubtedly was, his grouping of tribal sections is not always correct. I had his book (Agostini 1922–23) with me in the field and checked his tribal survey. I found that at several important points his ordering of the segments was incorrect. I should add that the differences between Agostini and myself are not due to the kind of changes discussed in this article.

stretching across to the village of Ajadabiya in the east, topples in undulations away into the flat expanses of the desert to the south. At all these points of segmentation, the territories occupied by the various sections are large and roughly defined, and the population aggregates supported on these territories run from over a thousand at one end to tens of thousands at the upper limits. The tertiary sections are numerically much smaller, some of them numbering as few as a hundred souls in all, and the territories to which they are attached are correspondingly smaller. The relationship between the numbers in this order of section, and the precise amount of water available in the local wells is an intimate one. If the population of one of these groups increases, or if the number of animals rises, or if the springs show a decline in the volume of water they give forth, or if the winter rainfall has allowed the storage in wells of only a small quantity of water, a rearrangement of the group must be effected. A significant alteration of any one of these components must mean that the local group must split to enable a new adjustment to be made in the relationship of man and animals to water.

Whatever changes occur within groups of any size, since the genealogy embraces the entire population, these must appear on the genealogy in some way or other. Now a genealogy is as rigid a framework, as fixed and final a pattern of grouping, as can be imagined. The impression that they are thus rigid and fixed, except for the addition of successive generations, is strengthened by the way in which the Bedouin use them. From their young boys to their old men, the Bedouin are expert genealogists, and the names of ancestors, for one reason or another, are never far from their lips. Names are kept alive by constant use, since all references to inter-group relationships must be in terms of these names. More than this, the Bedouin were proud to the point of boastfulness of their genealogical knowledge, and, wherever I travelled, the first request I had to comply with was to take down a large portion of a tribal genealogy. In recording their endless genealogies, one feature about them came to assume increasing interest; while there was remarkable unanimity with regard to most of the names given, there was one point of marked ambiguity—at the tertiary level of segmentation. I recorded genealogies in four tribes on an extensive scale, and in each tribe

ambiguity surrounding the actual names and their correct position occurred at about the fifth ascending generation. Whenever
this point was reached in the recordings, arguments would flare
up over the names to be included or excluded and over the relation of these names to those above and below, with the result
that for several people of the same segment there would be several versions of a genealogy which differed only at this one point.
An example of this sort is given below from the genealogy of the
Nasr section, which shows seven different versions of the arrangement of ancestors round about the fifth ascending generation
from the living.

The confusion at and around the fifth ascending generation
appeared with such regularity in the genealogies that I feel justified in referring to it as 'the area of ambiguity'. It seems likely,
moreover, that in any society where the lineage structure is
closely tied to the territorial disposition of groups, since the genealogy is so rigid, there needs to be in it somewhere an area of
ambiguity if it is to be related to reality. Without this ambiguity,
the form of the genealogy is too rigid to comprehend changes
which occur. This point in the genealogy came to assume critical
significance as the point where adjustments in it are made. Other
kinds of evidence point to the same conclusion.

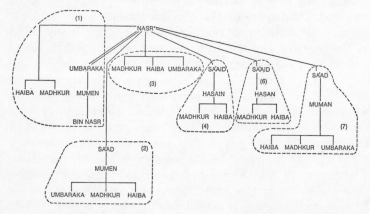

FIG. 18-3   GENEALOGY 3.   *There is another section, al-Dawwas,
which belongs to this group, but to include this as well would greatly
complicate the issue without giving any additional information.

There are, in Cyrenaica, three major status groups among the tribes: the noble or free-born tribesmen (*al-Hurr*), those who have been adopted or grafted on to a tribe (the *Laff*), and the clients (*Marabtin*).

Those who claim to be free-born also claim ownership of the natural resources. The *Laff* do not own these. They are people thought not to have originally been of the lineage of the tribe with which they are resident. They are found sometimes in ones and twos in the camps of the free-born, but sometimes constituting tertiary groups themselves. Now when such people have resided with their free-born hosts for several years and one of them has married one of the host's daughters, they are grafted to the genealogy at the point of tertiary segmentation, that is, where ambiguity occurs in the genealogy. Obviously, persons thus grafted to the lineage cannot be shown as descendants of one of the living or of the recently dead, remembered perhaps by some of the elders still living. It is equally true to say that they cannot be grafted to the lineage at a point superior to that of the tertiary segments, since this would involve recognition by a number of tertiary groups whose members may know little or nothing about them. When a person enters a new tribe, the only way in which he can do so is to go to live in a camp, and it is the concern of the people of that particular camp whether or not they accept him, since it is they who have to decide whether their resources are sufficient to support a newcomer. Once a man has been accepted as a full member of a tertiary section, membership of superior tribal sections is automatic, although to enter into tribal membership he requires the permission of members of a tertiary section only. To graft at a point superior to the tertiary would be the same as giving a man superior structural status, but without a camp in which to dwell. There is only one place for his incorporation, and that is where the ambiguity in the genealogy permits manipulation to include new lines. In this way the adoption of a person into a lineage does not offend the sense of kinship of the receiving group since the point of inclusion is an ancestor about whom little or nothing is known and whose authenticity is frequently doubted by some. What has been referred to as an area of ambiguity is, moreover, something of a jumble of names, and it is not a difficult matter, if a new line has to be attached somewhere along the line, to attach it to one of these names. Bedouin welcome, as members of their camps, practically anyone who wishes to join, even, in the case of one group, an Italian. The limit to this acceptance of members is, of course, the number of people who can be supported by the local resources. If people are being admitted freely to membership of a particular camp, this means that there is a local surplus of land and water, so that the number of grafts being supported by any particular section is a useful index of the extent to which the resources are being used. Conversely, as sometimes happens when grafted elements become numerous, or when the water supply, for various reasons, dwindles, it may be necessary to detach a grafted group. Such action is always the occasion of a violent dispute, usually over watering rights, and not infrequently fights break out. Whether or not the grafted group wins, from then onwards it will be forced to exist as an independent group, and a new tertiary section will have been born. No matter which of the processes involving grafts is considered—incorporation or detachment— both are contained within the framework of the tertiary section, without any effect on the rest of the structure.

The position of the clients, in the context of this discussion, is not unlike that of the grafts. Briefly, clients are men who are considered to have originated from a country other than Cyrenaica, and who for this reason cannot claim rights to land and water— at least this is the theory, although in some circumstances they are able to do so successfully. They are of various kinds, but they are not included in the genealogies given by the free-born. Clients are found grouped in two main ways. There are some large groups which constitute tribes in the sense that they display a genealogical and territorial organization like those of the free-born, and are usually to be found flanking the main tribes of the country on their borders. Some of these are powerful groups and enjoy considerable independence of action, but whatever their characteristics they none the less speak of themselves as 'for' or tied to the noble tribe whose territory includes theirs. Further, the sections of these client tribes have their special ties with tertiary sections of the noble tribes, which are not merely ties of sentiment, but which take the form of valuable mutual help in a number of situations. A whole client tribe, in the sense that it is occupying territory which cannot be said to belong to any particular section of their noble patron tribe, is tied to the patron tribe as such. Yet it is through the small tertiary segments that these ties are made effective. In this sense, a client tribe is a combination of small groups of people each group having specific relationships with defined tertiary sections, and participating in the tribe of their patrons through these relationships.

Secondly, clients are found distributed in small groups, sometimes no more than one or two men, but often in clusters large enough to compose a small camp. Practically all tertiary sections of the noble tribes have some clients either living with them or sharing their resources. While clients continue to reside with a particular tertiary section, it is the members of the latter who are responsible for them and vice versa. If, for example, one of the clients commits a homicide, the gathering of blood-money is the responsibility of the noble tertiary section to which he is attached, and vengeance can be exacted on any member of the noble section. In other circumstances, when the offender is a nobleman, then the clients of his group are the first to be approached for blood-money. Tied in this way to a particular tertiary section, they are not, however, compelled to reside with its members permanently. On the contrary, they may be forced to move. If, for example, there is a pressure on local water supplies, the first to feel it are the clients. Annually, they supplicate for the use of water, and if their patrons decide that there is insufficient to meet all needs, the request is refused, albeit reluctantly. Clients constitute a socially mobile group; they are the pawns in the annual readjustment of men to their resources. Whenever they move, they pass on to another tertiary section, which may be a collateral section of the one they have left or structurally far removed from it, but as soon as they leave one, their duties and obligations cease and are taken up anew with another structurally like group. It is because their attachment is to a tertiary section, and not to one of superior order, that they can be as socially mobile as they are, which in turn facilitates a more efficient adjustment to the ecological situation from year to year.

Small groups of clients move frequently, groups of adopted people less frequently, and groups composed of the free-born change their structural position only rarely. The latter change sometimes does, however, occur, and there is evidence to show that it does. For example, Agostini (1922–23, p. 323) in his tribal survey, records a section named Barsha as one of the groups stemming from Nasr.[12] In the genealogies I was given, the name did not appear, and even after some questioning, what information was known about it was concealed. Some time later the name cropped up accidentally in conversation, and I was then told that at one time it had been one of the Nasr groups, but that after a quarrel during a year of water shortage, the Barsha folk went to live with people with whom they had maternal connexions, and in whose territory there was ample water that year, and never returned. The group, a tertiary one, was detached from the tertiary point of segmentation in the genealogies, and tied on to a tertiary group of another tribe in its new homeland.

To summarize briefly the argument thus far, the mechanical devices of telescoping, fusion of names, the ejection of those names which cease to be of any social consequence, and the elision of names at or around the fifth ascending generation, taken together point to the importance of the tertiary order of segmentation in discussing the problem of maintaining the form of the genealogy constant in face of its natural tendency to alter; further, evidence of changes (adoption into a lineage, detachment from it, the inclusion and exclusion of clients) was presented, and this again led to the conclusion that the tertiary point of segmentation is critical in this respect. This being so, the manner in which change actually occurs, still remains to be shown, and this is best done, perhaps, by discussing the mode of proliferation of tertiary segments. In order to do this adequately, it is necessary to say something briefly about certain features of Bedouin marriage.

Among the Bedouin there exists a preferential form of marriage between a man and his father's brother's daughter. Parallel cousin marriage of this sort carries with it the exclusive right of a man to this cousin. Without his consent no one else can marry her, and to attempt to do so would be to risk the marriage arrangements being nullified after negotiations had almost been

[12] Barsha's position is incorrectly given as a sub-group of Haiba; it should be shown as structurally equivalent to Haiba. See also note 11.

concluded. I have been present on occasions when, after both parties have agreed to a marriage and the groom has collected most of the things necessary to present to the bride at the wedding celebrations, the girl's father's brother's son appears and demands the discontinuance of the arrangements; on one occasion, he did not appear until the actual day of the wedding, but was bought off with a cap, a cloak, and the promise of two sheep. The highest incidence for any form of marriage, moreover, is with the patrilineal parallel cousin, although not necessarily with the first cousin.

Parallel cousin marriage of this sort is not, however, the only form practised among the Bedouin. Much of the writing on Bedouin marriage leaves the impression that a solution of the problem of parallel cousin marriage (Murphy & Kasdal 1959) solves all the problems involved in their system of marriage. In addition to this form, there is a number of others; indeed there is another form of preferential marriage among them, which, although it does not have the compulsive character of parallel cousin marriage, is of major importance. I refer to cross-cousin marriage with the mother's brother's daughter. Such a cousin may be, of course, as a result of patrilineal parallel cousin marriage, a patrilineal parallel cousin as well. Such a cousin may be, on the other hand, a woman of another tribal section or of a different tribe altogether. A characteristic form of this marriage is that once it has been initiated, it is perpetuated in successive generations. Members of one line in a tertiary segment will, therefore, be building up kinship ties through marriage in one particular direction. At the same time, another line, by practising the same form of marriage will be weaving ties in a quite different direction. One direction these marriages could take might be to a tertiary segment of a collateral secondary segment; another might be to a primary segment of the same tribe, and yet another to people living in a date oasis. Only occasionally do marriages occur between collateral tertiary segments, and then there is usually some specific reason. In other words, when men marry outside the limits of their own tertiary segment, they leap-frog adjacent segments and marry into structurally more remote groups.

The result of these two marriage patterns is that the people of any summer camp will have descent lines cross linked by the bonds of marriage with parallel cousins, and at the same time cleaved by the maternal links established by repetitive cross-cousin marriage to different groups outside the segment. Thus, in one of its aspects, marriage makes of an agnatic group a group of cognates as well. 'Marry your paternal cousins and both your paternal and maternal relatives will be one,' to quote Bedouin sentiment on the matter. Within this agnatic group, nevertheless, two other clusters of kin exist—those with maternal connexions outside. In all, three areas of kinship can be defined,[13] although all the members of the segment will have the lineage bond of agnation in common. In normal circumstances, when split does not threaten the group, the bond of agnation, strengthened by parallel cousin marriage, takes precedence, although behaviour is significantly affected by maternal links at any time. There is, in the first instance, great jealousy between co-wives, which is passed on to their children. Each wife has her separate tent, and each is entitled to a strictly equal share of the husband's time they have in common. This applies similarly to favours he may grant his wives, and the distribution of his wealth among them. If, for example, the husband is the owner of a horse, he is re-quired to tether it outside the tents of his wives in strict rota-tion; if he retires for the night with one wife, the following night he must favour the other; if he buys dress material for the one he must buy a length of identical material for the other; if he bestows favours on the children of one the children of the other must be given equal consideration. Many such details are meticulously observed; but while many are observed most of the time, it is difficult to observe them all, the whole time. Any breach of the rules is quickly taken up by the wives, and quarrels ensue, leading not only to bitterness among the co-wives, but be-tween the offended wife and her husband, between the children of both wives, and between the children and their father. Often, when a man has co-wives, there is a marked discrepancy in age between them, for, when an elderly Bedouin marries a second

[13] The situation is not always as simple as this. Cross-cousin marriage may take more than two directions, and marriage within the segment might bring about great complexity, but the argument put forward above is not seriously affected by neglecting these details here.

wife he usually chooses a young girl of about twenty years. Children of the elder wife might be adult, therefore, when the children of the junior wife are infants. Great emphasis is placed on seniority, particularly among males, but strong emphasis is also placed on the equality of siblings and their equal legal status. Between brothers of widely differing ages, there is, then, this field of potential conflict. From an early date competitive, if not hostile, relationships develop between the sons of co-wives. Competition between half-brothers results not only from their mothers being co-wives: one group might be the sons of a divorced wife. The latter situation is often much worse, for the sons born of the divorced wife are now being fostered by a woman who is not their mother. A similar condition of things is brought about when a widower with sons remarries. Yet again, when a wife grows old and her sons have reached maturity, her husband may not divorce her formally, but merely 'throw her off his back'; she will then go to live with her grown sons, while her husband, in turn, takes a new wife, usually taking up residence in another camp for a time at least. It would be too much of a digression here to discuss the inheritance disputes, and the disputes over marriage and bride-wealth, which arise out of these various circumstances. Suffice it to note that such disputes are common and affect the alignment of people within a tertiary segment.

As half-brothers grow to maturity some of them will marry their maternal cross-cousins, and in succeeding generations some of their descendants will do likewise. In this way, a tertiary segment united by the bond of agnation, will also have within it smaller groups of kin having different sets of cognatic links. This group, as a residential unit, shows a very high concentration of agnates, and the Bedouin say with pride that members of the camps are always 'one' because of this agnatic bond, and indeed, the corporate identity of this group is strikingly displayed in many circumstances. It does not take precedence in all circumstances, for, built into agnation, with the heavy burden of duties which go with it, are serious stresses and strains which in some circumstances regularly come out into the open. In yet other circumstances cognatic kinship affiliations appear to be dominant, causing friction among agnates. A man, for example, may permit

his maternal kinsmen to use the land and water facilities of
his lineage; his agnates may give ready consent or bicker about
it, but when it becomes necessary to clean a well, disputes are
almost certain to break out in the camp between those who argue
that their maternal relatives should not be expected to assist in
its cleaning and those who insist they should as an acknowledgement of the use they have made of it. In these circumstances
maternal links divide agnates. Conversely, if it becomes necessary for some of the same men to use the water and ploughland
of their maternal kin, their agnates are only too pleased that
they are able to do so, because the pressure on their own resources is relieved. In these circumstances, the maternal link
strengthens the agnatic group. When, to give another instance,
blood-money has to be gathered, it is the duty of all agnates to
contribute equally, and no member of the group, rich or poor,
can contract out of this obligation without sacrificing his membership of the group. Payments of blood-money are witness of
the strength of the notion of 'oneness' among agnates, in one
sense, but in so far as they are compulsory, they point also to the
weakness in the relationship. Maternal kin are not directly concerned in this, but they can and do make contributions. In this
context two aspects of agnation appear, and the value of the
maternal link is emphasized. Again, maternal kinsmen are not
directly concerned in inheritance disputes, but they are expected
to intercede for their sister's sons, who often use their mother's
brother's tribal brand on their own animals. During disputes of
this kind, blame is thrown on to the maternal kinsmen for their
interference in matters which, properly speaking, are not their
business. In marriage, however, events take quite a different
turn. The responsibility for providing a man with a wife is first
that of the father, and secondly of the members of the tertiary
section; the father takes the initiative, and his agnates assist, not
only in the negotiations, but also in defraying the heavy costs of
the wedding festivities, the various gifts that precede it, and the
bride-wealth which follows. The mother's brother is also a key
person in all these arrangements. He enters into the negotiations,
assists with the entertainment on the wedding day, and makes a
substantial contribution to the bride-wealth. On the wedding day,
there is no kinsman to compare with the mother's brother; a few

weeks later, he is reviled for demanding a long overdue instalment of his daughter's bride-wealth. He is the person who can be approached freely, to whom love tales can be told, from whom help can be expected, who gives support in disputes, and who also upbraids, who punishes, who withholds, who acts as a pull-away from the agnatic group. An agnate demands help, and also compels the fulfilment of obligations. An agnate is a man with whom relationships are formal, particularly if he is a senior. He is, too, the person who unfailingly, though perhaps grudgingly, gives help when it is most required; who, regardless of the merits of the case, defends one against external opposition; and who is always available at each life crisis. A kinship link is not to be defined by any one particular mode of behaviour. Each is a cluster of different sorts of behaviour, one form taking precedence in these circumstances, another in other circumstances, and so forth.

The little clusters of kindred can be defined clearly in any of the camps. It is customary among the Bedouin for those who are most closely linked as kindred to pitch their tents close to each other. For example, if a man has two recently married sons, their tents are pitched on either side of his, with the ropes of their tents crossing the ropes of their father's tent. More distantly related kin will be more distantly placed, and here and there, breaks in the continuity of the lines of tents are to be observed, corresponding as a rule to breaks in kinship. Each large camp in this way can be viewed as two or more nuclei of kindred. The camp as a whole is dominantly composed of agnates, but they are disposed in such a way as to show clusterings of varying kinship composition. Characteristically each cluster has a separate name, often a female name which refers to a common mother of the cluster, or of the head of the leading family in it. When these relatively large camps break up with the onset of the rains and disperse to form small camps of five to seven tents for winter pasturing, they will be seen to correspond almost identically with the kin clusters of the larger summer camp. Again, a tertiary segment may have two wells for its own use. In a particular year there may be sufficient water in one of them to meet the needs of the whole group, and its members then live together in one camp; the following year both wells may have to be used, and the camp of the previous summer will split up, roughly half going to one well, and the remainder to the other. It is usually an easy matter to predict, at least in a general fashion, how the group will divide, as long as the details of kinship are known; the camps will be composed of members of two sets of patri-lines in the tertiary segment, who will also represent two discrete clusters of cognatic kindred. If, therefore, a tertiary group increases in numbers to the point where a split in the lineage is inevitable, here then is the line of split, along a line, that is, of kinship cleavage and lineage differentiation. 'Men make the tribe; women divide it,' is an oft-quoted saying among the Bedouin, but this, like most sayings, tells only part of the truth, as we shall see.

It is possible to show where on the genealogy change takes place, and it is possible to indicate the lines cleavages will follow, but the proliferation of a lineage does not occur merely because the possibility exists for it to do so. A group must, clearly, break up if the number of its members significantly exceeds that which can be supported by the available natural resources; water is the prime cause of the proliferation of lineages. Granting this, a group remains an undifferentiated corporation until occasion arises when its members, or some of them, can demonstrate unequivocally that they are no longer bound by its conditions of membership. There is a number of occasions when this can be done, some of which are discussed below.

The test, *par excellence,* of corporate affiliation is the acceptance of the responsibility to pay blood-money. Refusal to accept this is the same as renouncing membership of the group. Individuals are sometimes excluded from membership in this way. There are occasions too, when the payment of blood-money involves renunciation by more than one or two individuals. If membership of a section has increased to the point of splitting, and should a homicide occur within it, one of the kin clusters within the group might demand blood-money from the other. Nothing could make the statement of split clearer than this. The most impelling condition of membership of the tertiary group is that 'we pay as one and receive as one', a condition which, of course, excludes payment within the group. Any two groups between which the demand for blood-money has been made are, therefore, by definition, separate tertiary groups.

When a member of a group or his wife dies, there are specific days on which kin of various sorts should attend the mourning ceremonies, which extend over a period of a week. Allowance is made for those who may be away temporarily, although they are expected to hasten to the mourning camp as quickly as possible. Agnatic kin are expected not only to be present on the appropriate day, but are required to offer gifts consistent with their relationship to the bereaved; agnates of the tertiary segment are expected to offer a sheep, while some cognates ought to bring a goat and others a quantity of sugar and tea. At one funeral in a camp where I was resident, soon after the death occurred, the main concern of its inhabitants was whether or not certain men of their section would attend the mourning rites and bring appropriate gifts with them. These men lived at the time in another camp a few miles away, as they had been doing for several years past. They did not come when they were expected, and when they finally arrived at the end of the week they brought with them gifts of sugar and tea only—gifts which were totally inappropriate for agnates of the group. They were, in fact, now no longer members of it, and my neighbours were able to tell me, 'They have branched off from us. We will never live together again.' The lineage had proliferated and this was the first occasion for showing it.

Wide-spread in Cyrenaica is a cult of saints. The number of saints' tombs varies from tribe to tribe, there being fewer among the camel herders of the semi-desert than among the cow-herding, almost sedentary, folk of the plateau area. Whatever the number, the members of the group that venerates a particular saint make an annual pilgrimage to his tomb, and sometimes more frequent pilgrimages are made. In one area there were two men, accepted by their respective kin groups as leaders, who vied against each other for the leadership of their section. One of them had been a famous warrior during the Italian wars and, after being injured, fled to Egypt where he lived for seventeen years, until he returned to his homeland in 1947. The other had also fought against the Italians, failed to win renown, was a captive for a time, later released, and subsequently appointed leader of his section by the Italian authorities. The first, during his period of exile, had become impoverished. The second during his years of freedom had prospered. As far as their personalities were concerned, there was little doubt who was leader—the name of the former was known throughout the land. Now when the warrior returned from his Egyptian exile, his rival offered him a sheep as a gift. This act was wholly appropriate. Subsequently they continued to compete fiercely, but it soon became clear that the returned warrior was winning the greater support. In the face of this, the rival, in 1948, decided to break with tradition by staying away from the annual pilgrimage to the tomb of the local saint. Instead, he and his followers made their pilgrimage to a different tomb in the vicinity of their camp, and later built a low wall round the tomb, whitewashed it, and made it known that henceforward they would regularly use it for pilgrimages. The two kinship groups of a tertiary section now had their separate saint's tomb. Some months later, the rival decided to move with his small group to an area in which they had not previously resided. It is the custom among the Bedouin when they pitch their tents in a place for the first time, that the people of the neighbourhood should bring them gifts to mark the event. The returned warrior, who had now become a close neighbour of his rival was obliged, like others, to offer the latter a gift; he was also obliged to return the gift of a sheep that he had been given on rejoining his section in 1947. He brought a gift within a few hours of his rival's arrival, but it was a goat.[14] The rival and his followers were furious, and the argument that the warrior was too poor to give more was dismissed summarily. This was the final insult. The donor, in return, had been given less than he had presented. The reciprocity of gift exchanges had not only been arrested, it had been reversed. From then onwards the two groups made no attempt to conceal their hostility and went their separate ways.

Disputes stemming from circumstances such as these are the occasions which mark the proliferation of groups, although in all three cases cited, difficulties over water supplies had preceded the outbreaks of quarrelling.

In this discussion of the ways in which proliferation of segments takes place, the emphasis had been put on the tug of war between the interests of people in their agnatic connexions and

[14] A goat is inferior to a sheep in gift exchanges.

the interests they have in their maternal relatives. Stated thus sharply, this is a distortion of the process. To speak of the principle of agnation conflicting with the principle of cognation or maternal origin is nonsense, as the facts included in the discussion show. Agnation is not one thing, but many. Within its scope are included such aspects of social organization as succession, status, inheritance, bride-wealth, blood-money, modes of domestic and political behaviour, and so forth; and each of these aspects, the closer we stick to reality, can be broken up into a number of components. The same can be said of cognation and maternal origin. All these principles, so called, are clusters of numerous component parts, which combine, in reality, in a kaleidoscopic number of ways. In one situation a component of one combines with that of another to strengthen it; in a different situation the one component may repel the other; in a third situation, a number of the components in one will combine to exclude those of the other, and so on. If, therefore, an understanding of the way in which lineage proliferation occurs is sought, a view of the process as a conflict between the principle of agnation and the opposing pull of maternal origin is quite erroneous. It is of use in predicting the direction of cleavage to know that within a tertiary group there are also clusters of kin which are defined roughly by maternal links, and this knowledge serves as a rough and ready guide in predicting what the composition of groups, after they have split away from the parent group, will be. If a more precise picture of this composition is desired, other and more complex kinship links and the behaviour which accompanies them must be taken into account. If a still more accurate picture is desired, details of inheritance disputes, debts of bride-wealth, the size of flocks and herds, and the like, must also be taken into consideration. If, finally, one has the opportunity to study groups after they have proliferated, the presence or absence of this or that man can often be explained only in terms of his eye for a pretty girl or a personal preference for neighbours.

The kind of change which has been discussed in this essay is not difficult to negotiate in genealogical terms. Earlier it was stressed that within the tertiary tribal sections, although they are always predominantly agnatic groups, clusters of cognatic

kin also exist. Two ways of naming these clusters are adopted—
all groups, whether they are elementary families, an odd assort-
ment of kindred sharing a common tent for reasons of expediency, or tribal groups, have a name. Sometimes these clusters are
named after a prominent living male, or a deceased kinsman of
the same kind. Sometimes these little groups are named after a
woman, perhaps the grandmother of the group.[15] Thus a small
group of two or three tents will be distinguished from another
similar cluster within the camp, and so on for a number of groups,
depending on the size of the camp. Most camps, however many
tents they contain, have names for progressively inclusive clusters of tents until a twofold named division is reached. Tertiary
segments that are forced to split contain therefore two groups
with names already attached to them. When a split occurs, the
name of the tertiary segment is pushed into the area of ambiguity
and the names of what were previously two clusters become the
names of two new tertiary segments, with a minimum adjustment in usage and a minor re-shuffle at the tertiary level of segmentation. Names cannot continue to be pushed into this area of
the genealogy interminably, otherwise it would gradually expand
into a vast pool of names. For a few generations the name dispensed with in this way becomes one of those ancestors about
whom there is argument when genealogies are given. In the
course of time, name after name is subjected to the process of
elision and eventually will cease to be of concern to anyone.

I now summarize the main points of the discussion. The evidence that has been examined suggests that the mechanical devices of telescoping, fusion of names, and extinction of lines do
not affect orders of segmentation superior to that of the tertiary
order, and that in conditions of a completely stable population,
these devices alone would suffice to retain the form of the genealogical structure. But, it was argued, conditions of complete stability cannot be assumed; the evidence of the present distribution
of population among the numerous tertiary groups clearly points
to marked fluctuations occurring within these small groups. This
being so, proliferation of these groups in some areas at some

---

[15] The naming of groups within a tertiary segment is an interesting study
in itself, but it would be outside the limits of this discussion to make more
than a brief mention of it.

times, must follow, and conversely, while proliferation takes place here, combination will be taking place elsewhere as the population of groups decreases. The condition which compels proliferation is the alteration in the relationship of man and animals to the natural resources; and when this alteration builds up to an acute pressure on water and land, one group of a divided segment must move off to seek water elsewhere.

The next task was to demonstrate where this kind of change occurred on the genealogy. The sudden irregularity in the number of segments at the tertiary order, compared with the uniformity at others, provided a clue. Other evidence also pointed to this as a significant order in this context: there is ambiguity displayed with regard to the identity and positioning of ancestors here; members adopted into a lineage are grafted on to it here; clients are attached to tertiary sections; groups of noblemen, when they are detached and move off to another tribe, break away at this point. This is where change occurs, but, it was agreed, in understanding the way in which it takes place, certain forms of marriage have to be taken into account. Particular emphasis was placed on cross-cousin marriage with the mother's brother's daughter, and to women outside the tertiary segment, since the effect of these forms of marriage is to produce two or more clusters of cognatic kindred in camps largely composed of agnates, and to emphasize the line of cleavage in a lineage segment. So that when, therefore, a split occurs, the line it takes is predetermined. Proliferation, even when necessary, does not finally come about, however, until an occasion permits the separation of groups to be demonstrated by a violation of the conditions of membership of a group. Details of three such occasions were offered: the demand for blood-money between agnates who previously had constituted a politically undivided section; behaviour contrary to the demands of agnatic kinship in attendance and gift-giving at funerals; and failure to participate in a pilgrimage to the saint's tomb of a particular section. But another query remained: how are the newly formed groups named? It was seen that names already in daily use by the small group of people concerned came to assume a new significance, while the name which had previously spanned them all is disregarded and pushed into the area of ambiguity whence later it is elided altogether.

Change due to the normal and inevitable process of proliferation is thus managed within the structural limits of the tertiary section without disturbing any of the superior orders in the system. The latter remain fixed over long periods, but the tertiary sections of a particular secondary action may be reduced in number over a few generations while another secondary section may show a corresponding increase in the number of its segments.

By combining the various factors involved in change, it is possible to understand the details of lineage proliferation, or at least to travel along a well signposted road. In the light of this analysis, moreover, it is unnecessary to assume a stable population in each and every segment over long periods; the mechanisms of readjustment allow for substantial irregularities and fluctuations in population. It is possible that they are also sufficient to contain significant increases in the aggregate population. They could almost certainly control minor fluctuations, but it is seriously doubted whether a population increase sufficient to produce a country-wide and acute water shortage could be met merely by the proliferation of tertiary lineage segments. But to deal with this problem other aspects of the Bedouin genealogy and details of Cyrenaican history, which have necessarily been omitted from this discussion, would have to be taken into account, and this is best left for another article.

BIBLIOGRAPHY

(Vol. I)

Abaev, V. I.

1959 *Grammaticheskii Ocherk Osetinskogo Yazïka.* Orjonikidze.

Abou-Zeid, Ahmad.

1966 "Honor and Shame among the Bedouins of Egypt." In J. G. Peristiany, ed., *Honour and Shame.* Chicago: University of Chicago Press.

Agostini, E.

1922–23 *Le Popolazioni Della Cirenaica.* Benghazi.

Alport, E. A.

1954 "The Mazb," *Journal of the Royal Anthropological Institute,* 84:34–44.

Andrae, Tor.

1956 *Mohamed, the Man and His Faith.* London: Allen and Unwin.

Asad, Talal.

1964 "Seasonal Movements of the Kababish Arabs of Northern Kordofan," *Sudan Notes and Records,* 45:48–58.

Aswad, B. C.

1963 "Social and Ecological Aspects in the Origin of the Islamic States," *Papers of the Michigan Academy of Science, Arts and Letters,* 48:419–42.

1967 "Lineage Discord and Continuity Among Sedentarized Pastoralists in the Hatay (S. Turkey)," Ph.D. Dissertation, University of Michigan.

Ayoub, Victor F.

1965 "Conflict Resolution and Social Reorganization in a Lebanese Village," *Human Organization,* 24:11–17.

Bacon, Elizabeth.

1958 *Obok.* (Viking Fund Publications in Anthropology, No. 25.) New York: Wenner-Gren Foundation.

Baladhuri, Ahmad al. (d. 892).

1916–24 *The Origins of the Islamic State.* (Trans. and annot. by

Hitti and Margotten, Studies in History, Economics, and Public Law. Faculty of Political Science, Columbia University, Vol. 68, 2 vols.) New York.

Barkali.
    1950 *Hebraisch für Jedermann.* Jerusalem.

Barnes, J. A.
    1954 *Politics in a Changing Society.* Oxford: Oxford University Press.

Barth, Fredrik.
    1953 *Principles of Social Organization in Southern Kurdistan.* Oslo: Universitetets Etnografiske Museum, No. 7.
    1954 "Father's Brother's Daughter Marriage in Kurdistan," *Southwestern Journal of Anthropology,* 10:164–71.
    1959 "Segmentary Opposition and the Theory of Games," *Journal of the Royal Anthropological Institute of Great Britain and Ireland,* 89:5–21.

Basset, André.
    1929 *La Langue Berbère.* Paris.

Basset, H.
    1920 *Essai sur la littérature des Berbères.* Algiers.

Basset, H., and Picard, A.
    1948 *Elements de Grammaire Berbère (Kabylie-Irjen).* Algiers.

Beliaev, E.
    1954 "Formation of the Arab State and the Origin of Islam in the VII Century." Paper presented by the Soviet Delegation at the 23rd International Congress of Orientalists. Islamic Studies. Editions of the Academy of Sciences of the USSR. Moscow.

Bell, Richard.
    1926 *The Origin of Islam in Its Christian Environment.* London.

Ben Daoud, M.
    1924 "Recueil du droit coûtumier de Massat," *Hesperis.*

Ben Daoud, M., and Montagne, R.
    1927 "Documents pour servir a l'étude du droit coûtumier du Sud-Marocain," *Hesperis.*

Benet, Francisco.
    1957 "Explosive Markets: The Berber Highlands," in Karl Polanyi *et al., Trade and Markets in the Early Empires.* New York: Macmillan.

Berque, Jacques.
    1957 *The Social History of an Egyptian Village in the Twentieth Century.* Paris: Mouton.

Biarnay, I.

1916 "Un cas de regression vers la coûtume Berbère chez une tribu arabisée," *Archives Berbères,* I.

Bittner, M.

1916–17 *Studien zur Shauri-Sprache.* (Kais. Akademie der Wissenschaft in Wien. Phil-Hist. Klasse. In Sitzungberichte, 179 and 183.) Vienna.

Blunt, Anne.

1896 *Bedouin Tribes of the Euphrates.* New York: Harper.

Bogardus, Emory S.

1938 "Social Distance and Its Practical Implications," *Journal of Sociology and Social Research,* 22:462–76.

Bohannan, L.

1952 "A Genealogical Charter," *Africa,* 22:301–15.

Boulifa.

1905 "Le Kanoun d'Adni," *Travaux et Memoires publiés en l'honneur du XIVe Congrès des Orientalistes par l'École Supérieure des Lettres d'Alger.*

Bourrilly, J.

1932 *Éléments d'Ethnographie Marocaine.* Paris.

Bousquet, George.

1954 "Observations sociologiques sur les origines de l'Islam," *Studia Islamica,* II:231–47.

Braidwood, R. J., and Howe, B. (*et al*).

1960 "Prehistoric Investigations in Iraqi Kurdistan," *Studies in Ancient Oriental Civilization,* No. 31. Chicago: University of Chicago Press.

Braidwood, R. J., and Willey, G. R., eds.

1962 *Courses Toward Urban Life.* Chicago: Aldine.

Briggs, L. C.

1960 *Tribes of the Sahara.* Cambridge, Mass.: Harvard University Press.

Buhl, F.

1953 "Al-Medina," *Shorter Encyclopedia of Islam.* Ithaca: Cornell University Press.

Burkhardt, J. L.

1831 *Notes on the Bedouins and the Wahabys.* London.

Caussin de Perceval, A. P.

1948 *Essai sur l'historie des Arabes avant l'Islamisme.* Vols. 1, 2, 3. Paris: Librairie de Firmin.

Chemali, I.

1916 *Gli Abitanti Della Tripolitania.* Tripoli.

Coon, C. S.

  1953 *Caravan: the Story of the Middle East*. New York: H. Holt.

Cowan, D.

  1958 *Modern Literary Arabic*. Cambridge: Cambridge University Press.

Cowley, A. E.

  1949 *Gesenius' Hebrew Grammar* (ed. Kautzsch), 2nd ed. reprint. Oxford.

Cunnison, I. G.

  1956 "Perpetual Kinship: Political Institutions of the Luapula Peoples," *Human Problems in British Central Africa*, Vol. 20, pp. 28–48. Journal of the Rhodes-Livingston Institute.

  1957 "History and Genealogies in a Conquest State," *American Anthropologist*, 59:20–31.

  1966 *Baggara Arabs: Power and the Lineage in a Sudanese Nomad Tribe*. Oxford: Clarendon Press.

Daumas, E.

  1853 *Moeurs et coûtumes de l'Algerie*. Paris.

  1869 *La vie arabe et la société musulmane*. Paris.

De Boucheman, Albert.

  1934 "Matériel de la vie bedouine, recueilli dans le désert de Syrie: Tribu des arabes Sba'a," *Documents d'Études Orientales*, Vol. 3. Paris.

Dickson, H. R. P.

  1949 *The Arab of the Desert*. London: Allen and Unwin.

  1956 *Kuwait and Her Neighbors*. London: Allen and Unwin.

Doughty, Charles.

  1936 *Travels in Arabia Deserta*. London: Jonathan Cape.

Doutte, E.

  1905 *Merrakech, Comité du Maroc*. Rabat.

Dresch, Jr.

  1941 *Commentaries des cartes sur les genres de vie de montagne dans le massif central du Grand-Atlas*. Tours.

Dupree, Louis.

  1966 "Aq Kupruk: A Town in North Afghanistan," American University Field Staff Reports: *South Asia Series*, 10: nos. 9 and 19.

Duveyrier, H.

  1864 *Les Touaregs du nord*. Paris: Challamel.

Eberhard, Wolfram.

  1954 "Change in Leading Families in Southern Turkey," *Anthropos*, 49:992–1003.

English, Paul Ward.

1966 *City and Village in Iran: Settlement and Economy in the Kirman Basin.* Madison: University of Wisconsin Press.

Evans-Pritchard, E. E.

1940 *The Nuer. A Description of the Modes of Livelihood and Political Institutions of a Nilotic People.* Oxford: Clarendon Press.

1949 *The Sanusi of Cyrenaica.* Oxford: Clarendon Press.

1951 *Kinship and Marriage among the Nuer.* Oxford: Clarendon Press.

Farsoun, Samih K.

1970 "Family Structure and Society in Modern Lebanon," in L. Sweet, ed., *Peoples and Cultures of the Middle East,* Vol. II. New York: Natural History Press.

Firth, R.

1936 *We, The Tikopia.* London: George Allen and Unwin Ltd.

Flannery, Kent V.

1965 "The Ecology of Early Food Production in Mesopotamia," *Science,* 147:1247–56.

Fogg, W.

1939 "A Tribal Market in Spanish Morocco," *Africa,* XII, no. 4.

1940 "A Moroccan Tribal Shrine and Its Relation to a Near-by Tribal Market," *Man,* no. 124.

Forde, C. D.

1948 "The Integration of Social Anthropological Studies," *Journal of the Royal Anthropological Institute,* 78:1–10.

Fortes, M.

1945 *Dynamics of Clanship among the Tallensi.* London: Oxford University Press.

1949 *The Web of Kinship among the Tallensi.* London: Oxford University Press.

1949 *"Time and Social Structure: An Ashanti* Case Study in Social Structure," in *Social Structure,* M. Fortes, ed., pp. 54–84.

1953 "The Structure of Unilineal Descent Groups." *American Anthropologist,* 55:17–41.

Fortes, M., ed.

1949 *Social Structure.* Oxford: Clarendon Press

Foucauld, Ch. de.

1888 *Reconnaissance au Maroc,* 1883–84. Paris.

Freedman, M.

1958 *Lineage Organization in Southeastern China.* London: University of London, Athlone Press.

Fried, M. H.

   1957 "The Classification of Corporate Unilineal Descent Groups,"
   Journal of the Royal Anthropological Institute, 87:1–30.

   1960 "Evolution of Social Stratification and the State," in S. Dia-
   mond, ed., *Culture in History, Essays in the Honor of Paul Radin.*
   New York: Columbia.

   1961 "Warfare, Military Organization and the Evolution of Society,"
   Anthropologica, N.S., Vol. 3, No. 2, pp. 134–47.

Frolova, V. A.

   1960 *Belujskii Yazïk.* Moscow.

Geiger, W., and Kuhn, E.

   1895–1903 *Grundriss der Iranischen Philologie,* Vol. 1. Strasbourg.

Gellner, Ernest.

   1957 "Independence in the Central High Atlas," *Middle East
   Journal.*

   1963 "Saints of the Atlas," in J. Pitt-Rivers, ed., *Mediterranean
   Countrymen.* Paris.

Gilbertson, G. W.

   1923 *The Balochi Language.* Hertford.

   1929 *The Pakkhto Language.* Hertford.

Gluckman, M.

   1955 *Custom and Conflict in Africa.* Glencoe, Ill.: The Free Press.

Goffman, Erving.

   1956 "The Nature of Deference and Demeanor," *American Anthropologist,* 58:473–502.

Granqvist, Hilma.

   1931 *Marriage Conditions in a Palestinian Village.* Helsingfors.

Grierson.

   1921 *Linguistic Survey of India,* Vol. 10. Calcutta.

Guarmani, Carlo.

   1938 *Northern Nejd: a Journey from Jerusalem to Anaiza in Qasim.*
   (Trans. Capel-Cure, Introduction and notes by D. Carruthers.)
   London: Argonaut Press.

Hamiddullah, M.

   1938 "The City-State of Mecca," *Islamic Culture,* 12:253–76.

Hanoteau, A.

   "Essai de Grammaire Kabyle." Alar, n.d.

Hanoteau, A., and Letourneux.

   1872–73 *La Kabylie et les coûtumes Kabyles.* 3 vols. Paris.

Hart, David M.

   1970 "Clan, Lineage, Local Community and the Feud in a Rifian

Tribe," in L. Sweet, ed., *Peoples and Cultures of the Middle East,* Vol. II. New York: Natural History Press.

Hay, W. R.

1921 *Two Years in Kurdistan.* London.

Hirschfeld, Hartwig.

1883 "Essai sur l'histoire des Juifs de Medine," *Revue des Etudes Juives,* Vol. 7. Paris.

Hitti, Philip.

1960 *History of the Arabs.* London: Macmillan.

Hole, F.; Flannery, K. V.; Neely, J. A.

[In press.] "Early Agriculture and Animal Domestication at Deh Luran, Iran," *Current Anthropology.*

Horowitz, J.

1939 "Judaeo-Arabic Relations in Pre-Islamic Times," *Islamic Culture,* 13:161–96.

Hourani, George.

1951 *Arab Seafaring.* Princeton: Princeton University Press.

1952 "Did Roman Commercial Competition Ruin South Arabia?" *Journal of Near Eastern Studies,* Vol. II, no. 4, pp. 241–45.

Ibn al-Athir.

1930 *Al-Kamil fi al-Tarikh,* Vol. I.

Ibn Hisham, Abd al-Malik.

1900 *Al-Sira al-Nabawiya.* Ed. and annot. by M. al-Saqqa' al-Abyari and A. Sabli. 2nd ed., Vol. 1. Cairo.

Ibn Ishaq.

1955 *The Life of Muhammad.* (Trans. and annot. by A. Guillaume.) Oxford. (A translation of *Sirat Rasul Allah.*)

Ibn Khaldun.

1958 *The Maqaddimah.* (Trans. by F. Rosenthal.) New York: Bollingen.

1958 *Prolegomenen.* (Edited by M. Quatremere.) 3 parts. Paris.

Irons, W.

1965 "Livestock Raiding Among Pastoralists: An Adaptive Interpretation," *Papers of the Michigan Academy of Science, Arts and Letters,* Vol. L, pp. 393–414.

Jahn, A.

1905 *Grammatik der Mehri-Sprache in Sudarabien.* Vienna.

Jaussen, P. Antonin.

1948 *Coûtumes des Arabes au Pays de Moab.* Paris. (Reprint of original edition of 1903.)

Lagace, R. O.

1957 "The Formation of the Muslim State," *Anthropology Tomorrow,* Vol. 16, no. 1, pp. 141–55.

Lambton, A. K. S.

1953 *Landlord and Peasant in Persia.* New York: Oxford University Press.

1960 *Persian Grammar.* Cambridge: Cambridge University Press.

Lammens, Henri.

1914 "Le Berceau de l'Islam: l'Arabia occidentale a la veille de l'hegire" (Vol. I). *Scripta Pontificii Instituti Biblici,* Rome.

1924 *La Mecque a la veille de l'hegire.* (Melanges de l'université Saint Joseph, Vol. 9, fasc. 3.) Beirut.

1928 *Les Chrétiens à la Mecque à la veille de l'hegire: d'Arabie Occidentale avant l'hegire.* Imprimerie Catholique, Beirut.

Lammens, Henri, and Winsinck.

1953 "Mecca," *Shorter Encyclopedia of Islam.* Ithaca: Cornell University Press.

Laoust, E.

1920 *Mots et choses Berbères.* Paris.

Lattimore, Owen.

1951 *Inner Asian Frontiers of China.* New York: American Geographical Society Research Series, No. 21.

Leach, E. R.

1940 "Social and Economic Organization of the Rowanduz Kurds," *Monographs in Social Anthropology,* No. 3. London.

1954 *Political Systems of Highland Burma.* London.

1952 "The Structural Implications of Cross-Cousin Marriage," *Journal of the Royal Anthropological Institute,* 81:23–25.

Leeds, Anthony.

1963 "The Functions of War," in J. Masserman, *Science and Psychoanalysis.* New York: Grune and Stratton, Inc.

Leslau, W.

1938 *Lexique Soqotri (Sudarabique Moderne).* Paris.

Lewis, Bernard.

1950 *The Arabs in History.* London: Hutchinson.

1963 *Istanbul and the Civilization of the Ottoman Empire.* Norman: University of Oklahoma Press.

Lewis, G. L.

1953 *Teach Yourself Turkish.* London: English Universities Press.

Lhote, Henri.

1955 *Les Touaregs du Hoggar.* Paris: Payot.

Lichtenstaedter, E.

1942 "Fraternization in Early Islamic Society," *Islamic Culture,* 16:47–52.

Bibliography

Luc, B.

1911 *Le droit Kabyle.* Toulouse.

McCarthy, R. J., ed. and trans.

1953 *The Theology of al-Ash'arî.* Beirut.

Mackenzie, D. N.

1961 *Kurdish Dialect Studies,* 1. Oxford: Clarendon Press.

Maclean, A. J.

1895 *Grammar of the Dialects of Vernacular Syriac.* Cambridge.

Mair, Lucy.

1962 *Primitive Government.* Harmondsworth: Penguin Books.

Malov, S. E.

1951 *Pamyatniki Drevnetyurskoy Pismennosti.* Moscow.

Marçais, W.

1911 *Textes Arabes de Tanger.* Bibliothèque de l'École des Langues Orientales Vivantes. Paris.

Margoliouth, D. S.

1905 *Muhammad and the Rise of Islam.* London.

Maunier, R.

1926 *La Construction collective de la maison en Kabylie.* Institut d'ethnographie de l'Université de Paris, n. 3.

1927 "Recherches sur les échanges rituels en Afrique du Nord," *Année Sociologique,* nouvelle série, 1924/25. Paris.

1932 *Loi Française et Coûtume indigène en Algérie.* Paris: Domat-Montchrestien.

1935 *Coûtumes Algériennes.* Paris: Domat-Montchrestien.

1937 "Les groups d'interêt en Afrique du Nord," in *Annals Sociologiques,* coll. de *L'Année Sociologique,* fasc. 2. Paris.

Mayer, P.

1949 *The Lineage Principle in Gusii Society.* International African Institute, Memorandum 24. London.

Mead, George H.

1934 *Mind, Self and Society.* Chicago: University of Chicago Press.

Merton, Robert K.

1957 *Social Theory and Social Structure.* Glencoe, Ill.: Free Press.

Michaux-Bellaire, E.

1913 "Le Gharb," *Archives Marocaines,* XX.

"Makhzen," in *Encyclopedia of Islam.*

Michaux-Bellaire, E., and Salmon, G.

1905 "El Qcar el Kabir: Une ville de province au Maroc septentrional," *Archives Marocaines,* II.

1906 "Les tribus arabes de la vallée du Lekkous," *Archives Marocaines,* VI.

Mitchell, J. C.
1956 *The Yao Village: A Study in the Social Structure of a Nyasaland Tribe.* Manchester: Manchester University Press.

Mitchell, T. F.
1956 *An Introduction to Egyptian Colloquial Arabic.* Oxford: Clarendon Press.

Montagne, R.
1924 "Le regime juridique des tribus de Sud-Marocain," *Hesperis,* 4:313–31.
1924 "Une tribu berbère du Sud-Marocain: Massat," *Hesperis,* 4: 357–403.
1930 *Les Berbères et le Makhzen dans le Sud du Maroc.* Paris.
1931 *La Vie Sociale et La Vie Politique des Berbères.* Paris.
1932 "Notes sur la vie social et politique de l'Arabie du Nord: Les Shammer du Nejd," *Révue des Études Islamiques,* 6:61–79.
1935 "Contes Poetiques Bedouins," *Bulletin d'Études Orientales,* 5:33–120.
1947 *La civilisation du desert: Nomades d'Orient et d'Afrique.* Paris: Librairie Hachette.

Müller, V.
1931 *En Syrie avec les Bedouins.* Paris: C. Leroux.

Murphy, R. E., and Kasdal, L.
1959 "The Structure of Parallel Cousin Marriage," *American Anthropologist,* 61:17–29.

Murphy, R. F.
1962 "Deviance and Social Control II: Coleta," *Kroeber Anthropological Society Papers,* no. 27:49–54.
1964 "Social Distance and the Veil." *American Anthropologist,* 66: 1257–74.

Murray, G. W.
1935 *Sons of Ishmael.* London: George Routledge & Sons, Ltd.

Musil, Alois.
1926 *The Northern Heğaz.* New York: American Geographical Society.
1927 *Arabia Deserta.* New York: American Geographical Society.
1928a *Northern Neğd.* New York: American Geographical Society.
1928b *The Manners and Customs of the Rwala Bedouins.* New York: American Geographical Society.

Nicolaisen, Johannes.
1961 "Essai sur la religion et la magie touarègues," *Folk,* 3:113–62.

Niewenhuije, G.
1959 "The *Umma,* an Analytic Approach," *Studia Islamica,* Vol. 10.

Norbeck, Edward.
  1963 "African Rituals of Conflict," *American Anthropologist,* 65: 1254–79.
O'Leary, Delacy.
  1927 *Arabia Before Muhammad.* London: Kegan Paul.
Palgrave, W. G.
  1871 *Personal Narrative of a year's Journey through Central and Eastern Arabia.* London: Macmillan.
Park, Robert E., and Burgess, Ernest W.
  1924 *Introduction to the Science of Sociology.* Chicago: University of Chicago Press.
Patai, R.
  1962 *Golden River to Golden Road.* Philadelphia: University of Pennsylvania Press.
  1955 "Cousin-Right in Middle Eastern Marriage," *Southwestern Journal of Anthropology,* II:371–90.
Peters, Emrys.
  1960 "The Proliferation of Segments in the Lineage of the Bedouin of Cyrenaica," *Journal of the Royal Anthropological Institute,* 90:29–53.
  1963 "Aspects of Rank and Status among Muslims in a Lebanese Village," in J. Pitt-Rivers, ed., *Mediterranean Countrymen.* Paris.
Pitt-Rivers, J., ed.
  1963 *Mediterranean Countrymen.* Paris.
Polanyi, Karl, *et al.*
  1957 *Trade and Markets in the Early Empires.* New York: The Free Press.
Poppe, N., Jr.
  1962 *Uzbek Newspaper Reader.* Indiana University Publications Uralic and Altaic Series, Vol. 10. The Hague.
Rabin, C.
  1943 *Everyday Hebrew.* London: J. M. Dent & Sons.
  1951 *Ancient West-Arabian.* London: Taylor's Foreign Press.
Radcliffe-Brown, A. R.
  1952 *Structure and Function in Primitive Society.* Glencoe, Ill.: Free Press.
Rahimi, M. V., and Uspenskaya, L. V.
  1954 *Tajiksko-Russkii Slovar',* pp. 531–70. Moscow.
Randell, J.
  1962 "The Potential Development of Lands Devoted to Nomadic Pastoralism," in *The Effect of Nomadism on the Economic and*

Social Development of the People of the Sudan. Philosophical
Society of the Sudan.

Reckendorf, H.

1953 "Al-Ansar," in *Shorter Encyclopedia of Islam.* Gibb and
Kramers, ed. New York: Cornell University Press.

Rich, C. J.

1836 *Narrative of a Residence in Koordistan.* London.

Richardot, E.

1909 *Notes sur la touiza.* Algiers.

1935 *La mutualité agricole des indigènes de l'Algérie.* Paris.

Robertson Smith, W.

1903 *Kinship and Marriage in Early Arabia.* London: Adam and
Charles Black.

Robin.

1874 "Fetna Meriem," *Revue Africaine,* XVIII, n. 105.

Robinson, T. H.

1949 *Paradigms and Exercises in Syriac Grammar.* Oxford.

Rodinson, Maxine.

1957 "The Life of Muhammad and the Sociological Problems of
the Beginnings of Islam," *Diogenes,* 17:28–51.

Rosen, Lawrence.

1968 "A Moroccan Jewish Community During the Middle Eastern
Crisis," *American Scholar,* 37: no. 3.

Rosenfeld, Henry.

1964 "From Peasantry to Wage Labor and Residual Peasantry:
The Transformation of an Arab Village," in Robert A. Manners,
ed., *Process and Pattern in Culture: Essays in Honor of Julian
Steward.* Chicago: Aldine.

Sahlins, M. D.

1961 "The Segmentary Lineage: an Organization of Predatory Expansion," *American Anthropologist,* 63:322–45.

Savarese, E.

1926 *Le Terre Della Cirenaica.* Benghazi.

Schacht, Joseph.

1932 "Islam," in *Encyclopedia of the Social Sciences,* Vol. 8,
pp. 333–43. New York: Macmillan.

1955 "Pre-Islamic Background and Early Development of Juris-
prudence," in *Law in the Middle East,* Vol. 1 (M. Khadduri and
V. Liebesny, eds.) Washington, D.C.: Middle East Institute.

Schapera, I.

1956 *Government and Politics in Tribal Societies.* London: Watts.

Segonzac, Marquis de.

1899–1901 *Voyages au Maroc.* Paris.

1904–5 *Au Coeur de l'Atlas, Mission au Maroc.* Paris.

Service, E.

1960 "Law of Evolutionary Potential," in *Evolution and Culture* (E. Service and M. Sahlins, eds.), pp. 93–123. Ann Arbor: University of Michigan Press.

1962 *Primitive Social Organization.* New York: Random House.

Shemesh, A. B.

1958 *Taxation in Islam.* (Trans. of *Kitab al-Kharaj by Yahya.*) London.

Shibutani, Tamotsu.

1961 *Society and Personality.* Englewood Cliffs, N.J.: Prentice-Hall.

Simmel, Georg.

1950 *The Sociology of Georg Simmel,* K. H. Wolff, trans. Glencoe, Ill.: Free Press.

Smith, M. G.

1956 "Segmentary Lineage Systems," *Journal of the Royal Anthropological Institute,* 86:39–80.

Smith, S.

1954 "Events in Arabia in the 6th Century A.D.," *Bulletin of the School of Oriental & African Studies,* Vol. 16.

Soane, E. B.

1926 *To Mesopotamia and Kurdistan in Disguise.* London: John Murray. Second edition.

Southall, A.

1956 *Alur Society.* Cambridge: Cambridge University Press.

Spuler, B., ed.

1958 *Handbuch der Orientalistik,* Sect. 1, Vol. IV (Iranistik). Leiden.

1963 *Handbuch der Orientalistik.* Vol. 5 (Altaistik), part one (Turkologie). Leiden.

Stern, Gertrude.

1939 *Marriage in Early Islam.* London: Royal Asiatic Society.

Stirling, A. P.

1960 "A Death and a Youth Club: Feuding in a Turkish Village," *Anthropological Quarterly,* 33:51–75.

Suttles, W.

1960 "Affinal Ties, Subsistence, and Prestige among the Coast Salish," *American Anthropologist,* 62:296–305.

Swartz, Marc J.; Turner, V.; and Tuden, A.
1967 *Political Anthropology.* Chicago: Aldine.
Sweet, Louise.
1965a "Camel Raiding of North Arabian Bedouin: A Mechanism of Ecological Adaptation," *American Anthropologist,* 67:1132–50.
1965b "Camel Pastoralism in North Arabia and the Minimal Camping Unit," in A. Leeds & A. Vayda, eds., *Man, Culture, and Animals: The Role of Animals in Human Ecological Adjustments.* Washington, D.C.: American Association for the Advancement of Science.
Thompson, W. F. (trans.)
1839 *Practical Philosophy of the Muhammadan People.* London.
Torrey, C. C.
1933 *The Jewish Foundation of Islam.* New York: Jewish Institute of Religion Press.
Tritton, A. S.
1951 *Islam, Belief and Practices.* London.
Tucker, A. N., and Bryan, M. A.
1966 *Handbook of African Languages. Linguistic Analyses. The non-Bantu Languages of North-Eastern Africa.* Published for the International African Institute by Oxford University Press.
Ubach, E., and Rackow, E.
1923 *Sitte und Recht in Nordafrika.* Stuttgart.
Ullendorff, E., and von Soden, W.
1964 *An Introduction to the Comparative Grammar of the Semitic Languages.* Wiesbaden.
Various authors.
1959 *Philologiae Turcicae Fundamenta* (languages). Wiesbaden.
Vayda, Andrew P.
1961 "Expansion and Warfare among Swidden Agriculturalists," *American Anthropologist,* 63:346–58.
1962 "A Re-examination of Northwest Coast Economic Systems," *Transactions,* New York Academy of Sciences, Ser. II, 23:618–24.
Villiers, Alan.
1940 *Sons of Sinbad.* New York: Scribner's.
1948 "Some Aspects of the Arab Dhow Trade," *Middle East Journal,* 2:399–416.
Von Grunebaum, Gustave.
1916 *Medieval Islam.* Chicago: Chicago University Press.
Wakidi, Muhammad Ibn Umar al. (752–829).
1882 *Muhammad in Medina.* (Trans. and abbrev. by Wellhausen.) Berlin: Reimer.

Watt, Montgomery.

    1956 *Muhammad in Medina.* Oxford: Clarendon Press.

    1960 *Muhammad in Mecca.* Oxford: Clarendon Press.

    1961a *Muhammad, Prophet and Statesman.* Oxford: Clarendon Press.

    1961b *Islam and the Integration of Society.* London: Routledge and Kegan Paul.

Weingrod, Alex.

    1970 "Change and Stability in Administered Villages: The Israeli Experience," in L. Sweet, ed., *Peoples and Cultures of the Middle East,* Vol. II. New York: Natural History Press.

Wolf, Eric.

    1951 "The Social Organization of Mecca and the Origins of Islam," *Southwestern Journal of Anthropology,* Vol. 7, no. 4.

Wright, W.

    1951 *A Grammar of the Arabic Language.* (2 vols.) 3rd edition. Cambridge: Cambridge University Press.

Wysner, G.

    1945 *The Kabyle People.* New York. [Privately printed.]

INDEX